D1601107

THE QUESTION OF HUMANISM

THE QUESTION OF HUMANISM

Challenges and Possibilities

edited by

David Goicoechea,
John Luik, and Tim Madigan

PROMETHEUS BOOKS
Buffalo, New York

Published 1991 by Prometheus Books

With editorial offices located at 700 East Amherst Street, Buffalo, New York 14215, and distribution facilities at 59 John Glenn Drive, Amherst, New York 14228.

Copyright © by David Goicoechea, John Luik, and Tim Madigan

Library of Congress Cataloging-in-Publication Data

The Question of humanism / edited by David Goicoechea, John Luik,
    Tim Madigan.
         p.   cm.
    Includes bibliographical references.
    ISBN 0-87975-614-4 (hard)
    1. Humanism. I. Goicoechea, David. II. Luik, John.
III. Madigan, Tim.
B105.H8Q84   1990
144—dc20   90-25502
                                                                                CIP

Printed on acid-free paper in the United States of America.

Contents

Acknowledgments   7

Preface
  David Goicoechea   8

Introduction: The Question of Humanism and the Career of Humanism
  John Luik   15

PART 1: THE VARIETIES OF HUMANISM

1. Were Plato and Aristotle Humanists?
   Martin Andic   27

2. Roman Humanism
   Allan Booth   41

3. St. Thomas and Medieval Humanism
   Edward A. Synan   58

4. Christianity, Humanism, and St. Thomas Aquinas
   R. J. McLaughlin   70

5. What Is Renaissance Humanism?
   Martin Andic   83

6. William Blake and the Romantic Perception of Humanism
   Cecil Abrahams   99

7. Existentialism, Humanism, and Positivism
   Calvin Hayes   105

PART 2: THE CHALLENGES TO HUMANISM

8. An Old Question Raised Yet Again:
   Is Kant an Enlightenment Humanist?
   John Luik   117

9. Kierkegaard's Teleological Humanism
   Robert L. Perkins   138

10. The "Humanism" and the Humanism of Karl Marx
    Danny Goldstick   150

11. Marxism, Humanism, and Ecology
    James Lawler and Zaid Orudjev   162

12. Zarathustra and Enlightenment Humanism
    David Goicoechea   170

13. Heidegger: What Is Called Humanism?
    Richard S. G. Brown   179

14. What Now Little Man?
    Comedy, Tragedy, and the Politics of Antihumanism
    Samuel Ajzenstat   193

15. Foucault and the Question of Humanism
    Charles E. Scott   205

PART 3: THE ENIGMAS OF HUMANISM

16. Acting Human in Our Time
    Zygmunt Adamczewski   217

17. Pyrrhonism and the Concept of a Common Human Nature
    in Eighteenth-Century Aesthetic Thought
    Michael Cardy   223

18. The Human Person in American Pragmatism
    Richard P. Francis   235

19. Sartre and the Humanism of Spontaneity
    Monica C. Hornyansky   244

20. The Humanistic Implications of Liberation Theology:
    Juan Luis Segundo and Karl Marx
    Marsha A. Hewitt   253

21. The Modern Spirit and the Paradox of Humanism
    Kenneth Dorter   273

22. The Inevitability of Humanism
    Graeme Nicholson   295

23. Secular Humanism and Eupraxophy
    Paul Kurtz   308

Afterword: The Answer of Humanism
   Tim Madigan   326
List of Contributors   340

Acknowledgments

We would like to thank Mrs. Irene Cherington, Brock University Philosophy Department Secretary, for her help in preparing much of the manuscript, and Prometheus Editor Mark Hall, for his work in seeing the volume through to publication.

David Goicoechea
John Luik
Tim Madigan

Preface

David Goicoechea

An easy Humanism plagues the land;
I choose to take an otherworldly stand.
The Archimedean point, however small,
will serve to lift th' entire terrestrial ball.

John Updike, Midpoint

In the fall of 1986, at Monterey, N.L., Mexico, The Second World Congress of Christian Philosophy under the presidency of Dr. Agustin Basave Fernandez Del Valle discussed "Humanism and Christian Metaphysics in Our Times." The proceedings of that conference which have now appeared in five volumes again indicate the wide range of interest in humanism.

Upon returning from the conference, it seemed to me that many questions remained. Can a satisfactory assessment of the varieties of humanism be made? What are the present day challenges to humanism? What are the enigmas of humanism? These questions were explored by the Brock Philosophical Society at St. Catharines, Ontario, during the school years of 1987-88 and 1988-89. The following papers are the proceedings of that discussion.

VARIETIES OF HUMANISM

Already in Roman times Aulus Gellius made a key distinction between two kinds of humanism: the one signified by the word "philanthropy" and the other signified by the word *paideia*. The varieties of humanism might be understood in relation to these two original kinds. In Greek times it was from Promethean humanism that philanthropy sprang forth. It was from the humanism of the sophists that *paideia* came forth. Socrates, Plato, and Aristotle were in significant senses both antititanic and antisophistic. The doctrine of the golden mean would not mix with the tragic protest; nor could the notion that man is the measure of all things be harmonized with the standards of formal truth.

In Rome the distinction continued. Philanthropy gathered to a greatness around the Stoic *recta ratio*. All humans are of a family because they are collected by the Heraclitean logos which became right reason. Roman law could respect the laws of each people because of its Stoic belief in the brotherhood of all men. The Romans were practical and their pragmatism gave rise to their Stoicism; just as their Stoicism gave rise to their practicality. They practiced the Stoic humanism of an enlightened egoism or of a self-interested altruism. To live and let live, especially when all roads lead to Rome, was the most practical policy for all. At the same time the Romans were the first to institutionalize paideic humanism. The school curriculum was based on the great books of the rhetorical tradition. Greek rhetoric became Roman oratory. The Greek sophistic stream would have dried up had it not been channeled by the Roman aqueducts that kept the paideic waters flowing into Europe and the Americas, especially Latin America, ever since. In Rome the two kinds of humanism were distinct and even confrontational as Gellius indicates. And yet Cicero as a practical Roman would have no doubt argued that because of the paideic learning the Stoic philanthropy could work.

In Patristic times the two streams of humanism came together as they flowed into the Judeo-Christian waters. In that flow there is the Torah upon which a man should meditate day and night and find therein all of his delight. There is the prophetic message of social justice which was predominate from Amos and Hosea to Jesus. The chief message of the Torah was to do the will of God and a condition for that was to practice social justice. In the medieval synthesis the Greco-Roman *paideia* and philanthropy were seen as *praeparatio evangelica* for the law and the prophets which had been fulfilled in Jesus. Love of God and love of neighbor were interpreted as the ultimate principle of order. Thus the new philanthropy received a primacy over the new *paideia*. Love is the fulfillment of the law.

In Scholastic times, as the Christian social order became more stable, humanism as *paideia* grew in influence. With the Platonic renaissance of the twelfth century and the Aristotelian renaissance of the thirteenth century, *paideia* as *trivium* and *quadrivium* prepared the way for all students of medicine, law, philosophy, and theology. John of Salisbury was called "the humanist." Humanism was interpreted as the cultivation of the liberal arts. Scholastic humanism had a paideic purity that equalled that of Roman humanism.

But it was Renaissance humanism that became the paradigm for all time of paideic humanism. In Florence, the flow of free inquiry that began with the sophists, was institutionalized in Roman education, and became the university movement in the thirteenth century broke forth in a flood of creativity. The paideic source which became the *trivium* and *quadrivium* now no longer flowed forth into just philosophy, theology, medicine, and law; it permeated every recess of the entire culture. The classical rhetoric resonated in the sweet thunder of the oral tradition of the romance languages. It flowed forth in all the arts that became the chief educator for the general populace. Through Michelangelo, Leonardo, Raphael, Donatello, and others, western Europe received a paideic education quite different from the gothic and the romanesque.

The pendulum was not long in making restitution to philanthopic humanism. The great aesthetic growth of the Renaissance *paideia* invited the ethical backlash of the protestant reformers. A renewal of the prophetic claim for social justice swelled up and there was an outcry for the rights of all to life, liberty, and the pursuit of happiness. Enlightenment humanism emerged and gave birth to the French and American revolutions and the revolutions ever since, right down to the ones today in South Africa and the U.S.S.R. The Enlightenment lives on as the greatest concentration of philanthropic humanism. Out of it flow: Marxism as a humanism, existentialism as a humanism, and eupraxophy as a humanism. By working within the limits of reason alone, Enlightenment man wants to make this earth a better place for all.

CHALLENGES TO HUMANISM

Humanism has lived by the challenge and perhaps will die by the challenge. It began as a challenge of tragic protest with Prometheus. It continued its challenge through the sophists. It was challenged in return. Nietzsche claims that Socrates and Euripides took the sting out of the protest by Sophocles and Aeschylus. Plato and Aristotle certainly presented a formidable challenge to both the titanic excess and the sophistic standard of man as the measure of all things. In Rome the humanistic challenge became so successful that humanism acquired the power of the status quo. Roman law institutionalized philanthropy and Roman education institutionalized *paideia*. Humanism which was the challenger in Greece became the triumphant victor in Rome. But it was in turn dethroned and syncretized by the offspring of the prophetic protesters from Israel. They were a new sort of humanist who for centuries had challenged the elements of false religion and lax morality in their own kingdom. The upbuilding of Roman Christendom came about through the polemics of prophetic protest against Roman institutions and through the shaping of Judeo-Christian belief and practice by the Roman institutions of philanthropy and *paideia*. Eventually, philanthropy became institutionalized in canon law and *paideia* in the *trivium* and *quadrivium*. New challenges met those medieval institutions and in the Renaissance *paideia* became more than institutionalized; it became acculturated. Then philanthropy stepped forth and became embodied in modern technology and the capitalistic social order.

In postmodern times Enlightenment humanism is being seriously challenged. This challenge began with Immanuel Kant. In his three critiques he was the greatest philosopher of Enlightenment humanism. He laid the epistemological, ethical, and aesthetic framework of the Enlightenment attitude. But then he wrote his book on *Religion Within the Limits of Reason Alone.* He discussed the problem of radical evil and self-deceit. He concluded that man is in need of grace if there is to be redemption. Humanism in both its ethical or philanthropic form and its aesthetic or paideic form has always proceeded within the limits of reason alone. In his book on religion Kant, the great Enlightenment humanist, began to argue against his own humanism. He argued for the necessity of a theism which could make humanism possible. Nietzsche, Heidegger, and Derrida have followed Kant in deepening the serious charges against humanism.

Nietzsche exposed the dangers for the human if humans limit themselves to reason alone. He stressed the Apollonian and Dionysian sources of the truly great for mankind. He did make a most powerful criticism of Christian Platonism from the viewpoint of Enlightenment humanism. But in turn he made perhaps the most telling criticism of Enlightenment humanism from his own postmodern perspective. Enlightenment humanism is as much entangled in ressentiment as is Christian Platonism. It does not proceed from the primacy of a receptive Yes and Amen saying. It begins not only with a No to the Divine, but also with a No to existence as it is at present. It believes in the myth of progress and that it can make things better with instrumental reason. Nietzsche offers a poetic, rhetorical, and philosophic criticism of Enlightenment poetry, rhetoric, and philosophy.

In our times, perhaps Martin Heidegger's *Letter on Humanism* will prove to be the most significant publication concerning the question of humanism in its varieties, challenges, and enigmas. Heidegger challenges humanism from the perspective of the proper dignity of man within the ontological framework. In his thinking as thanking and not as calculating he argues that each western humanism is grounded in metaphysics or is the ground of a metaphysics. All humanisms are tied to the assumption that man is the rational animal. This metaphysical limitation has been the essence of Roman humanism, Renaissance humanism, Enlightenment humanism, Marxist humanism, existentialist humanism, and the Christian humanisms of our day. By implication for Heidegger the Greek philosophers, the Scholastic philosophers, and Heidegger himself are not humanists. They do not give the primacy of being to reason. These philosophers each had a principle which was ontologically prior to the human and to the rational. The human will receive its proper dignity only through that thinking which is properly thankful for the gift of Being. Humanisms are forgetful of Being and therefore not properly grateful. For man to live in his highest dignity it is not enough for him to think of himself as a rational animal as all the humanisms do. For Heidegger *homo* begins to become *humanus* when he lets himself be reclaimed and governed by Being.

The postmodern French thinkers such as Bataille, Foucault, Deleuze, and Derrida also present their various challenges to humanism. Derrida, in his deconstruction of the metaphysics of presence, exposes the violence and the ethnocentrism of humanism insofar as it is connected with logocentrism, ontocentrism, epistemecentrism, phallocentrism, etc. Derrida, in his essay on "The Ends of Man" in *Margins* characterizes French thought from 1945 to 1968 as totally humanistic. In their humanistic insistence Derrida claims that his countrymen did not even notice the challenges to humanism of Hegel, Husserl, and Heidegger. The focal point of Derrida's challenge to humanism has to do with what he calls "reading us." Kant never worked out a conception of the "we", but Hegel's "we" took him beyond humanism. Husserl's transcendental subjectivity and Heidegger's *Dasein* are developed in the direction of a *Mitsein* that seeks to deconstruct ethnocentricity. However, they remain caught in the phenomenological metaphoricity of lighting, clearing, presence, truth, and house of Being that is violently confining. Thus, Heidegger still urges the privileging of the oral over the written and all the attendant privilegings. Derrida wants our solicitation to go as far as to solicit readings of us. He finishes his essay on "The Ends of Man" by recalling Zarathustra who overcame his humanism of pity by turning his back on the distress of the higher men so that they might behold each other in the face to face of the overman.

ENIGMAS OF HUMANISM

Just as theism calls forth antitheists that theism might grow, so humanism calls forth antihumanists that humanism might grow. Thus, John Updike takes an antihumanistic stand. He seems to be of like mind with Kant, Nietzsche, Heidegger, and Derrida in judging humanism to be too violently inhumane. This death wish of humanism has perhaps always been its root enigma. But the enigmas of humanism run so deep that as one tries to say what they are he is led more and more to question what they are.

Within the philanthropy of Promethean humanism the enigma was already apparent. The rebel Prometheus and the tyrant Zeus clashed in a confrontation of wills. Prometheus wanted to be autonomous and to take for mankind the properties of the gods. His excess resulted in his suffering. Aeschylus understood that suffering as that which makes men wise even if against their will. By willfully seeking to control human destiny the tragic hero would get only wisdom instead. But that wisdom is a gift against man's will. Is it impossible that Prometheans ever get what they bargain for? Nietzsche would certainly think that pity never works. But Nietzsche did think that tragedy works and so did Aristotle for different reasons.

Aulus Gellius and the Romans did not seem to trust either Promethean humanism or tragedy. Gellius saw humanism only as *paideia* and not as philanthropy. But sophistry too has its enigmas. That the perplexities of *paideia* are as great among the Greeks as are those of philanthropy becomes evident when one asks such a questions as: were Plato and Aristotle humanists? Plato did have as much a love-hate relationship with the sophists as he did with the tragedians. He censored Protagoras and Lysias as much as he did the Titanic story of Prometheus. And yet Plato had a great place for *paideia*. In his essay on Plato's *Pharmacy,* Derrida translates the *paideia* of Plato as play. One might think of it as the play of free inquiry. Plato's Socrates according to Derrida is the spitting image of a sophist. But the difference between them makes all the difference. There can be three logics: of all work and no play, of restricted play, and of free play. Did the sophists go off in the direction of all work and no play? Lysias seems to have argued for sex without love because he mistrusted the uncertainties of freedom that love might entail. Is there a danger that free inquiry when it confines itself to the limits of reason alone, loses the possibilities of free play? Is the work ethic of the Enlightenment humanists a belated implication of the all too limited Protagorean measure?

The Promethean paradox of Aeschylus makes clear that the willfulness of Prometheus wins for him only a wisdom which he receives against his will. The sophistic paradox as presented in the *Phaedrus* shows that if one limits eros to the confines of reason alone then he loses the freedom of the play of free inquiry. But the paradox of Greek humanism becomes most poignant when the two kinds are thought together. Prometheus is a mask for the excesses of Dionysus at play in his healthy, happy, humorous joy. Protagoras is a somber, serious, and sober spokesman of Apollo whose *paideia* becomes pathetic in its lack of play. Can the humanisms of compassion and of sophistication mix? That is the core enigma of humanism which the Greeks have bequeathed us.

The Romans solved the problem with their genius for institutionalization. In Greece the philanthropists were protestors from the margins who pestered the Aryan tyranny. The paideic sophists were wandering rhetoricians who taught the established professionals but never became established. Rome took Promethean pity as refined by Heraclitus and the Stoics and codified it into Roman law. Rome took rhetorical *paideia* and embodied it in Roman education. Rome's driving energy sought to establish the Pax Romana! Roman law and Roman education worked together in instituting that ultimate institution of peace at any price. But with the Roman transformation of humanism a new enigma arose. How can humanism become institutionalized? Are not both philanthropy and *paideia* voices of protest from the margins rather than the central voice that keeps the margins in line?

Patristic Christianity made headway because of the prophetic protest against the injustices of the Roman Babylon. Augustine in his *City of God* argued that Rome fell because of impiety and injustice. But with Augustine there arose the theism-humanism paradox. The prophetic voice of Israel which was analogous to the tragic voice of Greece eventually became institutionalized into Roman Catholic law. Thus, there remained the center-margin paradox. But compounded with it there arises the question as to how well the prophets of theism might be authentic voices of humanism. The question of the humanism of liberation theology is to be asked at this point.

The Renaissance gave rise to humanism's aesthetic-ethical polemics. The southern *paideia* of the rhetorical tradition was met head on by the northern philanthropy. It took great wealth to finance the artistic grandeur of the Italian Renaissance. The confrontation became focused on indulgences. They were the symbol of religious taxation that provoked Luther's ninety-five theses. With Promethean protest Luther cried out against the institutionalizing art of *paideia*. Promethean humanism revolted against paideic humanism.

In the Enlightenment there arose the ambiguities of the paradox of ethics-within-the-limits-of-reason-alone and a less restricted ethics. Kant first discovered the limitations of working within the limits of reason alone. He saw that to overcome radical evil ethics had to ultimately be a gift of grace. Kierkegaard saw that genuine ethics had to be based on faith. The romantics,

Nietzsche, and Derrida, all deconstruct the metaphysics of presence as the basis of ethics. Derrida thinks that ethics should be based on the face to face encounter which alone provokes violence but also alone prohibits it.

In our time the enigma of humanism has to do with the universalistic and individualistic tendencies of *paideia* and philanthropy. At the Brock conference this immediately became clear in the discussion of Dr. Adamczewski's inaugural address on "The Peril and the Potential of Humanism." He told us that as a student in Poland he had elected to study the humanities. He came to feel at home with the classical tradition that began in Greece and Rome. He said that when he visited the Louvre the primitive and oriental art did not interest him. But as soon as he beheld the Greek art he felt at home. He was grateful for his humanistic education for bringing him to such a homecoming. In the discussion, Dr. Sinha, from India, asked if there was not something lacking in a humanism that is so particularizing. Should not a true humanism open one to the universally human? Perhaps paideic humanism which thinks of itself as promoting the universal is quite narrow in its exclusive interest. Perhaps philanthropic humanism can be more universal. Perhaps the challenge of the rock bottom enigma has to do with appropriating both the particularizing *paideia*, which claims to be universal, and the more universal philanthropy.

Introduction

The Question of Humanism and the Career of Humanism
John Luik

In one sense, the title of this volume is splendidly apt, for it centers one's attention on perhaps the most indisputably central aspect of humanism, its simultaneous synoptic and contextual quality, that is its insistence on anthropocentric foundationalism, on the appropriateness of situating all that is crucially significant within the framework of the human. But in another sense, the title is to a degree misleading, or at least if not misleading then incomplete, for it tends to suggest that there is a recognizable entity, humanism, about which our concerns are for the most part only substantive, questions largely of evidence and viability. But as the authors of the volume are at considerable pains to argue, the question of humanism is as much a series of interrelated definitional questions about what humanism properly is, or in some instances was, as a neat set of substantive questions about the plausibility of a particular philosophical doctrine. In this sense, the career of humanism has been as much an effort to arrive at a consensus about what humanism is as an attempt to defend the viability of humanist claims. But even putting the question in this way is perhaps misleading, as if to suggest that questions of definition and questions of substance can be neatly separated: the sense that one assigns humanism quite obviously affects the plausibility of its program. In the end questions of definition and substance become virtually inseparable, if not indistinguishable.

At first glance, the papers in the first section, "The Varieties of Humanism," appear to belie this claim, as the authors for the most part appear to be concerned solely with historical, definitional questions about what we ought to take humanism to be. Thus, whether we take Kant's famous four questions —What is man? What can I know? What ought I to do? and What may

I hope?—as definitive of humanism, or Heidegger's more recent elaboration of the different senses of humanism—classical humanist learning and studies, anthropocentricism, the belief in rationality as the defining characteristic of humanness, and the concern with the human world in all of its aspects, humanitarianism—whichever definitional route one takes, there appears to be nothing problematic about such terms as Roman humanism, medieval humanism, Christian humanism, Renaissance humanism, romantic humanism, or even existentialist humanism. Or is there?

Professor Andic, in his essay "Were Plato and Aristotle Humanists?" concludes that the question of their inclusion in the humanist canon must be left open, unless we are to consider anyone a humanist who is "interested in the best life for human beings," something akin to Heidegger's humanitarian conception of humanism. But as Andic rightly asks, is humanism thus defined a useful category? Moreover, it is not simply the broadness of the humanist characterization that makes Plato and Aristotle difficult to position within the tradition; it is also their apparent unwillingness to endorse beliefs central to much subsequent humanist thought, to, as Andic puts it, "acknowledge the humanity of everyone, the capacity of each person to think and act of himself . . ."

If not then to Plato and Aristotle, perhaps it is to Roman humanism, what Heidegger calls the first humanism, that we should turn for humanist origins. "The first humanism, Roman humanism, and every kind that emerged from that time to the present, has presupposed the most universal 'essence' of man to be obvious. Man is considered to be an *animal rationale.*"* Professor Booth accepts Heidegger's claim but isolates the particular sense of rationality that Roman humanism exhibited. The Romans, Booth argues, accepted that man had the capacity to achieve individual perfection and "the capacity perfectly to assess and to guide all affairs, in their every dimension, as they touch upon man throughout the universe." This did not, however, like the humanism of subsequent centuries, require that the Romans had to empty the universe of the gods, Booth claims, nor did it mean a grudging human subservience to divine decrees. Rather, the Romans "forged not myths, but a meticulous array of rituals which aimed not so much to honor the gods as to manipulate them. So by the time the Romans developed a literature and adopted a mythology, they had already assured themselves of their ability to enlist, or rather coerce superior powers into the service of Rome."

This coercive sense of power, power displayed in such confident fashion even with respect to the gods, is, not surprisingly, absent from the unashamedly Christian humanism described by Professors Synan and McLaughlin in chapters 3 and 4. For Synan and McLaughlin there is a neat symmetry between the Kantian and Heideggerian definitions of humanism, at least with respect to St. Thomas, for in Thomas and his age we find a belief in the crucial significance of reason, in the necessity of knowledge and proper action, a love and concern for humankind, and a commitment to appropriate, if not always re-

---

*"Letter on Humanism" in Martin Heidegger, *Basic Writings,* D. Krell, trans. (New York, 1977), 202.

spect, the past. Still, one cannot but wonder whether there is some intellectual confusion here, in that the concepts of reason, knowledge, beneficence, indeed of human itself are being employed in quite a different sense, for the distance between the exuberant confidence of the Romans, whose humanism led them not so much to honor the gods as to use them, and the Christian humanist vision of St. Thomas, which, as Prof. McLaughlin notes, culminates in the "guidance of faith" that is "no denigration of reason," seems extraordinary. It is not that the Thomistic humanist vision is entirely incompatible with the classical humanist, for as McLaughlin notes, "If Thomas Aquinas is right, as we attempt to put our lives into good order, what we have first to do is give thought to what it is to be a human being and, in the light of such understanding, intelligently, freely, responsibly to struggle to achieve the highest human goods." So much the Roman humanist would allow. But the culminating, and to McLaughlin and Synan, the crucial claim, moves in a quite different direction. McLaughlin states, "If our intelligence leads us, as it leads Thomas, to affirm our creaturely status, then on a purely natural level, without our appealing to any privileged matters of faith, it also dictates that we be religious."

In his essay "What is Renaissance Humanism?" Professor Andic begs to differ, at least to the extent that he finds a humanism without religion to be coherent. For Andic, "humanism need not be religious, or irreligious, or moral, or immoral." Renaissance humanism, for Andic, is essentially the rebirth of what Heidegger calls the first humanism, Roman humanism, that is the preservation and cultivation of the ideals and culture of the classical world. As Andic quite properly notes, this preservative and cultivative side of Renaissance humanism has both a great merit and a substantial defect. The merit can be glimpsed in what we might call the recreative power of the classical past, as noted by no less a Renaissance humanist than Machiavelli.

> When evening comes . . . I return to my house and enter my study; and at my door I take off the day's clothing . . . . and properly dressed now I enter the ancient courts of the men of old where, received by them with affection, I feed on the only food that is mine and for which I was born, where I am not ashamed to ask them the reasons for their actions, and they in their humanity . . . answer me; and for four hours of time I am not bored, remember no trouble, no longer dread being poor or dying; entirely I give myself up to them.*

The defect, as Andic reminds us, also derives from that reverence of the past, a reverence that too often stifles the very use of reason that humanists consider man's unique possession. Andic quotes H. A. Mason:

> At best the scholars did little but possess the wisdom of the past as we might possess a set of copy-book maxims. The maxims certainly make us aware of a difference between the actual and the ideal, but they do not of themselves enable us to penetrate the actual; still less do they show us how to bring the actual nearer to the ideal . . . On the contrary, the very

---

*Quoted by M. Andic in chapter 5.

wealth of examples drawn . . . from these pagan moralists made it impossible
to see any object steadily. If you call to mind the most celebrated treatises
of the day, from More's *Utopia* to Machiavelli's *Prince* and ask: in what
spirit are general principles being brought to bear on particular questions
of the day; with what flexibility are the actual complexities of the real world
being handled, in short, how much thinking do they contain of the kind
that really advances any question, the answer must (I think) be that the
general principles are applied *a priori,* the particularities of the actual world
are either not taken into account or are not brought into fruitful relation
with general principles, in short that there is no genuine thinking, no precision
and delicacy of judgment, no real focussing of the mind—no looking steadily
at any object.

If reason is constrained by certain aspects of Renaissance humanism, modern humanism, from the Romantic period onward, offers at least the prospect
of its emancipation, according to Professors Abrahams and Hayes. Using
William Blake as the paradigm of romantic humanism, Abrahams argues that
reason and history can be genuinely liberating, freeing persons and nations
from the sterile and doomed circles of historical inevitability. While Abrahams,
following Blake, is more optimistic about reason's prospects, Hayes, focussing
on Sartre's claims for existentialism as a humanism, is more constrained. While
claiming not to make a contribution to Sartre scholarship, Hayes nevertheless
grasps the soft conceptual underbelly of existentialist humanism by noting
that despite its deep concern with the human, and more specifically with
appropriately human action, it yet cannot provide any *"concerted* guidance
in ethical matters."* Medieval humanism, the humanism of St. Thomas, can,
at the very least, provide an answer, cooperatively through faith and reason,
to the question of what the human good is. It is in the end, a good discovered,
not created by human persons. Contemporary existentialist humanism, if Hayes
is right, resolutely refuses any talk about morality being discovered, preferring
instead to speak of inventing right and wrong. Yet at the same moment in
which it speaks of creating right and wrong, it seems to suggest that the
instrument for such invention, reason, is in some sense crucially unequal to
the task. In the end, Hayes argues, we are left in a world without discovery
and in which invention is impossible, a world in which "anything is permitted."
    While the first groups of essays attempt to provide some historical per-
spective to the question of what humanism is, the second set of essays focus for the most part on criticisms of various humanist claims. This should
not be taken to suggest that the figures discussed, thinkers like Kant, Kierkegaard, Marx, and Heidegger, are necessarily to be placed within some cumber-
some and decidedly uncongenial collective called antihumanist, as many of
these critics of humanism might just as appropriately be seen as ultimate
champions of what they perceive to be genuinely humanist concerns. In this
sense the figures dealt with in "The Challenges to Humanism" are as much
concerned with defining humanism as with a critical appraisal of its substantive claims in that their very criticisms of the humanist career suggest once
again the conceptual ambiguity surrounding the label humanist even while
drawing them inescapably into the project of refashioning the humanist credo.

Perhaps the figures of this section should be thought of as reluctant humanists, or humanists at the edge, simultaneous critics and champions of the humanist cause.

The ambiguity of intention is perhaps most clearly observed in the work of Kant, whom I suggest possesses the most respectable humanist credentials. Despite his commitment to such Enlightenment beliefs as the emancipatory and objective power of reason, moral foundationalism, the inevitable spread of political liberalism and international order, if not good will, a commitment which has often led to his being portrayed as the paradigm humanist, I argue that Kant's anthropology is, in the end, unable fully to embrace the humanist agenda. What ultimately makes Kant a humanist at the edge, or even on a more radical reading a Christian humanist, is his belief in the reality of an evil within human persons so rooted and so fundamentally and inescapably subversive of the human project in all of its essential dimensions that it yields only to a faith in a divine grace that can complete the task begun by reason and morality.

Criticism of the more traditional humanist claims is also found in Kierkegaard's "teleological humanism," according to Professor Perkins. Afer a careful examination of Kierkegaard's critique of the "depth and grandeur of pagan, i.e., non-Christian humanism," where Socrates functions as Kierkegaard's humanist advocate, Perkins points to the essential differences that Kierkegaard's Chrisitan humanism presents from its classical predecessors. For Kierkegaard, genuine humanism focusses not on the notion of recollection, so central to Platonic thought, but on the "decisiveness of the moment" by which Kierkegaard, according to Perkins, "means that persons are entirely responsible for what and who they are because of the choices they make of themselves." Whereas Socratic humanism has nothing new to offer persons caught in the existential predicament, Christian humanism offers the "godman" who alone has the power to "recreate persons, and to lead them to a new beginning."

The two Marx pieces by Professor Goldstick and Professors Lawler and Orudjev provide a quite different assessment of humanism than that offered by the avowedly theistic program of Kant and Kierkegaard. Goldstick is interested in Marx's response to that element of humanism caught by Kant's question "What ought I to do?"—that is, Marx's "overall ethical motivation." Goldstick finds Marx a problematic traditional humanist in that Marx rejects the notion that *"conformity to human nature* cannot . . . provide a *reason* for calling anything 'morally good.' "

The reasons for such a rejection are to be found, according to Goldstick, both in Marx's discovery that the development of history is really nothing more than an ongoing remaking of human nature and in Marx's belief that making human nature the foundation for an ethical norm would prove, in the end, to be an inescapably conservative move. "To make *de facto* human nature— . . . the ultimate basis for the ethical norm is necessarily to end up endorsing as 'natural' the existent status quo, while confining what can be condemned as 'unnatural' to exceptional cases that deviate from its normal pattern."

Professors Lawler and Orudjev are also at pains to specify Marx's dissent from an abstract humanism which allows individuals to be sacrificed in the historical process to the general interests of humanity. "Against such abstract humanism," Lawler and Orudjev argue, "Marx and Engels defended 'real humanism': *'Real humanism* has no more dangerous enemy in Germany than *spiritualism* or *speculative idealism,* which substitutes "self-consciousness" or the *"spirit"* for the *real individual man . . .'* " Against such a humanism, a humanism identified both with Renaissance and Kantian thought, Marx and Engels propose a way in which the admittedly lofty notions of human personhood can be realized within the scope of communal life. For Lawler and Orudjev the Marxist critique of traditional humanist values is not directed primarily at the content of those values, but at the absence of any precision with respect to how such values are to be realized. For Marx such values are to be realized only in a society in which the "free development of each is the condition for the free development of all." But the problem with such an unblinking attention to the question of how such values can be realized opens up both Marx and Engels to the ecological critique of humanism, where the humanist assumption of "respect for the *human* individual . . . as the highest moral and political norm is increasingly criticized as a form of 'speciesism' . . . ," a theme also raised by Professor Dorter.

Equally unsympathetic to Enlightenment humanism, and perhaps to any kind of humanism, is Nietzsche's Zarathustra. According to Professor Goicoechea, "Nietzsche's *Thus Spoke Zarathustra* can be read as the paradigm postmodernist assessment of enlightenment humanism," wherein the "lion is the symbol of enlightenment humanism [and] the child is the symbol of postmodern Dionysianism." According to Goicoechea, Nietzsche perceives the enlightenment "no-saying" as much a form of nihilism as that found in Christian Platonism. Zarathustra, however, is not a nihilist as "his dramatic words and works show that the life affirming child can be born out of the death of the lion." The child, freed from the tyranny of both Enlightenment rationality and obsessive autonomy, can, Goicoechea claims, fully embrace the "love of eternal recurrence." "The Child's 'yes' saying is not only a playful and creative 'yes' saying. It is also a 'yes' and 'amen' saying. It is the saying of a sacred 'yes'. . . . He says, 'Let them return again and again.' He says that because he loves 'ennightenment' as much as enlightenment. In the night he can graciously and joyously receive all."

One of the most significant and yet at the same time more difficult figures to situate in the humanist/humanist critic terrain is Martin Heidegger. Professor Brown, in his "Heidegger: What Is Called Humanism?" argues that the clue to Heidegger's position with respect to humanism is to see the question of humanism within the context of a larger Heideggerian concern: namely, the question of the essence of human action. Heidegger's attack on traditional humanism, Brown suggests, is launched in "order to establish that thinking is the only genuine human activity and, therefore, it might be equally expected that thinking would present us with the requisite directives that are applicable to our active lives."

Heidegger's objection to the humanisms of the past is that their concern with human essence necessarily entangles them in a metaphysics, a metaphysics which ignores the fundamental question of "the relation of Being to the essence of man. . . ." Heidegger's humanism, then, must be a humanism that is, at least in some senses, radically unlike the traditional humanisms, a humanism "which understands itself from the standpoint of Being in its relationship to man." Brown suggests that this "curious kind of humanism" is best described as "original humanism," which Heidegger refers to as "mediating and caring, that man be human and not inhumane, 'inhuman,' that is, outside his essence." For Brown, such "original humanism" presents a number of substantive problems, the most serious being that "original humanism is riddled with the kind of vagueness and arbitrariness which could easily precipitate into inhumanism."

The questions of Nietzsche's Zarathustra are also, in part, the questions of Professor Ajzenstat in his "What Now Little Man? Comedy, Tragedy, and the Politics of Antihumanism." Ajzenstat returns us once again to the definitional problem in that he argues that to "raise the question of humanism is to ask, what it is, if anything, that gives value to human life." Ajzenstat sees the answers, even allowing for a bewildering variety of detail, dividing into "two broad categories," two categories that really suggest "two humanisms":

> The two humanisms I have in mind can be labelled the humanism of the
> ordinary and the humanism of the extraordinary. The upshot of the first
> is to see the value of life in the natural gratifications that make for com-
> fort and ease—being warm, well-fed, healthy, sexually satisfied, and sur-
> rounded by friends. The upshot of the second is to see the first as soporific
> and dehumanizing, as, in the words of Nietzsche's Zarathustra, 'poverty and
> filth and wretched contentment.' "

Despite the contradictory character of these two humanisms, Ajzenstat wants to argue that essential humanism is to be found in embracing both and that it is in tragedy that we find the "meeting place of the humanism of the ordinary and the humanism of the extraordinary."

The final essay in the section examines what Professor Scott finds to be the ambiguous status of Foucault within the humanist tradition. In one sense, Scott argues, Foucault is obviously part of the humanist tradition, in the sense that he stresses the importance of "traditional texts, practices, and institutions." But at a deeper level, Scott believes that Foucault stands against humanism in that he "departs from it by allowing his thought to be moved and formed by the gaps and fissures of the humanistic tradition rather than by an effort to achieve theoretical superiority on the questions of human nature and destiny." Still, Scott believes that Foucault's thought "does not advance or produce the ideas that characterize humanism," but at the same time it does nothing to refute such ideas either. Rather, it places them into question, through displaying their "uncertainty and self-contradictory" character, a move that in the end may be more humanistic than anything traditionally given that description.

The essays of the third section, "The Enigmas of Humanism," return to both the definitional and the substantive concerns raised by the first two groups of essays. While all of the authors save for Professor Francis show a certain sympathy with the humanist agenda, all are alive to the problems of the tradition outlined by the authors in the second group of essays. Thus, in his essay, "Acting Human in Our Time," Professor Adamczewski, beginning with Aristotle's concern with distinctively human conduct, conduct claimed by the agent as his own, examines the pressures that contemporary life brings to the problem of distinctive human action. As he notes: "It appears that a definite shift has taken place across history: that which used to fulfill adequately the human 'function,' reason, has been dehumanized into abstraction, while the opposing aspect of concrete immediacy has been adapted, in particular technically, to such sophisticated human inclinations as to disguise its original animality." These confluent pressures of distorted reason and disguised animality, arising in quite different ways, seriously undermine, according to Adamczewski, the essential characteristic of humanness, the owning of one's actions.

The same forces described by Professor Adamczewski, also serve to jeopardize the career of humanism in the twentieth century for Professor Dorter. Dorter argues that in the very process, mandated by human reason, of subordinating nature to our wills, the "tool by which we hoped to achieve dominion becomes the instrument of our own effacement, and as the power of human technology over nature increases, the place of the individual within the world becomes more problematic." The paradox of humanism is thus that through our characteristic human drive to assertion we "find ourselves subordinated to nonhumanistic principles," a process that in our time, as noted by Adamczewski, is made more frightening because it leads "in the direction of the mechanical rather than the natural." What Dorter seeks to discover is a way to be faithful to the humanist tradition while at the same time finding a way to minimize the limitations of that tradition. Though Dorter leaves open the direction that such an enterprise would take, he argues that it cannot take the traditional humanist route of affirming that "human beings are the highest beings in the universe" for such a move ultimately empties the universe of anything beyond the timely, a move, as Heidegger noted, that is in the end spiritually vacuous.

Perhaps the most unsympathetic essay in the group, unsympathetic precisely because of its fear that humanism as pragmatism is spiritually vacuous, is Professor Francis's piece on humanism in the context of American pragmatism. Pragmatism presents a vision of human nature, Francis suggests, where:

> Human nature is explained, in strictly humanistic terms, as a changing, always busy, episodic, biological, transient organism that solves problems intelligently along scientific lines, creates values in morally competing facts and ideas, is socially significant, interactionally free, aesthetically capable, and religiously encouraged."

Francis finds such a pragmatic humanism ultimately unsatisfying, particularly in the work of Dewey, because of its uncritical confidence in human reason, especially in science, its rejection of "abstract codes of ethics," a move that invites "behavioral chaos" and the ultimate impossibility of meaningful theistic experience.

Professor Cardy, while sharing Professor Francis' worries about meaningful and nonrelativistic moral codes, believes that the humanist career offers a variety of resources for allaying the frequent charges of its critics that humanism either has no ethic or possesses an unacceptable ethic. In his "Pyrrhonism and the Concept of a Common Human Nature in Eighteenth-Century Aesthetic Thought" Cardy examines the manner in which certain eighteenth-century thinkers attempted to maintain the century's commitment to humanity while at the same time avoiding the conceptual pitfalls that Cardy believes are inherent to Pyrrhonism. Cardy suggests that the Pyrrhonist approach is "anathema in ethics, but acceptable in aesthetics," and he attempts to show how the moral nihilism of Pyrrhonism, allegedly unavoidable in humanism, was "either absorbed into a theocentric view of the universe, side-stepped, or diverted into productive channels by the application of the method of experimental induction."

In the essays by Professors Hornyansky, Hewitt, and Nicholson we return, in part, to a series of thinkers dealt with in earlier essays in the volume. Professor Hornyansky in her essay, "Sartre and the Humanism of Spontaneity" provides a second and quite different look at Sartre's relationship to humanism. Hornyansky attempts to defend Sartre's thought from the criticisms suggested in Heidegger's "Letter on Humanism," suggesting that Heidegger's criticisms, while correct in one sense miss "the development of Sartre's thought which lifted it out of a sclerosed Cartesian duality and set it on a path which was then hard to foresee." Hornyansky believes that Sartre's humanism is "one of the most thoroughgoing and intense" largely because of his uncompromising insistence on locating the ultimate "urges, shaping, and limits of human action" within human consciousness. Human action, for Sartre, is *"elicited* by a vision of the future rather than *caused* by antecedent states of affairs," and as such human agency requires quite different explanatory principles than are used to account for natural events. And it is this, as Hornyansky rightly notes, that leads Sartre to reject the humanism of Marx. The difficulty with such a humanist approach, Hornyansky concludes, is that it fails to take account adequately of both custom and transcendence. "For such a mind nature, or the cosmos, or at its most grandiose, the idea of Being, also lacks any legislative force," with the result that our relation to transcendence is left dangerously obscure.

The question of the human relationship to transcendence is also central to Professor Hewitt's examination of the humanistic implications of contemporary liberation theology. As Hewitt observes "The central problem posed by humanism for Christianity, succinctly stated, is how to reconcile human autonomy and subjective agency with belief in an external, supernatural agency. . . ." Liberation Theology, through its attempt to reconcile the anthropologies, ethics, and concern for justice, though not perhaps the ontologies that resonate through both Marxism and Christianity, is one of the most important contemporary attempts to move the humanist-Christian dialogue forward in a manner that might offer some sort of at least provisional resolution to the tension between human autonomy and divine agency. Hewitt explores the problems inherent in such attempts by focussing on the work of the Latin

American theologian Juan Segundo. While it is clear that Segundo's intentions as a contribution to the Christian-Marxist dialogue are admirable, the specifics of his program, as Hewitt observes, suffer, perhaps irremediably, from the ontological tensions between Marxism and Christianity and Segundo's own failure to accept the radical character of Marx's atheism.

The final two essays in the volume bring us, not inappropriately, full circle, in that they at once return to the definitional question of humanism and to the substantive response of humanism to its critics. Professor Graeme Nicholson argues for what he describes as the inevitability of humanism, by defending the humanist position from some of its more strident contemporary critics: Heidegger, Althusser, and Foucault. Nicholson argues that even though Heidegger attempts to "displace man from the center of thinking, his thinking is after all obliged to reinstate a human at the center." Similarly, Althusser's analysis of society and economics fails, Nicholson suggests, precisely because he fails to take proper account of the nature of human beings. For Nicholson, Foucault's claim that the portrait of the human (allegedly a recent invention) will be ultimately erased is not sustained. "The human face and figure, while new in a certain way, when the play is enacted in our own day, and in the future, still will have an aura about them that recalls many others that we know from our long history."

Professor Paul Kurtz, while perhaps less sanguine about the inevitability of humanism, is equally concerned with both its definitional and substantive viability. To this end, Kurtz proposes a new term to describe humanism, eupraxophy, a term that, Kurtz argues, better captures the distinctive sense of what humanism is about. Kurtz acknowledges that "there are many variations of humanism: naturalistic, existential, Marxist, pragmatic, and liberal," and he is interested in "what is distinctive about the eupraxophy of modern-day secular humanism." While not claiming that humanism can only mean one particular thing, Kurtz wishes to suggest that there are four defining features of contemporary secular humanism: its method of inquiry, something that functions as the "basic principle of secular humanism"; its world view, that is its interpretation of the universe and the place of human existence within that universe; its fundamental ethical recommendations—courage, reason, and compassion; and its vision for social and political life which grows out of its ethics and includes a commitment to participatory democracy, the use of reason in the common life, and the importance of fundamental justice. In this sense, with Kurtz we conclude where we started, with Kant's notion of the crucial questions of humanism, with Heidegger's different senses of humanism, with the fundamental question of what humanism is, and indeed, should become.

PART ONE

THE VARIETIES OF HUMANISM

1

Were Plato and Aristotle Humanists?

Martin Andic

The first people to be called humanists, it seems, were the promoters of classical literature in fifteenth century Italy, such as Petrarch and Lorenzo Valla, and later and more generally the proponents of *studia humanitatis,* the so-called humanities, presenting the humane virtues and ideals of ancient Greece and Rome. What is it to be fully human and free and flourishing? they asked, and they thought they could answer this by considering the most civilized and natural of our ancestors before religion and school philosophy had interfered with them. Man is a part of nature, and whatever is natural for him is good, e.g., enjoyment; he is a social and political creature, and more active than reflective, so he need not always contemplate and conform himself to the order of things, but can sometimes form and transform it. Often quoted in this regard are the famous words of Pico della Mirandola (1463–1494) in the *Oration on the Dignity of Man,* in which the divine creator says to man:

> To you, Adam, we have fixed no place in the scale of created beings, no one face or task, so that you will take whatever place and face and task you choose. All other creatures are bound by the laws we have laid down for them, but you are not held in by any bounds, so that you will fix them for yourself. We have set you at the center of the world, so that from there you may easily look around at all there is in it. We have made you neither heavenly nor earthly, neither mortal nor immortal, so that you will make yourself into whatever image you find best. You can sink among the animals, or rise among the heavenly if you like.

This thought of the self-creation of man is not new; we find it, for example, in Boethius' *Consolation* 2.5 and 4.3 f., in Plotinus' *Beauty* 5 and 9, and in Aristotle's *Politics* 1.2; moreover, Pico's passage has a mystical tendency, as we see in the orator's comments on these words of the creator:

What boundless generosity of God the Father, and happiness of man to have what he chooses and be what he wills! Animals at birth bring with them from their mother's womb all they will ever have. Heavenly spirits from the beginning of time or soon thereafter are already what they will be forever. But man is born having within him by the gift of God the seed of every kind of creature, so that whatever he cultivates will grow and bear fruit in him. If he chooses a vegetative existence, he will be like the grass; if he chooses sensuality, he becomes like the beasts of the field; if he chooses understanding, he is turned toward heaven; if he loves wisdom, he will be an angel and a Son of God. But if he is not content in being any of these creatures, then in the center of his soul he can be united to God, in the mystery of God's unity at the center of all things and above them all.

There is, it has been said, a mysticism of ascent to a God beyond the world, and a mysticism of descent to the world from God and with God to shine with his light on everything. I do not know Pico's work well enough to say with confidence which direction it takes; but at any rate the tendency of much of the later humanism of the Renaissance was to celebrate man's life in *this* world. Through his science he can understand the cosmos by using his own senses and reason; that is, he can grasp it mathematically, and need not always be consulting authorities; through his religion he can improve his life here and now, and draw on all religions and philosophy as arising from a single divine inspiration. Later humanists distanced themselves from religion and the supernatural altogether, and more recently they have moved away from science and technology as well, and toward greater devotion to literature and the arts, history, ethics, and politics. We have thus seen pragmatism, communism, and existentialism presented as a humanism.[1]

Jean-Paul Sartre, in *Existentialism is a Humanism* (1946), defined existentialism as the position that "existence precedes essence, or . . . that one must begin with subjectivity. . . . Man is nothing else but that which he makes of himself." According to him, to be truly human is to act and choose without relying on any theory of human nature for a guarantee that one is right, since one's humanity and values are created by one's own choices and commitments, for which one must answer oneself. (This sounds like Pico.) The subjectivity and freedom of the *cogito,* for Sartre, is the only basis for humanism.

Jean Beaufret wrote about this to Heidegger, who replied in his "Letter on Humanism" (1947) that to be human is rather to stand in the light of Being beyond the finite beings of our experience; it is to take part in the light of Being, in other words to bring to light or to fulfill the relation of Being to the being of man and of all other beings; e.g., compared to beings, Being is nothing if it is concealed by them, while compared to Being, beings are nothing unless they make it present or manifest. To be a man is to become the thought of Being, a nonduality in which Being is at once object and subject, in a thinking that is neither practical (as Sartre suggests) nor theoretical (technical, metaphysical), but prior to both: it is thinking in which the world is not a machine but a world of day and night, of seasons, forests, lakes, mountains, and rivers, of waking and sleeping, growing up and growing old, falling ill and healing, of dying and giving birth.[2] As he writes elsewhere, being is giving, and thinking is thanking, not engineering a result or philosophizing in the sense of a technical analysis of beings, but acknowledgement and poetry and praise and silence.

The first humanism, says Heidegger, was a Roman appropriation of Greek *paideia,* or liberal education,[3] in which man was seen as always and everywhere a rational animal. "This essential definition of man is not false," he says, "but it is conditioned by metaphysics." For man is not simply one living creature among others, the one that can reason: he is the one who guards the truth of Being "in order that beings might appear in the light of Being as the beings they are." And thus the shepherding of Being is, for Heidegger, the only basis for humanism. His own definition of humanism is "meditating and caring, that man be human and not inhumane . . . a concern that man become free for his humanity and find his worth in it."[4]

Now I am not a Heidegger specialist and consequently will not hazard a fuller explanation of his thinking here; but I am interested in this idea of the classical origins of humanism and the suggestion that, insofar as they were metaphysicians and ignored the difference and relation of Being and beings, Plato and Aristotle were not humanists, at least in his sense of the word.[5] (Does Plato, I wonder, ignore the difference and relation of Being and beings when he writes, in *Republic* 6, that the Good is "beyond being" and truth and knowledge but is the cause of them all, as the sun is the source of bodies and light and vision but is other and greater than these?[6] Does Aristotle, when he says that the divine is "a principle whose very essence is actuality"?[7] Does Plotinus, who claims to be expounding both, when he emphasizes that the One is beyond everything yet is the source of all?[8] Heidegger, I take it, has his answer to all this: to treat Being as a cause or principle or source is already to limit or define it as a being.) I propose therefore to leave him to one side at this point and to turn my attention to them. Let us address the question What would they make of humanism? by asking What to them is a human being and his humanity? What is a good man and a good human life?

First, for Socrates and Plato (whom I shall treat together, following Emerson's remark that they "are the double star which the most powerful instruments cannot entirely separate"), the question would arise first with the Sophists, those wandering professors of wisdom and virtue who offer for a fee to teach people to become outstanding men and citizens by speaking persuasively to anyone about anything. The Sophists' theory of knowledge, so far as they had one, was skeptical, relativist, or nihilist, while their ethics and politics tended to be anthropocentric and secular, even materialistic, hedonistic, and egoistic.

The best example is Protagoras, whose words on truth are quoted by Socrates in the *Theaetetus.*

> Man is the measure of all things: both of things that are, that they are;
> and of things that are not, that they are not.[9]

Socrates goes on to reject this idea, not because it is anthropocentric so much as because it is relativistic and does away with the difference between knowledge and belief, since if whatever appears to any man *is* to him (as Protagoras says), then all appearances are true and real and all men are wise; and yet everyone distinguishes appearing from being, belief from reality, in regard to what *will* do good or harm in treating an illness, making wine, composing music, cooking a meal, or (and this is Protagoras' own specialty) persuading a jury. He also rejects it because it proves unstatable, since either it is false as soon as it appears false to anyone, or else it is unfalsifiable because one cannot assert it as the truth but only as what one believes, and then nothing can contradict it because it contradicts nothing.[10]

But Socrates would also reject the anthropocentrism of Protagoras' idea: even though the wise man is a better measure than the ignorant one, it is really not man but God who is for Socrates the true measure of all things: "Nothing imperfect is the measure of anything," he says in the *Republic;* it is true that he may not have Protagoras in mind here, but in *Laws* Plato's spokesman, the Athenian, remarks that "it is God who truly is for us 'the measure of all things,' much more truly than, as they say, 'man,' " so that whoever would be loved by God, must become like him in restraint and justice, since like loves (only) like.[11] As Plato often says, the divine is not jealous or envious of man but wants him to become as like itself as he can;[12] so too Socrates keeps saying that the gods do not forget the man who remembers them and becomes as like them as he can through justice and goodness.[13]

Now Protagoras also wrote a book on the gods, opening with the well-known agnostic words:

Regarding the gods I do not know whether they exist or not, nor what they are like. For many are the obstacles to knowledge [of them]: the darkness of the subject, and the shortness of human life.

For Socrates, however, it is evident both that there are gods and that they are good, whatever else they may be. When he begins to revise the religious mythology to be used in the education of the young guardians in *Republic* 2, he makes it axiomatic that divinity is truly good and the cause of all other good, and the cause only of good and not of evil as well. What beyond this the gods may be, according to him, is hard to say,[14] but it is clear at least that the Ideas are divine and so are the minds made divine by knowing them, and that these Ideas include especially the pure Forms of the virtues.[15] He treats God or the divine as if it were the same as the Idea of the Good itself in *Republic* 6, and the Idea of Life in *Timaeus* and *Phaedo,* somewhat the way Christians speak of Father and Son as two Persons of one God.

On the other hand, Socrates would agree that man has no knowledge of the gods; yet for him this has a different meaning. As he explains to the judges who will condemn him for impiety and ruining the young by teaching them to question everyone and everything and so to slander their elders, the god Apollo himself told him through the oracle at Delphi that no one was wiser than he; and after questioning himself and others and comparing his knowledge of his ignorance with others' knowledge of their technical knowledge but deeper ignorance of their moral ignorance, Socrates concluded that the god only meant him as an example and was really saying to all men through him that no one is wiser than he who, like Socrates, knows that he is not very wise, by contrast with the god who really is. It is thus the god who is the measure, since only he knows what the goodness is that makes men and their lives good; but since all men want to live well, they need to know and acquire this goodness, though they will not exert themselves to discover it until they are shown their ignorance and lack of it, and Socrates takes it that this is what the god wants him to do. The god wants him to sting people awake to think more of what they think, to make them realize that they have thought so little of the virtues that they say they think so much of, that they do not even know that they do not adequately know them, and so are not so wise and good as they imagine they are. This life of questioning and investigation and discussion is the only one worth living because only it draws near the goodness men need to live well.[16] Thus Socrates agrees that men have no knowledge of the gods and what they know, that is so long as they imagine they have it, without having worked to acquire it; but unlike Protagoras Socrates believes in knowledge and inquiry, as something both possible and necessary for their fulfillment,[17] and for him this searching and learning become the definition not only of the philosopher who is in love with the beauty of this goodness,[18] but also of man himself.[19]

Now in *Republic* 4 Socrates distinguishes three parts of the soul—appetite, spirit, and mind—though he also hints that there are as many parts as one needs to distinguish, and in Book 10 he suggests that in itself the soul may be really simply the *mind,* for we see the soul best when we consider it detached from the bodily life and identified with its best part and what it loves, the divine deathless eternal Ideas.[20] He has anticipated this move in the symbolic picture of the soul he draws in Book 9, as a man with an inner man within a lion within a dragon,[21] the whole man living best by subjecting through the practice of justice the brutal parts to "the human, or perhaps we should say to the divine." In other words a man most truly *is* not simply his soul but his mind, his most divine part.[22]

But there is a puzzle here: for what in him puts the inner man in charge of the dragon and the lion? Who or what is it that *harmonizes* his three parts or *turns* the soul from darkness to light, from sensible appearance to ideal reality and truth, or *makes* his soul follow the gleam of truth "with the whole of its being"?[23] What is the soul's *government, throne, tower,* or *guardhouse* that we turn, or fail to turn, over to mind rather than to spirit or appetite, and *who* decides?[24]

Perhaps this is a self or "I" that comes into being through a man's identification with mind, so that the harmony, conversion, and mastery are an act of that better self or mind, purified not so much from spirit and appetite as from the life dominated by them.[25] For as Socrates remarks:

> One who maintains that justice is better [than injustice] would say that all
> our words and actions should strengthen the man within the man. He will
> look after the many headed beast as a farmer looks after his animals, fos-
> tering and domesticating the gentle heads and preventing the wild ones from
> growing. With the lion as his ally, he will care for all of them and rear
> them by making them all friendly with each other and with himself.[26]

That is, he always only does what makes him a better human being, and
lets the rest go whenever it interferes with this. He is not an ascetic, therefore, but rather he lives the most truly enjoyable life that a man can live,
because it is the best and wisest.[27]

It follows that the best man is not merely a knowing mind, but *a just
man,* a statesman and educator, who willingly returns to the cave to help
others become just, a *philosopher* who does not only examine himself and
others in order to perfect his own soul, but who calls each to work for the
perfection of one's own.[28] When Socrates calls the best men godlike in *Republic* 6, he speaks of their moral virtues, their justice and restraint, and the
beauty of these, just as in the *Theaetetus* it is through justice that we are
to flee worldliness in order to become like the divine which, as Timaeus says,
generously wants everyone and everything to be such as it is.[29]

Religious writers have criticized Socrates and Plato for relying too much
on the human ability to become good of oneself, and ignoring the need for
divine help or grace. But perhaps they do not ignore it. Consider Glaucon's
challenge to Socrates in *Republic* 2 to show that justice is always better than
injustice for what it directly does to the soul of its possessor, so that one
both *can* and *should* choose it, even if one has the power to do what one
likes, or alternatively even if it leaves one powerless to avoid being wronged
by the unjust man who manages to exchange reputation and rewards with
him and to call his own injustice an act of justice. It looks as if no man,
but only a god, could suffer such wrongs without being defiled by them and
beginning to return them like-for-like, or at least meaning to hatefully.
Adimantus adds to this that poets, and parents and elders quoting them in
praise of justice, always only commend it for this reputation and reward,
so that they really teach people to be wicked but hide it: hence "only a man
of godlike character whom injustice disgusts, or one who has superior knowledge [of the harm it does the soul], avoids injustice" when he has the power
to do it. Socrates replies that the brothers "must be divinely inspired if you
are not convinced that injustice is better yet can speak for it as you have
done"; and in Book 6 he says twice in the same passage that it can only
be by divine intervention that anyone turns out well given present non-
philosophical modes of education.[30] Socrates seems to admit that justice looks
foolish and mad, if not impossible, from the viewpoint of the nonphilosoph-
ical and the unjust; but he agrees also that to those who believe in it and
pursue it, it is divine and blessed.[31] As we have seen, when he criticizes the
poetic theology of Homer and Hesiod later in Book 2, he insists that the
divine is truly good, and as such, it is the cause of all other good, rather
as if it *is* the goodness that makes us and our lives good, and we have no

other good apart from that which we receive from it; indeed in the *Euthyphro* he remarks that "there is for us no good that we do not receive from the gods."[32] So apparently to believe in justice is to believe in its divinity, its absolute and unambiguous goodness, to believe that we acquire it from the gods as theirs not ours. Moreover, the just man perhaps does not know his own justice, but only his need and desire and love for it, just as the wise man of the *Apology* does not know his own wisdom, or dare not claim any real knowledge of goodness such as that which the god alone can have, but only his own active aspiration for it.[33] His whole and only just activity is, in a sense, a passivity to the divine justice within him, or to the divine mind within him; in this respect he only works negatively, by doing nothing to interfere with what it does in and through him. This is why he cannot charge a fee for the advice he gives, since it is not his own; he only makes himself the spokesman for the god who intervenes in worldly life through him and who seeks to turn everyone into its own likeness.

Putting all this together, we can return to our question: Is Plato a humanist? I want to say, Well, no and yes: no, because his philosophy is not so much centered on man as it is on God or the divine Good; yes, because it is centered on man's relation to God and the divine Good, as the one true humanity and fulfillment and freedom. Moreover, the man who realizes this good for himself is the one who works to realize it for everyone, since it consists in a kind of communication, community, wholeness, and unity.

We can clarify this by turning now to Aristotle, about whom many similar things can be said.

To begin, Aristotle would agree that it is not man who is the measure, but the *good* man.[34] For man's practical wisdom and politics do not represent the highest kind of knowledge, since "in fact man is not the best thing in the universe,"[35] but rather the minds that move the solar and stellar spheres, and beyond these the divine mind itself. Apparently the highest knowledge is the knowledge of God and of what he knows, and our highest good is found in uniting ourselves as fully and as often as we can to this.

Our highest good, he explains further in *Nicomachean Ethics* 1.7, must be something humanly *attainable* by action, absolutely *final* or desirable always as an end only and never as a means to any other good, and *sufficient* to complete our life when taken by itself, that is, when taken as a final and formal cause of the goodness of all the other good things that we desire, so that we want them because they are either means to this or parts of it.

Aristotle says that we call it happiness, and proposes that it consists in doing something well and often that only men (among natural things?) do, or that makes them human, namely reasoning; and if men do this well in several ways, for example, deliberating, or theorizing, then it is reasoning well in the best and completest way, or with their best or highest part, as he adds later in 10.7.

There he shows that his candidate for man's highest happiness is the mind's wise contemplation. He does not say theorizing, because he thinks that beholding the truth is even more satisfying than working it out, as an actuality or fulfillment is better to us than the process of becoming actual.[36] In this he would disagree with Leibniz:

Therefore our happiness will never, and ought not, to consist in full enjoyment in which there is nothing more to desire, dulling our mind, but in a perpetual progress to new pleasures and new perfections,

and with Lessing:

If God held all truth in his right hand, and in his left the passionate lifelong pursuit of truth, though with the condition that I should always risk error, and if God said to me, Choose! I would take his left hand and say, Give me this, Father, the truth is for you alone!

and even with Socrates:

It is the greatest good for a man to discuss virtue every day . . . for the unexamined life is not worth living for a man. . . .

What would one not give, gentlemen, for the opportunity to examine the man who led the great expedition against Troy, or Odysseus, or Sisyphus, ... It would be an extraordinary happiness to talk with them, to keep company with them and examine them.[37]

For, Aristotle explains, we can contemplate more *continuously* than we can do any other thing, and more *enjoyably,* and *self-sufficiently* or without depending on any other men, and more *finally* or without aiming at any other good beyond it, and therefore as our most complete or fullest happiness. However, he goes on, and I quote:

Such a life would be more than human. A man who would live it would do so not insofar as he is human, but because there is a divine element within him [sc. mind]. . . . We must not follow those who advise us to have human thoughts, since we are (only) men, and mortal thoughts, as mortals should; on the contrary we should try to become deathless as far as that is possible and do our best to live by what is highest in us. . . . One might even regard it as each man's true self, since it is the controlling and better part. It would, therefore, be strange if a man chose not to live his own life but someone else's. . . . [Thus] a life of mind is the best and most pleasant [and happiest] for man, inasmuch as mind, above all else, is man.[38]

Aristotle goes on to state that the life of moral virtue is happy in another sense and is the best life for men as such; and here it looks at first as if he is comparing the contemplative and impractical or inactive life with the practical and noncontemplative one, as best and second best, respectively.

The man who leads the latter life, he says, is more dependent on others and on external goods, since he needs food for his body and money to buy it from others. He even needs money to practice the virtues of justice, generosity, and restraint. For money allows one to be just by meeting obligations to others, to be generous by giving them what they need, and to have the restraint not to take more than one needs. The gods, says Aristotle, do not need money, nor do they need to perform just, generous, and restrained actions; they can coherently be imagined only as contemplating and as rejoicing in men like themselves who honor and live by their minds as much as possible. (Might the gods enjoy seeing these morally good actions performed by men, or do they perform these good actions themselves eternally, begetting or inspiring them in us?)

I do not think, however, that Aristotle means that the best and most godlike and supremely happy men are never active, while the best merely human ones are never contemplative. There are not *two* lives, the second best perfecting the human and the best transcending it: there is *one* best life, perfecting the human by transcending it as often as possible; contemplation is promoted by practice and manifested in it by actions aimed at drawing others into itself, so that in a sense even practice *is* contemplation.[39] In other words, moral virtue is not a mere external *means* to intellectual virtue, and worthless in itself; rather it is an essential *part* of the life organized around contemplation as its meaning and goal.[40] The best man uses his mind as well as and as often as he can, and this means that he contemplates whenever possible and does whatever makes him do it better and more continuously. But even the very best man must rest and sleep and eat sometimes, and besides he is a social and political animal, who needs friends and family and fellow citizens, with whom he can work and think, and whom he can improve by his example of working and thinking. Thus, Aristotle remarks that while the contemplative is sufficient and can think by himself, "perhaps he could do it better if he had colleagues to work with him": better, that is to say, with more wisdom, and perhaps also with more courage, restraint, and justice, but therefore also with more enjoyment.[41] Perhaps the wiser he is, the less he needs to have colleagues to help him, but the more he needs to *be* a colleague to others to help them to act and think and live well. For a good man needs and takes pleasure in being a friend to others who not only acknowledge his good actions but also provide further scope for them insofar as by his example he shares in their good actions as partial agent.[42] The final section of the *Ethics* addresses the good man's need and desire to educate those among whom he lives. For "if the community neglects [this], it would seem incumbent on every man to help his children and his friends to attain virtue," and this will lead him to study politics and legislation.[43] Thus as a social and political animal the contemplative man will act, and the active man will theorize and contemplate: the best human life requires *both*, even if contemplation is its end. Let us remember that contemplation is in itself intensely active and demanding for the thinker,[44] as well as for others who find it attractive and allow it to transform their lives too. So even as a contemplative he will act, e.g., in teaching others or doing research with them on biology and politics and rhetoric as well as metaphysics and astronomy. Let us remember also that mind is needed for right action, to grasp that the good for man in general is contemplation, and to judge what it requires in particular circumstances.[45] And thus Aristotle concludes that the best and happiest men are "those who most love and honor mind, . . . who care for what is most dear to the gods, and who act rightly and nobly."[46]

The divine part of a man, his mind, says Aristotle, *is* man. This is what makes him fully human, since he needs to use this in all his activities, practical as well as intellectual. It is what makes him good at being a man, and its excellence constitutes the formal and final cause of his humanity, but also of his happiness, since this lies in the exercise of his best and most complete excellence. The supremely happy man therefore does not live austerely, but has family, children, and friends, and occasions to practice the virtues controlled by and manifesting mind.[47]

So is Aristotle a humanist? Once again, I think, we must say, no and yes: no, because the center of his philosophy is not man but the divine; yes, because the center is, more exactly, the divine mind in man, or man's assimilation to God's mind through the life organized around contemplation of it and what it contemplates, while working to communicate this life to all men and as much as possible to raise them to a life beyond the merely human. (Beyond the *merely* human, that is to say, beyond the all too humanly sensual, selfish, ambitious, envious, cruel, and false, and to the *fully* human, courageous, restrained, generous, friendly, truthful, just, and above all wise.)

Is *humanism,* then, a useful term to characterize the thought of Plato and Aristotle? I prefer to leave this question open. But perhaps both can be called humanists in the loose sense that they are interested in the best life for human beings, and it may be in this way that we should understand Socrates' remark that the philosopher practices death and Aristotle's that we should make ourselves deathless.[48] Both are speaking of a quality of life: Socrates means that we should die away *to* and *from* the bodily life, and live instead for the virtues and truth and wisdom, and be willing to die *for* this true life of the mind; Aristotle means that we should live as much as we can by this mind, for this is the presence in us of the mind of God, which is deathless. Both can admit that our being and mind come to an end in time, while saying that we should live by a mind that does not. Both can agree with Spinoza that

> A free man thinks of nothing less than death, and his wisdom is a meditation not on death but on life.[49]

As we have seen, this need not be a harsh ascetic life, indifferent to bodily enjoyment and social relationship, since at its best it includes everything that can be done rightly and well so as to make one a better human being and so manifest one's goodness and wisdom as to impart them to others.

But if any philosophy can be called a humanism that concerns itself in this way with the best life for man or has an ethics or politics—if even a god-centered religious philosophy is a humanism in making the most godlike life the most truly human one—then is this still a useful category? What does it exclude? Nihilism? But Nietzsche built, or tried to build, an ethics on the ruins of nihilism. Positivism? This rules out ethics and normative discourse generally as literally or scientifically meaningless. But perhaps it considers it liberating and good for man to do this. Mechanism? This says that in nature there is no good or evil, no right or wrong, only consequences, since men and living creatures are simply machines.[50] Could this be liberating? Surely not without qualification; humanism so understood would be a reproach.

Let us think again in this connection of Pico's words in the *Oration:* man, he says, is able to fix his own limits, and make himself into whatever he likes. Pico does not mean what Sartre means, that man has no essential nature, but rather that man can become like God in mind and character, in terms of Christian Platonism, and so fulfill his nature, if he chooses. Later humanists like Francis Bacon, who went the technological way, would take his meaning to be that man can become what he likes and do what he wishes, shaping the world to please himself. Three hundred years later we see that this refusal to acknowledge any objective bounds to man's ambition leads to the idea that man must do whatever he can and that whatever is possible is necessary, whether it be thermonuclear bombs or chemotherapy, organ implants or genetic engineering, factory farms or pesticides, artificial intelligence or electronic surveillance. Pico's God tells man that he is not held in by any limits but can fix them for himself—or rather the technologist can become a god, and the rest his slaves. Some modern humanists therefore have protested that this attitude creates an inhuman world and makes us inhuman beings with machine hearts (in the phrase of *Chuang Tzu* 13). Let us remember Pindar's advice, rejected by Aristotle,[51] to have human thoughts since we are only men, and mortal thoughts as mortals should. Let us recognize some natural limits to our ambition and desires and preserve our humanity and our world.[52] Let us try to be like God not in his power but in his goodness, and understand our humanity in the same way, doing no more to our fellow human beings and living creatures, to our planet, and to ourselves, than will make us better and wiser, not merely more powerful. Let us live, not severely but fully and enjoyably in a world that is more truly ours because it is not ours alone and because we are *not* the measure of all things.

This is to reject the humanism of unrestrained technology in favor of a humanism more like that of Christianity and other religions, of Plato and Aristotle, and of Pindar too, who in the Eighth *Pythian Ode* calls man "a creature of a day" and "a shadow's dream," and adds

> But when god-given glory comes
> A bright light shines on us and life our life is sweet.

Yet where Pindar speaks of the glory of victory in the games, celebrated in poetry such as his, Plato and Aristotle might talk of the blessedness of virtue and wisdom.[53] The light of these is comparable to the light of Being in Heidegger's thinking: a light in which things are seen for what they *truly* are, at their best and most godlike, because for men truth *is* godlikeness.

One thing more. Perhaps, we think, humanism should be universal and take in *all* men, and *all* women, excluding no one. But do Plato and Aristotle actually offer the best life to everyone? Xenophon's Socrates is an elitist; but Plato's Socrates calls everyone to pursue virtue through philosophy, though he expects many to ignore it; likewise Aristotle, who says in *Politics* 7.2, for example, that "evidently that form of government is best in which every man, whoever he is, can act best and live happily." Yet both Plato and Aristotle live in a city in which slaves outnumber free men 20 to 1 according to Athenaeus; modern scholars have said it is only about 1 to 1.[54] But even this seems to us too many. Plato never explicitly denounces slavery, although he clearly can and should do so.[55] In the *Statesman* he seems to reserve it for those who *cannot* rise above ignorance and grovelling subservience, just as exile and execution are only for the incorrigibly wicked. In *Laws* he writes that a man shows the quality of his justice by the way he treats his slaves: in dealing with those whom he can easily wrong he shows whether he truly loves right and hates wrong.[56] Similarly Aristotle cites the sage Bias' remark that "Ruling reveals the man"; but like Plato he seems to think that some men are naturally slavish and that slavery is right and best for them, although he considers the position that it is unnatural and wrong, and at one point he even cites an orator, Alkidamas, who said, "God has left all men free; nature has made no man a slave."[57] Shouldn't a humanist, we may wonder, acknowledge the humanity of everyone, the capacity of each person to think and act for himself, at least to suffer? And doesn't he show his own humanity by doing this, and refute it by refusing to?[58]

Yet let us not rush to judge Plato and Aristotle. It may be that they do not actively promote freedom for everyone, but it is arguable that they would desire it and seek it. Justice is giving each man his due. Socrates would say: it is giving each what he needs to make him just, good, and wise, whether directly by stopping him to question him, or indirectly by attractive example, a sort of final cause. But many are uninterested in what is right or best or true; they are led by their emotions, enslaved to them, and they will not learn of any life higher than the bodily one. They may have a capacity to think and act for themselves and to learn to do this well, but they will not develop it.[59] When these are in the overwhelming majority, and threaten the lives of those who would question their moral notions too closely, including their notions about their right to enslave others, it may easily seem as if the way of example is best. It is not without power.

Notes

1. See Paul Edwards, ed., *The Encyclopedia of Philosophy* (New York, 1973), 4.73.
2. Cf. John Caputo, *The Mystical Element* (1978), 263.
3. See for example the second century grammarian Aulus Gellius, *Attic Nights,* trans. John Rolfe (Loeb Classical Library, 1927), vol. 2, 457:

> Those who have spoken Latin and have used the language correctly do not give to the word *humanitas* the meaning which it is commonly thought to have, namely, what the Greeks call *philanthropia,* signifying a kind of friendly spirit and good-feeling towards all men without distinction; but they give to *humanitas* about the force of the Greek *paideia;* that is, what we call *eruditionem institutionemque in bonas artes,* or "education and training in the liberal arts." Those who earnestly desire and seek after these are most

highly humanized. For the pursuit of that kind of knowledge, and the training given by it, have been granted to man alone of all the animals, and for that reason it is termed *humanitas,* or "humanity."

4. Martin Heidegger, *Basic Writings,* ed. David Farrell Krell (New York, 1977), 200f.

5. Ibid., 194, 227, 232; 202, 224f.

6. Cf. *Sophist* 254ab.

7. *Metaphysics* 12.7 1071b20; cf. 2.1 993b9.

8. *The Good or The One* 1,6,9.

9. *Theaetetus* 152a.

10. Ibid., 169d–172c, 177c–179b.

11. *Republic* 6.504c, *Laws* 4.716c; cf. Matthew 5:43–48.

12. *Timaeus* 29e, 37c; *Phaedrus* 247a; *Epinomis* 988b; cf. Aristotle, *Metaphysics* 1.2 983a3.

13. *Republic* 10.613ab; *Apology* 41cd.

14. See *Apology* 35d, *Cratylus* 400d-la, *Philebus* 12c, *Timaeus* 28c.

15. *Phaedrus* 247ce, 249c, 250ac; *Phaedo* 78b–84b; *Republic* 10.611e; *Theaetetus* 176e–7a.

16. *Apology* 29de, 38a.

17. *Protagoras* 354d; *Theaetetus* 196d–7a; *Meno* 81de, 86bc; *Phaedo* 90c–1b.

18. *Symposium* 203b–4a; *Lesser Hippias* 369d, 372ad; *Republic* 5.475ce, 6.485d, 490ab.

19. *Phaedrus* 249bc; *Theaetetus* 153bc; cf. *Sophist* 262c: "a man learns."

20. *Republic* 4.435c–41c, 443e; 10.611–2a.

21. 9.588b–90d. There is a dragon in the soul, and a lion, as well as a man.

22. Ibid., 589d. Cf. *Phaedrus* 249cd; *Phaedo* 80a, 114d–5, 106d–7a; *Republic* 9.519ab, 527de; *Philebus* 28c; *Timaeus* 41cd and especially 90ad: "A man who has earnestly loved knowledge and true wisdom, and used his mind more than any other part of him, must think deathless and divine thoughts, if he wishes to attain truth, and so far as a man can share in deathlessness, he must wholly be deathless and since he ever serves the divine power and has the divine in him in place, he must be outstandingly happy."

23. *Republic* 3.443c–4a; 7.518b–96, 6.508cd; 10.611e.

24. Ibid., 8.550b, 553b, 560b, 561b; cf. 6.488 and *Phaedo,* 92e–4, 78c.

25. Cf. S. Kierkegaard, *Either/Or,* trans. W. Lowrie (Princeton, 1987), 2.217–21, 230, 262f.

26. *Republic* 589ab.

27. Ibid., 9.576e–8a; cf. 4.443c–5b, 1.352d–4a; *Phaedrus* 247ce, but also *Phaedo* 64–5a.

28. Republic 7.519–21b, 9.592; *Apology* 28e, 38a, 29d.

29. *Republic* 6.500b–1c; *Theaetetus* 176ac; *Timaeus* 29e; cf. *Republic* 1.335, 2.379ac; pseudo-Dionysius, *Divine Names* 4.1, 20: the good is communicative of itself and of being.

30. *Republic* 2.366e, 369a; 6.493a,e.

31. Cf. *Theaetetus* 176e–7a.

32. *Republic* 379ac; *Euthyphro* 15a; cf. Mark 10.17.

33. *Apology* 23ab; cf. *Euthyphro* 4e, 15cd; *Charmides* 164a.

34. Aristotle, *Nicomachean Ethics* 3.4, 10.5; cf. Plato, *Symposium* 186c.

35. *Nicomachean Ethics* 6.7 1141a22.

36. Ibid., 7.14 1154b28.

37. Leibnitz, *Principles of Nature and Grace* 18; Lessing, *Eine Duplik* quoted by Kierkegaard in *Postscript* 97f; Plato, *Apology* 38a, 41cd; see also *Phaedo* 79d, 89d, 81a, 84ab.

38. *Nicomachean Ethics* 10.7 1177b27–8a8; cf. 9.4 1166a17, 9.9 1168b35–9a3; see also *Rhetoric* 2.21 13.94b24: "Mortal creatures should cherish mortal, not immortal thoughts"; thus Pindar, *Isthmean Ode* 5.14–7: "Seek not to become Zeus . . . Mortal thoughts befit a mortal man;" *Pythian* 3.58–62: "From the gods we must expect things that suit our mortal minds, aware of our mortal minds, aware of the here and now, aware of our allotment. Do not yearn, O my soul, for immortal life! Use to the utmost the skill that is yours" (trans. Nisetich).

39. Cf. Plotinus, *Virtues* 3 and *Nature, Contemplation, and the One* 1f.

40. Cf. *Nicomachean Ethics* 6.12 144a17, 13 1145a7–12.

41. Ibid., 10.7 11177a35; cf. 1.8 1099a7–22.

42. Ibid., 9.9 1169b11–4, 1170a27–b19.

43. Ibid., 10.9 1180a31; cf. 1.9; 2.1; 4.1, 6; 5.1, 6; 8.8, 13.

44. Ibid., 7.14 1154b21, 10.4 1175a3, 10.7 1177a19.

45. Ibid., 6.5, 8f.

46. Ibid., 10.8, 1179a28f; cf. *Politics* 7.1 1323a27, 622.

47. *Nicomachean Ethics* 1.8, 9.9, 10.8 1178b36; *Rhetoric* 1.5.

48. *Phaedo* 64a; *Nicomachean Ethics* 10.7 1177b33.

49. *Ethics* 4.67.

50. Cf. Kant, first *Critique* A532–58; *Groundwork* III.

51. *Nicomachean Ethics* 10.7.

52. Cf. Plato, *Gorgias* 507d–86, *Republic* 1.349–50c.

53. *Theaetetus* 176–7a; *Nicomachean Ethics* 1.9, 10.7f.

54. Twenty to one or 400,000 to 20,000 is the estimate of Athenaeus (2nd century A.D.); modern scholars have revised the ratio down to about 1 to 1, or 20,000 slaves to 20,000 free men, or 60,000 free men and women, or 120,000 free men, women, and children. See A. H. M. Jones, *Athenian Democracy* (1957); cf. Victor Ehrenberg, *The Greek State* (1960), p. 33, and Ostwald's note to *Nicomachean Ethics* 9.10 1170b32. See also Plato, *Ion* 535de and *Symposium* 175e.

55. It is not *needed* in his ideal city in the *Republic*, since this includes citizens who give their brute labor in exchange for wages (3.37le, 4.434c, 5.463b). Moreover, it is not *permitted* either, for the only citizens whose own wisdom fits them to rule in fact may own nothing privately (3.461d-7, 4.419-21c). No one is born to serve others slavishly as the one task that he can alone or best perform for the common good, but everyone serves everyone in his own way, and the philosopher serves the character of all (4.423d, 7.519e-10). To allow the city, or the guardians collectively, to own slaves would seem to go against the spirit of this scheme (see 4.423b-5). The reference to slavery in the ideal city, therefore, is puzzling, and we are left to wonder why Plato does not take this opportunity to denounce it. See B. Calvert, *Classical Quarterly* 37 (1987): 367–72.

56. Plato, *Statesman* 308e–9a; cf. *Republic* 9.590–1a; *Laws* 6.777d.

57. *Nicomachean Ethics* 5.1; *Politics* 1.3–7; cf. 7.2 1324a34–7; *Rhetoric* 1.13; cf. *Nicomachean Ethics* 8.1 1155a17–22; 8.9 1159b27–32; 8.11 1161b2–8.

58. Cf. Kierkegaard, *Works of Love* 1.1, pp. 32f: "Like is known only by like."

59. Cf. *Republic* 7.517a, 518b–9b; *Nichomachean Ethics* 10.7 1179b4–1180a24.

2

Roman Humanism

Allan Booth

Humanism is quickened by the notion that intelligent man and his world are the focus and measure of all things. This doctrine, in its fullest acceptance, disbelieves that individual and group are subject to divine designs and constraints beyond human comprehension and control. Man assures himself instead that inherent in his rational nature lies a trait which allows and authorizes him to manufacture and direct his own destiny, freely and without divine meddling. This governing trait is moreover so focal a force as to obviate the risk that some limb of knowledge may develop a potency sufficient to wag the human, or rather the humanist being. For humanism grants to the governing trait, implanted securely within man and his management, the means to individual perfection and the capacity perfectly to assess and to guide all affairs, in their every dimension, as they touch upon man throughout the universe. Hence a crucial question: how may man best equip his intelligence to utilize this trait? Thinkers in fourteenth-century Italy, the acknowledged springboard for humanism's relaunch, found their answer in Antiquity: absorption of a liberal draught of *belles-lettres* seasoned with a dash of moral philosophies should position man to exercise, to its potential plenitude, his rational autonomy. This perspective explains itself readily. The Italian humanists were reacting against a social and intellectual stagnation sanctified by the Church, but they were as yet unaware of a situation where scientific advances could undo Christian dogmatism. So, quite naturally, they looked to their pre-Christian Roman past, whose predominantly literary culture concentrates upon man's known existence (rather than upon any hereafter) and betrays the pervasive conviction that divine powers should assist man to his ends and not *vice versa*.

Umanista, the term used in the late fifteenth century to designate the professional humanist, was applied initially to the teacher and student of rhetoric. This usage corresponds finely with the acceptation of the Latin term *humanitas,* to which Aulus Gellius, a favored author of Petrarch,[1] devotes the following note (*Attic Nights* 13. 17.1):[2]

> Those who have spoken Latin and have used the language correctly do not give to the word *humanitas* the meaning which it is commonly thought to have, namely, what the Greeks call φιλανθρωπία, signifying a kind of friendly spirit and good-feeling towards all men without distinction; but they gave to *humanitas* about the force of the Greek παιδεία; that is, what we call *eruditionem institutionemque in bonas artes,* or "education and training in the liberal arts." Those who earnestly desire and seek after these are the most highly humanized. For the pursuit of that kind of knowledge, and the training given by it, have been granted to man alone of all the animals, and for that reason it is termed *humanitas,* or "humanity."

The expression "liberal arts" may suggest quite a range of subjects to a modern reader unaware of ancient realities. Yet, as clearly emerges from Gellius' work and other sources, liberal pursuits in his day were limited to two principal areas: *grammatice,* that is, the study of grammar and literature (mainly poetry and history), and rhetoric. This cultural focus was reflected at the institutional level where the future Roman gentleman, scholar, or statesman was educated in boyhood by the *grammaticus,* or grammarian, the teacher of grammar and literature, and in adolescence by the rhetorician or, to keep his Latin title, the *rhetor;* such was usually the fullest range of liberal schooling.[3] So Gellius himself and his medieval interpreter would have understood the principal and cumulative polish in *humanitas* to come from refinement in rhetoric, from the command of expression and reasoning, from the understanding of human nature afforded by that study.

For the humanist sense of *humanitas* Gellius refers to Cicero, who wielded immense authority throughout the Renaissance. Now it was Cicero who consolidated in Latin thinking the idea that the complete human being in complete control is embodied, not in any metaphysician who seeks to explain and order reality by pursuit of the mystical, but in the perfect orator who knows how to recognize, sift, and apply knowledge beneficial to man. This orator, according to Ciceronian doctrine, would keep a mastery of all wisdom under the sensible and sense-making control of rhetoric (*De oratore* 3. 143): ". . . the consummate orator possesses all the knowledge of the philosophers, but the range of the philosophers does not necessarily include eloquence; and although they look down upon it, it cannot but be deemed to add a crowning embellishment to their sciences." The eloquent Cicero, who writes not without a trace of autobiographic eulogy, has no time for the claim that there be some higher wisdom, artistic, religious, scientific, or philosophic (to give "philosophy" its ancient range of sense), a force distinct from and superior to the scope of rhetoric. Indeed he inveighs against Plato's Socrates as "the source from which has sprung the undoubtedly absurd and unprofitable and reprehensible severance between the tongue and the brain, leading to our having one set of professors to teach us how to think and another to teach us how to speak" (3.61). And Cicero believes that an alert mind can readily assimilate the sum of human widsom (3.89):

Consequently, nobody need be afraid of the magnitude of the sciences on the ground that old men are studying them, for either they have come to them in old age, or their interest in their studies has lasted on to old age, or they are very slow learners. In fact my view of the situation is that unless a man is able to learn a subject quickly he will never be able to learn it thoroughly at all.

Of course, if man is to forge and direct his destiny, he must have the capacity to fulfill speedily and soundly his apprenticeship to this task; education, in the humanist perspective, should then consist of a concise course of study serving as a prelude to life of creative thought and action.

The identification of the ultimate in human achievement with the city-state of Plato's *Republic* ruled by philosophers could hold little appeal for Cicero. But the Roman statesman would not despise all Greek political thought. For he could find authority for his rhetorically dominated humanism in the doctrines of Plato's contemporary Isocrates, "the father of eloquence." (ibid. 2.10).[4] The latter eschewed the Platonic quest for absolute, immutable divine values and truths, placing all higher studies, including dialectic, in subservience to rhetoric, the subject for which he reserves the designation "philosophy." (cf. *Antidosis* 261–269; *Panathenaicus* 26–29). Discourse at the social level is the essence of man and the source of human blessings, avers Isocrates (*Antidosis* 253):

> For in all other powers which we possess . . . we are in no respect superior to other living creatures; nay, we are inferior to many in swiftness and in strength, and in other resources; but, because there has been implanted in us the power to persuade each other and to make clear to each other what we desire, not only have we escaped the life of wild beasts, but we have come together and founded cities and made laws and invented arts; and, generally speaking, there is no institution devised by man which the proper power of speech has not helped us to establish.

This declaration that man is a social animal who owes his progress in civilization to his reasoned speech has helped earn for Isocrates, in addition to the title "father of eloquence," that of "father of humanism."[5] This designation is supported too by the belief that Isocrates established rhetoric as the crown of a system of schooling which was then simply inherited by the Romans when they dominated the Greek world two centuries later. Thus in the touching but apologetic tribute met in his monumental history of ancient education, H.-I. Marrou writes: "c'est Isocrate, beaucoup plus qu'aucun autre, qui porte l'honneur et la responsabilité d'avoir inspiré l'éducation à dominante littéraire de notre tradition occidentale."[6] But is Isocrates' outlook sufficiently free from belief in a divine guidance of human affairs to deserve the designation "humanist"? And did he in fact establish the supremacy of rhetoric in ancient schooling and culture?

The words which Herodotus (8.144) places in Athenian mouths have Greeks marked apart from others and joined together by blood, language, religion and custom. In a recent essay, C. G. Thomas identifies two other traits of distinction which would have been too obvious for inclusion in this list: "the form of organized corporate life known as the *polis,* or city state, and the concept of humanism, its attendant view of the worth and purpose of human life"; the notion of hybris which demarcates the spheres of human and divine operations would have produced, moreover, a humanism that was not in conflict, but in harmony with religion.[7] Now Greek thought of the fifth and fourth centuries did indeed connect man's survival and progress with the development of the city-state; Plato's Protagoras could exploit acceptance of this idea in formulating his fable to justify the thesis that political virtue is teachable (*Protagoras* 320c–323a). Again, myths like that of Bellerophon, who, for his attempted ascent to heaven, was cast down to earth there to wander a deranged outcast from human society, provide warnings against hybris. But if a general belief in man's divinely appointed destiny to belong in a city-state be thus attested, was Greek man, even within this limit, to be the measure of all things, or was he further subject to divine control?

The *Iliad* and the *Odyssey,* which attained written form about 700 B.C. after the Greek invention of the alphabet, draw upon an oral heritage that explores the relationship between man and god; as in other cultures, so here the casting of the main lines of this relationship is set in a mythic age where divinities intermingle freely with mortals. Both epics at their outset invoke the aid of the Muse and so claim to be divinely inspired. No doubt such invocations might be dismissed as mere literary conceits. But the very subject matter of the Homeric poems endowed them with an aura of divine revelation. Homer's title "Educator of the Greeks" would never be challenged with success, and the epics were to remain basic texts in Greek education. There was, moreover, a general tendency to regard all poets as inspired figures and to accord them a didactic function and social responsibility; thus, in Aristophanes' *Frogs* (1009–1053), it is the defined role of the tragedian to teach men to be better citizens.

In debate, such poetry was naturally cited to support arguments which it would inspire with the blessed cogency accorded at certain times and places to biblical quotations. For example, in his attack on Timarchus, Aeschines rebuts thus the defense's anticipated exploitation of Homer to justify and glorify the accused's homosexual attachments (141; cf. Lycurgus, *Leocrates* 99-103):

> But since you make mention of Achilles and Patroclus, and of Homer and the other poets—as though the jury were men innocent of education, while you are people of a superior sort, who feel yourselves quite beyond common folks in learning—that you may know that we too have before now heard and learned a little something, we shall say a word about this also. For since they undertake to cite wise men, and to take refuge in sentiments expressed in poetic measures, look, fellow citizens, into the works of those who are confessedly good and helpful poets, and see how far apart they considered chaste men, who love their like, and those who are wanton and overcome by forbidden lusts. I will speak first of Homer, whom we rank among the oldest and wisest of the poets.

Having cited Homer to his advantage, Aeschines proceeds to make similar use of Euripides, "a poet than whom none is wiser." (151). In caring thus to furnish the jurors with divinely inspired instruction the orator was fulfilling, if somewhat mechanically and vicariously, a role granted him by poetic tradition.

Rhetorical prowess is celebrated as the Homeric hero's principal political virtue. Thus Phoenix, the mentor of Achilles, notes his duty to exercise his young charge in affairs of war and in debate where men can make their mark (*Iliad* 9. 440–444). The verbal powers of various heroes are remarked and, as one would expect, Odysseus, the man never at a loss, is well equipped with the gift of eloquence *(Iliad* 3. 216–224):

> . . . when nimble-witted Odysseus took the floor, he stood there with his head bent firmly down, glancing from under his brows, and he did not swing his staff either to the front or to the back, but held it stiffly, as though he had never handled one before. You would have taken him for a sulky fellow and no better than a fool. But when that great voice of his came booming from his chest, and the words poured from his lips like flakes of winter snow, there was no man alive who could compete with Odysseus.

While the Homeric poems allow for the development of such a gift by experience, the gift itself, like the poet's inspiration, is divinely bestowed.[8] It is the princes who have the prerogative and duty to address and instruct the people: in this office they appear divine, and they may receive divine instruction and aid when their eloquence is used to assist in the advancement of divine plans (cf. *Iliad* 2. 142–332; *Odyssey* 8. 165–177). So the speeches of the princes tend to be oracular (cf. *Iliad* 1. 199–244; *Odyssey* 2. 129–176).

The *Iliad* and the *Odyssey* establish, then, not only for the poet but also for the orator the role of divinely inspired educator. In the *Theogony* (75–103), the Greek *Genesis* composed about 700 B.C., Hesiod brings this situation from the mythic past to the social benefit of the world in which he lived. For he relates that, whereas Apollo through his step-sisters, the Muses, inspires poets, Zeus through these same goddesses, his daughters, grants eloquence to rulers at birth, so that, in dispensing justice, they may soothe their communities. In his other epic, the *Works and Days* (202–285), Hesiod further explains that a city-state will suffer loss or destruction at the hands of Zeus if its populace and leaders are corrupt and unjust; it is in fact a gift from Zeus, justice, that distinguishes man from predatory animal and permits him to flourish in a society. So the prosperity of the city-state rests on the just use of persuasive eloquence, the standard of justice being divinely ordained and the use of eloquence divinely monitored.

The lines of the traditional thinking may then be sketched thus: the gods grant man the quality of justice needed to promote community-life in the city-state; by inspiring poets the gods grant the general means to educate the citizen-body in its just duties; by granting eloquence to the leaders the gods assure the maintenance and dispensation of justice; the gods reward and punish men and their communities in accordance with their conformation to the imposed quality of justice. The question of man's role in a divinely controlled world is not answered explicitly in Greek mythology. But it is easy to discern in the works of Homer and Hesiod, the Greek bibles,[9] a general view that his purpose is to provide the gods with entertainment and nutrition. Such is an obvious explanation of religious festivals and sacrifices, and of divine concern for the human community: the gods have provided the means for a stable environment, the city-state, so that man may flourish and keep the gods fed and amused at regular intervals.

In this view of the world man is scarcely "the measure of all things." He does become so, however, in the strain of thought visible from the sixth century B.C., that holds the world to have been created and to be governed by chance; justice would then be a convention devised by man.[10] If this human convention allows human flourishing within the city-state, then the power of persuasion which facilitates acceptance of codes of justice and directs behavior in general could be identified as the governing trait in this humanist state. It may be tempting to assume that Isocrates' reasoning followed such a course. But the temptation should be resisted.

"Man is the measure of all things." The mention of humanism brings readily to mind this, the opening remark from the treatise on truth written by the sophist Protagoras, perhaps the most prominent of the itinerant professors who gravitated towards Athens in the fifth century B.C., offering instruction in various subjects, most notably in rhetoric. It was this same Protagoras who declared himself unable to decide about the existence of the gods, hampered as he was by the complexity of the question and the brevity of human life. In his rhetorical instruction Protagoras emphasized that all questions could be approached from opposite directions, and he was infamous for having demonstrated how the apparently weaker argument might be transformed into the stronger. One can readily understand then that Protagoras and his kind would be cast as threats to accepted decency and its religious foundations. Their pursuits and pedagogy are in fact mocked and attacked in Aristophanes' *Clouds,* where Socrates is presented as a composite of sophistic villainy, where Wrong Logic invokes mythic tradition and Homer to make the seemingly worse case appear the better, where Pheidippides, once graduated from sophistic training, despises received custom and, by twists of his tongue, justifies and glorifies actions recognized to be immoral.

Protagoras was condemned at Athens for impiety, according to a questionable tradition. But Socrates was certainly tried for refusal to recognize the gods of Athens, for introduction of novel deities, for corruption of the youth, and Plato (*Apology* 18b–19c) cites the *Clouds* as reflecting a hostile and widespread view of Socrates' beliefs and teachings. So, at the end of the fith century, Protagoras and other sophists were surely regarded at Athens as irreligious subverters of tradition. Isocrates began teaching in the early part of the fourth century; he was then in his forties. He was allegedly a pupil of Socrates and of several of the sophists. But his educational thinking, which may have been influenced by the reactionary mood, shows greater affinity to the traditional view of the role and inspiration of the orator than to any sophistic humanism.[11]

In the *Panegyricus* (23–33), reportedly the fruit of a decade's labor and dated to the close of the 380s, Isocrates connects the initial survival and the advancement of Athens with the reverence towards the gods displayed by the city's autochthonous inhabitants. In the *Areopagiticus* (29–30), dated to the early 350s,[12] he laments the lapse of traditional rituals which he sees as a cause for decline in a prosperity once constant through recompense of the gods. In his last composition, the *Panathenaicus,* he attributes the past greatness of Athens to "reverence in relation to the gods and justice in relation to mankind" (124) and affirms that "there is no one, who, among the ways of life, will not give preference to the practice of reverence in relation to the gods and of justice in relation to mankind and of wisdom in relation to all activities in general" (204). In his speech *On the Peace* (33), dated to the mid 350s, Isocrates expresses the belief that the pious and just fare better among gods and men and "pass their days in security for the present and have sweeter hopes for eternity" (33). This conviction appears too in the speech directing advice to Nicocles, who became ruler of Cyprus in the 370s. Isocrates exhorts him to render justice without bias, then adds (20): "In the worship of the gods, follow the example of your ancestors, but believe that the noblest sacrifice and the greatest devotion is to show yourself in the highest degree a good and just man; for such men have greater hope of enjoying a blessing from the gods than those who slaughter many victims." The speech which Isocrates places in the mouth of the same Nicocles begins by associating the study of rhetoric with reverence for the gods, with the practice of justice and with the cultivation of virtues. And, after eulogizing the civilizing force of eloquence, the speaker is made to conclude (9): "Therefore, those who dare to speak with disrespect of educators and teachers of philosophy [i.e., rhetoric] deserve our opprobium no less than do those who profane the sanctuaries of the gods".

This association between rhetoric, religion, and justice appears too in the *Antidosis,* written in the 350s. There Isocrates invokes the annual offering to the goddess Peitho, "Persuasion" deified, as an attestation of Athenian veneration for effective speech and of his detractors' impiety (249–250). The type of rhetoric he teaches habituates his disciples to think noble thoughts and to aim for just benefits (274–280). Those who gain unjust advantages should not be thought blest in any way (281–285):

> No, you ought to believe rather that those are better off now and will receive the advantage in the future at the hands of the gods who are the most righteous and the most faithful in their devotions, and that those receive the better portion at the hands of men who are the most conscientious in their dealings with their associates, whether in their homes or in their public life, and are themselves esteemed as the noblest among their fellows . . . This is verily the truth, and it is well for us to adopt this way of speaking on the subject, since, as things now are, Athens has in many respects been plunged into such a state of topsy-turvy and confusion that some of our people no longer use words in their proper meaning but wrest them from the most honourable associations and apply them to the basest pursuits. . . . They characterize men who ignore our practical needs and delight in the mental

juggling of the ancient sophists as 'students of philosophy', but refuse this name to those who pursue and practice those studies which enable us to govern wisely both our own households and the commonwealth—which should be the objects of our toil, of our study, and of our every act.

Here Isocrates clearly intends to present his pursuit of rhetoric as both a religious and a civic vocation, and he wishes, moreover, to impress upon the reader that the orator formed by his instruction will fulfill this vocation by obtaining the goodwill of the gods towards the Athenian city-state.

In Homer the individual orator might receive direct inspiration from the gods and so act as an agent in the furtherance of divine designs. In addressing Philip of Macedon, Isocrates recalls this possibility (149–150):

> . . . but if [my discourse] is up to the standard of my former publications, I would have you believe that it was not my old age that conceived it but the divine will that prompted it. . . . I think that you are not unaware in what manner the gods order the affairs of mortals; for not with their own hands do they deal out the blessings and curses that befall us; rather they inspire in each of us such a state of mind that good or ill, as the case may be, is visited upon us through one another.

In Homer the gods may not appear particularly just, but Hesiod certainly represents them as the dispensers of reward and punishment for just and unjust behavior, and so does Isocrates. The latter believes, as the texts cited above show, that upright individuals may gain rewards in an afterlife, and, if he admits that sinners may escape this world unpunished, he concurs with the Hesiodic conviction that the sinful community will perish through divine retribution (*On the Peace* 120): "for a man who is godless and depraved may die before paying the penalty for his sins, but states, since they are deathless, soon or late must submit to punishment at the hands both of men and of the gods." Thus unjust orators lead their cities to destruction.

Isocrates' world is not regimented perfectly by the gods; in the *Panathenaicus* (186) he explains that "if men of honest purpose sometimes come off worse in the struggle than men who desire to do injustice, we may attribute this to negligence of the gods." But Isocrates does place man under rather strict divine constraint in the use of his reason and in the direction of his affairs. Isocrates' stance is justified by his mythic account of man's creation and initial development, which may be reconstructed thus from the *Panathenaicus* (123–126) and the *Panegyricus* (21–33):

> Athens was the world's first city, founded by King Cecrops, and an autochthonous population sprung from divine seed sown in the goddess Earth. This people was naturally imbued with a speech and intelligence directed by justice and reverence towards the gods. These qualities won the goodwill of Demeter who granted the gift of agriculture to guarantee the survival and prosperity of the Athenians in this world and established religious rites to provide the hope of a happy afterlife. The city-state progressed using its

just powers of speech to conduct its affairs and to frame its basic legislation in line with divine will.

Consequently, it was men of birth, reputation, wisdom, and eloquence who benefitted the evolution of the state (cf. *Antidosis* 230–236; 306–308). But with the march of time the pristine purity of the people has been corrupted and speech is used perversely and sacrilegiously for unjust purposes. Isocrates' training is therefore necessary to habituate Athenians to speak and think in terms of ancestral values, to revert to the religious rhetoric of yore, and so to act in a manner likely to be in keeping with divine will.

Isocrates' ideal orator is thus subjected to curbs which contrast with the liberties attributed to Adam by the literal and humanist sense of the words of Pico della Mirandola in his *Oration on the Dignity of Man*. The title "father of humanism" were better reserved for one who acknowledged man to exercise over his own destiny a rational control untrammelled by divine fetters. But let us now pass to the second question. Did Isocrates establish for the study of rhetoric a position of cultural dominance throughout the Greek world? Does he thus merit the title "father of rhetoric" and thereby have a claim to have legitimized the supremacy of a system of thinking that was readily "humanized" by his successors?

"The power to speak well is taken as the surest index of a sound understanding, and discourse which is true and lawful and just is the outward image of a true and faithful soul," writes Isocrates in the *Nicocles* (7; cf. *Antidosis* 255). Now the good orator will know how to appraise the deeds of the past (celebrated by poets and historians), possessing "the ability to make proper use of them at the appropriate time, to conceive the right sentiments about them in each instance, and to set them forth in a finished phrase" (*Panegyricus* 9). He will not possess foreknowledge of the future (*Against the Sophists* 2), but he will make the best judgement at every turn (*Antidosis* 292): "For . . . those who have gained this power [of eloquence] by philosophy [i.e., by studying rhetoric according to his prescription] and by the exercise of reason never speak without weighing their words, and so are less often in error as to a course of action." If Isocrates' religious subservience is ignored, he can be made to recommend the sort of formation favored by the first Italian humanists.[13] But in fourteenth-century Italy, as in Rome from the end of the pre-Christian era, the acceptance of rhetoric's importance was reflected at the institutional level; there was schooling in rhetoric for those seeking a liberal education. It is far from clear, despite assertions to the contrary, that, from the time of Isocrates, the Greek world adopted schooling in rhetoric as the crown or even a regular part of a liberal education.

In the A.D. 70s, the emperor Vespasian established two chairs of rhetoric at Rome, one for Greek, the other for Latin eloquence. This action recognized rhetoric as the predominant intellectual pursuit of the Empire. Moreover, this emperor and his successors granted exemptions and privileges to rhetors, who were to be found throughout the Empire in all cities and towns of any importance, and to *grammatici* whose instruction was preliminary to rhetoric. Thus rhetoric reigned supreme in education, culture, and thought. Now this situation would extend back to Isocrates' time, according to Marrou (pp. 294–295):

> . . . ce caractère oratoire de la culture hellénistique n'est pas un fait premier et paradoxal qui aurait imposé à l'éducation de donner à la rhétorique la place de premier plan que nous lui voyons occuper. C'est un phénomène secondaire et dérivé. Le fait premier, c'est que depuis les Sophistes et depuis Isocrate, l'éloquence n'a jamais cessé, malgré toutes les révolutions politiques et sociales, d'être l'objectif principal de la culture supérieure, le couronnement de toute éducation libérale qui se voulait complète . . . depuis Isocrate, la rhétorique n'a jamais cessé d'être pratiquée comme la forme normale de l'éducation supérieure

Thus Marrou is certain that when the Romans subjugated the Greek East in the second century B.C. and, with the help of Greek influence, developed a literary culture, there was a simple transference to Rome of a long-established system of schooling in rhetoric (cf. pp. 389–390). In his book on Greek rhetoric G. Kennedy sees a different development.[14] Aristotle had recognized rhetoric as a subject worthy of a philosopher's attention, and thereafter some instruction in this subject might be received in Athenian schools of philosophy. Kennedy regards study of rhetoric at this level as an incidental part of higher education undertaken by the student in his late teens and twenties. In the two centuries after Aristotles' death, systematic schooling in rhetoric, on the other hand, would have become the central focus of a secondary education tackled by the student in his mid teens. But when the Romans subjugated the Greek East in the second century, they showed more interest in rhetoric than philosophy and thus caused a revitalization of the notion, dormant since Isocrates' death, that higher education should consist of the study, not of philosophy, but of rhetoric. Kennedy identifies the Greek Hermagoras who wrote a rhetorical handbook about 150 B.C. as the actual innovator of this higher education in rhetoric "not intended for young school-boys, but for advanced students" (p. 319). To its merit, Kennedy's reconstruction recognizes the importance of Roman influence. But were schools of rhetoric in fact a regular feature of Hellenistic education before the Roman conquest?

In the second half of the second century B.C., Polybius, a Greek politician, published a history of the rise of Rome. In this work (12. 25–28a) he attacks the historian Timaeus, who came to Athens in the closing decades of the fourth century and spent fifty years there. Polybius reprehends his predecessor for including in his work speeches which read like immature school-compositions. He alludes moreover in technical terms to exercises which formed part of the curriculum known to have been employed by schools of rhetoric in the first century B.C..[15] So these criticisms of Timaeus indeed suggest that schooling in rhetoric was an established element of education in the Greek world into which Polybius had was born about 200 B.C. Yet there is cause to ponder the accuracy of this inference.

Isocrates died at the start of the 330s B.C. after having taught rhetoric for half a century. So, if schooling in this subject was going to gain currency in liberal education throughout the Greek world as a result of Isocrates' example, it should surely have done so in his lifetime. But that no set pattern of secondary or higher education in rhetoric did evolve thus is indicated by Teles, a Cynic philosopher who wrote about the middle of the third century B.C. Drawing upon Crates, another Cynic who flourished in the latter part of the fourth and early part of the third century, Teles paints life as a web of woes from cradle to grave.[16] First the infant is maltreated by his nurse. Then, on reaching school-age, the child is conducted by his slave-supervisor to schools of athletics, elementary letters, music, and drawing. When he is older, he must attend teachers of mathematics, geometry, and horsemanship. When he attains the age of majority, as an ephebe, that is, a cadet citizen, he submits to teachers of athletics and armed combat as well as to the director of the gymnasium. Aged twenty and now fully adult, he is liable for military service. The primary cycle of studies is the same as that described by Aristotle as customary (*Politics* 8. 3. 1). The advanced mathematics of the secondary cycle correspond with the recommendations of Plato, and, since only youths from richer families could indulge in equestrian training, the described program is clearly the most extensive imaginable. The paramilitary training at the tertiary stage would probably begin at the age of eighteen, as it did in the Athens of the 320s where the Aristotelian *Constitution of Athens* (42) was written. But neither Crates nor Teles, who could readily have adjusted anything written by his predecessor, recognizes any standard secondary or higher stage of education in rhetoric or philosophy.

Interested Greeks of the third and second centuries B.C. could find sophists willing to teach them rhetoric; for example, there is extant a letter, dating from about 150 B.C., in which Attalus II of Pergamum honors the tutor of Attalus III who had been appointed because of his experience in teaching rhetoric.[17] Yet neither sophist nor rhetor figures in the list of intellectuals said to have reeducated the Greek world after their expulsion from Alexandria in the latter half of the 140s B.C. (Athenaeus *Deipnosophists* 4. 184):

> You, indeed, are not unaware that Menecles, the historian of Barca, and again Andron of Alexandria, in his *Chronicles,* record that the Alexandrians were the teachers of all Greeks and barbarians at a time when the entire system of general education had broken down by reason of the continually recurring disturbances which took place in the period of Alexander's successors. I say, then, a rejuvenation of all culture was again brought about in the reign of the seventh Ptolemy who ruled over Egypt, the king who received from the Alexandrians appropriately the name of Malefactor. For he murdered many of the Alexandrians; not a few he sent into exile, and filled the islands and the towns with men who had grown up with his brother – philologians [i.e., *grammatici*], philosophers, mathematicians, musicians, painters, athletic trainers, physicians, and many other men of skill in their profession. And so they, reduced by poverty to teaching what they knew, instructed many distinguished men.

The report, which would have any education above the elementary level disappear after the death of Alexander in 323, no doubt distorts truth to enhance the prestige of Alexandria. But clearly its authors do not write of a world that recognized rhetoric as its chief cultural pursuit.

Perhaps then Polybius thinks of exercises in rhetoric that might constitute part of the education offered by Athenian schools of philosophy; he does in fact criticize topics debated in the Academy (12. 26c). A series of inscriptions spanning from 123 B.C. congratulates Athenian ephebes first for their attendance at the schools of philosophy, then, from the 80s B.C., for having followed the instruction of rhetors and *grammatici* as well.[18] So there are grounds to believe that schooling in rhetoric did not begin to establish itself as a standard part of Greek liberal education before the Roman conquest of the Greek East in the second century B.C.

Some confirmation of this hypothesis may be found in Cicero's *De oratore, On the making of an orator,* written in the mid 50s B.C., when Cicero had already passed the climax of his career as a statesman orator. The dramatic date of the work is 91 B.C., and its principal speaker is Crassus, the censor who had closed down schools of Latin rhetoric at Rome the previous year. In the third book (93–95) Cicero has him explain that he did so because he felt that Greek *rhetors* gave a more profound instruction, but he has him foresee the Romans eclipsing the Greeks in eloquence. We are of course to understand that this prophecy has since been fulfilled in Cicero who expresses his own educational views through Crassus and claims to have effected the proper adaptation of Greek learning to Roman ends.

Crassus contrasts Greek and Roman emphases thus (3. 69):

> However, the streams of learning flowing from the common watershed of wisdom, as rivers do from the Apennines, divided in two, the philosophers flowing down into the entirely Greek waters of the Eastern Mediterranean with its plentiful supply of harbours, while the orators glided into the rocky and inhospitable Western seas of our outlandish Tuscany, where even Ulysses himself lost his bearings.

The immediate source of the flow of wisdom is the philosopher Carneades, who became head of the Academy in the first half of the second century B.C., and Crassus laments that the art of rhetoric derived from his teaching has lost depth at Rome. Not that Crassus himself has studied at length. His father had educated him carefully in boyhood, then he "came forward as a public advocate at an extremely early age, and when only one and twenty conducted the impeachment of a very eloquent and distinguished man—in fact public life was [his] education, and practical experience of the laws and institutions of the state and the custom of the country [his] schoolmaster" (74). During his quaestorship in Asia he had associated, however, with Metrodorus, a rhetor from the Academy, and he regards eloquence as "so potent a force that it embraces the origin and operation and development of all things, all the virtues and duties, all the natural principles governing the morals and minds and life of mankind, and also determines their customs and laws and rights, and controls the government of the state, and expresses everything that concerns whatever topic in a graceful and flowing style" (76).

He disbelieves that it is sufficient to learn off bare rules of rhetoric; the orator must study philosophy as well, "provided that we carry [its principles] over into the field of political science to which they belong and with which they are concerned, and, as I have said before, avoid spending an entire lifetime in acquiring them, but, after we have beheld the fountain-heads, which one who does not get to know them quickly will never know at all, then draw from these sources, whenever necessary, as much as the subject demands" (3. 123; cf. 87–89, 145–146). In this fashion, the Romans make proper use of Greek learning which the Greeks themselves have failed to exploit (131).

From Crassus' or rather Cicero's comments it would appear that rhetoric, generally a branch of philosophy in the Greek world up to the Roman conquest, had indeed been isolated and developed into a schooling independent of philosophy in response to Roman intellectual preference. In this case, it was the Romans, not the Greeks, who identified and established rhetoric as the final and perfecting stage of a liberal formation.

At the beginning of his tract *On Rhetoricians,* Suetonius records a decree of the Senate from 161 B.C. and a censorial edict of 92 B.C., both issued against the teaching of rhetoric at Rome:

> "As the result of a discussion about philosophers and rhetoricians, the senate decreed that Marcus Pomponius, the praetor, should take heed and provide, in whatever way seemed in accord with the interests of the State and his oath of office, that they not be allowed to live in Rome." Some time afterward the censors Gnaeus Domitius Ahenobarbus and Lucius Licinius Crassus issued the following edict about the same class of men: "It has been reported to us that there be men who have introduced a new kind of training, and that our young men frequent their schools; that these men have assumed the title of Latin rhetoricians, and that our young men spend whole days with them in idleness. Our forefathers determined what they wished their children to learn and what schools they desired them to attend. These innovations in the customs and principles of our forefathers do not please us nor seem proper. Therefore it appears necessary to make our opinion known, both to those who have such schools and to those who are in the habit of attending them, that they are displeasing to us."

In justifying their action the censors invoke an ancestral decision and ancestral custom. The decision evidently was that taken in 161 B.C., and the offense to Roman custom was the disruption by this schooling of the traditional apprenticeship to public life. The transition from boyhood to adult status, reckoned to occur about the age of sixteen, was marked by the exchange of a purple-bordered toga for the pure white toga of manhood. At this juncture, the young adult would be entrusted to the supervision of a senior statesman and he would learn by attending this mentor as he went about his business. This initiation to public life would last normally for a year. Thereafter the young adult was expected to busy himself with civic and military duties; Crassus notes his early forensic successes. The schools of Latin rhetoric were seen to distract young men from these activities and to encourage idleness.

The resolution passed by the Senate in 161 B.C. can scarcely have been directed at private tutors whose presence is so frequently reported at this period in the homes of the prominent. As in the 90s B.C., offense must have been caused by the opening of schools by enterprising Greek philosophers and rhetors; the Romans were generally not adverse to studying in Greek. The philosophers were then attempting to establish in the new capital of the Mediterranean world such schools as existed in various Hellenistic cities, but the Greek rhetors, in response to Roman demands on Greek culture, must have been launching a schooling somewhat novel in its limited focus.

Schools of rhetoric, both Latin and Greek, were accepted at Rome in the course of the first century B.C., and they were thereafter recognized to provide the crown of a liberal formation for youths which ended about the age of eighteen. They thus were allowed to occupy the first few years of officially adult life and, to a large degree, they supplanted the traditional apprenticeship to public life. This schooling, however brief, was believed to equip the individual with the powers of reason and expression required to direct his world. Thus the city of Rome provided a situation in which schooling in rhetoric, in general abeyance since Isocrates' venture, finally flourished. And it was the enthusiasm of the Roman masters for rhetoric that in turn infected the Greek East with a similar zeal. Such a pattern of evolution is reflected in Philostratus' work, *The Lives of the Sophists.*

In the A.D. 230s, Philostratus, a Greek from the island of Lemnos, compiled a biographic history of the sophists from the fifth century B.C. down to his own time. By "sophist" he understands one who taught rhetoric, but not all his subjects established schools or gave formal courses; in some instances the teaching seems to have been limited to a rather random association with a few disciples. Again, Philostratus divides his biographies into two streams, philosopher-sophists and rhetorician-sophists, explaining that "the men of former days applied the name 'sophist', not only to orators whose surpassing eloquence won them a brilliant reputation, but also to philosophers who expounded their theories with ease and fluency" (13; cf. 5). In the series of sophists proper, Philostratus names seven active in the fifth century. He identifies only two who began their careers in the fourth century, Isocrates and Aeschines. The latter is made a pupil of Isocrates and is said to have become a professional teacher of rhetoric on the island of Rhodes after retiring from political life at Athens. The veracity of this tradition may be doubted. Having dealt with Aeschines, Philostratus continues (63):

> We will pass over Ariobarzanes of Cilicia, Xenophron of Sicily, and Pythagoras of Cyrene, who showed no skill either in invention or in the expression of their ideas, though in the scarcity of first-rate sophists they were sought after by the Greeks of their day, as men seek after pulse when they are short of corn; and we will proceed to Nicetes of Smyrna. For this Nicetes found the science of oratory reduced to great straits, and he bestowed on it approaches far more splendid even than those which he himself built for Smyrna. . . .

Nicetes flourished in the second half of the first century of the Christian era. Fourteen sophists are commemorated after Nicetes, but Philostratus offers no more than three names for the three and a bit centuries separating Aeschines' death and Nicetes' birth. He could have found others to mention, but a knowledge that the study of rhetoric did not begin to flourish in the Greek world until well after the Roman conquest may have deterred him from searching too hard. Proud of his Greek heritage, Philostratus was not going to call Rome the "mother" or "foster-mother of rhetoric," but it was she rather than Isocrates who established the supremacy of this subject. Moreover, the Rome that promoted the importance of rhetoric had an outlook more humanist than that of Isocrates, or, for that matter, of Philostratus; for, true to Greek tradition, the latter has his most successful sophists divinely inspired.

According to tradition, Rome was founded in the 750s B.C.. The Romans regarded themselves as the people most reverent towards the gods, and they did elaborate a state-run religious machinery to ensure a fruitful harmony between the city and divine powers. But, unlike the Greeks, the early Romans did not establish an oral mythology to explain the nature of the gods and the role of man. Thus, when the Romans did begin to develop a literature in the late third and second centuries B.C., they simply made free use of Greek mythology. By this borrowing, they eventually did produce a polished national mythology which showed them divinely destined to rule the world. But this dominion, in native religious thought as opposed to any variation inherent in the imported in mythology, resulted from the Romans' directing the gods rather than vice versa. The early Romans had accepted that gods and men existed in the world and had discovered, to their own satisfaction, the means to effect the coexistence most profitable for themselves. It may in fact have been the desire to obtain this relationship that averted mythological speculation, which seems inevitably to betray human uncertainties and weaknesses; the early Romans would have seen little need to arm the gods with information that might be deployed against them; so they may consciously have avoided formulating the view so common in mythologies that man is somehow an abject dependant of the gods. In any case, the Romans forged, not myths, but a meticulous array of rituals which aimed not so much to honor the gods as to manipulate them. So, by the time the Romans developed a literature and adopted a mythology, they had already assured themselves of their ability to enlist, or rather coerce, superior powers into the service of Rome. At every turn, human inventiveness may be seen devising ways to harness these powers. Success was attested by Rome's conquests and her dramatic expansion in the third and second centuries B.C. So, when the Romans dominated the Greek East, they were a people confident in the supremacy of their rational powers and assured of the rectitude of their humanist outlook. They did not need the Greeks to teach them how to think, but they were in a position to evaluate the Greek intellectual heritage and to pluck therefrom what they considered useful. Not surprisingly, instruction in the art of speaking was judged useful; for, in a quick and tractable fashion, it helped the young Roman organize and express the human thought that ruled the world.

A Cicero was free, then, from the religious blinkers worn by an Isocrates.

Now Cicero was an oratorical giant at Rome, the perfect example of the rhetorically trained statesman; his modesty has not prevented him from telling us so much. He had, however, fought a vain struggle to maintain the Republic, and he lost his life through his outspoken hostility to Antony. The latter acted in this execution with the consent of Octavian, whom Cicero had tried to exploit, describing him as a gullible but dispensable necessity. In fact Octavian snatched a giant share of supreme power at the age of eighteen and later, under the name Augustus, he was to exercise supreme power for some forty-four years over Rome's "restored" Republic; it was under his patronage that such luminaries of Latin literature as Horace and Virgil flourished. This Octavian had equipped his intellect by studying rhetoric in Latin and Greek with Marcus Epidius and Apollodorus of Pergamum. Here, for the humanist who cared to reflect, was a confirmation of the basic validity of Cicero's doctrine: schooling in rhetoric could indeed adequately arm man's intellect to use that natural trait which should accord him perfect control of his world and destiny.

"What has Horace to do with the Psalter, Virgil with the Gospels and Cicero with Paul?" This question in Jerome's twenty-second letter introduces the future saint's account of the famous dream where, in his early twenties and not long after his conversion to the ascetic way, he saw himself before the throne of judgment. Asked to profess his faith, he answered that he was a Christian. "Thou liest," came the reply. "Thou art a Ciceronian, not a Christian. 'For where thy treasure is there will be thy heart also.' " Jerome swore to renounce pagan literature for ever. Now Jerome lived to learn of the sack of Rome by Alaric in A.D. 410 and to witness the start of the final disintegration of the Western Empire. To a fourteenth-century humanist with a nascent historical perspective, Jerome's lifetime would mark a prelude to the cultural stagnation of the Middle Ages. So, in the early Renaissance, Jerome's reported dream can only have promoted veneration of Cicero as a prophet of humanist values and respect for the resilience of the humanist society of Rome in the last century of the pre-Christian era. This veneration and respect was well directed; for the humanist outlook is more Roman than Greek.

Notes

1. Cf. L. D. Reynolds and N. G. Wilson, *Scribes and Scholars* (Oxford, 1968), 109.

2. Most translations are borrowed from the editions of the respective authors in the Loeb Classical Library. Please note that in the case of Philostratus reference is made to the page numbers of the Loeb edition. The translations of Homer and Herodotus are drawn from the Penguin Classics series.

3. Cf. M. L. Clarke, *Higher Education in the Ancient World* (London, 1971), 6–7.

4. "That Cicero was greatly indebted to Isocrates for his general theory of culture" is argued by S. E. Smethurst, "Cicero and Isocrates," *Transactions of the American Philological Association* 84 (1953): 253–320.

5. Cf. W. Jaeger, *Paideia: the Ideals of Greek Culture*, trans. G. Highet (Oxford, 1944), vol. 3, 46–47.

6. *Histoire de l'éducation dans l'Antiquité*, 6th ed. (Paris, 1965), 132.

7. "The Legacy" in *Paths from Ancient Greece*, ed. C. G. Thomas (Leiden, 1988), 10.

8. The point is well made by F. Solmsen, "The Gift of Speech in Homer and Hesiod," *Transactions of the American Philological Association* 85 (1951): 1–15.

9. Cf. Herodotus 2.53.2: "But it was only—if I may so put it—the day before yesterday that the Greeks came to know the origin and form of the various gods, and whether or not all of them had already existed; for Homer and Hesiod, the poets who composed our theogonies and described the gods for us, giving them all their appropriate titles, offices and powers, lived, as I believe, not more than four hundred years ago."

10. Cf. W. K. C. Guthrie, *The Sophists*, vol. 4.1 of *A History of Greek Philosophy* (Cambridge, 1969), 55–84.

11. Isocrates' religious views are typical of his time; see J. D. Mikalson, *Athenian Popular Religion* (Chapel Hill, 1983). For an assessment of Isocrates' educational outlook which does not connect it so closely as does mine with mythological and religious traditions, see E. Rummel, "Isocrates' Ideal of Rhetoric: Criteria of Evaluation," *Classical Journal* 75 (1979): 23–35.

12. See R. W. Wallace, "The Date of Isocrates' *Areopagitikos*," *Harvard Studies in Classical Philology* 90 (1986): 77–84.

13. H. L. Hudson-Williams entitles a study of Isocrates' educational aims and methods "A Greek Humanist," *Greece & Rome* 9 (1940): 166–171.

14. *The Art of Persuasion in Greece* (Princeton, 1963), chapters 1 and 5.

15. Cf. J. Fairweather, *Seneca the Elder* (Cambridge, 1981), 108–109.

16. For text and translation see E. N. O'Neil, *Teles, the Cynic Teacher* (Missoula, Montana, 1977), 54–57.

17. For a translation of this document see S. F. Burnstein, trans. and ed., *The Hellenistic Age from the Battle of Ipsos to the Death of Cleopatra VII*, vol. 3 of *Translated Documents of Greece and Rome* (Cambridge, 1985), no. 90.

18. Cf. C. Pélékidis, *Histoire de l'éphébie attique des origines à 31 avant Jésus-Christ* (Paris, 1962), 266–267.

3

St. Thomas and Medieval Humanism

Edward A. Synan

On August 4, 1988, the *Buffalo News* ran an informative and surprising column: At a meeting of the Humanist World Congress, which had been held the evening before in Amherst, New York, the assembled humanists had inducted into their Humanist Hall of Fame the television comedian Steve Allen. Everything that Allen was reported to have said to his interviewer from the *Buffalo News* justified the award. From our point of view, one of the best things Allen said is that "Thomas Aquinas and Thomas More were part of the humanist tradition."[1]

Both Thomas Aquinas (1225–1274) and Thomas More (1478–1535) were accepted as first-rank scholars by their extremely disparate worlds. Aquinas lived in a period when western Europeans were digesting an unaccustomed diet of scientific and philosophical Latin translations from the Greek of such ancients as Aristotle and Proclus, and even small portions of the Dialogues of Plato. Translations were necessary because few contemporaries of Aquinas knew Greek.

More, on the other hand, was a co-worker in a wide community of scholars who knew Greek well, but who had serious reservations about the value of the Latin scholasticism that had flourished in the day of Aquinas, a scholasticism to which Aquinas had made notable contributions.

Neither More nor Aquinas used the word "humanism." More, in his celebrated letter to Martin Dorp (1485–1525), spoke of "the revival of good literature," *bonas renasci literas,* and to his friend, in the same letter, wrote that "if you also, one day, turn to a knowledge of the Greek tongue—which I strongly desire. . . ."[2]

Aquinas, in contrast, was interested in Greek for the sake of technical philosophy and science. We shall spend a long time looking for an interest in Greek literature like *that* held by Brother Thomas. Even his very serious control of Latin, as will be seen, was put mainly to technical rather than to literary uses.

The moral of all this is that those who organized this program on humanism are supported by Steve Allen, above all by his inclusion of Thomas Aquinas in the ranks of humanists. Furthermore, if Steve Allen was right to call both Aquinas and More "humanists" (as I should like to think he was), then the terms "humanist" and "humanism" must be broad enough to cover two very different sorts of scholar. In consequence, the terms cannot be what medieval logicians and metaphysicians called "univocals," that is, the terms cannot convey an identical meaning and reference every time they are used. Neither can they be explained away into the opposed limbo of "equivocity," by a denial that in their diverse uses there is a subtle community. The two epochs, the Middle Ages and the great Renaissance, produced undeniably diverse cultures: Did they have nothing at all in common? If both cultures were humanistic, then there must have been at least two humanisms. It is perplexing to think that cultures so different can sail under the same flag of "humanism."

Should Thomas Aquinas rise from his tomb to give an account of this use of one term for two truly diverse realities, he would surely do so by an appeal to his theory of analogy. The realities are genuinely two; they are not the same, but in a significant way they are related to each other. Thus bad generals lose their men to no purpose and bad chess players lose their men to no purpose; but the "men" of one and "men" of the other are by no means identical. So it is that "humanism" in the thirteenth century was far from identical with "humanism" in the fifteenth and sixteenth centuries. This is not to say that the two cultural achievements were totally incommensurate with each other. Like human soldiers lost at Waterloo and the squandered ivory pieces of an inept chess player, the two humanisms are related positively in a way that unites them in their very differences and yet distinguishes them in their very similarities. Both can be lost, but how diverse that eventuality is! Both had a value, but how disparate the worth of a human life and the worth of a crucial rook or pawn! In every way in which those "men" differ, they are at one; in every way in which we discern similarities we see at the same moment irreducible diversity.

The aim of this essay is no more than to set some points of reference for boundaries within which it may be possible to identify those aspects of Thomas Aquinas that may permit us with justice to term him a representative of "medieval humanism." Because Aquinas is accessible to us only through his writings, we are authorized to begin, but not necessarily to end, by weighing his putative humanism on a literary scale.

Now literary humanism has been seen traditionally as a matter of education in Latin and in Greek literature. Normally such an education marks the primary and secondary levels of schooling rather than the postsecondary level. A humanistic education is by definition not a professional education, unless, of course, we include the professional training of a university classicist.

In the case of Aquinas this exception can hardly be sustained. His professional training was in theology, a discipline that in his time was scholastic and technical, shot through with the conceptions and procedures of a logic that was still developing and completing the austere analyses of Aristotle and of the Stoics. We have but to remember the strictures of Renaissance humanists against the medieval schoolmen (and Sir Thomas More joined in that chorus with the very letter already cited) to be secure against any temptation to include scholastic theology among the sources from which Brother Thomas might have drawn a humanistic education in a literary mode.

On the other hand, Thomas Aquinas received his primary education between the ages of about five and fourteen from the Benedictine monks of the great monastery on Monte Cassino. Despite our total ignorance of the precise procedures, texts, and goals that were held in honor by those monks, there is incontrovertible evidence, clear in what Aquinas would write during a most productive lifetime, that he had mastered to a notable degree the Latin half of a traditional literary humanism. We shall return to the issue of Greek.

Here a word of caution must be inserted. It is true that Aquinas is the author in a real sense of almost a hundred works, many of them multivolumed in our printed editions. A number of those works, however, have come down to us in a form called by the medievalists *reportationes,* "reports." These were written, not by the author, but by those who had heard the author lecture. An instance of this (and of its contrary) is known to every medievalist: the *Sentence* commentary based on the Paris lectures by John Duns Scotus (1266–1308). These have come down to us under the title: *Reportatio Parisiensis,* the "Paris Report." In contrast, the work by Duns at Oxford on the same material, but gone over and revised by the author himself with an eye to publication, formerly called the *Opus Oxoniense,* is now more accurately styled: the *Ordinatio,* "the edition set in order" by the Master himself, not merely "reported" by those who had heard him lecture. It will be conceded that the quality of Aquinas' Latin cannot be judged by evidence that stems from his *reportationes* but must be based on works the Latin of which is his own.

As a small boy at Monte Cassino Aquinas learned to read and speak Latin. This was a practical necessity. In the thirteenth century, Latin was the language, not only of the international Church, but also of science, of learning, of diplomacy. An extreme instance of this last is a letter in the papal archives from a Mongol minister of state and addressed to Pope Honorius IV (1285–1287). This letter conveyed an invitation: The Pope might wish to join in an offensive military alliance with the Mongols against the Moslem caliphate of Egypt; their prey, caught between Mongols from the east and papal forces from the west, would be easy to defeat. The "Latin" is so barbarous that its modern editor thought it right to append a French translation:[3] it was necessary for thirteenth-century diplomats to write in Latin even when this was impossible!

On the theme of bad Latin it must be noted that our distinction between the Latin literature of the so-called "golden age" (the principate of Augustus (27 B.C.–A.D. 14) and that of the "silver age" (a period that ends with the reign of the Emperor Hadrian, A.D. 117–138) was unknown to the Middle Ages. Indeed, the value judgment implicit in the use of two unequally precious metals to qualify the two literary periods would have seemed perverse to the medievalists. Golden-age writers were pagan to a man; the fathers of the Church, products of the late imperial school system—Jerome and Ambrose and Augustine—fall into what, on this basis, must have been an even less respectable era. Later than the "silver age," the age of the Fathers would thus have been of less value. On the contrary, the Fathers of the Church thought of their time as the "Sixth Age"[4] of the world when the preaching of the Gospel had transformed the inhabited globe, if not into an earthly paradise, at least into a world in which the God of Abraham, Isaac, Jacob, and Jesus was held officially in high regard.

This is not to imply that the Latin scriptures sacred to humanists, the literary achievements of Roman antiquity, were not esteemed throughout the medieval period. Although the party-line humanists of, say, the Florentine Academy may not have been excessively grateful for this fact, every text they had inherited from Latin antiquity owed its survival to the painstaking work of copyists. Those copyists were often enough monks. Those pious drudges worked in the *scriptoria,* the "writing-rooms," of their monasteries to preserve the traces of a culture that had preceded what was thought of then as the *translatio studii,* the "transfer of learning," from Athens and Rome to the western barbarians. In this the monastic scribes were doing precisely what one monastic founder in Italy, the pious and cultured Senator Cassiodorus (ca. 485–580), had prescribed for them; he had even composed an elementary schoolbook to help them do it well, a *De orthographia,* "on correct writing."[5]

In this tradition the monks on Monte Cassino when the five-year-old Thomas Aquinas arrived for an education had both extensive library holdings and the skill to use them. They clearly succeeded in their efforts to teach the school boy from Roccasecca to read and to write Latin. His Latin is fluent and correct. To judge the prose of Aquinas in context, it is illuminating to compare a page by Aquinas with a page by Duns Scotus. To read the latter seemed to one medieval reader a *fractio capitis,* a "skull-breaker," owing both to his subtle thought and to his tortuous expression. So also, a comparison with William of Ockham (ca. 1300–ca. 1349) must give the palm to Aquinas for his smooth and sinewy Latin prose. No doubt it was easier for those students whose first language was a contemporary Italian dialect, rather than a northern tongue, to excel in Latin. Bonaventure (ca. 1217–1274), an almost exact contemporary of Thomas Aquinas, wrote mellifluent Latin; he was an Italian from Bagnorea. Whatever the explanation, Aquinas and Bonaventure wrote better Latin than did most of their competition.

Because Latin was still a living language, however, the Latin of the century of Aquinas and Bonaventure was no longer the Latin of Cicero (106 B.C.– 43 B.C.) and Quintillian (A.D. 40–ca. 118). It was marked by less demanding syntactical conventions: *quod* with a subjunctive, for instance, often did service for the infinitive with an accusative, and a postclassical vocabulary developed to handle new conceptions, new inventions, and new themes. It was a malleable language, calculated to horrify a doctrinaire humanist of the quattrocento. Perhaps it will be enough to remark that fifteenth- and sixteenth-century humanists did succeed in reviving the splendid periods of Cicero and in making normative what Augustine had called the "stateliness of Tully," *Tulliana dignitas,* to which, for a moment, he compared unfavorably the "Itala" Latin Bible (*Confessions* 3, 5, 9). The price of their triumph in making "golden age" Latin the standard for the future was not inconsiderable: it was to render Latin a "dead" language.

For the single institution of modern times in which Latin remains a normal means of communication, the central offices of the Roman Church, the late Cardinal Bacci found it necessary to issue from time to time supplementary word lists of acceptable Latin terms for which the past gave no direct help. My mother once saved a story from the *New York Times* on one such innovation, for she knew from long experience that Latin had played some role in my getting through the minefields of university and seminary; she rightly thought I would be interested in what the Cardinal had proposed. It turned out that he had given his blessing to a Latin term for "television." When necessary to mention the device in Latin, the Cardinal announced, one could say *televisio*—hardly a surprise and hardly a perfect solution, to be sure, for its ancestry is clearly mixed. Greek "distance" and Latin "seeing," *tele* and *visio,* may not constitute a verbal equivalent of *filius spurius,* but one might have hoped for straight Latin or straight Greek, perhaps *visio longissima* or, had the word not been preempted for an earlier invention, *teleskopos.*

As might have been guessed, the Latin of Aquinas was already a "learned" language, hardly to be understood by the general population, even in Italy where late Latin had changed the least. One of the virtues that contemporary biographers of Brother Thomas thought worthy of mention when his name was being considered for canonization is that he preached to the people in a language they could understand; what is more, he saved all subtleties for the lecture hall and eschewed them in his homilies to the people.

One way to estimate the quality of the Latin education of Aquinas is to compare the use he made of it with what a pope who died about nine years before the birth of Aquinas had done with his own classical education. Pope Innocent III, who began to rule the Church when he was 37 years old in 1198, was to die in 1216. Like Saint Thomas Aquinas, Pope Innocent was the scion of an aristocratic family, indeed of one a rank above that of the Aquino line, for the pope's father was a Count whereas the father of Aquinas was but a knight.

Like Thomas, the future Pope Innocent began his education with Benedictine monks, but at a monastery in Rome. From Rome he proceeded to Paris for the study of theology and then to Bologna to study law. His classical education, therefore, like that of Aquinas, must have been received at the hands of Benedictine monks. Innocent's ability to write Latin prose seems roughly comparable with that of Aquinas as is the single specimen of Latin poetry that has come down to us from the pen of Innocent. This is a hymn in honor of the Virgin Mary, written in the accented and rhyming verse the Middle Ages favored.[6] Such a verse form is to be found in the hymns for the feast of Corpus Christi, now ascribed with growing confidence to Brother Thomas.

In contrast to Aquinas, however, Innocent III has given evidence of a serious acquaintance with the quantitative prosody of the ancient Latin poets.[7] To my knowledge, as much cannot be said of Thomas. The pope, for instance, cited classical poets much more frequently than did Aquinas, so much so, in fact, that it does not seem possible to account for the pope's readiness with an apt couplet from classical poetry by appeal to florilegia; such collections, or their equivalent, easily account for the relatively limited use by Aquinas of the Latin poets.

Beyond the frequency with which the pope made use of golden-age poets (he cited at least forty authors and, owing to several citations of the same lines, did so on at least forty-eight occasions), a qualitative aspect must be added to this quantitative norm. This last is more than impressive.

On some occasions Innocent was notably free in the way he manipulated his material. At times he would cite two lines, excised from two poems by the same author, and present them as a couplet with no indication to his reader that their juxtaposition was not the work of the poet cited. Even more freewheeling, he often did the same thing with lines from poems by two different authors and this with no intimation to reader or auditor (his sermons are not without poetic decorations) that the two lines are not from the same hand. Finally, and this is the most revelatory of all, here and there he adjusted a word or two of the received text in order to make his own point more sharply.

What is significant in this perhaps excessively personal use of classical poetry is that on no such occasion did Innocent fail to preserve the meter. This is, of course, particularly telling when he adjusted the order of words or put one of his own in place of his poet's term. It is not credible that Innocent should have done this so often and without a slip had he not understood the poetic conventions followed by Virgil and Horace and Ovid and the rest. Yet, as has been noted, Innocent did not follow the classical prosody in the single example of his own verse which we possess.

Now Brother Thomas, too, cited on occasion lines of classical Latin verse. A serious, if preliminary, study of this by an erudite modern scholar, C. M. J. Vansteenkiste, O.P.,[8] has found only five classical poets cited by Aquinas, and this on a total of only twenty occasions, although to this census perhaps a paraphrase or strong echo of a line from Plautus, *Miles gloriosus* 37, ought to be added. It must also be remembered that both Innocent and Thomas counted the *Disticha Catonis* as instances of classical verse, as indeed did all medieval scholars, and not without reason. In fact, the *Distichs* are the work of an author from the third or fourth century of the Christian era. It remains true for them both, nonetheless, that citing the *Distichs* was an expression of esteem for one whom all then perceived as a classical author. With the Plautus echo, the Aquinas census of authors rises from five to six and the list of his citations from twenty to twenty-one.

There is no evidence, parallel to what has been provided by Pope Innocent, to show that Thomas was familiar with classical, quantitative meters, although, of course, its absence does not exclude the possibility that the monks at Monte Cassino had taught their students what their confreres in Rome had taught when the future pope was under their instruction. On only one detail might Thomas Aquinas be thought to have surpassed Innocent in fulfilling a "humanist" condition: Thomas cited three Greek authors, but through the mediation of Jerome or of the Sacred Scriptures themselves. This detail, therefore, cannot be adduced as evidence that Thomas Aquinas knew any Greek.

This observation invites us to ask whether Thomas may not, after all, have had at least some measure of Greek at his disposal. Authoritative voices in our own time, those of Martin Grabmann[9] and of Roberto Weiss,[10] have been reluctant to rule out the possibility, but positive evidence seems to be extremely feeble. It is, of course, not possible to argue that the often fanciful Greek "etymologies" given by Aquinas argue ignorance of Greek on his part. He knew Latin well, but often enough indulged in totally groundless efforts to explain the roots of Latin words as indeed Augustine had done before him. Both were victims of popular, but unscientific, guesses on the origins of terms—in the case of Aquinas, Isidor of Seville's or those of Peter Helias.

With this caution in place, it remains difficult to identify any positive evidence that Aquinas rejoiced in a knowledge of Greek, however modest. Much as etymological errors in explaining Greek terms are no evidence against his having known some Greek, so his more than once repeated observation, for instance, that because the Greek language has no ablative case for nouns and pronouns a Greek genitive is used where a Latin author would have used the ablative. Aquinas was correct on this point, to be sure, but this is the sort of thing he could have heard at table or read in the marginal glosses of a manuscript.

An 1895 article[11] made an orderly assault on the thesis that Brother Thomas knew some Greek and, *pace* Weiss and Grabmann, despite its age and its brevity, seems still to be valid in promoting a negative conclusion. Read closely, the scholars who promote an affirmative solution of this issue do not go farther than to claim its possibility; they do not establish its actuality. We are authorized to adopt the Scots verdict: "Not proven" or, in a more scholastic formula: *a posse ad esse non valet illatio.*

Much as Pope Innocent has provided a useful control on Aquinas and his use of Latin poetry, so John of Salisbury (ca. 1151–1180) who became the Bishop of Chartres, can provide a useful control on the question of whether Aquinas knew any Greek. For this twelfth-century humanist, who wrote excellent Latin prose, according to the same Robert Weiss, "is known to have picked up the rudiments of Greek from one of the Greek-speaking inhabitants of Santa Severina in Calabria during his sojourn in South Italy."[12] In support of this confident statement Weiss adduced three references to John's *Metalogicon Libri* III: 1, 15; 3, 5; and 4, 2.

True enough, all three make mention of a *Grecus interpres,* a "Greek interpreter," but to have employed an interpreter is hardly evidence that John knew Greek; it runs in the opposite direction. Besides, John's account of the meaning of his translator's summons: *Analetiza hoc* is not reassuring on the claim that John had "picked up the rudiments of Greek." Having noted correctly, 4, 2, that "what the Greeks call 'analytic' we (that is, Latin speakers) can call 'resolutory' " John went on to indulge in linguistic phantasy. This is particularly visible in his own precision that his interpreter was accustomed to say this "especially concerning composite expressions," for composites, to be sure, demand analysis or resolution into their components if they are to be understood fully. Having been right thus far, John went on to introduce two howlers: the Greek *ana,* he asserted, means "equal" and *lexim,* presumably the root in his eyes of the second part of the composite *analetiza,* John claimed means "expression." Greek does have a word from which we have borrowed our word "analysis": it means "a breaking-up" and the roots at stake are *ana,* "up" and *luo,* "loosen." What seems to have happened is that the Greek interpreter made a kind of Latin loan-word imperative of *analuo* to go with the Latin *hoc,* as in English we should say: "Analyze this!" Nor do the other two citations proffer any evidence at all that John rejoiced in the "rudiments" of the other classical language.

If we should stay with Latin, the literary humanism of John cannot be impugned. His excellent Latin would not have drawn the fire of the most antimedieval quattrocento humanist. Let us hasten to acknowledge that John is superior to Thomas Aquinas in his demonstrated skill at Latin prose composition. It must, at the same time, be conceded that John wrote with a freedom denied to Brother Thomas. The latter was bound by scholastic literary forms of the most constricting sort. One of these was the stylized "disputed question" and another the *ad literam,* "to the letter," exposition of scriptural, Aristotelian, Boethian, or Proclean texts, all in the service of theology.

After having dissented from the views of scholars as distinguished as Martin Grabmann and Roberto Weiss on whether Thomas Aquinas may have known any Greek, it is a debt of honor to remark on a most defensible observation of Weiss that bears on a very significant achievement by Aquinas in the area of internal literary criticism.

With all his world, Thomas Aquinas had from the beginning of his career ascribed to Aristotle a small book of metaphysical aphorisms, circulating in Latin translation under the title *Liber de causis,* "The Book about Causes." In 1268 a Latin translation (by the Dominican William of Moerbeke) of Proclus' *Elementatio theologica* became available to Aquinas. He recognized that the shorter *Liber de causis* has been excerpted from the *Elementatio* and had itself come into the Latin world via a translation from the original Greek into Arabic.

Of this accomplishment Roberto Weiss wrote that it is "a spontaneous and natural development of classical studies as pursued during the later Middle Ages." Even more strongly, the modern editor of the Thomistic exposition of the *Liber de causis,* H. D. Saffrey, O.P., who counted the words of Weiss just cited "a felicitious expression," proclaimed in his own name that: "Then the dawn of Humanism began to glow . . ."[13] This, to be sure, is high praise. In this instance of Thomistic insight both Saffrey and Weiss have seen a first exercise of the internal criticism of a text in order to correct a misapprehension as to its author. Both recognized (and Saffrey adduced examples) that this methodology is an essential component of Renaissance scholarship and thus of humanism of a literary sort.

May it not be taken as an ungracious pressing of an advantage that here I observe that their enthusiasm may have led them into somewhat excessive praise. Aquinas was able to do this only because William of Moerbeke had provided him with a Latin version of Proclus. If to be a humanist is to cultivate Latin and Greek, then Aquinas seems to have shown only half of what is required: a control of Latin, facile and clear, but heavily scholasticized. Still, if to be a humanist in a literary sense is to be able to manipulate the techniques of internal criticism, then indeed Brother Thomas is a first harbinger, however remote, of the cultural rebirth to come.

Renaissance humanism, it will be conceded, is often the beneficiary of impassioned rhetoric; it is associated with a world view that esteems the individual rather than the community. Far from restriction to the area of language, the term "humanism" can evoke much else besides: sculpture, painting, architecture, and engineering, wealthy patrons, and new perspectives on government and religion. Humanism thus conceived glorifies the name of the commanding artist or architect in contrast with the anonymous medievals who could produce a cathedral, but leave no indications as to the names of the individuals, artists or architects, whose achievement it was.

At its worst, a humanism of the individual slips easily into a cult of personality, careless of community and of the common good. At its best, however, such a humanism can offer a deeply grounded respect for the person as against what we now designate "the mass-man," for the concrete single individual as against the universal abstraction, "humanity," so easily loved by a philanthropist who dislikes most of the persons met in the day's round. In such a benign humanism, the world view at stake would reject two partial views of the person. One, excessively spiritual, would take us for angels, imprisoned in machines of flesh; its contrary, excessively materialistic, would make us to be no more than clever beasts. Is such a "metaphysical humanism," *sit venia verbo,* not more basic and more accessible to the wide range of humanity than is the Graeco-Roman literary humanism that can flourish only within western Europe and its cultural dependencies?

Where would Thomas Aquinas fall in this range of "humanisms"?

No doubt the reader has already guessed where the sympathies of the author must lie. Here it will be argued that the sympathies of Thomas Aquinas would lie there as well. Having paid our debts to "literary humanism," let us move to more fundamental grounds for thinking of Aquinas as a humanist.

The ways we write and the language we use are surely superficial and contingent devices when set against the structure of each and of every human person. Spiritual and intellectual, to be sure, we are also material and biological and mortal. To evoke once more the analogy between soldiers and chessmen, human individuals, as seen by Thomas Aquinas resemble each other in their real differences and differ in their similarities. All of us speak and all of us think, yet how different is Swahili from French, how diverse the reflections of an astronomical physicist from those of an infant exploring a world that can be little more than a mother and a crib and a self.

It is hard to imagine that Aquinas could have given any human tongue—Latin or Greek or his native dialect—the all but mystical superiority assigned by Renaissance humanists to their supple and beautiful Latin, to their poetic yet precise Greek. We have heard the encomium of Brother Thomas as a preacher who did not talk down to his congregation, but rather talked to them and in the process spared them the subtleties of his university discourse. What of the great Renaissance humanists and their inner-circle mentality, their inner-circle languages, their contempt for scholars of their immediate past?

Even the beautiful "chancery" handwriting in which those humanists wrote reveals and, in a sense, denudes their limitations. Because the oldest manuscripts of the classics had been written in Carolingian times and in hands now classified as "Carolingian minuscule," the humanists inferred wrongly that what they were reading was the handwriting of the ancients. They would imitate not only the Latin of Virgil and of Tully, they would adopt the very handwriting (as they erroneously identified it) of those worthies.

Let it not be thought that we are free to condemn in our turn the great humanists because we know better where and when the Carolingian minuscule originated. In any case, their mistake has been a "happy fault," a *felix culpa,* for it has given us our two lower-case type fonts, our so-called "roman" and "italic" alphabets. It has been our good fortune that they despised the late-gothic hands and replaced them with what we read on our printed pages. All this we know, thanks only to the scholarship of the seventeenth century, steadily advancing from that day to this, and advancing still. It was not only Bernard of Chartres, as reported by John of Salisbury, who had to confess that moderns are as "dwarves, seated on the shoulders of giants" and so seeing farther than do those indispensable giants.[14]

All of this would have struck Thomas Aquinas as secondary and accidental. That a language, or two languages, should define the good life for humans must have seemed to him—had so outlandish a claim been made in his hearing—an all but incredible aberration. What would have counted with him is that we can speak at all and that because we "speak" within, we have something to say externally in our various languages.

Here the term "we" is truly universal: it embraces, actually or virtually, all our race. Because this human race can think of itself and speak of itself as "we," Aquinas saw that we are irredeemably social. As Aristotle had seen before him, the human sum is greater than its parts; there is a qualitative advance when we found a family, a village, or a city. A city can approximate a world; "Rome" named a city *par excellence* and it also named an empire of world-wide scope. In one gesture the pope blesses "the City and the world," gives his benediction *urbi et orbi.*

This entailed that Friar Thomas saw all of us, himself included, within the range of a realistic optimism. "Realistic" because he knew that our race is capable of, even prone to, the worst sort of aberration from laws that our freedom permits us to flout. Where we have known, or now, at least remember Hitler, he had heard of Ghengis Khan and of the pyramids of human skulls left in the track of apparently invincible Mongol armies. He knew about usurious loans in a primitive economy and deceptive merchants; he knew about teachers who betrayed the eagerness of their students with bizarre and covert theorizing they feared to sustain in the presence of their colleagues. He knew that the desperation of the poor returns all private property to the state of common ownership. The starving man who took a rich man's loaf was no thief in the eyes of Brother Thomas.

Nor did this entail a blanket condemnation of the rich. King Louis IX, at whose table he had sat, was rich and a saint; Abraham's wealth did not diminish the patriarch's sanctity.

The human person of Aquinas, integrally taken, is an "image" of the

Holy One. If our "likeness" to our Source has been distorted and darkened, this is now reparable for it has been repaired in principle: our race, he saw, has fallen, but it has been redeemed.

Here the thirteenth-century Aquinas, a humanist in his fashion, joins hands across the centuries with Michaelangelo and Leonardo and Erasmus. What do they have in common?

It is something more basic than Greek meters or Latin prose style. It is a vision of the human as incarnating the Eternal Word in an infinitely diminished, but infinitely precious form. By a paradox, humanism ends in faith in the Holy One for each of these primary representatives of the movement. It has begotten the *Summary of Theology* and the Vatican Stanze, the unbearably majestic Moses in the Gesu at Rome, the *Adagia* of Erasmus, and the never to be exhausted theme of Madonna and Child. Is it a paradox that humanism should end with divinity? No doubt it is, but a paradox is nothing less than an unexpected vision of what we had long looked at, but had not yet "seen."

Notes

1. Under the heading "Allen Calls Humanism Compatible with his Belief in God," Anthony Cardinale of the *Buffalo News,* 4 August 1988, quoted Steve Allen on the humanism of Aquinas and More; on 18 August a letter from Allen corrected three incidental errors in the original story.

2. Thomas More to Martin Dorp, 21 October 1515, in *The Correspondence of Sir Thomas More,* ed. Elizabeth Frances Rogers (Princeton, 1947), 34, line 232 and 63, lines 1232–1238.

3. M. Prou, ed., *Les registres d'Honorius IV* (Paris, 1886), fascicule 2, coll. 346, 347, n. 489.

4. See, v.g. Augustine, *The City of God,* book 22, chapter 30.

5. PL 70, 1239–1270.

6. For the text of Innocent's hymn, see: PL 217, 917–920.

7. See my "The Classics: Episcopal Malice and Papal Piety" in the *Proceedings of the Twentieth Annual Conference, The Classics in the Middle Ages* (Binghamton, N.Y.: 1990), 379–402.

8. " 'Versus' dans les Oeuvres de Saint Thomas" in *St. Thomas Aquinas, 1274–1974. Commemorative Studies* (Toronto, 1974, vol. 1), 77–85.

9. ". . . Io non voglio qui discutera la questione non ancora sciolta e di non facile soluzione se ed in quale misura Tommaso comprendeva il greco. Io inclino piu ad una riposta affermativa alla questione . . ." M. Grabmann, *Guglielmo di Moerbeke, O.P. il traduttore* (Rome, 1946), 69, 70.

10. ". . . it is likely that St. Thomas himself had not been quite without Greek." R. Weiss, *Medieval and Humanist Greek. Collected Essays by Roberto Weiss* (Padova, 1977), 11.

11. L. Schutz, "Der hl. Thomas von Aquin und sein Verständniss des Griechischen," *Philosophisches Jahrbuch* 8 (1895): 273–283.

12. ". . . John of Salisbury is known to have picked up the rudiments of Greek from one of the Greek-speaking inhabitants of Santa Severina in Calabria during his sojourn in South Italy." *Medieval and Humanist Greek,* 9.

13. R. Weiss, *The Dawn of Humanism* (London, 1947), 21, cited by H. D. Saffrey, O.P., in his edition of *Sancti Thomae de Aquino super Librum de causis expositio* (Freibourg/Louvain, 1954), xxiv.

14. "Dicebat Bernardus Carnotensis nos esse quasi nanos gigantium humeris insidentes, ut possimus plura eis et remotiora uidere, non utique proprii uisus acumine aut eminentia corporis, sed quia in altum subuehimur et extollimur magnitudine gigantea." *Metalogicon* 3, 4.

4

Christianity, Humanism, and St. Thomas Aquinas

R. J. McLaughlin

THE QUESTION

The topic for investigation here is the relationship between humanism and religion: ought the religious person to be a humanist and ought the humanist to be religious? That the two are at least compatible can be argued from the earliest Christian literature—works by Justin Martyr, Clement of Alexandria, St. Basil the Great, to mention a few[1]—as it can also from the much later literature of the Renaissance, literature associated in a special way with modern humanism. The celebrated humanists of the fifteenth and sixteenth centuries, even when they were reacting against abuses in the Catholic Church, were not rejecting religion, any more than their heroes from antiquity were atheistic. We recall Erasmus (with his ideal of a *philosophia Christi*) and St. John Fisher (patron of my own college in Rochester, bishop and cardinal, and the only man elected chancellor of Cambridge University for life) as men dedicated to human values and to Christianity at the same time.[2] Cicero, that model humanist of the ancient world, was no atheist; and it was on the basis of his teaching that St. Augustine could argue that every irreligious society is by that very fact an unjust society.[3] Neither were Plato or Aristotle godless men. Read all that is said about the gods and religious worship in the *Laws;*[4] and consider too Aristotle's warning in the *Nicomachean Ethics* that, unless we struggle heroically to be godlike, we shall not succeed in being even human.[5] In our own time Pope Paul VI, inspired by the philosopher Jacques Maritain and the theologian Thomas Aquinas, affirmed that the only true humanism is a Christian humanism.[6] From a wide variety of sources, therefore, we hear that religion and humanism are quite compatible.

70

Still, there are problems. Reflect first on the fact that Christianity, like any authentic religion, requires its members to maintain a sense of their radical subjection to the divine, a sense that of themselves they are nothing and can do nothing, that any good qualities they may possess or good that they may do is traceable to God as to its ultimate Cause. "What is man that Thou are mindful of him?" asks the Psalm (8:5). "Without me," says Christ, "you can do nothing" (John 15:5). And from the earliest days of the Christian Church to the present, the constant theme is: "He must increase, I must decrease" (John 3:30). Granted that, if man is indeed a creature of God, it is no derogation from human excellence for him to admit his creaturely status; still and all, the Christian who takes this fact seriously will be animated, it seems, by a spirit quite other than that which moves those humanists who are inclined to celebrate what man is and can accomplish. Singled out for special praise by the Christian is the person who abandons the *agora* for the hermitage or monastery; the Greek ideal of the doer of mighty deeds and sayer of great words is replaced in a Christian scheme of things by the ideal of the suffering servant. Humility, self-effacement, even obscurity become things to be sought. The more fervently religious a person is, the less of a humanist it seems he will be.[7]

But the problem goes deeper. No one is a Christian who does not assent unqualifiedly to dogmas beyond the power of the human mind to discover or corroborate—dogmas to the effect that God is triune, that the Second Person of the Trinity became man and lived among us, that He continues His mission in time through a Church, that those who live as God wills us to live will be rewarded with an eternity of rapturous enjoyment of His Divine Self. But today thinkers celebrated for their humanist outlook express impatience with such "dogmatic" assertions and relegate such beliefs to the category of "mythological illusions," preferring to put their reliance, they say, on the critical use of scientific reason.[8] According to them, the Christian, who is content to say "I believe" is no humanist.

Furthermore, just as the Christian must regulate his *thinking* according to the official dogmas of his Church, so he must regulate his *behavior* according to the moral teaching of his Church. From Abraham to the present, the truly religious man is one who is obedient to God and God's spokesmen. But the signers of the 1973 "Humanist Manifesto" assure us that ethics needs no theological sanction and warn that the traditional faiths encourage dependence rather than independence. Paul Kurtz tells us, "The only authority is the authority of intelligence,"[9] and the hallmark of authenticity is self-commitment.[10] So humanism, which insists on the autonomy of the person, seems incompatible with a religious outlook, which calls on a man to be submissive to external direction, to be obedient to his God and God's Church.

ON BEING HUMAN

However divergent our understandings of humanism, we can agree, I suppose, that it is fundamentally a moral view, an attitude toward the conduct of life, a call to a way of living that respects the most important human values. What I want to do in this essay is to consult the one whom I consider to be the premier Christian theologian and to investigate the connection in his doctrine between the promotion of human goods and religion.

St. Thomas Aquinas begins his reflections on right living by setting before us an idea of what it is to be human. And, remarkably for this very authoritative representative of what is often said to be a highly authoritarian religious tradition, what he emphasizes in human nature as particularly significant for morality are the very points that today's humanists stress—viz., that man is intelligent, that he is free, that he is responsible. So speaks Thomas in the "Prologue" to the moral part of the *Summa Theologiae,* in which he may be supposed to be setting down the keynote of his moral theology. It has been pointed out that, where Thomas could have spoken of our freedom under God, his preference in that Prologue for speaking of us as like God cannot be without significance.[11] We *too,* he says, are *"suorum operum principium,"* the originators of our own acts. As he proceeds to develop this moral doctrine, he stresses that the good for man is always *"secundum rationem":* "according to reason."[12] Ignorant and stupid people may often be very good people, close to God; but their goodness must be in spite of their ignorance, not because of it. For there is no moral virtue without prudence, practical wisdom, good sense about what is to be done.[13] Each of the cardinal virtues, on which turns the whole moral life, is a different way of introducing intelligence into our operations.[14] Among the virtues we find obedience, yes; but it is only one virtue among many and not the principal virtue.[15] And never blind obedience, Thomas tells us. Any proper law, of man or God, demands our respect; but not every edict of civil or ecclesiastical authority deserves to be called a law. It needs to be a reasonable directive. And if an edict falls short of being reasonable, disobedience may be permissible, or even demanded.[16]

Thomas would agree with Sartre that our moral decisions are, in a sense, ours and ours alone; that though we may seek the advice of people whom we think wise, in doing so we have, to some extent anyway, already taken a moral position by choosing one counselor rather than another; and that, whatever that counselor says, the final choice will be ours, not his.[17] Perhaps Thomas is readier than Sartre to admit that we are at times dominated by forces beyond our control, so that some of the things we do we do without merit or culpability.[18] Ordinarily, however, we are not without resource;[19] and we act in a properly human way only when we intelligently commit *ourselves* to this or that course of action. Here we approach what Thomas means by "acting conscientiously": acting *cum scientia,* with knowledge.[20] The reasonable man will be open to all sorts of advice from all promising quarters. As member of a particular church, he will be especially interested in what this moral teacher has to say, but in the end the choice will be his, not his spiritual counselor's, not his bishop's, not the pope's.

Some young people are upset when Church leaders, or teachers of ethics, speak out clearly on moral issues, saying perhaps quite emphatically that abortion on demand is an evil policy, that capital punishment is wrong, that the relatively affluent are morally obliged to assist the indigent. They object as though such pronouncements infringed on their liberty, when in fact these are matters of instruction, not coercion. The defender of personal liberty should, after all, be at least as respectful of the teacher's liberty to label choices evil as of his own liberty to make evil choices. Sometimes, of course, men in authority attempt to defend the truth by force, as when the government of Alberta penalizes a man for teaching that the holocaust never occurred and when the Church denies certain scholars the privilege of teaching as Catholic theologians in Catholic institutions. Though Thomas Aquinas allows that authorities must at times appeal to force—perhaps in situations in which you and I would not readily countenance it—his basic disposition is the authentically humanist one of preferring to rely on rational persuasion.[21]

Reason, freedom, personal responsibility—to the extent that these are litmus tests for the authentic humanist Thomas Aquinas clearly passes. But you may want to object, along with many of today's humanists, that it is religion that skews the Thomistic picture such that it becomes hard to recognize Thomistic humanism as humanism.

ON BEING RELIGIOUS

How Thomas arrives at the conclusion that being fully human itself requires us to be religious is the next element of his philosophy that we must advert to. Basically his reasoning is that of St. Augustine in the *City of God,* that suggested by Cicero in the *De Re Publica* and hinted at by Plato in the *Euthyphro:* justice requires religion.[22] The point may be appreciated through comparison of the honor that we pay God with the honor that we give our parents. Filial respect or piety, we call the latter. The son or daughter who is indifferent to her parents, who does not cultivate a loving concern for them, who is not the least bit deferential to them, who ignores the sickness or loneliness or poverty of their old age is not a son or daughter any of us would admire. We see selfishness and a lack of love at work here. But we see something else besides—a real injustice, a failure to pay a debt, not just to confer a gratuity. Without parents, after all, none of us would have been born. It is they who fed us, housed us, nursed us through illnesses, lavished affection on us, saw to our education, disciplined us in virtuous living, generally did what they could to bring us to that level of maturity at which we could look after ourselves. To such benefactors, common decency says, we owe a return for the inestimable goods that we have received. Now, if we have a debt in justice to our human parents, the immediate causes of countless benefits to us, how much more of a debt have we to God, the ultimate cause of all that we are and have, Him who calls us and our parents forth from nothingness and showers all kinds of goods upon us, from happy family to friends, to education, to satisfying work, to this glorious universe that is our home, Him whose greatest blessing, Christian faith assures us, is the destiny He has established for us with Himself. To God, therefore, will be due an honor infinitely higher than that which we accord our parents. To be disposed to pay this debt, as far as we are capable, is precisely what it is to be religious.[23]

And what does being religious involve? The analogy of filial respect continues to be helpful. We can imagine a son or daughter who values the things that her parents value: who applies herself diligently to her job and is honest in her business dealings, who is quick to come to the aid of people in distress and is regularly busy doing for others—in short, one who loves her neighbor. But if this daughter seldom bothers to talk with her parents, generally fails to thank them for their kindnesses, neither asks their help nor offers hers, we will have difficulty supposing that she really loves *them* rather than just happens to love the things that they love. Here, I suggest, we can see what religion is basically about: our cultivating within ourselves a sense of subjection to God and indebtedness to Him and our stirring up within ourselves appropriate sentiments of gratitude. Being religious may entail doing things for our neighbor, just as a son's love of his parents may prompt him to be courteous to other people, to be truthful, sometimes to put himself at risk to save others from peril. So acts having directly to do with something other than our obligations to God, while remaining acts of kindness or truthfulness or bravery, become acts of religion when done out of reverence for God. They are commanded by religion, St. Thomas explains, without being the primary expressions of religion.[24] First and foremost, religion is reverence for God and expresses itself in acts of devotion (the will promptly to do what God wills) and prayer (an asking of God's help that confesses our dependence on him who is the author of all goods).[25] And since we are bodily creatures, says Thomas, our obeisance to God naturally takes a physical form in public acts of adoration.[26]

Two conclusions emerge from these reflections on religion. One is that for a fully human life we need to cultivate more than human values. We need to be open to the superhuman. Anyone who recognizes the existence of God and yet fails to be regularly mindful of Him, not bothering to enter into conversation with Him, not bowing down in awe and gratitude—any such person is morally corrupt. Just by reason of being human we are obliged to be prayerful. The second conclusion is almost as important. Though being religious has to do primarily with our relation to God, the fact is that the more we try to bring our wills into accord with the divine will, the more our love of Him will extend to all the things that He loves—to all men, to all creatures. So while it will make sense for some people to turn aside from many of the good things in this world—from wealth, from marriage, from independence—and to dedicate themselves to God in a special way through vows of poverty, chastity, and obedience; and while some holy people, like a John the Baptist or a Therese of Lisiuex will castigate their bodies in ways that might look inhuman in order to achieve the kind of self-discipline that will strengthen them to be of one will with God, such turning away from created goods must never involve any denigration of the worth of God's handiwork. God loves creatures into existence, all of them; we too should love them. Especially we should love human beings, who, alone among material things, give evidence of being valuable for their own sake.[27] So religion, far from being a distraction from this life's pressing concerns, far from being an impediment to a full-blown humanism, is a factor giving us deeper, more compelling reason to work for the benefit of all humanity.[28]

ON BEING A BELIEVER

Of course, some readers may doubt precisely what I have assumed: that God exists or at least that we can prove it. These are issues that I don't intend to press directly for two reasons: one, that most readers probably are already familiar with the arguments that I consider best, those of Aquinas;[29] and two, that satisfactory clarification of them is beyond the limits of this brief inquiry. Let me say only, that, if one has difficulty with these arguments, the reason, I suspect, is not that one finds the premises wrong or the logic faulty but that the God to whose existence I have been referring is still a hidden God; and we all, Thomas Aquinas included, find it very difficult to suppose that we really know what we are talking about when we talk about things beyond the range of our senses.[30] So no sooner does Thomas, starting from sense data, conclude that a trans-empirical God exists than he hastens to assure us that he does not know what it is to be as God is.[31] Apparently Thomas is less bothered than are many today by the fact that he has proved to exist a he-knows-not-what, by his inability to give God a face or in any way confirm his conclusion in sense experience. Here we touch on a point of considerable importance, I think, for understanding how a genius like Thomas Aquinas, along with the vast majority of philosophers until fairly recent times, could think the existence of God demonstrable and yet so very many philosophers today think just the opposite. In the modern era something has happened to change the picture. And that something has nothing to do with the discovery of mistakes in Thomas's reasoning. What is new is what is meant by knowledge. Without going into detail, I suggest that the enormous success of positive science since Copernicus has led us to think of mathematical physics as providing the paradigm for all knowledge. And because techniques of verification play so prominent a role there, we begin to suspect that any talk of the unverifiable is somehow intellectually suspect.[32] But Thomas, following up on the Aristotelian theme that the verb *to know* is said in many ways, forcefully insists that it is an intellectual sin to attempt to proceed in one discipline with the method proper to another.[33] To those who reject all God-talk as meaningless, because unverifiable, Thomas asks, just what is wrong with reasoning from the sensible to the insensible. Something akin to this goes on even in physics, when the astronomer, noticing an irregularity in the orbit of some heavenly body, concludes that at a precise point in space there must exist a center of gravity, though no light emanates from the spot for him to behold. Thus the "black holes" of space. What is this but positing the existence of the unobserved to explain the observed?[34] Why should the procedure of the philosopher or theologian or St. Paul (Rom. 1:20) be any the less intellectually respectable when he concludes to the existence of an unexperienced and radically unexperienceable cause of all the things that he does experience?

Any fledgling undergraduate can read Thomas Aquinas's "five ways" and understand the words. But really to make the arguments one's own, that will be another matter, involving a disciplining of the mind so that it can work effectively at the requisite level of abstraction, be clear in its concepts, and rigorous in its reasoning, be good at recognizing the issues and asking the right questions. Not everyone is naturally fit for such accomplishments. And those who are need years of training for the task. Even then, they will make mistakes. What did Aristotle say about our ability to know the things of God? Our minds are to the divine what the eye of the owl is to the sun— blinded by its superluminosity. But because such knowledge is required if we are to see ourselves for what we are and rightly organize our lives, it is fitting that God has spoken to us in a special way, revealing things about Himself and our relation to Him that are indeed naturally knowable. So comments Thomas Aquinas in the very first article of the *Summa Theologiae*. And he adds that, since God has in fact established for us a destiny above the requirements of our nature and thus beyond the capacity of the intellect naturally to discover and since knowledge of this end is indispensable for the direction of life, the necessity of revelation becomes even clearer.[35] All of this is as we might expect: that an intelligent and loving cause should at one time or another communicate with those of his creatures who are intelligent. And so we come to another element important for understanding the human condition—faith.

The assent of faith is not the "Yes, maybe" of fallible human opinion responding to persuasive though less than compelling evidence but the "Yes, certainly!" of the one who has no doubt that He who speaks to him speaks the truth.[36] Were the situation otherwise, were it for the sake of something held as merely probable that the believer was ready to go to the lions or cross or gallows, the secular humanist's case for the irrationality of belief would have greater force. St. Thomas sees nothing unreasonable in a revealing God or in a believing human being. Of course, he sees no way of proving that it is God who speaks or that what is said is necessarily true. To assent on these two scores is precisely what it is to be a believer.[37] Now, if the foregoing reasoning is sound, it is no denigration of reason to expect it to submit to the guidance of faith. For the point is not that we should ever abandon reason in the interests of faith. In a sense we believe, Thomas teaches, only because it is reasonable to believe, even though what we believe we have no evidence for asserting. Thus I cannot prove that Christ is the incarnate Word of God the Father, but I find it reasonable to believe this (for reasons not germane to this discussion). And if I am glad to be a believer, it is not because I, any more than Thomas or Augustine or Anselm or any Christian theologian, think faith an end in itself; it is a means to an end. We don't believe in order always to go on believing but in order eventually to under- stand. There is nothing anti-intellectual about this notion of faith. Just as the man making his first visit to Brock University must initially take it on faith that there is indeed a Brock University (about which he has heard re- ports from sources that he can hardly suppose to have conspired to deceive him) and only subsequently, once he has reached his destination, no longer relies on faith, so analogously the Christian believes in God in order finally to come to see God, face to face, in that beatifying intellectual vision of which the evangelist spoke (in words that the humanist John Fisher recalled as he went to the gallows): "This is eternal life—to *know* Thee, the only true God . . ." (John 17:3).

CONCLUSION

If Thomas Aquinas is right, as we attempt to put our lives into good order, what we have first to do is give thought to what it is to be a human being and, in the light of such understanding, intelligently, freely, responsibly struggle to achieve the highest human goods. If our intelligence leads us, as it leads Thomas, to affirm our creaturely status, then on a purely natural level, without our appealing to any privileged matters of faith, it also dictates that we be religious. That God has spoken to us in a way requiring faith in him is nothing that the philosopher can prove, but that such communication should occur is something that the philosopher can see as fitting, indeed, as necessary if our true destiny transcends the requirements of our nature and if awareness of this end is indispensable for the correct ordering of our lives. I recommend to every reader of whatever school of thought a study of the writings of Thomas Aquinas, a profoundly religious human being and a determinedly human man of religion.

Notes

1. See in particular Justin Martyr's *Dialogue with Trypho,* Clement's *Miscellanies,* Basil's treatise *To Young Men on Making Good Use of Greek Literature.* Although Tatian and Tertullian offer a contrary witness, showing antagonism to the kind of humanism emanating from the pagan philosophers, they are minority voices. For bibliographical information and a good summary treatment of humanist tendencies among the Christian apologists and Fathers in the first several centuries of the Christian era, see Etienne Gilson, *History of Christian Philosophy in the Middle Ages* (New York, 1954), chaps. 1–3 and accompanying notes.

2. Desiderius Erasmus, *Enchiridion Militis Christiani, Opera Omnia,* (Hildesheim, 1622), Tome V. Cf. Werner Jaeger, *Humanism and Theology* (Milwaukee, 1943), 65–66, an admirable little essay on a theme close to that of this paper and predictably rich in classical scholarship. Edward Surtz, *The Works and Days of John Fisher* (Cambridge, 1967).

3. Augustine, *De Civitate Dei* 19.21.

4. On the existence of gods, their care for men, and the requirement of our honoring them, see Plato, *Laws* 10. The text from *Laws,* 2.653cd, which Josef Pieper sets at the beginning of *Leisure: the Basis of Culture* (London, 1952), merits quotation here too: "But the gods, taking pity on mankind, born to work, laid down the succession of recurring feasts to restore them from their fatigue, and gave them the Muses, and Apollo their leader, and Dionysus, as companions in their feasts, so that nourishing themselves in festive companionship with the gods, they should again stand upright and erect." For a good summary treatment of Plato's attitude toward the

gods and religious worship, see G. M. A. Grube, *Plato's Thought* (Boston, 1958), 150–178.

5. In *Nicomachean Ethics* 7.1145a 15–27, Aristotle contrasts brutishness with a virtue that is "heroic and divine." Later, in 10.7, after concluding that man's ultimate good consists in contemplation (apparently of divine things) so far as this is possible, he wonders if such a goal is not unreasonably high, and answers: "But we must not follow those who advise us, being men, to think of human things, and, being mortal, to think of mortal things, but must, so far as we can, make ourselves immortal, and strain every nerve and fibre to live in accordance with the best thing in us . . . " (1171b 31–1178a 1).

6. Pope Paul VI, Christmas Message, December 25, 1969. Cf. Jacques Maritain's, *True Humanism* (London, 1938). See especially the "Introduction."

7. From the earliest days of the Church to the present we see deeply religious people going literally or figuratively into the desert, abandoning ordinary commerce with their fellows. Though in recent years the discipline of most religious communities has been appreciably relaxed, the Catholic Church still recommends that people aiming at the perfection of religious life consider divesting themselves of their private property, forswearing all sexual activity, and surrendering much of their personal autonomy through solemn vows of poverty, chastity, and obedience. The lives of the saints abound with stories of self-abnegation that can be expected to appall the contemporary humanist (think of St. Simon all that time perched atop a pillar); and even if many such stories about the saints are not the literal truth, their very existence testifies to a conception of religious devotion that is hard to reconcile with anything we are likely to call humanism. Many manifestations of religious devotion we can dismiss as aberrant (e.g., the rovings bands of flagellants in the fourteenth century); but Thomas a Kempis' *De Imitatione Christi,* which has a fair claim to being representative of something closer to mainstream religious devotion (of being at least an important tributary thereto), might be thought to display inordinate fear of human accomplishment, lest pride ensue, to encourage forgetfulness of public virtue in its stress on the private, and, particularly, to be distrustful of reason: "I would rather feel compunction than know its definition" (1.1).

8. Cf. *Humanist Manifestos I and II* (Buffalo, 1973). "We need to extend the uses of the scientific method . . ." (14); "We believe . . . that traditional dogmatic or authoritarian religions that place revelation, God, ritual, or creed above human needs and experience do a disservice to the human species. Any account of nature should pass the tests of scientific evidence; in our judgment the dogmas and myths of traditional religions do not do so" (15–16). See also Paul Kurtz, "Is Everyone a Humanist?" in *The Humanist Alternative,* ed. Paul Kurtz (Buffalo, 1973), especially 178, 183–186. Although in this essay Professor Kurtz argues against using the term *humanist* of theists, in more recent statements (cf. "On the Misuse of Language: A Response to Paul Beattie," *Free Inquiry* 6/1 [1985–86] and Kurtz's Brock University address of November 1987) he prefers to distinguish two main categories of humanist: those who accept the existence of God and the obligations of religion and those who do not. The latter brand of humanism, his own, he likes to call "secular." The change in vocabulary is helpful. If our question were purely a definitional one, we could stop here. But the substantive issue of the relation between being human and being religious would persist.

9. Paul Kurtz, "Is Everyone a Humanist?" 184.

10. Jean-Paul Sartre, *Existentialism and Humanism,* trans. Philip Mairet (London, 1960).

11. Ignatius T. Eschmann, O.P., "St. Thomas' Approach to Moral Philosophy," *Proceedings of the American Catholic Philosophical Association,* 31 (1957): 25–36.

12. See, for example, *Summa Theologiae* (hereafter cited as *ST*), I-II, 19, 4, c; 21, 1, c; 63, 2, c; 71, 6, c; 90, 1, c.

13. *ST*, II-II, 51, 2, c; *De Virt. Comm.*, 6, c; *De Veritate*, 14, 6, c.

14. Of the four cardinal virtues prudence has the first rank, being defined as a perfected ability for acting in a reasonable manner here and now (*ST*, I-II, 57, 4). It is said to be *"principalior"* to the other three; it is presupposed by them—justice being a perfected ability for introducing reason into acts of the will with respect to others, temperance being a disposition to introduce reason into the concupiscible appetite, fortitude a disposition to introduce reason into the irascible appetite (*ST*, I-II, 61, 2). For a superb study of the preeminence of prudence among the cardinal virtues see Josef Pieper, *Prudence* (New York, 1959).

15. Thomas treats obedience as a virtue contained under justice. Its distinguishing characteristic is that it presupposes a command, expressed or implied. In the strict sense of *obedience*, the virtue requires that one intend to fulfill a command, though, in a looser sense, just the doing of what is commanded is enough to warrant calling a man obedient (*ST*, II-II, 104, 2). Clearly with respect to obedience to other men there are innumerable virtuous acts that are not suitably matters of precept (*ST*, I-II, 96, 3). And if the human superior should command contrary to God's ordinances or if he should exceed his authority, obedience is not due (*ST*, II-II, 104, 5). Where God's commands are concerned, Thomas allows that obedience, despite its subordinate status as a potential part of justice, takes a certain precedence over other moral virtues (cf. n. 24, below). The reason is that the obedient man for the sake of cleaving to God contemns not just possessions or goods of the body but that spiritual good which is his very will. And the more that a man contemns for the sake of adhering to God, the greater the virtue (*ST*, II-II, 104, 3).

16. *ST*, I-II, 90, 1; 95, 2.

17. *De Veritate*, 17. The entire question is devoted to conscience; articles 3–5 are especially relevant. See also *ST*, II-II, 104, 5, on the obedience due superiors.

18. *ST*, I-II, 6.

19. *ST*, I-II, 94. In Article 4 St. Thomas explains that, however uncertain and confused we may be about how we should live, the first principles of morality are never entirely expunged from our awareness. Cf. Jacques Maritain, *Man and the State* (Chicago, 1951), 93.

20. *ST*, I, 79, 13.

21. Cf. Yves Simon, *The Nature and Functions of Authority* (Milwaukee, 1948).

Against the interpretation of Thomistic texts advanced here one might object on two counts. The first is that, given the lack of any real distinction in God between knowing and willing (*CG*, I, 45, 73), the insistence on the primacy of the rational element in law is not ultimately defensible. But granted that everything that God knows to be actual he also wills to be, and vice versa, it is also true that, even in God, as we are constrained to understand him, will logically presupposes intellect: it is appetite for the *understood* good (*CG*, I, 72). That understood good is nothing other than the Godhead itself, in the willing of which God wills whatever else he wills. This brings us to the second objection, which is none other than the central problem of Plato's *Euthyphro:* does God will things other than himself because they are intrinsically lovable, or are they lovable because God wills them? If we say the latter, we seem to imply that God's preferences are arbitrary and whimsical. On the other hand, if we make the divine preferences depend on something other than God himself, we seem to imply that the first cause is himself caused, a contradiction. Creation, as Thomas understands it, is the establishment of things in a relationship of absolute dependence on the uncaused cause. Neither God's knowledge nor his willing can in any way be determined by things other than himself. His willing causes other things to be lovable. So how does Thomas avoid the imputation of irrationality in God? Just why does God will this to be rather than that? Like human choices, but more so, God's choices are hidden. Why he wills one thing rather than another is an impenetrable mystery. But we do know that, since he is sufficient unto himself and yet wills other things to be, he must will them out of sheer generosity, sheer beneficence (*CG,* I, 74–98). The situation is analogous to that of the demiurge in Plato's *Timaeus,* save for the fact that for Thomas the ideas that provide a ground of reasonableness have no existence independent of the divine intellect, of the divine substance.

22. Augustine, *De Civitate Dei,* 19, 21; Plato, *Euthyphro* 12e–16a.

23. Justice is a disposition to render to others what is *due,* and what is due is an *equal* return. Religion is only imperfectly contained under justice; for while it gives honor to God, as is due, the return is in no way equal to what has been received (*ST,* II-II, 80, 1). Though we sometimes speak of "religion," probably meaning "Church," as something that people can "belong to," St. Thomas presents it as a quality of soul residing in those who are said to be religious, thanks to which they are steadily disposed to, and have a perfected ability for (it is a *habitus*), certain good activities (it is a *virtus*) (cf. *ST,* I-II, 49–50, 55). As religion should not be confused with Church, which is a society rather than a *habitus* (cf. Jacques Maritain, *Man and the State,* pp. 150–1), neither should it be confused with faith, which, along with hope and charity, is theological rather than moral, having as its object God, who is our end. Religion has as its object, not God, but the worship (*cultus*) that we direct to God and is thus concerned with things referred to the end rather than the end itself (*ST,* II-II, 81, 5).

24. To the religious person there is no wrongful act that he will not be willing to characterize as "irreligious." The contrary good acts would, therefore, appear to be religious acts and *religion* but another name for virtue in general. For those who think of religion as a special virtue it will not be enough to say that morally good acts become religious by being done with a view to eventual union with God; for this might be thought to be the end of the moral life precisely as such (*ST,* II-II, 81, 6). The problem is compounded for St. Thomas by the Letter of James, which tells us that "religion pure and undefiled before our God and Father is this: to visit orphans and widows in their trials and to bear oneself uncontaminated by this world" (1:27). Even according to the sacred text, therefore, the things that religion is concerned with seem no different from the objects of such virtues as mercy and temperance. St. Thomas answers that, "since virtue is directed to the good, where there is a special kind of good, there must be a special virtue." The honor that we give God is a special kind of good. To be religious is to be virtuous in a different way from that of the dutiful son or the dutiful citizen, from that of the temperate man or the brave man. But the acts of other virtues can be viewed not only as means of achieving human fulfillment (which is the perspective of ethics generally) but also as dutiful service of God (which is the perspective of religion) (*ST,* II-II, 81, 4). And insofar as our acts are thus "directly and immediately ordered to the honor of God," by them we approach closer to God than we do by acts of the other moral virtues taken by themselves. In this way religion, while remaining in a sense derivative from justice and prudence, "is superior to the other moral virtues" (*ST,* II-II, 81, 6).

25. *ST,* II-II, 82, 2; 83, 3.

26. *ST,* II-II, 81, 7; 84.

27. Cf. *CG,* III, 112. Cf. R. J. McLaughlin, "Men, Animals, and Personhood," *Proceedings of the American Catholic Philosophical Association,* 59 (1985): 166–181.

28. Jesus explicitly rejects the suggestion that one can truly love God and not love one's neighbor (1 John 4:20). So the presence among us of people who maintain the appearance of being dutiful worshippers but who ignore the needs of their fellow men is a scandal to religion. Nothing, of course, prevents individuals who doubt or deny the existence of God from outdoing the religious man in their loving service of other men. For an interesting account of how professedly nonreligious people can be religious by implication, see Joseph Owens, *Human Destiny* (Washington, D.C., 1985), especially 64–76.

29. *ST,* I, 2, 3; *CG,* I, 13.

30. *ST,* I, 84, 7–8.

31. *ST,* I, 3, 4, ad 2m; 12, 12; *In Boeth. de Trin.* VI, 3–4. Notice that, if the problem is one concerning the very intelligibility of sentences about God, faith is in the same predicament as philosophy; for "the light of revelation is received in us according to our mode of knowing" (ibid., 3, c).

32. Since Copernicus sciences have become progressively more mathematicized. Now, the fact that mathematics does not deal with real things but with mental constructs derived from physical reality and given a purely ideal existence in the mind means that, to the very extent that sciences are mathematical in character, they are concerned with something other than the real world. Naturally the scientist coming to the conclusion of his mathematical reasoning will want to turn back to the real and confirm or disconfirm his mathematical hypothesis in sense experience. For the conclusion will be no more secure than the original intuition of a certain mathematical character to the real. Cf. E. A. Burtt, *The Metaphysical Foundation of Modern Physical Science* (New York, 1955). Sciences that are not thus dependent on mental constructs but stay focused on the real will not have the same need of verification in sense experience. Cf. St. Thomas, *In Boeth. de Trin.* V–VI; Jacques Maritain, *The Degrees of Knowledge* (New York), 136–173, and "The Ways of Faith," in *The Range of Reason* (New York, 1952), 205–218.

33. Thomas Aquinas, *In Boeth. de Trin.,* VI, 2, c. Cf. E. Gilson, *The Unity of Philosophical Experience* (New York, 1937), which traces in a variety of thinkers the unhappy consequences of trying to impose on all thinking the spirit and methodology of a particular discipline.

34. Cf. Mortimer Adler, *How to Think about God: A Guide for the Twentieth Century Pagan* (New York, 1980), 98.

35. Cf. *CG,* I, 3–5; *ST,* II-II, 2, 3–4.

36. Josef Pieper shows clearly that even when the belief in question is not religious we may distinguish sharply between belief and opinion. He tells of a person who hears from a stranger that his brother, lost and presumed dead in war, is really alive. As long as the person hearing the news is hesitant, saying only that he presumes so but must check the facts, the bearer of the good tidings can fairly say, "In other words, you don't believe me." *Belief and Faith* (New York, 1963), 14–15.

As Thomas explains, sometimes it is the object that moves the intellect to assent, either because it is immediately evident, as in an act of basic understanding, or because it is rendered evident by other things, as in scientific demonstration. At other times, when evidence, mediate or immediate, is insufficient to establish the truth, the intellect still assents, moved to do so by a free act of the will. But why would one choose to assent in this case? Perhaps because he thinks that the evidence shows one side of the question probable: he assents, but with a fear of error; this is the state of mind called opinion. Or his assent may have nothing to do with the evidence:

he may choose to assent simply because of his confidence in the person who reveals the information to him; this is what Thomas means by faith. *ST,* II-II, 1, 1 and 4; 2, 1. Now, the fact that this confidence, in proportion as it is real and total, should prompt the believer to say yes to anything that the revealer says understandably frightens the secular humanist. His religious counterpart can agree that no mere mortal talking about matters accessible to human investigation should be accorded this unreserved confidence. The unqualified character of religious faith presupposes that He who speaks stands infinitely higher than any human witness and is omniscient. Moreover, to insist that religious faith involves firm conviction is not to suppose that the mind of the believer has the complacency of the knower who has followed an inquiry to its conclusion and now rests content in the truth. Faith, Thomas explains, does involve a certain unease, that of the person who is still longing to see for himself, who still has many questions to run over and over in his mind. *ST,* II-II, 2, 1; cf. Josef Pieper, *Belief and Faith,* 21–24, 43–50.

37. *ST,* II-II, 2, 2.

5

What Is Renaissance Humanism?

Martin Andic

What is Renaissance humanism? What is the Renaissance, and what is a humanist? Is the Renaissance over? Are we all, or should we be, humanists today? Or Renaissance men?

Historians argue whether there was a Renaissance at all and not just a continuation of trends begun in the Middle Ages, or whether there was only one and not several, such as that of Romanesque Provence in the tenth and eleventh centuries or France in the twelfth and thirteenth; or if one Renaissance then what it was and whether it was an achievement or a failure. In what follows I shall simply follow the majority and call the period between 1300 and 1600 in Western Europe a Renaissance in the general sense of a rebirth or revival of culture, as the writers of that period called it themselves.[1] Taking the leading role in this rebirth were the so called humanists, such as Francesco Petrarch (1304–74) and Lorenzo Valla (1407–57), assisted by such philosophers as Marsilio Ficino (1433–99) and Pietro Pomponazzi (1462–1525), whom I shall briefly discuss further on. Now in an important respect Ficino and Pomponazzi were not, or were not only, humanists, nor were the humanists as such philosophers. The humanists were writers and historians, moralists and political men who argued with school philosophers about the meaning and aims of education, saying that the proper study of man is not the *dialectic* that wins arguments about such things as the Zenonian paradoxes of continuity and division pursued in Aristotle's *Physics,* but rather the *practical wisdom* that rules oneself and one's community, that knows truth and enjoys beauty, through the study of literature and history and ethics. Thus Petrarch writes of dialectic:

> I know that it is one of the liberal arts and a stepping stone for those who want to rise higher. . . . It sharpens the intellect, marks off the path toward

truth, and teaches how to avoid fallacies. . . . But a wayfarer who forgets the goal he has set to himself because the road is so pleasant is not sound of mind. . . . Occupation with dialectic may cover a part of this road; it ought never to be the goal. . . .[2]

and he goes on in words recalling those of Callicles in Plato's *Gorgias* (484–6d) to mock at old men who still play the games of boys with boys.

Now the studies urged by these humanists were in fact the humanities, or *studia humanitatis,* which developed the humane virtues of classical Greece and Rome.[3] These studies included grammar, rhetoric, poetry, history, and moral philosophy but not, like the medieval "liberal arts," logic and the *quadrivium* (arithmetic, geometry, astronomy, and music, four of the five mathematical sciences required by Socrates in *Republic* 7: actually his five count plane and solid geometry separately); nor, like the "fine arts" of the eighteenth century, did they include the visual arts, music, dancing, and gardening.[4] And while they retained ethics, they left out metaphysics and philosophy of nature, as well as theology, law, and medicine, all standard subjects in the cycle of the medieval university. The humanists thus took the part of rhetoric in the ongoing rivalry between philosophy, which *thinks* truly or at least truthfully about everything, and rhetoric, which *speaks* and *writes* well about verything, going back to the rivalry between Socrates and Plato and Gorgias and Isocrates.[5]

The humanists were generally tutors and teachers in secondary schools, where their subjects became a core curriculum or foundational requirement for work in other subjects; they were often notaries and executive secretaries or chancellors to princes or cities, in which role they were called upon to compose Latin documents, letters of invitation or thanks, speeches for welcoming visitors or dedicating public works or for state weddings or funerals, poems of praise, orations, or histories; sometimes they were rich or noble amateurs in these now fashionable subjects. They recovered Latin and Greek manuscripts, edited and copied or printed them, translated Greek into Latin, or Latin into vernacular languages; they wrote commentaries, textbooks, and studies of grammar (or what we should call philology today); they cultivated and taught a smooth style, a taste for simplicity, clarity, and concision, sometimes at the expense of real insight and precision. Searching for the most accurate manuscripts and the original intentions of their classical authors, they developed standards of historical criticism (one early sensational fruit of which was Valla's exposure in 1449, as a clumsy forgery, of the so called Donation of Constantine, giving the Roman Empire to Pope Sylvester.) The humanists recovered the writings of Lucretius, Tacitus, and some of Cicero, while disseminating those of Virgil, Ovid, Seneca, and Boethius; they translated into Latin most of what was left of Greek poetry, history, and politics, as well as the philosophy of Plato and the Neoplatonists, Sextus Empiricus, and the apocryphal literature of Pythagoras, Orpheus, Zoroaster, and Hermes. They developed the humanist Roman lettering (taken from Carolingian minuscule, which they mistook for ancient Roman), and the humanist cursive we call italic. Many worked as proofreaders and editors in the new industry of printing books, or were actually publishers themselves (e.g., Aldus Manutius, Henri

Estienne also known as Henricus Stephanus, he of the marginal reference numbers in Plato).

In their writings the humanists show an inclination toward the dialogue, the terse essay or treatise rather than the commentary piling up arguments better or worse, toward the letter and the invective or attack; and they think their own experience and thought worth emphasizing, in which some have seen an individualism or subjectivism flowering in the essays of Montaigne, who repeatedly says that he writes always only of himself:

> So, reader, I am myself the substance of my book. . . . My sole aim is to reveal myself. . . . I do not portray [my subject's] being, I portray his passage. . . . Just as good men do the public a service by showing them a model to imitate, I shall perhaps do likewise by showing them what to avoid. . . . I take so much pleasure in being judged and know that it is almost indifferent to me whether I am admired or criticized. . . . I speak of myself exclusively. . . . I study myself more than any other subject. This is my metaphysics, this is my physics. . . . I would rather understand myself well by self-study than by reading Cicero. In the experience that I have of myself I find enough to make me wise, if I were a good scholar. Anyone who recalls the violence of his past anger, and to what a pitch his excitement carried him, will see its ugliness better than in Aristotle, and will conceive a juster hatred for it.[6]

By the mid sixteenth century humanists were more aware of modern progress in technology and science and knowledge of the earth, and they engaged in literary controversies over the relative superiority of ancients and moderns, who excelled in sciences though never perhaps in arts.

Humanists love to pile up not arguments but classical quotations and allusions, but as a result they often strike us as superficial and thin, rather than deep and dense. Often it seems to us that they have nothing much to say, but say it with style and grace and a rich display of learning. Here is the judicious assessment by H. A. Mason:

> At best the scholars did little but possess the wisdom of the past as we might possess a set of copy-book maxims. The maxims certainly make us aware of a difference between the actual and the ideal, but they do not of themselves enable us to penetrate the actual; still less do they show us how to bring the actual nearer to the ideal. . . . On the contrary, the very wealth of examples drawn . . . from these pagan moralists made it impossible to see any object steadily. If you call to mind the most celebrated treatises of the day, from More's *Utopia* to Machiavelli's *Prince* and ask: in what spirit are general principles being brought to bear on particular questions of the day; with what flexibility are the actual complexities of the real world being handled, in short, how much thinking do they contain of the kind that really advances any question, the answer must (I think) be that the general principles are applied *a priori*, the particularities of the actual world are either not taken into account or are not brought into fruitful relation with general principles, in short that there is no genuine thinking, no precision and delicacy of judgment, no real focussing of the mind   no looking steadily at any object.[7]

For genuine thinking we have to go on to the philosophers of the Renaissance proper, the best of whom followed, as we might expect, Plato or Aristotle or both. I shall say something about Ficino and Pomponazzi, who mainly follow Plato and Aristotle respectively; but first I shall briefly review the transmission of these Greek philosophers down to Renaissance Europe.

In the Latin West only parts of Plato's *Timaeus* had survived into the Middle Ages in the excerpts and commentaries of Cicero and Chalcidius, and the passages of Plotinus presented by Victorinus; but the general content and spirit of Platonism and Neoplatonism was preserved by Augustine, Boethius, pseudo-Dionysius, and John Scotus Eriugena. In the thirteenth century, there became available Latin translations from the Greek of Plato's *Meno* and *Phaedo,* Proclus' commentary on the *Parmenides,* and the Neoplatonic *Book of Causes* attributed to Aristotle; but not until the fifteenth century were there Latin versions by Leonardo Bruni of the *Republic, Gorgias, Phaedrus,* and *Laws,* and then of the whole of Plato and Plotinus by Ficino, who also translated the so called Hermetic and Pythagorean literature, offering courses and discussions of these at his Platonic Academy in Florence.

As for Aristotle the Latin West had initially only Boethius' translation of the *Categories* and *Interpretation* (with commentary by the Neoplatonist Porphyry), until there became available in the eleventh and twelfth centuries translations from the Arabic and Byzantine Greek of most of his writings with extensive commentaries by Alexander and the Neoplatonist Simplicius and Galen, as well as by Avicenna and Averroes (he of the notorious teaching of the unity of all active intellect, though he actually worked to purify Aristotle of Neoplatonic elements). By the mid thirteenth century Aristotle set the curriculum in philosophy at the universities of Europe as well as the Arabic countries, not only because of the manifest quality of his thought but also because of its seeming completeness, its systematic and encyclopedic nature. Aristotle set the problems and the methods for resolving them, the terminology and definitions, and the themes for commentaries and questions.

The influence of Aristotle continued into the Renaissance and even increased especially in Italy, where Petrarch, who himself preferred Plato, wrote that Aristotle was better than his translators and commentators; the Aristotelian Pomponazzi rejected the Averroistic unity of intellect while arguing that the soul's deathlessness was unprovable by reason; and Jacopo Zabarella, said to be one of the best and most lucid of Aristotle's commentators ever, discussed his method in the terms of analysis and synthesis which so influenced Galileo.

Platonism, on the other hand, never seriously challenged Aristotelianism in the universities, though it did influence literature through the theory of love developed by Ficino, who also admired Aristotle, and by Shakespeare; through Pico's explicit blending of Plato with Aristotle, Christian and Arabic thought, and the Jewish Cabala; and through Giordano Bruno's erotic poetics and cosmic vitalism; while in its emphasis on the certainty of mathematics and the comparison of learning to recollection, Platonism worked on in Galileo, and thereafter in Berkeley, Coleridge, Shelley, and Emerson. Rennaissance Platonism did not usually oppose itself to Aristotelianism but often combined with it and with other traditions, and it has taken longer to be separated out by itself.

The humanists, by the way, were not essentially pagan, irreligious, or secretly atheist, any more than the philosophers whom they inspired were. The humanists wanted to get back to an accurate study of the sources, to get past the questionable commentaries and doubtful translations to the classics themselves: there were Christian humanists who returned to the Bible and Church Fathers with a better understanding of the ancient languages and texts both sacred and profane, for example, Petrarch, Valla, Manetti, Erasmus, Melanchthon, and even Calvin who worked on the text and commentary of Seneca (not to mention Luther who retranslated the Bible into German but ignored pagan writers). Petrarch himself revered Augustine and composed his most personal work, *The Secret Conflict of My Cares,* as a dialogue between himself and Augustine as guide. And in a famous letter describing his climb of Mount Ventoux he tells how, overcome by the wonderful view from the top, he drew Augustine's *Confessions* from his pocket and opened it at random to the words,

> "Men go to admire the high mountains, the great floods of the sea, the huge streams of the rivers, the shores of the ocean, and the wheelings of the stars—and neglect themselves." I was stunned [Petrarch goes on to say,] and I told my brother, who wished to hear more, to let me be, and I closed the book, angry with myself that I still admired earthly things, although I should have learned long ago even from pagan philosophers that "nothing is wonderful but the soul compared to which if it is great nothing else is."[8]

Augustine was also a favorite of Ficino and Nicolas of Cusa and the Protestants, though not of Erasmus who had edited his text and drew criticism from both Catholics and Protestants for preferring Jerome's reading of the Bible to his.

The great philosophers and scientists of the Renaissance however, as said above, were not, or not only, humanists, that is philologists and historians. They had classical training and aspirations, but they also had originality and incisiveness, an ability to think things through for themselves. We see this if we briefly compare the humanist Valla with the philosophers Ficino and Pomponazzi who have genuinely interesting things to say. Valla's philosophical writings display much wit and padding; he argues like Boethius that human freedom is consistent with divine foreknowledge, but expressly sidesteps the question whether this freedom of ours is really possible if God's will is the cause of everything;[9] he defends a Christian Epicureanism, whereby we should do good because of the eternal pleasures of heaven that it will bring; and he offers to reduce logic to a part of rhetoric, or what we should ordinarily say in Classical Latin, more perspicuous even than Classical Greek.

In Ficino, on the other hand, we have a much more fresh and insightful mind. In his *Platonic Theology,* he emphasizes man's central position and mediating role in the universe: as agent of the divine thought and love, man encompasses and shares in everything from highest to lowest:

> [The soul] is the greatest of all miracles in nature. All other things below God are always one single thing, but the soul is all things together. So it may rightly be called the center of nature, the middle term of all, the series of the world, the face of all, the bond and juncture of the universe.

According to Ficino, man's purpose is divine contemplation and love; and so, arguing like Kant, Ficino says that since few of us attain it in this life, there must be a future life in which all who seek it and begin the climb to it will enjoy it for always (since it would take forever for us to do what we were made to do, we must have forever): otherwise all our search and climb is in vain and human life is pointless, so that the best of all the animals has the worst life of them all since he alone cannot attain what he lives for. Each of us must work for this himself by himself, yet we are lifted to it by our mutual love and friendship, which is an implicit love of God, since he is always present in the love with which we love one another in spirit and in truth: that is, he is the third between any two friends, uniting and watching over them and raising them to himself.[10] Love is in a sense our very humanity (as well as our divinity), and we prove our own by acknowledging that of every other man, and loving others as our equals. Thus Ficino writes,

> Nero was not a man but a monster, and human in skin alone. For had he really been a man, he would have loved other men as members of the same body. . . . That is why I think wise men have called by the name of man himself only that virtue that loves and helps all men as brothers . . . that is, humanity.[11]

This philanthropy implies a tolerance of religious differences, for while Christianity is the best religion of course, religion is natural to men and part of their humanity. Each religion addresses the one true God, and the variety of them all adds to the beauty of the world.[12] For if love is our very humanity, it is also our divinity. As Ficino constantly says, love makes the soul of man something divine. He writes to Lorenzo de'Medici:

> Take care never to despise humanity, nor to consider it merely earthly and human, for humanity is a being of beauty, of celestial origin, and the greatest joy of god in heaven.[13]

And in the opening words of his well-known *Letter to the Human Race,* he says,

> Know thyself, divine race clothed with a mortal garment![14]

The thought is echoed in Shakespeare's *Twelfth Night* (5.1.243–5): "A spirit I am indeed; But am in that dimension grossly clad which from the womb I did participate." This brings into focus something essential in humanism, that it not only can be variously religious, but is *egalitarian,* in making excellence and nobility for everyone as a human being and not only for everyone of good or noble birth, provided one is raised in the excellences of a human being: kindness, gentleness, humility, fairness, courage, wisdom. As Werner Jaeger says,[15] it extends an aristocratic ideal to all.

Pomponazzi, an Aristotelian professor of philosophy at the University of Bologna, agrees with Ficino that man is at the center of the world and (with Pico) that man can become either temporal or eternal as he chooses. But placed in the middle between angel and beast, he can really know only about bodies, and so he cannot prove his soul's deathlessness even though God reveals it to faith. (This is the source of the misleading notion that Pomponazzi believed in a double truth that is false in philosophy but true in religion.) There is much that man cannot know. Indeed Pomponazzi compares the philosopher to Prometheus, in that while trying to understand divine secrets he is eaten up by constant anxious thoughts, cannot eat or drink or sleep, is mocked by nonphilosophers as a fool, and harassed by the Inquisition as a nonbeliever.[16] In fact, says Pomponazzi in his controversial book *The Immortality of the Soul,* chapter 14, man's purpose is not contemplation perfected in a life beyond death but moral goodness, or character. For while few men are wise, and even animals are practical, every man can and should be good: he is not angry when we say that he is not a good metaphysician or a good builder, since there is no blame in this, but only when we say that he is not a good man, or not just or restrained; consequently this is where the fulfillment and task of any man is: in other words, not in the contemplation that few men can achieve, but in the practice of the moral virtues that all can acquire and that makes them human. Moreover, even though a heavenly reward hereafter is promised by God, a man can and should be good simply because this is good to be. This is the reward of goodness that is essential to and inseparable from it, and that is even diminished by any external or accidental reward, or the hope of it, just as the evil itself of injustice is the punishment essential to and inseparable from it, and even diminished by any external and accidental punishment. One is therefore a better man if one is good simply because of the beauty of it and the ugliness of evil, than if one is moved by hope of good or fear of evil to come to his immortal soul. Here Pomponazzi is following Plato and Boethius, and anticipating among others Kant, Kierkegaard, Emerson, Lev Shestov, and Simone Weil. I quote, for example, from Shestov:

> Socrates affirmed that virtue has no need of reward, that it is of little importance whether the soul is immortal or not, that the virtuous man obtains everything that he needs from the good. But I think that Socrates . . . stopped midway, and that the good will not be content with such signs of humility. He should have taken still another step; he should have admitted that the virtuous man has no need of the immortality of the soul and renounced immortality completely . . . he should have admitted that Socrates is mortal, since already here on earth he has obtained from the good everything that he could wish, but that Alcibiades and those who resemble him are immortal. The good gives them nothing or very little, and they exist by another principle which, in the course of this earthly life, does not succeed in accomplishing its promises, and postpones the accomplishment of them to another life. . . . A hundred lives deprived of the good, no matter how happy they may be, are not worth one single life in the good, no matter how painful or horrible it may be.[17]

Pomponazzi also anticipates Kierkegaard in his argument, found in his book on *Causes of Natural Wonders,* that the value of prayer lies not in its outward effects but in its inward ones, the pious mind it creates in the person who prays; but perhaps he found this thought in Augustine.[18] Like Ficino, Pomponazzi also emphasizes the solidarity of man whereby each through his own good actions contributes to the good of all, for man is good if and only if each man is.[19] These are serious and thoughtful positions, supported by interesting arguments and suggestive examples. Pomponazzi was a professor, and he wrote like a professor, showing in his writing some of the faults of the school philosophy in which he was trained. He is less engaging than Ficino. But he is generally worth the effort to understand him.

There are other good philosophers of this time: Bernardino Telesio with his double soul, his sensualistic epistemology, and his account of space and time as absolute and parallel; Francesco Patrizzi, the successor to Ficino with his Platonistic philosophy of nature; Nicolas of Cusa with his nondual vision of God, his learned ignorance, his God as not other, resuming Plato and pseudo-Dionysius and Eckhart; Giordano Bruno with his infinite universe of innumerable worlds like our own centered on the sun, his art of memory, his heroic love and frenzy drawing the soul to God through and beyond suffering and death, himself burnt at the stake in 1600 by the Inquisition, telling his judges, "Perhaps you who pronounce my sentence are more afraid than I who receive it." Renaissance philosophy deserves our attention.

Having pinned up this cartoon of humanism and philosophy in the European Renaissance, I want to try to answer the other questions that I put at the head of this essay. First, are we all, or should we be, humanists today? Perhaps the question seems frivolous, if we think of a humanist as a bookish person, in effect an historian or philologist, a student of the classics of Greek and Roman literature. But let us remember that the humanists were concerned above all with these classics as humane studies that we need above all others.[20] If we need to think through what it is to be a good human being and citizen (as Socrates puts it in *Apology* 20b) and to live a fully realized, flourishing human life—if, that is, we need to understand and realize ourselves in our humanity and to cultivate those humane virtues that make us fully human beings—then where better to begin this self-study than with those precious records of outstanding men and women drawn from the treasury of Latin and Greek history and literature, in order to learn by imitating their deeds and avoiding their failures to become such as they are?[21]

Consider what these studies meant to a Florentine historian in the early sixteenth century writing in political exile. He rises with the sun, he says, and goes to see how the woodcutters get on with their work and listens to their bad luck stories; then he wanders to a spring and then to his aviary, there to read in Dante or Petrarch or in Ovid or Tibullus of their loves and to think of his own. He goes on to the inn by the roadside to chat with passers by, hear the news, and observe mankind. Then after dining at home with his family on the poor produce of his farm, he walks back to the inn to pass the time playing at cards and dice with the innkeeper, the butcher, the miller, and the furnace tenders, quarrelling and exchanging insults and abuse as they argue over pennies in voices raised loud enough to be heard miles away. And so with these trifles he keeps his brain from mouldering and satisfies the malice of fate, content to let her drive him along this road to see if it will not be ashamed of what it does.

When evening comes [he continues], I return to my house and enter my study; and at my door I take off the day's clothing, covered with mud and dirt, and put on regal and courtly garments: and properly dressed now I enter the ancient courts of the men of old where, received by them with affection, I feed on the only food that is mine and for which I was born, where I am not ashamed to ask them the reasons for their actions, and they in their humanity [sc. kindness] answer me; and for four hours of time I am not bored, remember no trouble, no longer dread being poor or dying; entirely I give myself up to them.

And because Dante says it does not lead to knowledge when we hear but do not remember [*Paradise* 5.41], I have noted everything in their conversation of use to me, and have composed a little work on princedoms, where I go as deeply as I can into considerations on this subject, discussing what a princedom is, what kinds there are, how they are won, and kept, and lost. . . .

This is, of course, Niccolo Machiavelli writing to Francesco Vettori (10.xii.1513) about the beginning of the composition of *The Prince,* at about the same time as the *Discourses on Livy* in which curiously enough he writes almost all the same hard-headed maxims and reflections from the viewpoint of republican government as he formulates from the perspective of autocracy in *The Prince.* I will mention Machiavelli again as a Renaissance thinker, but here I cite him as a humanist who knows and loves the past and means to learn from it how to think and live in the present. While working on his history and politics, he invites the great men of the past—Livy, Tacitus, Sallust, Polybius—into his imagination and holds Latin conversations with them. (Petrarch too writes letters to Cicero and Livy; and Dante records a visionary tour of the other world guided by Virgil through Hell and Purgatory up to the Earthly Paradise, though not beyond to the Heavenly Paradise reserved for Christians.)

Now this can become pathological, if we lose ourselves in our studies of and admiration for the great men of the past, and neglect to live ourselves.[22] If we are too intent on our heroes, we can fail to consider our families and fellow citizens, the nonscholars and unlettered people of our own and other countries, the great and small men and women of other past and present cultures beyond Europe and North America, not to mention other intelligent species of living things with whom we share the world, such as whales and wolves. Our historical vision, if it is not historical enough, can make us blind and thoughtless and even inhuman. On the other hand, we surely enrich our lives, our imagination, and our humanity if we know something of how exemplary individuals of other times and places have acted and spoken, written and thought.

Dr. Johnson defended the study of Greek and Latin and spoke of its value to people even in the ordinary dealings of life, conceding that there may be cases in which such learning is useless: " 'for instance, this boy rows us as well without learning, as if he could sing the song of Orpheus to the Argonauts, who were the first sailors.' He then called to the boy, 'What would you give, my lad, to know about the Argonauts?' 'Sir (said the boy), I would give what I have.' Johnson was much pleased with this answer, and we gave him a double fare."[23] Evidently learning may be valuable and enriching even when of no practical or material use.

History alone will not make us wise and good, but neither will ignorance of history. We can live too much in the past, but we live more fully if we make it our own past and even part of our present by making Socrates and Plato and Aristotle (for example) our contemporaries, our models and sources of energy, as Machiavelli did Livy and Caesar. We can draw strength not only from them and their words and deeds, but from their ideals too.

This is a defense of humanism as it was understood in the Renaissance, an active study of classical antiquity (and perhaps other times and cultures too) in order to find solutions to our own problems. It is not necessarily any defense of the humanism that has become a question today, the radical humanism that is said to dehumanize man and his world. How did the one lead to the other? We can surmise the answer by considering a typical definition from a modern study of Socratic humanism:

> By humanism we mean the type of thought that is centered on man himself, that raises questions concerning his ultimate nature, and that tries to answer them without transcending the limits of what is human. In this sense humanistic thinking is the cultivation of man, his self-cultivation and self-unfolding into full humanity.[24]

This suggests that man should understand and cultivate himself by himself, letting man be man and God be God: but does that mean ignoring the religious dimension in man, or does it mean taking this fully into account? We sometimes picture the humanist in the first way, trying to do everything for himself, aspiring as we say to be a Renaissance man, that is to say a many sided genius,[25] original and free, exulting in his creative powers as he forms and transforms his world in the image of himself, and himself in the image of his self-chosen ideals. In ruling others he is good—compassionate, faithful to his word, kind, guileless, and devout—when he can, but he knows how to be evil when he must;[26] in studying nature he looks for knowledge that gives him power over it;[27] in his painting and sculpture, his architecture and music he displays himself no longer simply as a child of heaven but magnificently in the full flower of manhood.[28] He loves personal glory, freedom and mastery, and thanks to the compass, gunpowder, and the printing press he has whatever he wants and does whatever he can, with nothing to stop him: he has plenty and can get more without limit, he can stretch his powers without limit, he can perfect himself in any way he likes without limit.

The humanists and philosophers of the Renaissance we have considered here would mostly react to this picture with horror. This is not a man but a Titan, a meddler, and a vandal; his arts and sciences and his very humanity are diabolical, as divine things generally are without love.[29] When the fourteenth and fifteenth century humanists and philosophers said that man is placed in the center of the world and can become what he himself chooses, they did not mean that everything is permitted to him; they said that he is the middle, not as the *measure* of all things but as the *mediator* of the divine vision and love; just as when the Christian humanists cited the patristic saying that God became man in order that man might become God, they meant in the self-sacrifice of love and justice and not in the self-assertion of ambition and pride. They thought that God is fully divine only in man, that is to say in the full humanity of Christ in whom man is fully human, in the sense that Christ is our model of limitless love, not power; and that the closer a man approaches God in anything but compassion and justice, the less he is even a man.[30]

With all this in mind, I feel like saying: If we should be Renaissance men, it is in the sense of being equal to everything, inviting and welcoming everyone into the life of "the spirit of truth in love"[31] that builds a common world for us all to live in together, in common pursuit of that goodness that makes us and our lives good and humane and in this way truly human. Many would argue that the Renaissance is over in that we have forgotten this connection between the two meanings of humanity, as it were biological and ethical and/or religious. But the Renaissance is not over yet for us if we recover that understanding and, acting on it, take part in the rebirth of humanity in this normative sense of humane values and culture.

Perhaps I have said too much.

But perhaps again I should not close without once more citing Nietzsche who also loved classical antiquity though perhaps not Greek philosophy nor in the end[32] even Greek literature as compared to Latin and French.

> *The journey to Hades.*—I, too, have been in the underworld, like Odysseus, and shall be there often yet; and not only rams have I sacrificed to be able to speak with a few of the dead, but I have not spared my own blood. Four pairs it was did not deny themselves to my sacrifice: Epicurus and Montaigne, Goethe and Spinoza, Plato and Rousseau, Pascal and Schopenhauer. With these I must come to terms when I have wandered long alone; they may call me right or wrong; to them will I listen when in the process they call each other right or wrong. Whatsoever I say, resolve, or think up for myself and others—on these eight I fix my eyes and see their eyes fixed on me.
>
> May the living forgive that occasionally *they* appear to me as shadows, so pale and somber, so restless and, alas, so lusting for life—while those men there seem so alive to me as if now, *after* death, they could never again grow weary of life. But *eternal aliveness* is what counts: what matters "eternal life" or any life!

These words are from the early *Mixed Opinions and Maxims* (1879, #408) translated by Walter Kaufmann who notes that Nietzsche later wrote that his ancestors were Heraclitus, Empedocles, Spinoza, and Goethe, that is, leaving out Epicurus and Montaigne, Pascal and Rousseau, and even Schopenhauer and Plato. His remark here at any rate is highly reminiscent of Machiavelli in the passage I cited earlier, and also of Pomponazzi and Shestov. Nietzsche too studied the ancients in order to learn how to live and become fully human, but was it to learn humane values? I think that he would say that he did, though not in a sentimental sense.[33] Consider the opening lines of another early writing of his:

> When one speaks of humanity, the idea is fundamental that this is some-thing which separates and distinguishes man from nature. In reality, however, there is no such separation: "natural" qualities and those called truly "hu-man" are inseparably grown together. Man, in his highest and noblest capacities, is wholly nature and embodies its uncanny dual character. Those of his abilities which are terrifying and considered inhuman may even be the fertile soil out of which alone all humanity can grow in impulse, deed, and work.
>
> Thus the Greeks, the most humane men of ancient times, have a trait of cruelty, a tigerish lust to annihilate—a trait that is also very distinct in that grotesquely enlarged mirror image of the Hellenes, in Alexander the Great, but that really must strike fear into our hearts throughout their whole history and mythology, if we approach them with the flabby concept of modern "humanity." . . . the Greeks considered it an earnest necessity to let their hatred flow forth fully; in such moments crowded and swollen feeling relieved itself: the tiger leaped out, voluptuous cruelty in his terrible eyes. . . .[34]

Nietzsche can be seen as a Renaissance thinker, and even as a humanist, in wanting to go back to the sources, to look afresh at nature itself, in order to learn all that is in man, worst and best, in order to use *all* in the service of what is best, of human excellence. Let us remember that his ideal types are self-overcomers, self-masterers—the artist, the philosopher, and the saint— and that his heroes include (especially) Goethe, Machiavelli, and Thucydides.[35]

I conclude then that humanism need not be religious, or irreligious, or moral, or immoral. Humanism can be an excellence or a fault: one can be too much of a humanist, or not humanist enough. The case of Nietzsche reminds us that humanism can be a healthy protest against dogmatism, sophistry, hypocricy, falsehood, inhumanity. One can love human beings and see nothing human as alien, and still be a critic of humanism and humane values, as of religious, or moral ones, in the way that Socrates is himself a critic of philosophy, and Jesus a critic of religion.[36]

Notes

1. Apparently the first to do so was Giorgio Vasari in the preface to his *Lives of the Most Excellent Italian Architects, Painters and Sculptors from Cimabue to Our Own Times* (1550), remarking that by emphasizing that "the ages resemble na-ture as shown in our human bodies; and have their birth, growth, age and death," he hopes that today's artists will recognize "the progress of the renaissance [*rinascita*] of the arts and the perfection to which they have attained in our own time."

2. Petrarch, *Letter to Tommaso Caloria* 12.iii.1335.

3. Cf. Cicero, *Archia* 2.3, *Murena* 61, *Republic* 17.28: "only those are men who are perfected in the arts proper to humanity"; Aulus Gellius, *Attic Nights* 13.7: humanity is what the Greeks called *paideia* and we education and training in the liberal arts, for "those who seriously desire and pursue these are most highly humanized."

The word "humanism" itself was first used by the German J. T. Niethammer in 1808 in a debate about the importance of studying the classics, and it was applied to the Renaissance by George Voigt in 1859 in a book called *The Revival of Classical Antiquity or The First Century of Humanism.*

4. See P. O. Kristeller, *The Cambridge History of Renaissance Philosophy* (Cambridge, 1988), 113. I am indebted to Kristeller for many details.

5. Rhetoric has always been a more popular study than philosophy, and it has been noted that most of the literary men of the generation after Plato studied not at his exclusive and esoteric Academy but at the school of Isocrates from which Cicero says they emerged like the army of heroes out of the Trojan horse: see *Oratory* 2.94. Rhetoricians tend to be moralists and call themselves philosophers, while philosophers have their own philosophical rhetoric: thus Isocrates in *Against the Sophists* and *Antidosis;* Socrates in *Phaedrus* 269c–79; *Euthydemus* 304b–7; *Gorgias* 504de, 507c–8c, 527c; *Republic* 3.398–403c, 412a, 9.591cd, 10.598e, 607e; and Aristotle, *Rhetoric.* We should also recall here Hume's proposal to reconcile the two, with an "easy" philosophy presenting "abstruse" truth, in the first *Enquiry,* section I.

6. *Essays,* "To the Reader," 1.26.10; 3.2.1–8; 3.8.1, 10, 65; 3.13, 24, 27.

7. *Humanism and Poetry in the Early Tudor Period* (1959), 111, 199f.

8. *Letter to Francesco de'Roberti,* 26.iv.1336; Petrarch is quoting *Confessions* 10.8, and Seneca, *Letters* 8.5; cf. Socrates in *Gorgias* 482bc; *Phaedrus* 228c–9a; Plotinus 5.1.1.; Boethius CP 2.5.

9. Cf. Descartes, *Principles* 1.39–41.

10. This is the famous theory of Platonic love: love lifts each to the divinely beautiful good so that he gives birth to his own beautiful excellence which is what he truly is and in which he lives deathlessly (*Symposium* 199c–212b); each loves those here with whom he followed the same god or divine excellence there (*Phaedrus* 244–57b). Michaelangelo is echoing this in part when he writes that love turns our weak eyes to beauty which leads the soul alive to whatever heaven there may be.

11. *Works* 635.

12. Cf. Wittgenstein's remark to Drury, "All religions are wonderful," in *Recollections of Wittgenstein,* ed. R. Rhees (Oxford, 1986), 117: I owe this quotation to Roy Finch and set beside it another from Simone Weil: "We should conceive the identity of the various traditions, not by reconciling them through what they have in common, but by grasping the essence of what is specific in each. For this essence is one and the same." *Notebooks* (1965), 2.502.

13. *Letters* 5.805.

14. *Works* 1.659.

15. *Paideia* (1939), 1.417 n.6.

16. *Fate* 3.7.

17. *Athens and Jerusalem,* trans. B. Martin (Athens, Ohio, 1968), 4.44.

18. *Confessions* 2.23, 11.1; cf. Kierkegaard, *Purity* 2.

19. *Immortality* 13.

20. Cf. Cicero, *Divination* 2.80: "It is your judgment, then, that those empty of human knowledge (*humanitatis*) are the authors of divine science (*Divinitatis*)!"

21. Thus Hoelderlin in *Hyperion* (1797/1799), trans. Willard Trask, 79–97, a passage climaxing in the following lines:

> Like an immense shipwreck, when the gales have been hushed and the sailors have fled and the corpse of the shattered fleet lies on the sandbank unrecognizable, so before us lay Athens, and the forsaken pillars stood before us like the bare tree trunks of a wood that at evening was still green and, the same night, went up in flames.

Here, said Diotima, one learns to accept one's own fate in silence, be it good or bad.

Here, I continued, one learns to accept all things in silence. Had the reapers who mowed this grainfield enriched their barns with its stalks, nothing would have been lost, and I should be content to stand here as a gleaner—but who was the gainer? . . . they have dragged away the columns and statues and sold them to one another . . . for their rarity . . . (But the spirit of all that beauty) had perished even before the destroyers descended on Attica. Not until houses and temples have been deserted do the wild beasts dare to venture into gateways and streets.

For him who possesses that spirit, said Diotima, Athens still stands like a blossoming fruit tree. The artist can easily restore the torso for himself.

22. See again Augustine, *Confessions* 1.13: "I memorized the wanderings of Aeneas but failed to remember my own, I learned to weep for Dido who killed herself for love while I was dying parted from You, my God and my Life, and did not weep for myself." See further Nietzsche, *The Use and Abuse of History*, trans. P. Preuss (1980), 7: "We require history for life and action, not for the smug avoiding of life and action, or even to whitewash a selfish life and cowardly, bad acts. Only so far as history serves life will we serve it; but there is a degree of doing history and an estimation of it which brings with it a withering and degenerating of life."

23. Boswell, *The Life of Samuel Johnson LLD*, 30 July 1763 (Everyman ed.), 1.283.

24. Laszlo Verényi, *Socratic Humanism* (New Haven, 1963), 1.

25. Cf. Socrates' criticism of the many-sided sophist or "complete man" in *Greater Hippias* 281b; *Lesser Hippias* 363e-4a, 366c-8; *Republic* 10.598cd; *Sophist* 232-5a; *Statesman* 291c; but let us notice that the wise statesman the philosopher aspires to be will have as such to *be* many-sided: *Euthydemus* 278e-82d, 288d-93a; *Charmides* 171d-2a, 173-4d; *Republic* 6.503c-6b; *Statesman* 304b-5d. He must know the right use and good of the many arts and sciences.

26. As Machiavelli says in *Prince* 18.

27. So Bacon in *The Great Instauration*.

28. So that as Frithjof Schuon remarks, "When standing in front of a Romanesque or Gothic cathedral, we feel that we are at the center of the world; when standing in front of a Renaissance, Baroque or Rococo church we are merely conscious of being in Europe": *The Transcendent Unity of Religions* (Wheaton, Ill., 1953), 84n.

29. As Simone Weil says in *Intimations of Christianity among the Ancient Greeks*, 171.

30. Thus Simone Weil in *Notebooks* 2:

Mysticism is the only source of the humane virtues. (438)

Must not every renaisssance be explained by some outside influence, if it is true that the more perfect cannot proceed from the less perfect?

Whence will *our* renaissance come to us, who have emptied and defiled the entire globe?

From the past alone, if we love it.

The Languedoç. There is nothing to compare with a native civilization (*patrie*) that is dead and cannot possibly be revived (there is no Great Beast to cope with). (445f; cf. *Republic* 6.492f.)

All our spiritual ills come from the Renaissance, which betrayed Christianity for the sake of Greece, but, having sought in Greece for something of a different nature from Christianity, failed to understand what was truly Greek. The fault lies with Christianity which believed itself to be different from Greece.

We shall only remedy this evil by recognizing in Greek thought the whole of the Christian faith.

We must do away with the very notion of humanism, and at the same time what is opposed to humanism, by recognizing the fact that [true] humanism is the Christian faith. (465f.)

The errors of our times are the result of Christianity minus the supernatural element. This is due to "laicisme" (secularization) and in the first place, to humanism. (502; cf. 227, 302f, 615f.)
31. Weil, *The Need for Roots* (New York, n.d.), 253.
32. See *Twilight,* "What I Owe to the Ancients," #2.
33. Cf. Shelley's wonder at the *scale* of classical architecture:

We have been to see Pompeii . . . I was astonished at the remains of this city; I had no conception of anything so perfect yet remaining . . . [the] public buildings are everywhere marked by the bold & grand designs of an unsparing magnificence. . . . The day was radiant & warm. Every now & then we heard the subterranean thunder of Vesuvius; its distant deep peals seemed to shake the very air & light of day which interpenetrated our frames with the sullen & tremendous sound. This scene was what the Greeks beheld. (Pompeii you know was a Greek city.) They lived in harmony with nature, & the interstices of their incomparable columns, were portals as it were to admit the spirit of beauty which animates this glorious universe to visit those whom it inspired. If such is Pompeii, what was Athens? What scene was exhibited from its Acropolis? The Parthenon and the temples of Hercules & Theseus & the Winds? The islands of the Aegean Sea, the mountains of Argolis & the peaks of Pindus & Olympus, & the darkness of the Beotian forests interspersed? . . . On each side of the road beyond the [eastern] gate are built the tombs. How unlike ours! They seemed not so much hiding places for that which must decay as voluptuous chamber[s] for immortal spirits. They are of marble radiantly white, & two especially beautiful are loaded with exquisite bas reliefs. . . . These tombs were the most impressive things of all. The wild woods surround them on either side and along the broad stones of the paved road which divides them, you hear the late leaves of autumn shiver & rustle in the stream of the inconstant wind as it were like the step of ghosts. The radiance & magnificence of these dwellings of the dead, the white freshness of the scarcely finished marble, the impassioned or imaginative life of the figures which adorn them contrast strangely with the simplicity of the houses of those who were living when Vesuvius overwhelmed their city. . . . I now understand why the Greeks were such great Poets, & above all I can account, it seems to me, for the harmony the unity the perfection the uniform excellence of all their works of art. They lived in a perpetual commerce with external nature and nourished themselves upon the spirit of its forms. Their theatres were all open to the mountains & the sky. Their columns that ideal type of a sacred forest with its roof of interwoven tracery admitted the light & wind, the odour & the freshness of the country penetrated the cities. Their temples were mostly upaithric [sc. open to the air, roofless]; & the flying clouds the stars or the deep sky were seen above. O, but for that series of wretched wars which terminated in the Roman conquest of the world, but for the Christian religion which put a finishing stroke to the ancient system; but for those changes which conducted Athens to its ruin, to what an eminence might not humanity have arrived!

This is an excerpt from his letter to Thomas Love Peacock, 23–24 January 1819, no. 471 in *Letters,* ed. F. L. Jones (Oxford, 1964), 2.70–6. The passage is enthusiastic but not, I think, sentimental.
34. *Homer's Contest* (1872), trans. W. Kaufmann.

35. *Schopenhauer as Educator* 5 and again *Twilight* 10.2.

36. See *Matthew* 23; and Plato, *Euthydemus,* especially 275ab, 282d-3b, 295e, 301c, 304e, and 303b-7; also *Apology* 19a, 25c-6a, 30b, 38a; and *Phaedo* 60c-1b.

6

William Blake and the Romantic Perception of Humanism

Cecil Abrahams

William Blake's lifespan corresponds with some of the most violent and cataclysmic events of European history. During this period his own country was involved in war with France, the American War of Independence, and the Napoleonic Wars. Moreover, industry moved to the factory, farming enlarged its scale, and iron and coal became the backbone of British industry. The population doubled from seven to fourteen million people. Living in the heart of the revolutionary world of the skilled London craftsmen where, as E. P. Thompson says, "Dissent was being preached by Dealers in Old Clothes, Binders, Sheep-Head Sellers, Church-painters, Manglemakers, Footman, Toothdrawers, Perukemakers, Phlebotonists, Breeches-makers, and Coal-weavers",[1] Blake found it easy to believe that events occurring in the latter decades of the eighteenth century fitted in well with his belief that the Orc cycles with their self-generated tyranny had come to the final stages of history.

The Orc cycles, so aptly named by Northrop Frye,[2] are the ever-narrowing circles of history which contain the solids and the voids, the Satanic mills which degenerate to the ultimate "white dot" of Satanic abstraction and vindictiveness. The circles narrow to the static center from which they generate themselves. History is, rightly seen, one whole.

Blake believed that history began with the fall of Albion, who is both the unified man and England. As unified man, Albion contains the four Zoas: Tharmas, man's instinct; Urizen, man's reason; Luvah, man's passions; and Urthona, the imagination of man. In unity, these Zoas or four living creatures work together to ensure Albion a dynamic vision. But when Albion falls, he scatters into forms indicative of a complicated spiritual confusion, and the Zoas become a parody of their eternal relationships and Albion becomes their prey. For Blake, history is the story of Albion which stretches from Africa to the dark abyss of eighteenth-century Europe. Blake sees the religious, political, mystical, social, economic, and psychological movements of all time and in all cultures as one identity.

If history were determined through the Orc cycles alone, then mankind would be bound like Ixion to the wheel of time. Orc's birth is dependent on the forms of repression which exist within man or society. Man in the state of Orc recognizes that the first stage of revolt is the destruction of the forces which suppress him, and thus, in the early stage of the Orc revolt and triumph, new hope abounds and there is a flowering of imaginative culture. But man in the Orc state is overcome by Urizen's hypocrisy (hidden self-contradiction), and he is divided into meek worm and raging man.³ The raging man, isolated and mystified, further contradicts himself and becomes a self-destructive serpent.⁴

Blake describes seven Orc cycles, each one gradually declining and making a less imaginative beginning until the "white dot" of Satanic opacity is reached. Logically, the Orc cycle, once it becomes Satan's "white dot," will slip into complete materialization and hopelessness. But in Blake's perception of history each Orc cycle is integrally bound to an epoch of history or what he calls the "Seven Eyes of God."⁵ Each "eye" represents a major epoch of history, epochs which disintegrate and follow one another until the final apocalyptic epoch of Christ. During each epoch an Orc cycle or cycles occur. The first three cycles occur in Africa, the next two in Asia, and the last two in Europe-America. The Orc cycles narrow down to what Blake calls the Christ epoch of history. Here the pattern is ended when the imaginative forces take control of life by reawakening sleeping man. Because that regenerative "eye" lives in the bosom of every man, man must reverse Albion's action which caused the Fall. History, therefore, is the sleeping giant, the One Man, and the human imagination is Eternity, to which time is a mere reflection though fallen man thinks it is the reality of history.

While other romantic observers looked upon the events of the late eighteenth century with hope and despair, Blake's deeply rooted perception of the journey of history from Beulah to Ulro, gave him a more confident perspective on the crises of his time. He firmly believed that mankind was in the final Orc revolution which was a necessary stage to generate the activity and social action that would return Albion to oneness. For him, now "the Eternal Hell revives,"⁶ the age of the prophet has come to pass, and the poetic, imaginative figure can counteract the static tyranny of the time. This is the "great moment in time" when the imaginative eye can see "a world in a grain of sand," when chronological time and space, which is history, disappears from visionary perception.

The crises in Europe and America were not only inevitable but necessary for history to be destroyed. Furthermore, all of the actual events which occurred were seen as integrally bound to one another: they were all part of the process of history, the error which would finally be revealed in Europe where the Sabbath of history began and would end.

The Europe of the late eighteenth century was an immensely dissatisfied place where the traditional authority of the monarchy, the church, and the scientific community was seen as tyrannous and needed to be challenged and overthrown. It seemed as if the "old mountains of France" (in Blake's words) and England were indeed fading away. Dr. Richard Price's view that "The times are auspicious" was held in common by a large number of people in France and England. Voltaire and Rousseau attacked the established control of the Church and State and called upon downtrodden Frenchmen to unite against the "beasts of prey." In England, the English insisted on their right to free speech and when George III tried to gag the newspaper editorials of John Wilkes, the citizens saw this action as the king's wish to prevent free speech and a general outcry ensued for civic and Parliamentary reform, freedom of the press, freedom from the press gangs, a larger loaf, and solidarity with the "Liberty Boys" of Boston and Philadelphia. For nearly a decade, the London tradesmen and artisans demonstrated for Wilkes at the hustings and dragged him in triumph through the streets whenever he was victorious. Often the demonstrations turned into riots.

Blake shared this feeling of radicalism and in almost every poem he wrote he warned those who oppress people that their oppression would result in revolution. Whereas Blake shared the general romantic perception and response to what they perceived to be the tyrannical regimes of England and France, he extended the romantic perception by his deeper belief in the Orc-cycle theory of history and by his inevitable faith that mankind will be restored to its original condition. For Blake, the Garden was already planted and sown inside man's soul before the Fall occurred. Hence, every action away from the unfallen garden is but a perversity. For romantic poets such as William Wordsworth and Percy Bysshe Shelley, the cleansing of the Garden through the destruction of those who defiled it was the main aim. Because once the garden was cleaned up it would flourish without hindrance.

For Blake, America was both mythical and historical. Following the mythological theories of his time, Blake believed that in the "Golden Age" before the Fall humanity dwelt in peace in Atlantis. But the Fall produced a chaotic world of floods which overwhelmed Atlantis. In this way Atlantis was separated from man by the Atlantic Ocean, and it is only when this ocean disappears that man will be rejoined with this golden civilization. And this will occur when the Americans have defeated the tyranny of George III in America and have joined their revolutionary fervor to the English and inspired them to restore Edenic love and freedom to England. Since in his own time a new English civilization was growing in America, it did not take Blake long to appreciate this significant event, and he both encouraged its continuity, and drew inspiration in imagery and thought from it.

Blake's task was to explore Urizenic tyranny for what it was, and in the European environment of enslavement, war, revolution, and liberation, the classical stalemate between Urizen and Orc seemed still the best way to define Orc's position and Blake's awareness of it. Thus the poem "America" is filled with imagery contrasting "warlike men" with "swords," "spears," and "muskets hiding in encampment and castles." The enslaving "chains," "whips," and "dungeons" are opposed by the "rending" of the chains and the release of man from the "whips" and the "dungeons." The fiery redness and flames of wrath of the honest rebel are opposed to the whiteness, hoariness and flames of hypocrisy of the oppressor. The heat is contrasted with light, and the Lion opposes the Wolf.

The difference in this battle between Orc and Urizen is that we are in the final Orc cycle of history and the battle is seen as part of the creative power of Los. Los does not only succeed to redeem Orc, rebellion, he also reclaims Urizen, tyranny. Thus Blake sees not only the destruction of the ancient regime but he reiterates the inevitability of history to run its course. The clash now is between Orc and Urizen as Albion's "wrathful Prince / A dragon form, clashing his scales" who "flame[s] red meteors round the land of Albion beneath."[7] The vision of history as four continents had led Ein-tharmon, the emanation of Los, earlier, to perceive the Fall of man in Africa as a continuous event. The vision of Washington, which perceives "a heavy iron chain" (the "mind-forg'd manacles" that enslaved the English) descending "link by link from Albion's (England's) cliffs across the sea" to reduce Americans to the same sorry state as the Europeans,[8] is part of the same narrative of fourfold history. It is the happening in Europe that determines the course of history. It is the English monarchy that causes oppression in America. It is "Satan" (England, George III) who "first the black bow bent,"[9] who causes the unjust war.

Orc's declaration to the spectrous Angel that "Empire is no more"[10] is truly one of the boldest and most triumphant announcements in all of Blake's poetry. Here, finally, after many early indications in Blake's work, victory is claimed over tyranny, over war-like, restrictive Empire-building, the dominion over man which Urizen and other tyrants search for. This victory is identified by Orc with the resurrection of Jesus, suggesting that further Orc-Urizen battles will not occur. Like Jesus, Orc is a revived God who is also Man (that is, Orc as "an eternal form of the imagination"), and Orc's renewal is as radical as that of the Jesus of orthodoxy. Hence Orc breaks not only the grave as Jesus did in his resurrection, but, more importantly, he destroys the limitations of the fallen body and can indeed call upon man to "rise and look out." Now "the fiery joy," which is the sexual gate that will consume the other four gates of the "law-built heaven,"[11] is set free to "burst the stony roof," the teaching by Urizen that sexual love is "Sin." Therefore, Orc announces with triumph, "For everything that lives is holy, life delights in life; / Because the soul of sweet delight can never be defil'd."[12] In this manner Orc assumes that he has laid to rest the most pernicious cause of fallen man's enslavement.

The Orc described by Blake here, although a figure of "Wonder," is not as yet Los, the true imaginative power who has not only Orc's revolutionary spirit, the fire (because all imaginative activity is a challenge to the establishment), but who has the prophetic ability (the light) to lead man out of the doomed cycle. "Orc is not," as Rose points out, "imagination but raw energy and not love but sexual power, he is Luvah in the night of this world. . . ."[13] Orc, bereft of imaginative light, can only meet Urizen on his own ground, namely that of violence, power, and force with the strongest side claiming victory. Blake describes Urizen, as well, in fiery, war-like imagery. Urizen "burns in his nightly tent"; he gives off "Sullen fires"; and he "glows with blood."[14] The irony that Blake points out here, though its true meaning is missed by the conventional mind, is that Orc unredeemed by Los is an "Antichrist" figure,[15] because his rebellion is not organized to lead to imaginative social and political positions. The battle is, as so often in the battles of the Zoas, a fight for "power and dominion," which is not only one of the causes of the Fall, but which does not permit freedom and brotherhood for all mankind. Like Orc or Urizen, man can perceive his regeneration only in terms of war-like and reactionary battles such as the ones Urizen and Orc have waged in every Orc cycle of history.

Having reached the moment of crisis when Orc is finally able, on a visible and physical level, to blow "the trump of doom" and claim success over Urizen, the rest of the poem "America" deals with the spreading of this victory to Europe where the Last Judgment is to occur. This is why the "foreheads" of "Washington/And Paine and Warren" are "rear'd toward the east,"[16] an indication that the battle has been won in the West (America) and is now to be taken to Albion's own shore in the East. The Angel and England's defeat is signified by the weeping of the Angel and the refusal by the American colonies to respond to England's call for war: "No trumpets answer; no reply of clarions or of fifes:/Silent the Colonies remain and refuse the loud alarm."[17] This is the pivotal point of "America." The "vast shady hills between America & Albion's shore" are removed and this leads to the hope of regeneration for all mankind which is expressed in the last plate of the poem. The removal of the "vast shady hills between America and Albion's shore" effectively reunites the shattered halves that occurred in the flood of the Lost Atlantis myth. Now the "thirteen Angels" or American colonies, having heard Orc's message of inspiration and revolution, become "fiery" and burn "indignant" "with the fires of Orc" and throw down the scepters of tyranny and natural religion as Orc did earlier. "Boston's Angel" recognizes that the deceptive "God" who "writes laws of peace & clothes him in a tempest," and the "pitying Angel" that "lusts for tears and fans himself with sighs," and the "crawling villain" who "preaches abstinence" but "Wraps himself/In fat of lambs"[18] are the false villains who have driven men like himself into the wilderness. Therefore he decides defiantly to break this cycle of imprisonment by refusing to follow anymore: "no more I follow, no more obedience pay." His defiance is followed by the casting off of "robes," and his speech is not only similar in tone and defiance to Orc's, but he unites the American colonies in action with the tearing off of the robe or flesh in the act of resurrection of Jesus Christ that Orc imitates and identifies with in an earlier passage.

In the poem "America," it is the ironic sending of the "diseases of the earth"[19] by Albions' Angel which leads to the final destruction of the forces of tyranny. The "diseases of the earth" are similar to the plagues that Jehovah sent against Egypt. Unlike the ten plagues which had been sent to destroy the declining and repressive African civilization, the plagues are sent unjustly and ironically strengthen the American people and defeat the oppressive forces. This victory of the Americans is felt in England where "the

Bard of Albion," the hypocritical villain who sings restriction's praise, refusing to accept Albion's defeat hides "in his cave . . . / And a cowl of flesh grew o'er his head, & scales on his back & ribs."[20] Refusing to accept the true meaning of Orc's victory, the followers of Albion, their spirits fraught with "Leprosy," turn into "the sneaking serpent." The "sneaking serpent" walks "In mild humility" waiting for the opportune moment when the wrathful of the world are unable to sustain the conditions of their victory. This is, of course, what has happened in every previous Orc cycle. It is Urizen who is the serpent at the bottom of the tree. Urizen is truly an "Antichrist" demon; through his deceptive action he draws Orc down with him to the bottom and turns a fiery Orc without Los's light into a serpent form. Urizen unredeemed is unimaginative. Therefore, though defeated, Urizen repeats the action of seeming humility which had been so successful in the first six Orc cycles. Thus his false "tears in deluge piteous" and his "Weeping in dismal howlings before the stern Americans"[21] are meant to create pity for himself and to deceive the Americans to the extent that he would not be truly identified as their tormentor. But the American revolution occurs in the Jesus epoch of history, and although Urizen is able to hide Orc's meaning from the rest of Europe until the French Revolution and thus continue to govern the wrathful of the world, he cannot annihilate the essential meaning of the American triumph. The promise is clear: the final end of Urizen and his followers will come "when France [has] receiv'd the Demon's light."[22]

NOTES

1. E. P. Thompson, *The Making of the English Working Class* (London, 1963).
2. Northrop Frye, *The Fearful Symmetry* (Boston, 1947).
3. William Blake, "The Four Zoas," 7:323
4. Ibid., 7:323–324.
5. Ibid., 28:351.
6. William Blake, "The Marriage of Heaven and Hell," 3:149.
7. William Blake, "America," 3:197.
8. Ibid., 3:197.
9. William Blake, *Notebook,* 420.
10. William Blake, "America," 6:198.
11. Ibid., 16:203.
12. Ibid., 8:199.
13. Edward J. Rose, "Goodbye to Orc and All That," *Blake Studies* 4 (Spring 1972): 135–151.
14. William Blake, "America," 3:197.
15. Ibid., 7:198.
16. Ibid., 9:199.
17. Ibid., 10:200.
18. Ibid., 11:200.
19. Ibid., 13:201.
20. Ibid., 15:202.
21. Ibid., 16:203.
22. Ibid., 16:203.

7

Existentialism, Humanism, and Positivism

Calvin Hayes

INTRODUCTION

While neither existentialism nor positivism can be said to be as influential as in their heydays, they still exert at least a residual influence on contemporary philosophy. The purpose of this essay is to reexamine a traditional philosophical problem which not only has not been solved satisfactorily by either of the above theories but, according to many, has not yet been solved by *any* contemporary theory. The problem will be approached through one of Jean-Paul Sartre's well-known essays, "Existentialism is a Humanism." The solution will be found via a detour into a very different essay. It is a problem flowing logically from one of the central contentions of contemporary humanism—that man creates his own values.

It is *not* the purpose of this essay to make a contribution to Sartre scholarship. It is, rather, to attempt to contribute to ongoing problems in meta-ethical theory. I will begin then by defining the problem, sketching the key elements in Sartre's essay relevant to his 'solution,' wander off on an apparent detour, and then return to Sartre's essay.

THE PROBLEM DEFINED

In the final section of *Being and Nothingness* Sartre[1] says:

> Ontology itself cannot formulate ethical precepts. It is concerned solely with what is, and we cannot possibly derive imperatives from ontology's indicatives.

This is a very cryptic comment on the ontological, epistemological, and logical problems of meta-ethics. They can be described under several guises: the problem of moral truth, the problem of moral knowledge or moral skepticism, and the closely related problem of relativism. These will be defined more sharply after we present a cursory summary of the key elements in Sartre's essay that have a crucial bearing on them.

The key ideas relevant to the problem are: (1) Sartre's much cited dictum that "existence precedes essence," (2) his discussion of Kant's two categorical imperatives—the universalizability principle and the means-end principle, (3) the dilemma faced by Sartre's friend in World War II, and (4) his thesis that we freely invent our values—we do not *discover* them or receive them as either divinely revealed or natural objects.

The problem of moral truth can be posed starkly: can our moral judgments *be* either true or false? If they can be, can we *know* whether they are? The positivist answer to this was strictly parallel to its answer to the similar question in regard to metaphysics. The challenge of moral skepticism rests on *three* pillars all of which appear to be endorsed by Sartre—they are *logical, epistemological,* and *ontological.*

The *logical* point rests on a claim usually traced back to David Hume, i.e., we cannot deduce an "ought" from an "is." This seems to be acknowledged by Sartre in his contention that we cannot possibly derive imperatives from ontology's indicatives. This is just the point behind R.M. Hare's well-known views on moral rules, viz., that they consist of universalizable prescriptions that can neither be deduced from nor be incompatible with any factual assertions. This may be one of the few areas in which existentialism and analytic philosophy agree.

It is a point equally well-entrenched among social scientists: it is the logical basis of Max Weber's fact-value distinction and similar distinctions made by Lionel Robbins, Arnold Brecht[2], and numerous other social scientific theories and, it would seem, the majority of philosophers as well.

The *epistemological* pillar of moral scepticism is one on which surprisingly existentialism and positivism also seem to agree. I say "surprisingly" because, when it comes to theory of knowledge, they appear to be poles apart. Positivism, after all, is the most epistemically puritanical or stringent of theories of knowledge. Existentialism seems to be a much more permissive theory of knowledge—both its critics and its defenders would seem to agree that it is much less rigorous or stringent in its logical and epistemic standards for truth, knowledge, and ontology.

Yet Sartre appears to accept the sceptical tone of standard positivist critiques of ethical theory. To appreciate the problem let us state an extreme principle—that endorsed by pure positivism—to see just why ethics, from this perspective, is in difficulty. The well-known positivist criterion of meaning allowed only two types of cognitively meaningful assertions: analytically true statements and empirically verifiable sentences.

While this turned out to be too stringent, it is not too difficult to see why ethical prescriptions are suspect even when we water down the requirements. Traditional ethical theories did not overly worry about this challenge (nor, for that matter, do modern ones)[3] since they simply posit some type of source of moral knowledge such as intuition, oral sense, conscience, or divine revelation.

It is a crucial premise in the case for moral scepticism that we have no such reliable sources of moral knowledge. Sartre, while he never explicitly states this, appears to agree in at least one case—that of a putative divine revelation. He is very sceptical of any claim to base knowledge of right and wrong on a divine book or revelation or scripture.[4]

The third pillar is *ontological*—the denial that values, especially moral values, have any objective ontological status; this also conflicts with most traditional moral theories. Here is where the connection between Existentialism and humanism (in its secular garb) is most apparent. Moral values are not rooted in God or nature or the universe or a platonic realm of being but are created by humans for human purposes.

This entails a rejection of any and all objective accounts of ethics, whether traditional theism (duty, i.e., God's will) or Platonism, natural law theory, or even Aristotelianism which Alasdair MacIntyre has attempted to revive partly it seems to overcome the problems being discusssed here.

We now can see the problem more clearly and also see in its starkness the ultimate problem it seems to entail. Given the above three premises it would seem to follow that there is not and cannot be such a thing as moral truth, if we accept something like a correspondence theory of truth, for there is nothing to which our moral judgments can *refer*. There are no objective values nor objective moral properties.

Sartre then faces what seems to be the stark outcome of this—what I term the DNA conclusion (for Dostoevsky-Nietzsche argument)—that "if god does not exist then anything is permitted". Whereas the conclusion clearly bothered Dostoevsky, it equally clearly was welcome to Nietzsche. Sartre, interestingly, is neither delighted nor worried but embarrassed.[5]

Notice also how Sartre's initial premise becomes relevant too, i.e., that there is no human nature. He cannot adopt (as MacIntyre would have us do)[6] an aristotelian account of human nature and a teleological theory of virtue based on it.

At this point we should look at the connection between scepticism and relativism. It would be useful to distinguish between two types of relativism, since the two are often confused. One is the "anything goes" type of relativism, the other is better described as situation ethics and, despite the hoopla about it in the 1960s, is actually a trivial consequence of most traditional theories.

The more interesting challenge is by far from the former type. It seems to follow ineluctably from the three key premises we have enunciated. Note that it constitutes a serious problem not only for traditional ethical theories but for modern ones also—utilitarianism, kantianism, and for vaguer, less coherent theories such as humanism—again whether secular or religious doesn't matter.

HOW TO DERIVE AN IS FROM AN OUGHT

The main theses of this paper are (1) Sartre fails to solve the problem as defined; however (2) no one else has either because (3) they have attempted to solve it in the wrong way. What I mean by (3) is that, while philosophers have either tried to deduce an "ought" from "is" (or given up on that possibility and tried something else), they have not tried doing the reverse, i.e., deducing an "is" from an "ought" and seeing whether moral judgments could be *refuted* even if they *can't* be *verified* or proved.

I do not have the temerity to suggest that all previous philosophers have been equally mistaken and now at last here is the one and only correct answer. On the contrary my own solution builds on the work of several philosophers. In particular, in insisting on a purely deductivist solution to the problem I agree largely with Aristotle, Kant, and Gewirth in their ethical theories and with Karl Popper in his anti-inductivist theory of scientific method.

However, Sartre is not completely wrong either. He is correct about (1) the crucial nature of the universalizability principle (which he however misuses), and (2) his contention that we freely invent our values, provided this is not understood in an intentionalist or constructivist fashion (to borrow Hayek's[8] term). In addition, Sartre does not sufficiently distinguish values and ethics, a common failure among social scientists also. Finally (3) he is correct about the logical point: we cannot derive imperatives from ontology's indicatives.

Now it is important to note that both (2) and (3) are together essential to make this a problem. It could be said that we freely invent our mathematical and scientific theories; in fact it *has* been said and is indeed a truism. The difference, of course, is supposed to be that we have *logical* and *experiential* reasons to accept or reject them unlike the case with ethics. We have, it is said, good reasons to believe $7 + 5 = 12$ or that elephants have trunks whereas we do not have logical and/or empirical reason to believe or reject claims such as "adultery is immoral", "cruelty is wrong" or "apartheid is unjust".

Without the *logical* gap we could justify our ethical theories indirectly by proving some is-statement and then deducing a moral prescription. Further the logical gap would not matter if we have independent good reasons for our moral judgments.

Now it won't do, as James Rachels says,[9] that moral truth lies with the proposition for which the best reasons can be given. This is insufficient since it avoids the problem of the *referent* of moral truth and also won't do since the concept of good *reasons* needs to be explained better also. Here we come to the heart of the matter: most accounts of rationality in modern philosophy (whether epistemic or ethical) are justificationist or foundational. This leads to our detour.

HUME ON IS, OUGHT, AND INDUCTION

While in his recent work on ethical theory MacIntyre has been highly critical of Hume's moral theories, in his earlier works he was much more favorably inclined. Hume, Aristotle, and the scholastics were the good guys whereas Kant, Plato, and the protestant reformers were the bad guys.[10]

This is because the former rooted their ethics in concrete human nature rather than abstractions imposed from without. What is significant for us is not MacIntyre's change of opinion but his comments on Hume's is-and-ought passage that provoked a lively debate. It is not, however, the *exegetical* debate with which we are concerned but a *logical* point MacIntyre makes in explaining his interpretation.

This has to do with the parallel between two perplexing philosophical problems: induction and the is-ought problems. Interestingly, they are both usually traced to Hume although both could equally well be credited to Leibniz[11] who, in 1702, wrote a letter to Queen Charlotte in which, *at the very least,* he adumbrated both problems. However, we are concerned mainly with MacIntyre's point about the alleged logical gulf between is and ought.

He refers to a critique made of theistic ethics by Nowell-Smith who, commenting on a certain argument by a bishop, said that theistic ethics doesn't just rest on theological premises *alone* but on a *moral* premise such as "we ought to obey God." MacIntyre's comment[12] on this is worth quoting in full:

> I can only make sense of this position by supposing that underlying it there is an assumption that arguments must be either deductive or defective. But this is the very assumption which underlies Hume's scepticism about induction.

The basic principle I am concerned with here is that (A) arguments are either deductive or defective. MacIntyre rejects this and endorses Strawson's "solution" to the problem of induction. At this point MacIntyre made the wrong move. It is *not* necessary to accept a nondeductivist solution to the problem of induction when there exists a reasonable deductivist alternative.

In order to avoid getting too sidetracked it will be admitted that a much longer argument is needed to defend this claim, so I will leave it in the form of a challenge. The deductivist solution I have in mind is Popper's. It rests on his *asymmetry* principle, a logical truism. Since I am primarily concerned with meta-ethics a long discussion of induction is neither necessary nor desirable, all I really need is the asymmetry argument applied to moral reasoning.

The asymmetry principle holds that, while there can exist logical gulfs between two statements, sometimes the *logical gulf is one-way only.* Consider, e.g., the two statements "Dale is a mother" and "Dale is a female."

Clearly the former entails the latter without the latter entailing the former. Popper argues that the same exists in the case of facts on the one hand and theories or universal laws[13] on the other hand.

We cannot (as Hume pointed out) deduce a theory or universal law from a finite number of facts and so cannot *verify* or prove or *justify* our theories. We can however derive facts from our theories or laws and *refute* or criticize or *falsify* our theories as Popper argues. My main argument is that unless the same can be done in ethics then we can't rationally decide between our competing moral theories, but if we can, then rational choice in ethics is possible.

Two subsidiary points need to be made, one logical and another philosophical. It could be claimed—as MacIntyre, Stove, Strawson, Black, Salmon, and others have done—that a nondeductivist solution is both necessary and possible. However, the challenge I would leave is how to distinguish a valid inductive argument from a nonsequitur or an enthymeme or fallacy or what I prefer to term "seductive logic": a system of arguments with some true premises, and a conclusion that appears to follow but does not from the premises.

The philosophical reservation I have has to do with reason in ethics. I agree with those (especially social contract) theorists who seem to feel that *subjective* reasons in ethics[14] are just as good as *objective* reasons. We all have good subjective reasons for wanting at least a minimal moral and legal code accepted in our society. What I wish to suggest is that we can also have good objective reasons as well WITHOUT HAVING TO SOLVE the problem of the *objective referent* of our moral judgments.

Here a parallel with the problem of mathematical truth might be useful. We have good objective reasons for most of our mathematical truths, indeed the best objective reasons the human race has yet devised, but we are very unclear and uncertain about the objective referent of numbers, sets, points[15], and other mathematical "objects".

In order to make this type of negative solution work, we would need to be able to deduce consequences from our moral prescriptions that could be subjected to criticism. I would suggest *three* different types of such possible implications—*existential* implications, as well as those based on the *ought-implies-can* principle, and the *universality* principle.

Sartre does use the last named, as Hare does, and it seems to have a firm logical basis.[16] Its major problems have to do with *application,* but this is a problem common to *any* use of this principle which, as Hare points out, transcend just ethical areas. It is (as Hare again points out) the logical basis of the golden rule[17] which in turn rests in part on *subjective* reasons, i.e., what you want or better *don't* want others to do to yourself. Before examining this more closely, however, I would like to examine the other types of implications.

In regard to the first type consider the following:

(1) Close the door.
(2) Execute all witches.
(3) We ought to be pious.

Interestingly all three have implications *without having to be either true or false.* It won't do to reply that these are not implications but presuppositions.

It is just as legitimate to criticize the presuppositions of a theory as it is to criticize the non-presuppositions, and further the most trivial of all logical principles is "p implies p." If p is one of the presuppositions of a theory T, clearly then p is necessary to T and therefore T implies p.

In the above case we obviously have the presuppositions that there is a door which is open, and that there is a God or gods who can be objects of piety.[18]

The second is more interesting in some ways since it illustrates the logic of moral reasoning well. Consider the following "practical syllogism":

(I) We ought to execute all witches.
(II) Sylvia and Mary are witches.
(III) Therefore we ought to execute Sylvia and Mary.

Notice that the *logic* is flawless. What is problematic, of course, are the premises. But the problem is not so much in (I) but in (II). (I), in *modern* logic, doesn't entail that witches exist, but clearly (II) does. It does not of course follow that we ought *not* to execute Mary and Sylvia, but it does follow that we don't have reason to in this argument if (II) is false, which it is if (IV) "there are no witches" is true.

Criticism of moral arguments (as is *all* criticism) then is multi-dimensional: it involves *logical, factual, theoretical,* and *dialectical* considerations. Consider the following set of prescriptions:

(a) The state ought to enforce perfect equality.
(b) Society ought to eliminate all sources of discontent.

It seems clear that both run into insuperable difficulties with the ought-implies-can principle. (a) is clearly self-contradictory since (a-1) "Perfect equality" entails *inter alia* no inequalities of *power* (a-2); for the state to enforce *anything* it must have *more* power than the citizens. As for (b) it would seem to be impossible for a combination of psychological, sociological, historical, and philosophical reasons.[19]

The most interesting examples of all are the following:

(A) All people have *negative* rights and duties.
(B) All people have *positive* duties to all other persons.
(C) All people ought to perform whatever positive duties they have.

It would take far too much time to argue the point in detail, but it seems to me a plausible case can be made for the following: all three pass the universalizability test but (C) fails the ought-implies-can test. Therefore on rational grounds (A) and (B) are superior to (C). Since I am working on much longer detailed arguments to try to show this, I will merely leave it to the reader to assess the validity of the claim for now and also leave this qualifying note—unless some such type of argumentation is possible then the rationality of ethics is suspect.

CONCLUSION

Let me finish then on a comment about Sartre's use of the *universality* principle, the role of *subjective* reasons, and a modification of Kant's use of his own principle. In an ideal, best of all philosophically possible universes, we could use the strict versions of Kant's principle; i.e., we would will as acts all and only those principles whose maxim we can will as a universal principle where the "can" (and cannots) are *purely* logical.[20]

Now most uses of Kant's principles, such as Hare's and its use in applied ethics,[21] rely on combining this principle with *consequentialist* reasoning. I don't wish to get sidetracked onto the meta-ethical debates about teleological versus deontological systems, but I do side with the "subjectivist" who feels that we cannot avoid bringing in subjective reasons into our ethical reasoning. Again the point will not be elaborated now. In fact, I almost wish or hope I am wrong, but I don't see how a purely a priori ethic is possible in the Kantian sense.

But this is one reason why it is crucial to state the golden rule and the universality principle on which it rests (according to Hare) in *negative* rather than positive terms.

The *positive* version of the golden rule would lead to the absurd consequence of my giving everyone a cup of coffee whereas the *negative* version only entails that I refrain from inflicting various harms and/or wrongs[22] on everyone else, i.e., not killing, injuring, torturing, etc. other people and not making exceptions unless there are very good reasons to do so.

Now let us apply this to Sartre's example of the troubled student's dilemma about what to do during World War II. Should he stay with his mother or go away to help the resistance? Sartre refuses to tell him and asserts that the problem has no solution in any ethical scripture such as the Bible or Kant.[23] Perhaps he is right, but my question would be: Why does Sartre give him *only two* choices? After all he could have defected to the Nazis! Would Sartre be as indifferent *to that choice?*

This is the real problem with subjectivism, scepticism, relativism, and yes, humanism in ethics. It cannot give us any *concrete* guidance in ethical matters. This is the real problem with Nietzsche's approach and why, up to a point, Dostoevsky was correct to be worried about an "anything is permitted" implication of an ethical argument or moral theory.

But while relativism, skepticism, and radical subjectivism seem inevitable given the logical, epistemic, and ontological premises we began with, I have tried to argue that we can avoid this conclusion without rejecting those premises, *if* we adopt a *negative* rather than positive solution to the is-ought problem. Just as we can solve the problem of induction without fideism, dogmatism, or authoritarianism so we can solve the problem of the rationality of morality without similar or parallel moves in meta-ethics. And *if* we *can't,* then we don't get the "warm fuzzies" of contemporary "humanism"—we *do* get Dostoevsky's "anything is permitted."

Notes

1. J. P. Sartre, *Being and Nothingness*, 765.
2. Arnold Brecht has a very thorough discussion of the problem in his *Political*

Theory. Robbits has a brief discussion in his *Nature and Significance of Economic Science.* Weber discusses it in his essays on value neutrality.

3. Since I have been primarily teaching applied ethics the last few years, I have become familiar with several books in the areas of business ethics, social philosophy, etc. While they usually discuss egoism, subjectivism, relativism, and theism, they usually avoid the is-ought problem or solve it by the smorgasbord approach—offering students a wide selection of theories, generally utilitarianism, Kant, Rawls, rights, social contract, etc.

4. "Existentialism is a Humanism" in Walter Kaufmann, *Existentialism from Dostoevsky to Sartre* (Magnolia, Mass., 1984), 353.

5. Ibid., 353.

6. Especially in *After Virtue: A Study in Moral Theory* (South Bend, Ind., 1984), and his recent *Whose Justice? Which Rationality?* (South Bend, Ind., 1988).

7. The best example of this probably is the injunction against killing. There have been numerous exceptions made to the general rule against taking human life and the same can be said about property rights, rules against lying, the violation of right to liberty, etc.

8. The idea is basically that, while morality, language, law, and other social institutions are human products, they are not *consciously,* deliberately *constructed* creations. See Friedrich A. Hayek's *The Constitution of Liberty* (Chicago, 1978) and his three-volume *Law, Liberty and Legislation* (Chicago, 1978).

9. In his essay on "Euthanasia" in *Matters of Life and Death*, ed. Regan (New York, 1986), 48.

10. This seems to be the gist of his "Hume on 'Is' and 'Ought' " in *Hume: A Collection of Critical Essays*, ed. V. C. Chappell (South Bend, Ind., 1968), 263–64.

11. *Leibniz Selections,* 361.

12. "Hume on 'Is' and 'Ought,' " 244.

13. This is extensively argued in *The Logic of Scientific Discovery* (New York, n.d.), and *Conjectures and Refutations* (New York, 1968).

14. The distinction may not be that easy to articulate but is easy to illustrate. We have, supposedly, good objective reasons to believe the Pythagorean theorem, Napoleon died in 1821, and e = mc.^{2} We have good subjective reasons to value our own life, liberty, and health. We have both objective and subjective reasons to desire food, exercise, and money.

15. Another interesting parallel could be drawn between *instrumentalism* in the philosophy of science and *prescriptivism* in ethics. According to the former, while our scientific theories can be neither true nor false, they must be compatible with the evidence as well as logically consistent. Thus, it must be possible to derive true and false consequences from a theory without that theory itself being true or false!

16. Hare argues this in *The Language of Morals*. The main point is that logically we are forbidden to use the term "red" of 2 objects of indistinguishable color in one case, but not the other. The same is true of the term "good."

17. In his article "Abortion and the Golden Rule" in *Philosophy and Sex,* ed. R. Baker and F. Elliston (Buffalo, 1984), 231ff.

18. Once again philosophers have approached this issue *backwards.* True we cannot logically go from (I) (The) God(s) exist to (0) We ought to be pious, but it seems plain that *if* we accept (0) we are *logically* committed to accept (I) and *if* we reject (I) we are *logically* committed to rejecting (0).

19. Neither (a) nor (b) are manufactured examples although even if they were they would still illustrate the logical point being made.

20. Since writing this I have come across an interesting example of a similar

wish applied to an area that would surprise most philosophers, i.e., modern physics. Some physicists express the wish for a mathematical theory of everything (TOE) like superstring theory that would be *almost synthetic a priori!* "The ultimate TOE would, ideally, need no recourse to experiment at all!" P. C. Davis and J. Brown, *Superstrings: A Theory of Everything?* (Cambridge, 1985), 7.

21. Rachels' essay "Euthanasia" is a good example of this. Even Gewirth's cogent *reductio ad absurdum* argument has to rely on the agent's (necessary according to him) *subjective* valuation of his own freedom and well-being.

22. The best way to define the difference between teleological and deontic theories is the following: In facing moral dilemmas the former tries to minimize *harms* whereas the latter tries to minimize *wrongs*.

23. In Kaufman, *Existentialism from Dostoevsky to Sartre*, 354–55.

PART TWO

THE CHALLENGES TO HUMANISM

8

An Old Question Raised Yet Again: Is Kant an Enlightenment Humanist?

John Luik

An essay about Kant as Enlightenment humanist labors under at least two significant, if not ultimately disabling, handicaps. The first is surely the definitional handicap of how we are to understand, not to say, make any sense of, the terms Enlightenment humanism and, indeed, Kant. Consider, for the moment, the Enlightenment. Which Enlightenment are we to speak about, the Enlightenment in France, England, Germany, the Enlightenment of the literary critic, the historian, the historian of ideas, the philosopher? As much contemporary scholarship has suggested, the term, like most historical generalizations, may in fact convey nothing because it conveys everything. And if Enlightenment were in itself not sufficiently problematic, consider the even greater difficulties associated with the phrase Enlightenment humanism. Was there, for instance, such a thing as Enlightenment humanism, that is a humanism recognizably different in shape and texture from, for example, Renaissance humanism? Did Enlightenment thinkers, or some Enlightenment thinkers, really conceive of themselves as humanists? And, if they did, what did they mean by the concept humanism?

But Enlightenment and humanism are only one aspect of the definitional problem, for there is also Kant himself, on his own an immensely difficult subject for a satisfyingly synthetic intellectual picture, and coupled with Enlightenment humanism, perhaps an impossibility. Kant's intellectual career admits of numerous tellings, and the plot lines do not always neatly converge. Thus, for instance, are we to find the humanist Kant in the first *Critique,* or within the complexities of the moral law, or, again, in the occasional writings on history and politics, or, perhaps, in the works on religion? In short, is there a way, or is there a coherent way in which the complexities and ambiguities of Enlightment humanism and Kant's intellectual career can be brought together? Is there anything that can be said about each within the context of the other that is not either a commonplace or a distortion?

One way around this definitional dilemma might be to posit a provisional definition of Enlightenment humanism and then to place a sample of the various "Kants," the Kant of the first *Critique,* the Kant of the second *Critique,* the Kant of the occasional essays in history and political philosophy, the Kant of the philosophy of law, and the Kant of the philosophy of religion, for example, against this definition of humanism in an effort to determine whether there might be at least a family resemblance, if not irrefutable kinship.

How, then, might we define Enlightenment humanism? By Enlightenment humanism we mean those men of letters, philosophy, and science, living in the years 1650–1800 who believed that the central concern of human existence was not the discovery of God's will, but the shaping of human life and society according to a set of universally acknowledged rational principles. To these thinkers, human dignity was a function not of man's allegedly divine origin, but of the ordering and rational possibilities of earthly existence. The end of man was neither the immediate adoration of God nor the heavenly city of the blessed, but rather the realization of those projects, suggested by reason and imagination, appropriate to this world. Thus construed, talk of Christian or more generally, religious, humanism, at least in the context of the Enlightenment, seems a contradiction in terms. Though immensely diverse in both interests and often intellectual program, what seems to unite the Enlightenment humanists, perhaps in a manner quite different from Renaissance humanists, is their enormous, and perhaps finally unjustified, confidence in the power of human reason to order a world and in their ready sense of responsibility for the consequences of reason's ordering.

In this sense, reason, for the Enlightenment humanist, was not simply the discovery of facts, but the creator of moral principles based in part on these facts. To a significant degree it was the exuberant confidence in what might be called the compulsive power of reason that explains the religious skepticism of the Enlightenment humanist. It is not merely that revealed religion lacked rational justification, but that in lacking rational justification it must needs be founded on faith, that is prejudice alone and prejudice could not but fail to divide men into warring intellectual camps. The religious sense, precisely because it lay beyond rational adjudication, must always be productive of fundamental disharmony, indeed war, whereas reason, while certainly creating intellectual contention, had at least the potential for securing peace.

What seems to define Enlightenment humanism is thus its confidence in, indeed its celebration of human autonomy, an autonomy secure through the creative and ordering powers of reason. In whatever direction one turns in an effort to capture the intellectual and indeed the emotional core of Enlightenment humanism, whether to its commitment to progress, its compassion for humanity and social reform, its championing of literary freedom, its interest in the classical past, its belief in the centrality of science and scientific method, all of these aspects of Enlightenment humanism derive from its confidence in and commitment to reason. And it is against this notion of the centrality of reason as the crucial measure of Enlightenment humanism that we must set the various strands of Kant's thought.

But having dealt with the first problem surrounding this topic, there is yet a second which is not simply definitional, but arguably substantive, namely, why ought an admittedly old question, adequately rehearsed and aptly addressed, be raised again? Surely, it might be suggested, if there is one area of Kant studies about which we may safely speak of a scholarly consensus, it is in this area of Kant as humanist. Kant is not unfairly described as the paradigm *Aufklärer,* the embodiment of the ideals of Enlightenment humanism, the first citizen of what Peter Gay has termed the "party of humanity."[1] Indeed, in whatever direction we turn, accepting the claims of a multidimensional Kant, whether to the Kant of the *Critiques,* the occasional writings or to Kant as scientist or educational critic there is surely a wealth of quite indisputable evidence for Kant as Enlightenment humanist. But is there really? The traditional reading of Kant as Enlightenment humanist rests on at least five pieces of interrelated evidence, some theoretical, some pragmatic, evidence that suggests a rather neat fit between the notion of humanism and the dimensions of Kant's thought. Let us pause to look at each of these pieces in turn.

The place to begin is undoubtedly with Kant's own manifesto of Enlightenment concerns, a manifesto arguably encompassing the central tenets of humanism, the essay "An Answer to the Question: What Is Enlightenment?" Here Kant claims that "Enlightenment is man's emergence from his self-concurred immaturity," with the "motto of enlightenment therefore: '*Sapere aude!* Have the courage to use your *own* understanding!' "[2] Kant makes the same point in the *Anthropology* where he speaks of the "unalterable commands," the most important of which is to think for ourselves.

> The most important revelation within man is leaving the tutelage for which he himself is responsible. Before the revelation others did his thinking for him, and he merely imitated them or let them lead him by guide ropes. Now he risks walking forward with his own feet on the ground of experience, even if he wobbles along.[3]

Without such a capacity to think for oneself, one is given over to the "heteronomy of reason," to prejudice,

> and the greatest of all prejudices is that of fancying nature not to be subject to rules which the understanding by virtue of its own essential law lays at its basis, i.e., *superstition.* Emancipation from superstition is called enlightenment. . . . For the condition of blindness into which superstition puts one, which it as much as demands from one as an obligation, makes the need of being led by others, and consequently the passive state of reason, pre-eminently conspicuous.[4]

The same concern with the individual's active use of understanding and reason, the same belief that only reason can be the key to fundamental autonomy, is to be found, of course, in the Preface to the first edition of the *Critique of Pure Reason,* where Kant, in commenting on the critical temper of the times, argues that "our age is, in especial degree, the age of criticism, and to criticism everything must submit."[5] It is the critical spirit, that is to say the rational temper, that in its quite fearless adjudication of any problem provides the foundation for autonomy. The central Enlightenment tenet of the conceptual weddedness of reason and autonomy, reason unswayed by any appeal other that rational justification allowing the individual to decide for himself, is thus equally central in Kant's thinking.

A second piece of evidence for Kant's Enlightenment humanism is to be found in the generally neglected philosophical anthropology, not simply the *Anthropology from a Pragmatic Point of View,* a course manual for Kant's lectures in anthropology given at Königsberg, but the entire anthropological dimension of his work. Indeed, one of the strongest evidences of Kant's humanist pedigree is to be found in the claim, contentious in some respects, but obvious in most respects, that the conception that provides the underlying coherence to the various strands of his philosophical enterprise is a philosophical anthropology founded on an understanding of persons as simultaneously inhabiting two orders, the order of nature and the order of freedom. It is this concern with persons, persons in their cognitive dimension, persons in their historical and political dimensions, persons in their moral and religious aspects, that provides the basis both for a definitive Kantian *Weltanschauung* and for Kantian humanism.

In both the *Logic* and in an important letter of 1793 to C. F. Staudlin, Kant sets out his intellectual agenda, an agenda centering not on three, but on four questions.

> . . . the plan I prescribed for myself, a long time ago, calls for an examination of the field of pure philosophy with a view to solving three problems: (1) What can I know? (metaphysics). (2) What ought I to do? (moral philosophy). (3) What may I hope? (philosophy of religion). A fourth question ought to follow, finally: What is man? (anthropology, a subject on which I have lectured for over twenty years).[6]

Aside from the fact that Kant here treats even the first question as metaphysical rather than epistemological, it is important to note that it is this outline, not Kant's after-the-fact reconstruction of his conceptual development, "but the recounting of a plan—prescribed . . . a long time ago"—which governed the development of the critical philosophy. Moreover, all of the questions focus quite obviously on human nature—What can man know? What ought he to do? For what may he hope?—with the fourth question, as Kant suggests, pulling together, as Kant attempts to do in the final part of his *Anthropology,* the somewhat disparate aspects of personhood that emerge from the answers to the previous questions.

Two letters, one to Moses Mendelssohn is 1766 and the other to J. S. Beck in 1791, corroborate the importance of human nature in Kant's thinking suggested by his reduction of philosophy to the famous four questions noted above. In the letter to Mendelssohn, Kant suggests that his central philosophical preoccupation is whether there is, or indeed, can ever be, sufficient data to be able to understand how "the soul is present in the world . . ."

> If, for the time being, we put aside arguments based on the propriety or on the divine purposes and ask whether it is ever possible to attain such knowledge of the nature of the soul from our experience—a knowledge sufficient to inform us of the manner in which the soul is present in the universe, in relation both to matter and to beings of its own sort—we shall see whether *birth . . . life,* and *death* are matters we can ever hope to understand by means of reason.[7]

Kant is certainly interested in knowledge, but epistemology is cast here in the context of personhood in that it is knowledge of the 'nature of the soul,' its birth, life and death, which is Kant's real interest.

The letter to Beck, in which Kant attempts to convince him to undertake the task of writing a summary of Kant's works, strikes a similar note of anthropological primacy. "Now what can serve better for this and for a lifetime than investigating something that concerns the whole nature of man, especially if one has the hope of making some progress from time to time by a systematic effort of thought. Besides, the history of the world and of philosophy are tied up with this enterprise. . . ."[8]

The centrality of human nature in Kant's conceptual agenda is even more apparent in the passage from the *Logic* where after listing the four questions of a "cosmopolitan philosophy," Kant notes that the first three are in fact really anthropological questions themselves.

> The field of philosophy in this cosmopolitan sense may be reduced to the following questions:
> 1. What can I know?
> 2. What ought I to do?
> 3. What may I hope for?
> 4. What is man?
> The first question is answered by *metaphysics,* the second by *morals,* the third by *religion,* and the fourth by *anthropology.* In the end, all may be related to the fourth.[9]

This is not to suggest that Kant always conceived of his work as primarily anthropological, as directed toward man in the broadest sense. His conversion to a philosophical anthropology aimed at securing the "rights of mankind," both conceptual and political, seems to have been occasioned by his reading of Rousseau during the early sixties.

> By inclination I am an inquirer. I feel a consuming thirst for knowledge, the unrest which goes with the desire to progress in it, and satisfaction at every advance in it. There was a time when I believed this constituted the honor of humanity, and I despised the people who know nothing. Rousseau corrected me in this. This blinding prejudice disappeared. I learned to honor man, and I would find myself more useless than the common laborer if

I did not believe that this attitude of mine can give a worth to all others in establishing the rights of mankind.[10]

But it was not simply Rousseau's general enthusiasm for mankind and his belief in the significance of philosophical anthropology that attracted Kant, but his recognition that beneath the vagaries of historical man there was, accessible to the patient observer, an essential man. "Among the multitude of forms assumed by man," Kant notes, "Rousseau first discovered man's deeply hidden nature and the concealed law by the observation of which providence is justified."[11] Kant's debt to Rousseau has often been chronicled in terms of the notions of will, obligation, contract, equality, rights, and freedom, but Rousseau's real importance to Kant might lie not so much in particular philosophical notions as in his conviction about the foundational character of a theory of human nature. In this sense, of course, Kant's commitment to anthropology is not unique, even through his conception of personhood may well be.

The belief in the significance of human nature for philosophical reflection is evident as well in Kant's own outline of his ethics lectures for the winter term of 1765–66 where he notes that

> in ethics I always consider historically and philosophically what *happens* before I point out what *ought to happen*. I shall make clear the method by which one must study *man*—not the man who, through the variable form which his chance condition impresses upon him, is distorted and as such has almost always been misjudged by philosophers, but the abiding *nature* of man and its unique position in creation.[12]

This notion of an abiding trans-historical nature of man as distinct from its historically conditioned particular manifestation as the only proper foundation for philosophy is also found in the first *Critique* in a passage devoted explicitly to political philosophy. At the beginning of the Transcendental Dialectic, in a discussion of Plato's *Republic*, Kant is sharply critical of those who suggest that Plato's perfect commonwealth is nothing more than a perfect vision, incapable of realization. Rather than dismissing the idea as impossible, "we should . . . be better advised to follow this thought, and, where the great philosopher leaves us without help, to place it, through fresh efforts, in a proper light."[13] Judged from an empirical perspective, which focuses on the "hindrances," the "adverse experiences" which count against the realization of Plato's idea (and by extension Kant's own version of it as well), such a political order does appear visionary. But in deciding whether this goal is indeed capable of fulfillment we must "abstract from the actually existing hindrances, which, it may be, do not arise unavoidably out of human nature, but rather are due to a quite remediable cause, the neglect of the pure ideas in the making of the laws." Political philosophy in particular and philosophy in general, Kant argues, can thus proceed only after it has considered the "abiding nature of man."

But it is not merely Kant's conception of enlightenment and the crucial anthropological dimension of his work that serve to justify his humanist standing: it is also his commitment to two other pieces of Enlightenment dogma, moral foundationalism and the objective and ultimately emancipatory character of reason. By moral foundationalism we mean the belief that reason can generate certain indubitable moral principles whose status as indubitable must be acknowledged by all rational agents. Such principles are not the product of divine revelation or intuition or indeed experience but are necessary in the sense that without them the moral experience of human persons is impossible. In this sense they function as the moral corollaries to Kant's necessary conditons for experience of any kind since without them coherent moral experience is a conceptual absurdity. For Kant there are, of course, at least two such indubitable foundational moral principles: first, persons as ends in themselves and second, the absolutely central place of freedom in the lives of human persons. The notion of a person, or for Kant, man, as end in himself, makes its most explicit and extended appearance in the *Foundations of the Metaphysics of Morals.* There Kant maintains that "Man, and, in general, every rational being exists as an end in himself and not merely as means to be arbitrarily used by this or that will. In all his actions, whether they are directed to himself or to other rational beings, he must always be regarded at the same time as an end."[14] The centrality of freedom is what ultimately grounds this status as end, as within the world of our experience it is only human persons who, in sharp distinction from the determination that structures the natural world, can freely set and achieve ends, and thus in so doing legitimately become objective ends in themselves. Here, then, in the first component of his moral foundationalism is one of Kant's most famous humanist claims: the unique value of human persons is to be found in their status as self-determining ends. The humanist, whatever else he may be, recognizes a fundamental moral and ontological ordering as between persons and things and accepts as a consequence of that ordering a nonnegotiable commitment to treating persons as ends, never as things.

There is, however, more to Kant's position than the mere assertion of indubitable moral principle, however definitive of humanism: there is also the belief in the objective character of reason itself, that is, the ability of reason to stand outside of the conflicting perspectives generated by subjectivity and observe things as they "are." Kant acknowledges the immense difficulty involved in such an undertaking, but he nevertheless argues that reason must, at least in principle, possess such a character. For instance, in both the third *Critique* and in the *Anthropology* Kant argues for what he terms the "maxims of *common human understanding,* maxims that define human rationality."

Common human understanding . . . is looked upon as the least we can expect from any one claiming the name of man. . . . By the name of *sensus communis* is to be understood the idea of a *public* sense, i.e., a critical faculty which in its reflective act takes account . . . of the mode of representation of every one else, in order, *as it were*, to weight its judgement with the collective reason of mankind, and thereby avoid the illusion arising from subjective and personal conditions which could readily be taken for objective, an illusion that would exert a prejudicial influence upon its judgement. This is accomplished by weighing the judgement, not so much with actual, as rather with the merely possible, position of everyone else, as the result of a mere abstraction from the limitations which continually affect our own estimate.[15]

From this idea of common human understanding Kant deduces three maxims. The first and third reflect the active role of reason in freeing one from tutelage to the opinions and beliefs of others, namely to think for oneself and to think consistently. The second, however, focuses on reason's capacity to view the world from the objective perspective.

> As to the second maxim . . . this . . . still indicates a man of *enlarged mind:* if he detaches himself from the subjective personal conditions of his judgement, which cramp the minds of so many others, and reflects upon his own judgement from a *universal standpoint* which he can only determine by shifting his ground to the standpoint of others.[16]

This capacity of "shifting his ground to the standpoint of others," latent in most persons, involves the moral quality of objectivity, or as Kant calls it here, the "idea of a *public* sense." Rationality is thus not simply autonomous thought, or indeed coherently ordered thought, but thought that is possessed of cognitive empathy in that it is devoid of the illusions of subjectivity arising from contingent situations and reflects upon its own judgments from a "universal standpoint." Reason can, as it were, free us from the blinding bias of self-interest and allow us to see the world as it objectively is. Autonomy is thus checked by objectivity. Or, seen in a slightly different way, autonomy and objectivity merge in the sense that the autonomy about which Kant speaks is the autonomy from the determination of one's action by the principle of self-love, the autonomy which structures its judgments according to the universality of the moral law.

Persons then assume their foundational importance for Kant the Enlightenment humanist because of their wholly unique instantiation of freedom and reason, objectivity and morality. Together freedom and reason are virtually unbounded; together they are emancipatory from self, others and the natural world. As Kant notes in the second thesis of the "Idea for a Universal History from a Cosmopolitan Point of View": "Reason in a creature is a faculty of widening the rules and purposes of the use of all its powers far beyond natural instinct; it acknowledges no limits to its projects."[17]

Similarly, in the first *Critique,* freedom is described as having the power to "pass beyond any and every specified limit,"[18] in part because in the end it is the "inner principle of the world." Freedom and reason must, however, be joined with morality and objectivity for the realization of genuine personhood. Indeed, it is freedom and reason that make morality in the sense of freely chosen conformity to the objectivity of the moral law possible. Only reason and freedom properly exercised can free persons from their cognitive and moral egocentricity—what Kant refers to as the "maxim of self-love"—and allow them to see both the world and themselves from the most general and comprehensive, that is to say from the most objective position available. Self-love—the "propensity to make the subjective determining grounds of one's choice into an objective determining ground of the will in general"[19]—is the main source of man's failure to become an end of absolute value in that it is what renders moral objectivity and moral autonomy impossible. Self-love, Kant argues, makes genuine thinking, genuine freedom, genuine objectivity, and hence, genuine personhood impossible, for it abrogates unprejudiced thought, enlarged thought, and consistent thought—the maxims of common human understanding—simultaneously. The possession of what Kant calls a "public sense"—the "critical faculty which in its reflective act takes account . . . of the mode of representation of everyone else, in order . . . to weight its judgement with the collective reason of mankind . . ."[20]—is impossible, for self-love destroys our ability for "putting ourselves in the position of everyone else" and enthrones rather than checks the illusions that arise from "subjective and personal conditions." As the second *Critique* puts it:

> We find . . . our nature as sensuous beings so characterized that the materials of the faculty of desire (objects of the inclination . . .) first press upon us; and we find our pathologically determined self, although by its maxims it is wholly incapable of giving universal laws, striving to give its pretensions priority and to make them acceptable as first and original claims, just as if it were our entire self.[21]

Only the moral law, it seems, can "exclude the influence of self-love from the highest practical principle"[22] and check "self-conceit" since the "idea of the moral deprives self-love of its influence and self-conceit of its delusion. . . ."[23] Reason and freedom, morality and objectivity thus provide at least the potential for that "goodness of the heart"[24] that in the end is, in the best humanist tradition, "wholly his own work."[25]

And it is the fact that this goodness of heart can be no other than his own work that points to the fifth piece of evidence supporting the traditional reading of Kant as Enlightenment humanist, the fact that within the critical philosophy one cannot specify theoretically a world in which the proposition "God exists" can be known to be true, the fact that Kantian theology, if we even speak of such a thing, can provide one with neither knowledge nor necessary belief.[26]

Kant's fundamental epistemological tenet is that no valid argument can establish anything theoretical about the nature of the world except as an object of possible experience. Human beings are conditioned, finite, and incomplete for Kant not only in the more obvious Christian sense of moral impediments, but in cognitive capabilities as well. It is this epistemological limitation which insures that there can be for Kant no valid argument from empirical premises for God's existence. God simply cannot be made an object of cognition as natural phenomena can. Nor can there be a successful argument of a strictly logical sort, for Kant rejects the ontological argument. Within the bounds of the first *Critique* and, more specifically, the "Transcendental Dialectic," Kant must reject any theological knowledge of God because such "knowledge" assumes that God can be dealt with in the same way that finite things are dealt with in the spatial, temporal world.

This emphasis on the limitations of human knowledge is underscored in the *Critique of Judgment* where Kant attempts to provide a hypothetical account of the divine mind. While human intellect is always discursive, knowing things systematically, the divine mind, according to Kant, is intuitive, apprehending truth immediately and totally. Thus God has a knowledge of himself, of the world, and of man immediately, while man has only the idea of God, the idea of the world, and the idea of the world sequentially united. The subject/object distinction, which is fundamental to human cognition, is not an element of the divine intellect. The fact that man cannot even conceptualize such an intellect, much less know it, only serves to reiterate the impossibility within the Kantian context of knowing God as an object of rational inquiry.

If Kant's epistemological arguments about the limitations of reason are correct, then the epistemic gap between God and man cannot be bridged. If Kant is correct there cannot be any knowledge of God, and thus faith in the most obvious sense cannot have any content, and most certainly cannot have the content specified in rationalistic theology. Indeed, if Kant's program is pushed to its logical limits, there would be no way in which man could even conceive of the externality of God, much less claim to know it to be the case.

This humanist case for the impossibility of religious knowledge is not, moreover, simply confined to the first and third *Critiques*. In "What Is Orientation in Thinking?" for instance, Kant places the entire discussion of the "concept of a First Being" within the context of a discussion of the "need of reason . . . to presuppose and assume something which it may not pretend to know on objective grounds." The "need of reason," Kant argues, provides us with nothing more than a "subjective ground" for believing in the existence of God. Kant goes on to speak of rational belief in God's existence as "a subjectively sufficient assent associated with the consciousness that it is an objectively insufficient assent; therefore it is contrasted with knowledge."[27] He observes that "no use of reason can change the belief into knowledge," and later that "pure rational belief can never be converted by all the natural data of reason into knowledge, because the ground of assent in this case is merely subjective. It is only a necessary need of reason to presuppose, not to demonstrate, the existence of a highest being and so long as we are men, it will remain so."[28] Kant does acknowledge that the postulate of reason is in no respect inferior to knowledge, but this, of course, does not confer upon it the status of knowledge. "But the rational belief, which rests on the need of reason's use in a practical sense, could be called a postulate of reason, not as if it were an insight sufficient to all thelogical requirements of certainty, but because this assent (when everything in man is morally arranged) is in degree inferior to no cognition even though in kind it is wholly different."[29] Belief while thus subjectively sufficient is objectively insufficient and hence not knowledge.

In the transcendental employment of reason . . . while opining is doubtless too weak a term to be applicable, the term knowing is too strong. In the

merely speculative sphere we cannot therefore make any judgments whatso-
ever. For the subjective grounds upon which we may hold something to
be true, such as those which are able to produce belief, are not permissible
in speculative questions, inasmuch as they do not hold independently of all
empirical support, and do not allow of being communicated in equal measure
to others.[30]

One finds the same conclusion in the third *Critique* where the moral
argument is again discussed. Kant argues here that one can claim to know
neither that there is a final end of nature nor an author of nature.

Now the question arises: Is it not possible to substantiate the objective reality of the conception of a final end in a manner that will meet the theoretical requirements of pure reason? This cannot indeed be done apodictically
for the determinant judgment. Yet may it not be done sufficiently for the
maxims of theoretical judgment so far as reflective? This is the least that
could be demanded of speculative philosophy, which undertakes to connect
the ethical end with physical ends by means of a single end. Yet even this
little is still far more than it can even accomplish.[31]

In a later passage, Kant is even more specific about the epistemological
status of belief or faith, and the postulates as mere assumptions.

But since we cannot procure objective reality for this conception from a
theoretical point of view, it is a mere matter of faith on the part of pure
reason. . . . But assurance in matters of faith is an assurance from a purely
practical point of view. It is a moral faith that proves nothing for pure rational knowledge as theoretical, but only for it as practical and directed to
the fulfillment of its obligations. It in no way extends either speculation or
the practical rules of prudence actuated by the principle of self-love. . . . This
does not make the cognition of the latter (supreme Object) any knowledge
or any opinion of the existence or nature of these conditions, as a mode
of theoretical knowledge, but as a mere assumption, confined to matters
practical and commanded in practical interests, on behalf of the moral use
of our reason.[32]

And in the second *Critique* Kant suggests that "with all the exertion of
our reason we have only a very obscure and ambiguous view into the future; the Governor of the world allows us only to conjecture His existence
and majesty, not to behold or clearly prove them. . . ."[33] Kant also speaks
of its being "morally necessary to assume the existence of God"[34] but affirms that such an assumption is merely a "hypothesis, i.e., a ground of explanation."[35] Thus even within the context of the moral argument, the postulates as assumptions are hypotheses, not knowledge.

Despite the central importance of reason and freedom, morality and the
perspective of objectivity, and the seeming impossibility of any genuine religious knowledge in establishing Kant's humanist position, there is yet a final
triad of evidence from Kant's political, historical, and religious writings that
completes the humanist portrait.

What emerges from works such as "The Idea," *The Conjectural Beginning, The Third Critique* and even certain parts of *Religion Within the Limits of Reason Alone* is an argument for a reasoned prospect of success in the long-term humanist project of blunting if not completely taming nature's recalcitrance to the human projects of securing domestic equity and prosperity and international tranquility—what Kant calls republicanism and cosmopolitanism, and of bringing the wills of most persons under the sovereignity of the moral law. Although on one level it is much too simple a characterization, on yet another it is not unfair to suggest that Kant sees the success of these humanist hopes as contingent on the development of reason and freedom. In this sense one can speak of a primary and a secondary strand of Kantian humanism with the secondary strand conceptually derivative from the primary. The primary strand, which is the most theoretical, consists in Kant's general anthropological perspective and in his respective claims about the value of persons that emerge from this perspective, most specifically, his belief in a version of moral foundationalism and the objective character of reason. The secondary strand, which is at least in some sense far more pragmatic, suggests what one might be justified in hoping for from the ultimate development of human reason and freedom. Thus, for instance, history, viewed in the appropriate fashion, reveals the "realization of Nature's secret plan to bring forth a perfectly constituted state as the only condition in which the capacities of mankind can be full developed, and also bring forth that external relation among states which is perfectly adequate to this end."[36]

Indeed, our confidence in reasons and freedom, or at least our hope in reason and freedom, allows us even to posit an idea "of how the course of the world must be if it is to lead to certain rational ends."[37]

> . . . if . . . one carries through this study, a guiding thread will be revealed. It can serve not only for clarifying the confused play of things human, and not only for the art of prophesying later political changes, but for giving a consoling view of the future (which could not be reasonably hoped for without the presupposition of a natural plan) in which there will be exhibited in the distance how the human race finally achieves the condition in which all the seeds planted in it by Nature can fully develop and in which the destiny of the race can be fulfilled here on earth.[38]

Reason and freedom thus provide one with a justified optimism, a hope, to use Kantian language, about the ultimate prospects of humanity. At other times, of course, it is not simply reason and freedom alone but reason and freedom under the "tutelege" of Nature that calm our conceptual and existential anxieties about final human success.

> The friction among men, the inevitable antagonisms, which is the mark of even the largest societies and political bodies, is used by Nature as a means to establish a condition of quiet and security. Through war, through the taxing and never-ending accumulation of armament, through the want which any state, even in peacetime, must suffer internally, Nature forces them to make at first inadequate and tentative attempts; finally, after devastation,

revolution, and even complete exhaustion, she brings them to that which reason could have told them at the beginning and with far less sad experience, to wit, a step from the lawless condition of savages into a league of nations.[39]

But whether alone as an exclusively human achievement or in conjunction with Nature, reason and with it freedom are sufficient to secure seemingly without even divine assistance, inasmuch as such an intervention would serve to fatally compromise human freedom, the progressive realization of culture, civil freedom, and international order. As Kant notes in the "Idea for a Universal History":

> At present, states are in such an artificial relation to ambitions of states. Furthermore, civic freedom can hardly be infringed without the evil consequences being felt in all walks of life, especially in commerce, where the effect is loss of power of the state in its foreign relations. But this freedom spreads by degrees.
>
> Enlightenment comes gradually, with intermittent folly and caprice, as a great good which must finally save men from the selfish aggrandizement of their masters. . . .
>
> In the end, war itself will be seen as not only so artificial, in outcome so uncertain for both sides, in after effects so painful in the form of an ever-growing war debt . . . that cannot be met, that it will be regarded as a most dubious undertaking.[40]

Thus, whatever the vagaries of the historical process, with both its progress and its relapse, "the human race has always been in progress toward the better and will continue to be so henceforth."[41]

Despite the seemingly impressive conclusiveness of much of the evidence that suggests Kant is best pictured as a central figure in the history of humanism, we wish to argue that such a reading ignores a major reappraisal during the last decade of Kant's intellectual life. This reappraisal centered on the fundamental character of human persons, and it suggests that Kant's relationship to humanism is really extraordinarily pragmatic. Furthermore, it argues that if Kant is to be called a humanist at all, it is only with the clear understanding of how decidedly marginal is his position with respect to traditional humanism. Indeed, perhaps the most compelling way of conceiving of Kant's relationship to humanism is to think of him as a humanist at the periphery of the tradition, as an ambiguous humanist who argues for persons as cognitively ambitious, yet epistemologically finite, driven by instincts yet able to set ends, enjoined to perfection yet radically evil, desirous of certainty yet forced to settle for faith, responsible yet needing divine assistance, unsocial yet enjoined to find their place in a moral commonwealth.

The occasion for Kant's reappraisal of the human prospect was his 1793 work *Religion Within the Limits of Reason Alone* (hereafter *Religion*), his last major conceptual project aside from the *Metaphysics of Morals*. Though Kant is interested in a variety of questions in *Religion*, the most significant of these is the problem of what he terms "radical evil." This is not to suggest that the problem of evil was some late career obsession for Kant. Whether from his early experiences as part of a Christian community rooted in the belief in comprehensive evil not simply as theological dictum but self-evident moral fact, or whether from his systematic explorations of the moral law within, or indeed, from a careful consideration of the historical record or the implications of the doctrine of human responsibility and freedom, Kant was never able, despite his most optimistic humanist formulations, to frame a conception of persons that omitted evil as at least partly constitutive of his nature. As he observes at the beginning of *Religion*, the Enlightenment optimism, founded on science, education, and reason, that saw mankind's progress towards perfectability as forever assured was not "deduced from experience."

> All agree that the world began in a good estate, whether in a Golden Age, a life in Eden, or a yet more happy community with celestial beings. But they represent that this happiness vanished like a dream and that a Fall into evil . . . presently hurried mankind from bad to worse with accelerated descent. . . . More modern, though less prevalent, is the contrasted optimist belief . . . that the world steadily . . . forges in the other direction, to wit, from bad to better. . . . If this belief, however, is meant to apply to *moral* goodness and badness . . . it has certainly not been deduced from experience; the history of all times cries too loudly against it.[42]

But if evil has been a part of Kant's anthropology from the beginning, why is the extended discussion in *Religion* such a threat to his humanism? The answer is to be found in the fact that Kant's previous discussions of evil, in the *Lectures on Philosophical Theology* and the *Conjectural Beginning*, tend to place evil's origin in man's inexperience with both reason and morality, in his *Rohheit*, his incomplete mastery of his inclinations. Considered in this fashion evil could be accommodated, though not without some conceptual tension, within the optimism of works such as *An Old Question* that easily affirmed that the "race has always been in progress toward the better and will continue to be so henceforth." Evil could thus be glossed as immaturity, as but a temporary feature of the lives of persons.

Within *Religion*, however, such a perspective is impossible for here we have not merely the evil that arises from what Kant calls "animality," not simply the evil linked to the inappropriate expression of the "sensuous inclinations" or the corruption of some "predisposition to the good," but evil that is radical in the sense of corrupting the foundation of the moral personality. And it is the corruption that destroys Kant's Enlightenment humanism.

But what does Kant mean by the corruption or "perversity of the human heart?" Such perversity is not the failure consistently to follow one's incentives, or the adoption of mixed incentives, but the reversal of the "ethical order among the incentives of a *free* will; and although conduct which is lawfully good (i.e., legal) may be found with it, yet the cast of mind is thereby corrupted at its root (so far as the moral disposition is concerned), and the man is hence designated as evil."[43] Evil then is radical in the first sense for

Kant in that it is foundational: it is a corruption of the "subjective determining ground of the will,"[44] that is to say in the source of all actions, not simply the corruption of certain individual evil acts. Indeed, an individual's particular acts may for Kant escape the characterization of evil without in any respect diminishing the character of radical evil itself, for Kant is speaking of two quite different actions, the "intelligible action," which is morally imputable, of reversing the ethical order of the incentives, and the sensible, empirical actions that follow from this reversal.

> The propensity to evil . . . is an act in the first sense . . . and at the same time the formal ground of all unlawful conduct in the second sense, which latter, considered materially, violates the law and is termed vice . . . and the first offense remains, even though the second . . . may be repeatedly avoided. The former is intelligible action, cognizable by means of pure reason alone, apart from every temporal condition; the latter is sensible action, empirical, given in time.[45]

Thus to speak of man as evil in this foundational sense is to predicate to him a moral as opposed to a physical propensity to evil, a propensity which is imputable to no one but himself.

> Man is *evil*, can mean only, He is conscious of the moral law but has nevertheless adopted into his maxim the . . . deviation therefrom. He is evil *by nature*, means species; not that such a quality can be inferred from the concept of his species (that is, of man in general)—for then it would be necessary; but rather that from what we know of man through experience we cannot judge otherwise of him, or, that we may presuppose evil to be subjectively necessary to every man, even to the best.[46]

But evil is not simply radical in the foundational sense of a corruption of the "determining ground of the will"; it is also radical in terms of the ordering, of the priority that one assigns to one's incentives to moral action. Kant believes that persons simultaneously adopt two contradictory incentives for acting—the incentives of the moral law and the incentives of sensuous nature. Whereas the incentives of the moral law order one's actions in accordance with the law's requirements of objectivity, rationality, and universality, the incentives of sensuous nature order one's actions in accordance with the "principle of self love." Radical evil is not the simultaneous adoption of these quite contradictory incentives but the *subordination* of the incentive of the moral law to the incentive of self-love.

> Man (even the most wicked) does not, under any maxim whatsoever, repudiate the moral law in the manner of a rebel (renouncing obedience to it). The law, rather, forces itself upon him irresistibly by virtue of his moral predisposition; and were no other incentive working in opposition, he would adopt the law into his supreme maxim as the sufficient determining ground of his will; that is, he would be morally good. But by virtue of an equally innocent natural predisposition he depends upon the incentives of his sensuous nature and adopts them also (in accordance with the subjective principle

of self-love) into his maxim. If he took the latter into his maxim *as in them-selves wholly adequate* to the determination of the will, without troubling himself about the moral law (which, after all, he does have in him), he would be morally evil. Now, since he naturally adopts *both* into his maxim, and since, further, he would find either, if it were alone, adequate in itself for the determining of the will, it follows that if the difference between the maxims amounted merely to the difference between the two incentives (the content of the maxims), that is, if it were merely a question as to whether the law or the sensuous impulse were to furnish the incentive, man would be at once good and evil: this, however, (as we saw in the Introduction) is a contradiction. Hence the distinction between a good man and one who is evil cannot lie in the difference between the incentives which they adopt into their maxim (not in the content of the maxim), but rather must depend upon *subordination* (the form of the maxim), *i.e., which of the two incentives he makes the condition of the other.* Consequently, man (even the best) is evil only in that he reverses the moral order of the incentives when he adopts them into his maxim. He adopts, indeed, the moral law along with the law of self-love; yet when he becomes aware that they cannot remain on a par with each other but that one must be subordinated to the other as its supreme condition, he makes the incentive of self-love and its inclinations the condition of obedience to the moral law; whereas . . . the latter, as the *supreme condition* of the satisfaction of the former, ought to have been adopted into the universal maxim of the will as the sole incentive.[47]

Or as the *Second Critique* described it:

We find . . . our nature as sensuous beings so characterized that the ma-terials of the faculty of desire (objects of inclination . . .) first press upon us; and we find our pathologically determined self, although by its maxims it is wholly incapable of giving universal law, striving to give its pretensions priority and to make them acceptable as first and original claims, just as if it were our entire self.[48]

Radical evil is thus radical in this second sense for Kant in that what he calls the law of self-love is made determinative of one's maxims, and thereby of one's moral life, in place of the moral law.

This fundamental reversal of the proper order of the incentives of the moral life is something that is so subversive of moral personality that were it not for a particular feature of human nature, Kant believes, conscience would not allow it to proceed. Only because of man's capacities for self-deception does conscience acquiesce in the subordination of the moral law to self-love.

This *innate* guilt . . . which is so denominated because it may be discerned in man as early as the first manifestations of the exercise of freedom, . . . this guilt may be judged in its first two stages (those of frailty and impurity) to be unintentional guilt . . . but in the third to be deliberate guilt . . . and to display in its character a certain *insidiousness in regard to its own good and evil dispositions*, and, if only its conduct has not evil consequences . . . does not trouble itself about its disposition but rather considers itself justified before the law. (emphasis mine)[49]

Thus the third aspect of the radical character of evil for Kant is the "insidiousness" of its character, its self-deceiving capacity that hides from the agent the fact that self-love, not the moral law, has become the basis of his actions. To a certain extent this self-deception originates in man's imperfect rationality, a rationality that in this instance is used against human ends in that it mistakenly believes that it can simultaneously adopt two quite incompatible foundational maxims. Self-deception has at least one root then in reason's powers to disguise the inherent contradictions between the moral law and the law of self-love. And this deception is rendered even more probable by the fact that judged strictly in terms of consequences, an agent's actions might not appear to diverge from the requirements of formal morality.

> Yet, even this reversal of the ethical order of the incentives in and through his maxim, a man's actions still may prove to be as much in conformity to the law as if they sprang from true basic principles. This happens when reason employs the unity of the maxims in general, a unity which is inherent in the moral law, merely to bestow upon the incentives of inclination under the name of *happiness*, a unity of maxims which otherwise they cannot have. (For example, truthfulness, if adopted as a basic principle, delivers us from the anxiety of making our lies agree with one another and of not being entangled by their serpent coils.) The empirical character is then good, but the intelligible character is still evil.[50]

Thus, we adopt the imperative of truth-telling not because we believe that truthfulness is necessarily right in the sense of following from the logic of the moral law, but because for the sake of happiness we wish to be relieved of the anxiety consequent to telling lies. Even while our actions are indistinguishable from conformity to the moral law, our motive is not conformity to it but rather conformity to our reading of self-interest.

Beyond the abnegation of moral personality, the reversal of the proper ordering of the incentives, and the dimensions of self-deceit, there is, however, one final aspect of the radical character of evil, that is its inextirpability, at least through human efforts. Though Kant speaks of moral revolution and moral reform, however extensive these might be in instituting a program of radical good, they are finally unable to remove radical evil. The best that is to be expected is that it can be overcome in the sense of acknowledged and held in check.

> This evil is *radical*, because it corrupts the ground of all maxims; it is, moreover, as a natural propensity, *inextirpable* by human powers, since extirpation could occur only through good maxims, and cannot take place when the ultimate subjective ground of all maxims is postulated as corrupt; yet at the same time it must be possible to *overcome* it, since it is found in man, a being whose actions are free.[51]

Conceived of in this fashion, it will be observed how the idea of radical evil as foundationally constitutive of human personhood undermines Kant's Enlightenment humanism in the most fundamental ways. Man's entire distinctiveness, according to Kant, is to be found in his capacities for rational freedom, for setting and acting on ends that transcend the natural, causally determined order of the phenomenal world. But in radical evil, persons allow the incentives of sensuous nature to have priority over those of the moral law and in so doing they lose precisely what is their most important characteristic. Radical evil for Kant renders persons virtually incapable of genuinely free and thus moral actions; it is reason's corruption of man's essential personhood.

But it is not simply man's ability to set ends in distinction from the natural world, what might be called Kant's idea of negative freedom, that constitutes man's uniqueness; it is also what might be described as positive freedom, his ability to set ends in accordance with the universal and objective character of the moral law. And it is this capacity for objective action that radical evil also renders tenuous through its connection with self-love. Radical evil precisely because it is the subordination of the moral law—the only guarantor of genuine freedom and with it genuine selfhood—to the law of self-love, so that the moral law becomes the maxim for actions only when it coincides with self-interest, destroys the very possibility of the moral enterprise. Self-love rather than the moral law as the foundational maxim of one's perception of the moral universe and of one's actions subverts morality precisely because it is only through the objectivity of the moral law that genuine freedom is to be found. In a very real sense then, self-love makes genuine thinking, genuine freedom, genuine objectivity, and thus genuine personhood impossible, for it abrogates at once all of the maxims of common human understanding—unprejudiced thought, enlarged thought, and consistent thought. Only the moral law provides us with the ability to put "ourselves in the position of everyone else"; only the moral law checks the illusions that arise from the "subjective and personal"; only the moral law can "exclude the influence of self-love from the highest practical principle and check "self-conceit."

In the end then, objectivity, the objectivity of the moral law with its formal conditions of universalizability and its demands for the neutral perspective, provides Kant with the only mechanism by which freedom, and with freedom, the humanism of the Enlghtenment, can be saved. Without man's voluntary submission to the laws of freedom, his propensity to treat his own interests as either exceptions to the moral order or as constitutive of the entire moral universe cannot be contained. Radical evil in the shape of self-love quite literally destroys the capacity of persons to understand the character of the moral law in providing the necessary formal conditions that make moral, social, and even political experience possible.

In this sense, too, the radical character of evil also threatens the basic humanism of Kant's conception of man as an absolute end, in that man's possession of the status of absolutely valuable end is founded on his capacity to adopt the universality and the objectivity of the moral law. The essence of the moral person for Kant is the capacity for acting freely without the constraints of the subjectivism of self-love and the narrowness of moral egocentricity. But in destroying one's capacity for according priority to the moral law, for excluding self-love from its determining role in one's moral life, radical evil destroys one's standing as an end of absolute value.

Radical evil is thus not some merely interesting but ultimately peripheral late-life intellectual obsession for Kant that has little if any bearing on the nature of his Enlightenment humanism. All of his Enlightenment confidences and hopes, whether his belief in historical progress, his faith in education, in the maleability of human nature, in the prospects of political reform or in the ultimate triumph of the objective and autonomous character of human reason are decisively shaken by the concept of radical evil.

It might, however, be objected that the picture that we have sketched with respect to the character and influence of radical evil in the lives of persons though true is nonetheless crucially incomplete in that it makes no mention of Kant's doctrine, equally present in *Religion*, of moral revolution, or if not revolution, at least moral reform. Surely, it might be argued, we can give full standing to the destructive consequences of radical evil while at the same time noting Kant's quite sincere belief in the possibilities of moral reform. And if we can provide some certainty of at least the possibility of reform, we can save, as it were, Kantian humanism.

While a detailed examination of the possibility of moral change in Kant is beyond the compass of this paper, there are two considerations that appear to argue decisively against the prospect of rescuing Kant's humanist project. First, none of the various strategies that Kant considers for moral reform, whether arguments centering on the invulnerability of *Wille*, on the logic of moral responsibility, on the assistance of conscience or the empirical evidence of the life of Jesus and the notion of a vicarious atonement, none of these in the end are conceptually satisfactory. All of them flounder on the fact that an escape from radical evil requires a cognitive revolution in which persons recognize that a reversal of the proper order of incentives has taken place at the foundation of their moral character, a revolution that is in principle impossible due to the pervasive character of self-deceit. It is after all, not merely that we have adopted the principle of self-love as determinative of our moral perspective; it is that we fail to recognize that we have done so. Indeed, it is this failure that makes radical evil "inextirpable by human powers."

But what of nonhuman powers? Can the value, autonomy, dignity, and ultimate prospects of human persons be saved in the end through divine intervention? There is much in *Religion* that suggests that Kant believes that divine intervention, grace as he terms it, can in the end accomplish that which is beyond the power of natural persons. Such grace, to be sure, is completely beyond our conceptual grasp, and we are allowed nothing more than the hope that it might be granted to us. But hope is surely allowable within the structure of Enlightenment humanism, or at least Kantian Enlightenment humanism, for it is hope that ultimately provides the epistemological underpinning for the entire humanist enterprise.

But grace, and with grace hope, cannot save Kantian humanism, for the reliance on divine intervention to solve the problem of radical evil, an evil that only man is responsible for, destroys the very notion of human autonomy and responsibility, and hence worth that it was designed to rescue.

In the end, Kantian humanism is destroyed by the notion of radical evil, for if it embraces a theistic salvation mediated by grace, then it abandons the very essence of its humanist program, namely human ability and accountability; and if it eschews a theistic salvation, it can find no ultimately satisfactory solution for an evil that is so radical as to render the human project impossible.

Notes

1. Peter Gay, *The Party of Humanity: Essays in the French Enlightenment* (New York, 1971).
2. Immanuel Kant, "What Is Enlightenment?" in *Kant's Political Writings,* ed. H. Reiss (Cambridge, 1971), 54.
3. I. Kant, *Anthropology from a Pragmatic Point of View,* trans. H. Gregor (The Hague, 1974), 97.
4. I. Kant, *Critique of Judgement,* trans. J. Meredith (Oxford, 1928), part 1, 152.
5. I. Kant, *Critique of Pure Reason,* trans. N. Kemp Smith (London, 1929), 9.
6. I. Kant, *Philosophical Correspondence,* trans. A. Zweig (Chicago, 1967), 205.
7. Ibid., 57.
8. Ibid., 179.
9. As quoted in L. Goldmann, *Immanuel Kant* (London, 1971), 130.
10. As quoted in L. Beck, *Critique of Practical Reason and Other Writings in Moral Philosophy* (Chicago, 1949), 7.
11. Ibid.
12. P. Schilpp, *Kant's Pre-Critical Ethics,* 2nd ed. (Chicago, 1960), 8.
13. *Pure Reason,* A 312.
14. Kant, *Foundations,* 86, G.5. IV, 428.
15. Kant, *Judgement,* part 1, 151.
16. Ibid., 152.
17. I. Kant, "Idea for a Universal History from a Cosmopolitan Point of View" in *On History: Immanual Kant,* ed. L. W. Beck (New York, 1963), 13.
18. Kant, *Pure Reason,* A 317, B 374.
19. I. Kant, *Critique of Practical Reason,* trans. L. W. Beck (New York, 1956), 77.
20. Kant, *Judgement,* part 1, 151.
21. Kant, *Practical Reason,* 77.
22. Ibid.
23. Ibid., 78.
24. Kant, "Idea for a Universal History," 14.
25. Ibid.
26. For a fuller account of this argument regarding Kant's religious epistemology see J. C. Luik, "The Ambiguity of Kantian Faith," *Scottish Journal of Theology,* 36. The argument of this essay represents a change of perspective about the nature of Kantian faith.
27. Kant, "What Is Orientation in Thinking?" in *On History,* 300.
28. Ibid.
29. Ibid., 300–301.
30. Kant, *Critique of Pure Reason,* B851.
31. Kant, *Critique of Judgement,* 454.

32. Ibid., 470. Emphasis mine.
33. Kant, *Critique of Practical Reason*, V 147.
34. Ibid., V, 125.
35. Ibid.
36. Kant, "Idea for a Universal History," 21.
37. Ibid., 24.
38. Ibid., 25.
39. Ibid., 18–19.
40. Ibid., 22–23.
41. I. Kant, "An Old Question Revived Again: Is the Human Race Constantly Progressing?" in *On History*, 148.
42. I. Kant, *Religion Within the Limits of Reason Alone*, trans. by T. Greene and H. Hudson (New York, 1960), 15.
43. Ibid., 25.
44. Ibid., 26.
45. Ibid., 26–27.
46. Ibid., 27.
47. Ibid., 31–32.
48. Kant, *Practical Reason*, 77.
49. Kant, *Religion*, 33.
50. Ibid., 32.
51. Ibid., 32.

9

Kierkegaard's Teleological Humanism

Robert L. Perkins

Just as the expert archer's arrow leaves the bowstring and has no rest before
it reaches the target, so the human being is created by God with God as
his aim and cannot find rest before he finds rest in God.[1]

Thou hast made us for thyself, Oh Lord, and our hearts are restless till
they repose in Thee.[2]

Buber said that the word God "is the most burdened of all human words."[3]
Though not so burdened as the word God, the word humanism shows the
strain of a long history and varied interpretations.[4] These cannot be reviewed
here. The object of this paper is, quite briefly, to state and argue for Kierkegaard's teleological humanism. Why think of Kierkegaard in relation to
humanism? Recently an anthology of the writings of Christian humanists appeared, and it contains no selection from Kierkegaard.[5] Obviously, not everyone thinks of Kierkegaard in connection with Christian humanism. One of
the central theses of this paper is that Kierkegaard belongs squarely in the
tradition of Christian humanism. Moreover, he belongs in the Platonic and
contemplative wing of Christian humanism.

The best way to approach Kierkegaard's humanism is through the figure
of Socrates, whom Kierkegaard used polemically against the age, constructively
to elucidate the depth and grandeur of pagan, i.e., non-Christian, humanism,
and finally in contrast with Christian humanism.

No Christian philosopher ever raised Socrates so high or denied his lofty
achievements so completely.[6] As Harold Sarf has observed, "He [Kierkegaard]
pursued in his own mind an intense dialogue with Socrates about how life
ought to be conducted, about the nature of the knowledge that can improve
man's moral character, and pointed out the factors that account for health

and illness in the soul and state. He found in Socratic discourse a living language relevant to the dilemmas of the modern era."[7] Socrates is Kierkegaard's code word for the highest and most profound human achievements in morality and inwardness. "O Socrates," Kierkegaard confided in his journals, "you were and are, after all, the only philosopher in the realm of the purely human."[8] We will examine several reaches of the theme of the purely human, for our humanity is better or less well used. Socrates is the criterion by which Kierkegaard judges the successes and failures of the purely human. The theme of Socratic and human inwardness is used polemically against the age: its effete aestheticism, its romanticism, its ethics, its religious expression, and its politics.

SOCRATES AND THE AGE

Kierkegaard's broad critique of romanticism has been documented, to only a minor degree, and that primarily in relation to Hegel.[9] Here we can only suggest the use Kiekegaard made of Socratic humanism as a critique of romanticism. Kierkegaard's view of romanticism was more negative than positive. Yet he so totally absorbed its spirit and its literary methods that he was able in the first volume of *Either/Or* to reveal its soft, even sordid, underside and to do so without preaching or lecturing. The literary expression of the book perfectly matches that of the romantics, and at the same time it undercuts romanticism's claims to be a form of life higher than bourgeois existence. There is perhaps no better way to express the contrast between the romantic and Socrates than to quote one of Kierkegaard's romantic persona, "I do not care for anything. I do not care to ride, for the exercise is too violent. I do not care to walk, walking is too strenuous. I do not care to lie down, for I should either have to remain lying, and I do not care to do that, or I should have to get up again, and I do not care to do that either. *Summa summarum:* I do not care at all."[10] Two more different personae than the effete and self-indulgent romantic and Socrates could hardly be imagined.[11]

Kierkegaard recognized that the romantic movement was far more than a literary phenomenon. It was also highly doctrinaire in presenting a new morality. In his thesis, *On the Concept of Irony with Constant Reference to Socrates,* Kierkegaard said that romanticism was an attack not only upon the prudery of the times, but was also an assault upon all morality and ethics.[12] In opposition to this onslaught against the established order, Kierkegaard set the Hegelian view of Socrates as the founder of morality. Kierkegaard criticized Socrates because he had no understanding "of a total system of actuality."[13] Later he repented of this charge against Socrates,[14] and emphasized even more thoroughly the fact that Socrates' greatness lies in his attempt to know himself in his individuality. This becomes clear in Judge William's praise of Socrates' effort "to develop himself into a paragon of virtue."[15] Kierkegaard says in his own name that Socrates came time and again to the good, that coming to the good was an ever repeated activity, i.e., Socrates did not have the good as a possession but rather as a task.[16] Judge William explains this effort as a withdrawal from life, as a refusal to engage in metaphysical ruminations, and as a decision not to act outwardly, but rather to act inwardly.[17] It is this understanding of Socrates' inwardness and subjectivity that is the source of that tired cliché of Kierkegaard as an individualist who has no social philosophy. It is his understanding of Socrates as the founder of morality[18] that is the paradigm of the individual who concentrates upon himself and his own moral integrity.

At this point we have come a good distance in our understanding of Kierkegaard as a humanist, for the presentation of Socrates in the dissertation and in *Either/Or* has shown a progress from the rapacious and irresponsible sophists who will express their will whatever the cost to others and from the frivolous, self-indulgent efforts of the romantics to escape from the world's problems by practicing an effete and self-indulgent aestheticism to the morally earnest Socrates engaged in his task of knowing himself. Socrates' irony was directed against the sophists and everything existent.[19] Kierkegaard, the faithful Socratic, has directed Socratic irony against the ironists of his age, the romantics. Romanticism itself was a critique of the bourgeois form of life. Now let us turn to the self-complacent bourgeois and those who attempted to legitimate the bourgeois form of life as rational.

The most critical estimate of the bourgeois life is the description Kierkegaard gives of the complacent philistine.[20] In the Socratic portion of *The Sickness unto Death* Kierkegaard discusses the philistine as one who has no imagination, who lives by routine habit, "how things go, what is possible, what usually happens." The philistine is satisfied with "the trite and obvious, and is in just as much despair whether things go well or badly." This is "spiritlessness," and such persons "lack even the possibility of becoming aware of God."[21] In his journals Kierkegaard makes the distinction between the secular-minded and the sensual:

> It is, indeed, not specifically sensuality but it is out-and-out secular-minded-ness for a shopkeeper, a businessman, and the like to want to amass money; for a lawyer, a doctor, and the like, in short, a secular office holder, to covet worldly esteem—No, the sensuality, the debauchery comes first when one wants to be spiritual to boot, when one wants to gorge on worldliness and sandwich holiness in between. All this tear-jerking, all this ecstatic declaiming and describing of how truth has suffered in the world is—if one is himself secular-minded—sensuality.[22]

The philistine wants to enjoy "the benefits of religion" and have his secularism and sensuality to boot. It is precisely at this point that the aesthete and the secular-sensualist show themselves to be one, however different the facade. Both fear and reject the moral earnestness of Socrates' search for ultimate truth, the truth which is "really worth knowing."[23] These represent the lower form of life in Kierkegaard's reading of Socratic teleology. For both Socrates and Kierkegaard, persons were meant for more than the mundane, the secular, the sensual, and the trite. The "more" that Socrates sought and that was really worth knowing eludes the sophists in Athens and the bourgeois and the unthinking masses of Kierkegaard's Copenhagen, be they poets or inn keepers or prime ministers or bishops in the Danish state church.

Lest we think that Kierkegaard arbitrarily and self-righteously wrote off the bourgeois form of life, we should note that on occasion he had high praise for it. One expression of bourgeois life at its best is the character and moral philosophy of Judge William in *Either/Or* and in *Stages on Life's Way.* Contrary to what some may think, Kierkegaard had a very positive view of marriage and made it the paradigm of the ethical form of existence. Another context in which he gave high praise to bourgeois life is in *Fear and Trembling*[24] where he praises the religion of hidden inwardness as possibly the modern expression of the religion of paradox and absurdity, the paradigm of which is father Abraham. At their best the bourgeois form of life and the religion of hidden inwardness are authentic forms of life which involve responsibility, love, family, friendship, and the claims of civil society and the state. This is the high ground for bourgeois life, but one must surely note that it involves no visible religious qualities. The religious qualities of life are hidden in the subjective life of the bourgeois. The problem with hidden inwardness can be put in the form of a question: Did Socrates' earnestness cause him to hide his quest for what "was really worth knowing" or did he have to "go public" in the quest? The same question applies to the religion of hidden inwardness: can religion be, remain hidden, or must it finally go public? Turning to those who would attempt to rationalize the bourgeois life, Kierkegaard has a number of critical things to say. First, and most important, it must always be recalled that Kierkegaard's critique of bourgeois life is always tempered, like Plato's view of the merchant class, with the insight that the commercial and business classes are defined by their appetites or, in modern parlance, by their desires. Plato schemed to control the appetites, but Kierkegaard has no hope that the desires can be controlled. Thus attempts to rationalize the aesthetic life are vain. This leads to the loss of the value of life[25] and to the loss of the possibility of politics.[26]

In *Training in Christianity* (written in 1848, published in 1850) Kierkegaard expressed critical reservations regarding the religion of hidden inwardness and rejected it.[27] He had come to realize it was a sham created by the establishment to cover its self-deification by creating the illusion that we are all Christians, that, to use Reinhold Niebuhr's inspired phrase, that all good Danes are "moral men in an immoral society." These Christian criticisms of Danish bourgeois society and the Danish state church are founded upon a deepening awareness of the failure of the aesthetic as a form of the personal life and as expressed in the social order. These criticisms are noticeably dependent upon the Socratic critique of the age.

CONSTRUCTIVE SOCRATISM

Not only were Socrates and the Socratic categories used as a critique of the age, but they were also used constructively to model the form of the purely human at its highest, the universally human and the "highest between man and man."[28] Socrates is at once the most extraordinary and the most ordinary of men. "The truly extraordinary man is the truly ordinary man. The more of the universally human an individual is able to realize in his life, the more extraordinary he is. The less of the universal he is able to take up into his life, the more imperfect he is."[29] Socrates is for Kierkegaard the model of the universally human in its fullest expression.

The subject of the *Philosophical Fragments* is the attractiveness of humanism, and Socrates is the spokesman of humanism in Kierkegaard's thought. The humanism of Socrates is an idealized humanism derived from the ancient sources and enriched with insights from the Enlightenment and especially from Hegel. Kierkegaard's Socrates is not merely the witty and ironic Athenian, but is rather a man of moral and religious sensitivity and encompassing humanity. This is the Socrates that tempts us from being Christians.[30] Inherent in the Kierkegaardian interpretation of Socrates are many of the basic insights and interpretations of Plato's view of Socrates. Kierkegaard uses the Platonic doctrines in an unusual fashion to dramatize the differences between Socratism and Christianity and he does so with the utmost respect for the pagan and the Socratic, interpreting it always as the most complete example of the universally human. Let us briefly examine the doctrine of recollection to see how Kierkegaard handles it.

Recollection is used by Kierkegaard as the basic point of departure from the Socratic and in contrast to his own notion of the decisiveness of the moment. By this last expression, the decisiveness of the moment, Kierkegaard means that persons are entirely responsible for what and who they are because of the choices they make of themselves. This is certainly different from the Platonic doctrine of recollection, in which persons are naturally ignorant of the truth and can reclaim it through Socratic recollection or through the Delphic exhortation to "know oneself." In fact, Socrates is not necessary in the process of recollection, for a person is in principle in possession of the truth. A person is capable of solving her own problems and of delivering herself from all evils, moral and natural. Socratic and Platonic recollection is an exemplar and paradigm of the fundamental challenge to the Christian faith that humankind is competent to overcome all challenges. The challenge may be presented as a doctrine of the sufficiency of reason, of science and scientific progress, or an Hegelian (or Marxist) faith in historical progress or some combination of all.

However, if the moment is decisive and we are responsible for ourselves, if the problem is more than natural ignorance, and if we cannot unmake what we have made, then other remedies must be had. Whereas Socrates had no new information to give persons, the god-man is necessary and appears "in the fullness of time" to impart the "condition," to recreate persons, and to lead them to a new beginning. Recollection is the highest truth between man and man, but faith in the crucified is the only way to the truth about the relation between God and humankind if the human conditions described above obtain. Still, the humanism of Socrates is "simple, noble, and wise."[31] Socrates is for Kierkegaard the model of the fact that fundamental human insight into personal and social dilemmas is hard to come by, that the difficulty of fighting against ingrained and unchallenged social privilege and custom is dangerous, and finally that none of us "know anything really worth knowing."[32]

It is probably at this point of informed and ironic ignorance that Kierkegaard is closest to Socrates. However, Socrates, trapped by his irony, did not pursue the issue raised here far enough. Kierkegaard pursued the ironic ignorance of Socrates one step further. If we do not know anything really worth knowing, then it should follow that we are not really in possession of the moral truths Socrates thought recoverable by recollection. Neither would any truth learned by talking to poets, politicians, and craftsmen be decisive, for it is truth gained from others and not the inward subjectivity demanded by the oracle. (Know thyself.) Whether it was Plato or Socrates that slipped here we will never in this life know. A second issue, which even a Socrates could have observed, is the break between knowing the good and doing the good.[33] Kierkegaard actually blames the "Greek mind" for missing the issue, saying that Socrates is too great an ethicist to have missed it.[34] Yet, according to the record, miss it he did.

These issues surrounding the concept of recollection and the subsequent reflection on the difference between the Socratic and the Christian illustrate the high regard in which Kierkegaard held Socrates. Kierkegaard will not make Socrates a Christian in spite of himself. Socrates is the very paradigm of the pagan, and paganism is judged by Socrates just as Christians are judged by Christ. The deepest truth of Socratism is not, according to Kierkegaard, recollection. Kierkegaard explored the theme of recollection in the *Fragments* in order to distinguish Christian categories from idealism, and he used Socrates as the figure under which he characterized idealism. However, he could not give up his vision of the ironic and ignorant Socrates, and in the *Concluding Unscientific Postscript* Kierkegaard distinguished Socrates from Plato by saying that recollection is typically Platonic and that Socrates "concentrates essentially upon existence."[35] To analyze a purely Socratic (and non-Platonic) concept of truth coherent with an emphasis upon existence, Kierkegaard introduces the sentence, "The truth is the subjectivity."

First, a brief negative warning about this infamous (or famous) sentence. Kierkegaardian subjectivity is not romantic subjectivity with its arbitrariness, marginalism, and idiosyncrasy. "Subjectivity" is a ruled concept. As such it is neither relativistic nor nihilistic. It does enable one to give an account of the pluralism of religious and philosophical beliefs.[36]

Kierkegaard has no grief with what we may call "objective" knowledge as such.[37] The only possible problem with objective knowledge is that it can sometimes be construed to be the equivalent of or a substitute for subjective or essential knowledge. Objective knowledge has the tendency to turn every cognitive relation into a bipolar one in which there is an observer and an observed.[38] Subjective truth, on the other hand, requires that the person appropriate the knowledge and that the insight become a foundation for life. Socrates is the prime example, for Kierkegaard, of the subjective life and of the searcher for subjective truth. Yet in Socrates the subjective and the objective come together in a new way, and this is all important.

He (Socrates) puts the question (of immortality) objectively in a problematic manner: *if* there is an immortality. Must he therefore be accounted a doubter in comparison with one of our modern thinkers with the three proofs? By no means. On this "if" he risks his entire life, he has the courage to meet death and he has with the passion of the infinite so determined the pattern of his life that it must be found acceptable—*if* there is an immortality.[39]

In this quotation we see the intimate unity between objective knowledge and subjectivity. There is no subjective assertion that there is an immortality just as there is not one proof, much less three proofs, that there is such. Subjective desire cannot create worlds, neither mortal nor immortal ones. Subjective truth is the truth which becomes the foundation on which one builds one's life. Whatever is the case objectively, in the facts, Socrates has patterned his life acceptably *if* there is an immortality. If there is no immortality, then he has still patterned his life in the best possible model, as if expecting to be eternally what he is in time.[40]

Subjective knowledge is, then, a step inward and a step into the risks of life externally. Socrates may say that no ill can befall a good man, and in the death penalty no ill befell him from a Socratic point of view. The reason for this is that Socrates related himself at all times absolutely to his goal of truth seeking: he was related relatively to the relative and absolutely to the absolute. Socrates' divine vocation was to exist in an absolute relation to the absolute and in relative relations to the relative. Kierkegaard calls this existence relation resignation. To face the relative ends of life as if they were ultimate is to become a slave of the relative and temporal. It is to become an aesthete. On the other hand, resignation causes the individual to face the absolute *telos* as absolute, "not as one end among many."[41] We may not place God or the absolute telos, in this instance, Socrates' divine vocation, "on a level with everything else."[42]

The second and "essential" existence relation in the subjective life of the individual is suffering.[43] Kierkegaard's concept of suffering is complex and we will note only the major aspects of specifically religious suffering. Religious suffering further develops the dialectic of Socratic religious subjectivity. The characteristic of this suffering is that the person is unable to express absoluteness of the eternal and universal in the necessities and issues of life. "Just as resignation looks to see that the individual has an absolute direction toward the absolute *telos,* so does the persistence of suffering guarantee that the individual remains in the correct position and preserves himself in it."[44] Kierkegaard uses the concept of *Anfechtung,* spiritual trial, to designate religious suffering. If we think for one moment that we can express the absolute in the finite, then the concept of *Anfechtung* will cease to exist, for it is the same in the ethico-religious sphere as temptation is in the ethical with only one slight difference. That one slight difference is that in temptation it is the lower that tempts and in *Anfechtung* it is the higher that drives one back from the religious. This suffering is grounded in the fact that the individual is in his immediacy committed, and may even be absolutely committed, to relative ends. *Anfechtung* is the dying away from immediacy *(Phaedo)*, yet while dying away from it, fully realizing that one cannot by that sacrifice or by any other act ever express the eternal in time, spirit in flesh.

This suffering has its existential analogue in Socrates' irony, in the fact that Socrates knew that he knew nothing really worth knowing.[45] Theoretically it is analogous to the fact that matter resists form (*Timaeus*) and practically in the recognition that we cannot produce a just man till we have a just state and cannot have a just state till we have a just man *(Republic)*. Thus we see that the Socratic optimism of recollection has melted away into the realization that we cannot finally justify ourselves. I would argue that the development of the ethico-religious stage to this point in Kierkegaard is a valid extension of some elements of the Platonic picture of Socrates but in directions unknown to Plato. Still, there is a real question whether he has been untrue to the spirit of Plato's Socrates. After all, Plato was quite conscious of his decision to let Socrates drop out of the dialogues as an active leader and become a mere "yes-man." Perhaps Kierkegaard has been as true to the spirit of Socrates in his fashion and in the terms of Protestant Christianity as Plato was in the terms of Hellenism.[46]

In this way the Socratic optimism melts away into guilt, the third and final determinant of existential pathos in the *Postscript*. What began as a dying away from the world became then a suffering when we realized that we cannot express the absolute in the relative, and this finally produces guilt. "The consciousness of guilt is the decisive expression for existential pathos in relation to an eternal happiness."[47] But the consciousness of guilt lies still in the province of immanence, and guilt offers no resolution of itself. As a Jewish proverb expresses it, "Only a scoundrel forgives himself."

> If the breach (between God and man) is to be effected, the eternal must determine and define itself as temporal, as in time, as historical, whereby the exister and the eternal in time get eternity as an obstacle. This is the paradox.[48]

SOCRATES, KIERKEGAARD, AND CHRISTIAN HUMANISM

This is as far as we can continue with Socrates and Socratic humanism and teleology in Kierkegaard. Yet Kierkegaard argues that we must go further, that we will not rest till we "reach the target" which is God. Christians know that Socrates must be left behind, even as Dante leaves Virgil, and no one ever proceeded beyond Socrates more reluctantly than Kierkegaard. He asks, "Subjectivity, inwardness, has been posited as the truth; can any expression for the truth be found which has a still higher degree of inwardness?"[49] The answer to that question is summarized in the "Moral" that concludes the *Philosophical Fragments:*

> This project indisputably goes beyond the Socratic, as is apparent at every point. Whether it is therefore more true than the Socratic is an altogether different question, one that cannot be decided in the same breath, inasmuch as a new organ has been assumed here: faith, and a new presupposition: the consciousness of sin, and a new decision: the moment; and a new teacher: the god in time. Without these, I really would not have dared to present myself for inspection before that ironist who has been admired for millennia,

whom I approach with as much ardent enthusiasm as anyone. But to go
beyond Socrates when one nevertheless says essentially the same as he, only
not nearly so well—that at least is not Socratic.[50]

Another answer to the above question drives us deeper still into subjectivity than Socrates ever thought to go, that the subjectivity is the untruth.[51]
As interpreted by Kierkegaard, the journey from the aesthetic through the
ethical to the ethico-religious has not brought us to God but to a realization
that we are separated from God and to the realization that we cannot cross
over to God. To express the same in human terms is to say that we are
not at one with ourselves, that we suffer a tension between our ideals and
our moral reality. The reason that we cannot cross over to God or are mis-
related to ourselves, is sin, a word that is not necessary till this moment.
Kierkegaard's treatment of sin, is, again, like his treatment of all fundamental categories, detailed, and, again, we cannot pursue that detail here. Let
this suffice to summarize his analyses: we are responsible for the break between
ourselves and God and between ourselves and humankind as well as the mis-
relationship within ourselves.[52] The development of ethico-religious subjectivity does not need to address the issue of sin and indeed cannot, for sin is
a theological category that lies beyond Socrates and outside of the ethico-
religious.

Correlative with the consciousness of sin in its contrast with Socratic
ignorance is the distinction Kierkegaard makes between Socrates and the
teacher. The teacher, for all of Kierkegaard's artistry in presenting him in
the *Philosophical Fragments*, is none other than the God-man from Naza-
reth, a paradox in his own being and another possibility of offense to those
who do not believe.

These two elements, the consciousness of sin and the god become man,
complement each other as problem and answer. The response to these is either
faith or offense. With the coming of God in flesh, humanism is raised still
higher, for it is now possible to overcome the consciousness of guilt and to
fulfill our lives through faith. These categories belong to every person, for
"Christianity begins immediately with what every human being ought to
become."[53] What we ought to become is referred to above as (1) conscious
of sin, (2) faithful to the God-man, and now the third term must be added:
(3) loving. It is precisely in this context that the universally human takes
a new turn, for it is all too easy for love to be reduced to the immanent
as if Christian love were simply the highest and final development of friendship and eros. Rather, as Kierkegaard argues, neighbor or Christian love is
different from love conceived under the ethico-religious. It is to love as the
fulfillment of the universally human that we shall briefly turn.

Kierkegaard argues that the ethico-religious renunciation, the effort to
relate to the absolute absolutely and to the relative relatively has failed because
it is limited to finitude and so has an incomplete and inaccurate view of
what constitutes renunciation. Selfishness is in the heart of the immanent view
of man and love. Christianity attempts, and indeed has the power and authority
to alter and make persons what they should be.[54] Christianity can accomplish

this task, primarily, by transforming preferential love to self-giving and sacrificial love or, more briefly, neighbor love. Stanley Moore uses another term, spiritual love, when he writes, "Only spiritual love transcends natural determinations and inclinations, transcends the self-love wherein the beloved is only an extension of the lover's ego. Only spiritual love, then, posits the neighbor as truly the *other*."[55] The meaning of neighbor love is that all the love that one has for oneself is Christianly to be taken and bestowed upon the neighbor. This love is qualitatively different from friendship and eros, and, again, constitutes the possibility of an offense. One may say that instead of self-fulfillment, we are commanded to fulfill the neighbor.

Second, this love breaks with the inwardness expressed in Kierkegaard's interpretation and extension of Socratism. This love is what it does: it is known by its fruits. We recall that the ethico-religious was characterized by an inwardness that could not find adequate expression in the outward. The inner was not the outer, to parody an expression of Hegel. In Christian love there is also a desire to find expression in the outward, but here the desire bears fruit. To be sure, there is no act or series of acts that are unequivocally a work of love.[56] But one can believe that an act is a work of love in so far as one loves. One's own love is itself the proof that an act of another is itself a work of love toward oneself. "Love believes all things" and is never deceived.[57]

Third, the Christian concept of love is the final and highest expression of the inwardness of the person and it has this power because we are made in the image of that one who is Love Undiminished.[58] The nature of God and the nature of man are one and the same: love, self-giving love. This is the deepest subjectivity, the mystery of the Christian faith, the secret of creation and redemption. In the case of God, the inner does become the outer utterly and completely; less so with persons.

After the tortured journey through the aesthetic to the consciousness of sin, and from there to faith and the reconciliation of the person to God and to oneself, Kierkegaard's teleological humanism thus ends in a love that binds heaven to earth and on earth each person to his neighbor. Kierkegaard's teleological humanism ends where Augustine's ends, for we love nothing so much as to love and to be loved, and to be loved by God and to love God and through God to love the neighbor are the greatest of all loves.[59]

Notes

1. *Søren Kierkegaard's Journals and Papers,* trans. Howard V. Hong and Edna H. Hong, seven vols. (Bloomington, 1967–1976), no. 65.

2. Augustine, *Confessions* I: 1.

3. Martin Buber, *I and Thou,* trans. Walter Kaufmann (New York, 1970), 123.

4. This sentence is true unless Feuerbach's reduction of theology to anthropology is true. In that case the history of the word humanism is the same as the word God, only not so long a history, and is a demystified version of it.

5. Joseph M. Shaw, R. W. Franklin, Harris Kassa, and Charles W. Buzicky, *Readings in Christian Humanism* (Minneapolis, 1971). This book does not contain a selection from Kierkegaard, but it does contain a selection from N. F. S. Grundtvig

whose motto was "First the human, second the Christian." One can only wonder what was the criterion used to determine the category of Christian humanism.

6. *Christian Discourses* and *The Lilies of the Field* and *The Discourses at the Communion on Fridays,* trans. Walter Lowrie (New York, 1941), 245–246.

7. Harold Sarf, "Reflections on Kierkegaard's Socrates," *Journal of the History of Ideas* 44 (1983): 256.

8. *Kierkegaard's Journals and Papers,* no. 4299.

9. Robert L. Perkins, "Hegel and Kierkegaard: Two Critics of Romantic Irony," *Review of National Literatures* 1 (1970): 232–254.

10. *Either/Or,* trans. vol. 1, David F. Swenson and Lillian Marvin Swenson; vol. 2, Walter Lowrie, rev. Walter Johnson (Princeton, 1971), vol. 1, 19–20.

11. For an extended critique of Friedrich Schlegel on just this point, see Søren Kierkegaard, *The Concept of Irony with Constant Reference to Socrates,* trans. Lee M. Capel (Bloomington, 1965), 310–312.

12. Ibid., 306.

13. Ibid., 253.

14. *Kierkegaard's Journals and Papers,* no. 4281.

15. *Either/Or* 2:244.

16. *Concept of Irony,* 254.

17. *Either/Or* 2:245.

18. *Concept of Irony,* 246–256.

19. *"Det Bestaaende."* See *Concept of Irony,* 236.

20. C. Stephen Evans makes much the same point in his *Kierkegaard's 'Fragments' and 'Postscript,' The Religious Philosophy of Johannes Climacus* (Atlantic Highlands, 1883), 194.

21. *The Sickness unto Death,* trans. Howard V. Hong and Edna H. Hong (Princeton, 1980), 41.

22. *Kierkegaard's Journals and Papers,* no. 2752.

23. Plato, *Apology* 21d.

24. *Fear and Trembling,* trans. Howard V. Hong and Edna H. Hong (Princeton, 1983), 38–41.

25. *Either/Or* 1: 19–42.

26. Robert L. Perkins, "Kierkegaard's Critique of the Modern State," *Inquiry* 27 (1984): 207–218.

27. *Training in Christianity,* trans. Walter Lowrie (Princeton, 1941) 90, 208–209, 213–214.

28. *Philosophical Fragments* and *Johannes Climacus,* trans. Howard V. Hong and Edna H. Hong (Bloomington, 1985).

29. *Either/Or* 2:333.

30. Robert L. Perkins, *Søren Kierkegaard* (London and Richmond, 1969), 9.

31. *Kierkegaard's Journals and Papers,* no. 6871.

32. Plato, *Apology* 21d.

33. *Sickness unto Death,* 92–96.

34. Ibid., 93.

35. *Concluding Unscientific Postscript to the Philosophical Fragments,* trans. David F. Swenson and Walter Lowrie (Princeton, 1941), 184.

36. Robert L. Perkins, "Kierkegaard, a Kind of Epistemologist," *History of European Ideas* 12 (1990): 7–18.

37. Robert L. Perkins, "Kierkegaard's Epistemological Preferences," *International Journal for the Philosophy of Religion* 4 (1973): 197–217. Also, "Kierkegaards

erkenntnistheoretischen Präferenzen," in Michael Theunissen and Wilfried Greve, *Materialien zur Philosophie Søren Kierkegaards* (Frankfurt a. M., 1979), 385–407.

38. *Concluding Unscientific Postscript,* 118.
39. Ibid., 180.
40. Plato, *Apology* 41–42. This interpretation of the relation of subjectivity and objectivity is quite different from the usual. See Raymond L. Weirs, "Kierkegaard's 'Return' to Socrates," *The New Scholasticism* 45 (1971): 573–583.
41. *Concluding Unscientific Postscript,* 358.
42. Ibid., 359.
43. Ibid., 386–468.
44. Ibid., 396–397.
45. Ibid., 448.
46. We cannot spell out the details of Kierkegaard's views on suffering. A brief outline can be found in *Kierkegaard's Journals and Papers,* no. 4717. A better exposition can be found in Sylvia Walsh Utterback, *Kierkegaard's Dialectic of Christian Existence* (Ph.D. thesis, Emory University, 1975), 213ff.
47. *Concluding Unscientific Postscript,* 474.
48. Ibid., 474.
49. Ibid., 185.
50. *Philosophical Fragments,* 111.
51. *Concluding Unscientific Postscript,* 191.
52. Søren Kierkegaard, *The Concept of Anxiety,* trans. Reidar Thomte (Princeton, 1980); *The Sickness unto Death,* trans. Howard V. Hong and Edna H. Hong (Princeton: Princeton University Press, 1980). Among other good literature see Utterback, *Kierkegaard's Dialectic,* 112ff.
53. *Works of Love,* trans. Howard V. Hong and Edna H. Hong (New York, 1962), 174.
54. Utterback, *Kierkegaard's Dialectic,* 242.
55. Stanley R. Moore, "Religion as the True Humanism: Reflections on Kierkegaard's Social Philosophy," *Journal of the American Academy of Religion* 37 (1969): 15–25.
56. *Works of Love,* 30.
57. Ibid., 213–231.
58. Ibid., 19.
59. Far more complete as an interpretation of the concept of love in Kierkegaard is Sylvia I. Walsh's "Forming the Heart: The Role of Love in Kierkegaard's Thought" *The Grammar of the Heart,* ed. Richard Bell (San Francisco, 1988), 234–256.

10

The "Humanism" and the Humanism of Karl Marx

Danny Goldstick

On being asked to talk about Karl Marx at the Brock University conference on humanism, undoubtedly the most important topic I could have addressed would have been the practical question of humanism as regards society: that is, the relative merits of socialism versus capitalism; which is the social system where human life flourishes best? Instead of that, I am going to confine myself to the subject of philosophy as such—but without actually getting very philosophical. "Should I be textual or polemical," I asked Professor Goicoechea, and he said to be textual. So I have limited myself to quotations from the writings of Marx (and a few by Engels) with interpretive comments by me in between.

Let me start off with Karl Marx's humanism. I have in mind here his overall ethical motivation. Though strongly allergic to all *moralizing,* he certainly was very free with value judgements on people, policies, and institutions. But overall statements of what motivated him in his life-work are extremely rare. However, here is one, from a letter written to Sigfrid Meyer on April 30, 1867. He had just completed *Capital* and was travelling through Germany after having arranged for the book's publication there:

> Why I never answered you? Because I was perpetually hovering on the verge of the grave. Therefore I had to use *every* moment in which I was capable of work in order that I might finish the task to which I have sacrificed my health, my happiness in life and my family. I hope this explanation requires no further supplement. I laugh at the so-called "practical" men and their wisdom. If one chose to be an ox one could of course turn one's back on the agonies of mankind and look after one's own skin. But I should really have regarded myself as *impractical* if I had croaked without completely finishing my book, at least in manuscript.

Here Marx says it is the agonies of mankind that have motivated his life-work. That, if sincere, sounds like humanism. But there is hardly enough there to hang a scholarly lecture on.

Which brings me, accordingly, to the subject of Karl Marx and "humanism." I mean the *word* "humanism." a word very prominent in his writings of 1843–44, but scarcely seen after 1845. Marx's *Economic and Philosophical Manuscripts of 1844,* written in exile in Paris, are quite full of "humanism," as well as of Marx's first thoughts on starting to study economics and the literature of socialism and communism, and his initial theoretical response on actually encountering class-conscious, communistically minded workers for the first time. These Paris manuscripts of Marx were not to see the light of day in print until 1932, but later in 1844 (after studying more deeply, among other things, the role of the different social classes in the French Revolution) Marx wrote his first joint work with Engels, *The Holy Family, or Critique of Critical Critique, Against Bruno Bauer & Company,* a book based, according to its Preface, upon "real humanism," and this book actually came out early in 1845.

More than twenty years later, Marx had occasion to reread or at least again dip into *The Holy Family,* as we know from a letter he wrote from Hanover to Engels six days before the letter to Sigfrid Meyer already quoted. His host in Hanover, Marx writes,

> possesses a much better collection of our works than both of us put together. Here I also found *The Holy Family* again; he has presented it to me and will send you a copy. I was pleasantly surprised to find that we do not need to be ashamed of this work, although the cult of Feuerbach produces a very humorous effect upon one now.

It is time to pause and explain who Bruno Bauer and Ludwig Feuerbach were. They both were Young Hegelians, and both of them specialized in the freethinking critique of the Christian religion, criticizing Hegel himself for being Christian. Marx had been Bauer's associate up to 1842 and was then a strong and pretty uncritical admirer of Feuerbach up until shortly before he wrote in a notebook in 1845 the eleven brief "Theses on Feuerbach" which Engels published, after his death, in 1888. Although sharply critical of Hegel, both Bauer and Feuerbach employed the same sort of German-metaphysical *language* as Hegel, just as Marx himself did in his *1844 Manuscripts.* How Hegelian their actual views were is debatable. Where David Strauss in the mid-1830s had, in effect, founded "higher criticism" of the Christian Bible by tracing the formation of the Christ story to the gradual processes of folk myth, Bauer objected that the level of "self-consciousness" was far too low among the inarticulate masses to give rise to any theology; it took deluded geniuses, believing themselves divinely inspired, to make the Bible stories up *out of* the masses' vague conceptions. For his part, Ludwig Feuerbach theorized that the very concept of God was an anthropomorphic blunder, a projection of essentially human excellences, such as knowledge, power and love, into heaven, at the cost of thereby demeaning and impoverishing the lives of real human beings here on earth.

In 1841 Feuerbach published his book, *The Essence of Christianity*. In 1886 Engels remarked on its effect upon Young Hegelians caught between Hegel's systematic idealism, on the one hand, and unsystematic atheistic materialism, on the other:

> Then came Feuerbach's *Essence of Christianity*. With one blow it pulverised the contradicton, in that without circumlocutions it placed materialism on the throne again. Nature exists independently of all philosophy. It is the foundation upon which we human beings, ourselves products of nature, have grown up. Nothing exists outside nature and man, and the higher beings our religious fantasies have created are only the fantastic reflection of our own essence. The spell was broken; the "system" was exploded and cast aside, and the contradiction, shown to exist only in our imagination, was dissolved. One must himself have experienced the liberating effect of this book to get an idea of it. Enthusiasm was general; we all became at once Feuerbachians. How enthusiastically Marx greeted the new conception and how much—in spite of all critical reservations—he was influenced by it, one may read in *The Holy Family*.[1]

In fact, Feuerbach's atheistic outlook was close to what is now often called "religious humanism," a tendency sometimes found today within Unitarianism, for example. Feuerbach didn't quite advocate worshipping humanity, as Auguste Comte did, but he did favor a rhetoric of anthropocentrism which, in our more secular age, sounds distinctly religious.

At any rate, in their second joint work, *The German Ideology,* written in 1846 but unpublished until the twentieth century, Marx and Engels marked a parting of the ways with Feuerbach as well as with Bauer and the other Young Hegelians. The basic criticism made of all these German freethinkers was that their philosophies were still unmaterialistically "ideological," being ultimately addressed only to the realm of *ideas* as the key to human bondage and emancipation. The earlier *Holy Family* had already embraced materialism and communism but had not broken with Feuerbach. The actual "holy family" of that earlier book was in fact Bruno Bauer and his group, and in the *German Ideology* he is sarcastically referred to as "Saint Bruno." He had published an article on Feuerbach which also discussed the *Holy Family (Die heilige Familie)*. Marx and Engels write:

> Saint Bruno . . . now turns against the apparent "consequences of Feuerbach," the German Communists and, especially, the authors of *Die heilige Familie*. The expression "real humanism," which he found in the preface to this polemic treatise, provides the main basis of his hypothesis. He will recall a passage from the Bible:
> "And I, brethren, could not speak unto you as unto spiritual, but as unto carnal" (in our case it was just the opposite), "even as unto babes in Christ. I have fed you with milk, and not with meat: for hitherto ye were not able to bear it" (1 Corinthians, 3:1–2).[2]

"In our case it was just the opposite." The meaning, which no doubt is not to be taken very seriously, seems to be this: in 1845 Marx and Engels'

Young Hegelian readers were not yet mature enough to be fed out-and-out materialistic *meat* rather than mere "spiritual" *milk.*

Volume II of *The German Ideology* is devoted to a critique of what the authors call "German socialism" or "true socialism," a philosophically voluble derivative of French utopian socialism and communism which was then making the rounds in petty-bourgeois circles in Germany. It is possible to suggest that Marx himself had in 1844 been at least significantly influenced by this school of thought. The *Communist Manifesto,* written in 1847, devotes a special subsection to criticizing "German, or 'True', Socialism," which "went to the extreme length of directly opposing the 'brutally destructive' tendency of Communism."[3] The criticism here is mostly by way of ridicule. For example:

It is well known how the monks wrote silly lives of Catholic Saints *over* the manuscripts on which the classical works of ancient heathendom had been written. The German *literati* reversed this process with the profane French literature. They wrote their philosophical nonsense beneath the French original. For instance, beneath the French criticism of the economic functions of money, they wrote "Alienation of Humanity," and beneath the French criticism of the bourgeois State they wrote "Dethronement of the category of the General" and so forth.[4]

Here now are some quotations from that part of the 1846 book, *The German Ideology,* criticizing "true socialism":

To arrive at communism or socialism by way of metaphysics or politics, etc., etc.—these phrases beloved of true socialists merely indicate that such and such a writer has adopted communist ideas (which have reached him from without and have arisen in circumstances quite different from his) translating them into the mode of expression corresponding to his former standpoint, and formulating them in accordance with this standpoint.[5]

Thus "true socialism" is nothing but the transfiguration of proletarian communism, and of the parties and sects that are more or less akin to it, in France and England within the heaven of the German mind and, as we shall also see, of the German sentiment.[6]

. . . true socialism, which is no longer concerned with real human beings but with "Man," has lost all revolutionary enthusiasm and proclaims instead the universal love of mankind.[7]

The conditions actually existing in Germany were bound to lead to the formation of this hybrid sect and the attempt to reconcile communism with the ideas prevailing at the time. It was just as inevitable that a number of German communists, proceeding from a philosophical standpoint, should have arrived, and still arrive, at communism by way of this transition while others, unable to extricate themselves from this ideology, should go on preaching true socialism to the bitter end.[8]

There is no such biting attack on "true socialism" in Marx's Paris notebooks of two years earlier which we call his *1844 Manuscripts.* Nor is there any criticism of Feuerbach there. But of enthusiastic "humanism" there is plenty. We read, for example:

> . . . consistent naturalism or humanism is distinct from both idealism and materialism, and constitutes at the same time the unifying truth of both.[9]

Back to Engels in 1886 writing on Feuerbach, whom he criticizes, above all, for taking a wholly negative attitude to Hegel.

> Feuerbach smashed the system and simply discarded it. But a philosophy is not disposed of by the mere assertion that it is false. And so powerful a work as Hegelian philosophy, which had exercised so enormous an influence on the intellectual development of the nation, could not be disposed of by simply being ignored. It had to be 'sublated' in its own sense, that is, in the sense that while its form had to be annihilated through criticism, the new content which had been won through it had to be saved.[10]

Consider, for example, Feuerbach's attitude to Hegel's "negation of the negation." Hegel did not, to be sure, actually use the (Fichtean) terminology of "thesis-antithesis-synthesis," but in his "negation of the negation" concept he did view that which supersedes something as itself being eventually superseded by something else which, on a higher plane, effectively restores something of what was there originally. To this version of progress through struggle it is only too easy to object that it is surely far preferable to achieve the positive end-result directly, without having to pass through any phase of negation. As far as Feuerbach is concerned, the triadic movement in Hegel is simply a philosophical dressing-up of the Christian Holy Trinity. Here is what Marx wrote in his *1844 Manuscripts* about Feuerbach's attack on Hegel:

> *Feuerbach* is the only one who has a *serious, critical* attitude to the Hegelian dialectic and who has made genuine discoveries in this field. He is in fact the true conqueror of the old philosophy. The extent of his achievement, and the unpretentious simplicity with which he, Feuerbach, gives it to the world, stand in striking contrast to the opposite attitude [of the others].
> Feuerbach's great achievement is:
> (1) The proof that philosophy is nothing else but religion rendered into thought and expounded by thought, i.e., another form and manner of existence of the estrangement of the essence of man; hence equally to be condemned;
> (2) The establishment of *true materialism* and of *real science,* by making the social relationship of "man to man" the basic principle of the theory;
> (3) His opposing to the negation of the negation, which claims to be the absolute positive, the self-supporting positive, positively based on itself.[11]

However, in *Capital,* Volume I, chapter 32, Marx expresses himself rather differently. The historical phenomenon under discussion there is the way in which the capitalist system supplants individual handicraft production through an industrial revolution which centralizes the means of production and socializes labor to the point where capitalism itself is doomed since, for the first time in history, a mass class of the oppressed is "disciplined, united, organized by the very mechanism of the process of . . . production itself" and thereby prepared to act together effectively, once it sees the need, to fight for its own collective interests, and eventually to take over when the fluctuations of "misery, oppression, slavery, degradation, exploitation" get to be too much for it.

> The capitalism mode of appropriation, the result of the capitalist mode of production, produces capitalist private property. This is the first negation of individual private property, as founded on the labor of the proprietor. But capitalist production begets, with the inexorability of a law of Nature, its own negation. It is the negation of negation. This does not re-establish private property for the producer, but gives him individual property based on the acquisitions of the capitalist era: *i.e.*, on co-operation and the possession in common of the land and of the means of production.

Engels devoted Part I, chapter 13 of his 1878 book, *Anti-Dühring,* to a defense of this passage in Marx's *Capital* against Eugen Dühring's charge that it was the mere imposition of an arbitrary Hegelian schema upon reality. (Engels tells us in his Preface to the book's second edition, in 1885, after Marx had died, that he had read over the whole text to him in manuscript, and that Marx had contributed the greater part of a chapter to the book, Chapter 10 of part II.*) Although Marx does appear to be saying Hegel's "negation of the negation" concept is all wrong in his rough notes of 1844, and saying just the opposite in his *Capital* of 1867, there are in fact remarks in the *1844 Manuscripts* which describe the workers' revolutionary takeover as a "negation of the negation," but not at all on the sociological basis which Marx postulates in 1867; what it apparently meant to Marx in 1844 to call the workers' revolution a "negation of the negation" was a matter of registering how imperfect that necessary revolution was bound to be, though the shortcoming was something which could, he thought, be corrected later.

The next quotation from Marx's *1844 Manuscripts* comes from a passage where he has been discussing the pre-Darwin debate between biological creationism and geology and (alongside other, incompatible lines of argument) trying to wriggle out of the problem of origins by means of philosophy. (When

---

*The uneasy squirming of Terrell Carver's book, *Marx and Engels: The Intellectual Relationship*, is worth quoting here as an example of how a contemporary Western academic orthodoxy (that Marx somehow dissented from Engels' views on the dialectics of nature) can still be maintained by a stubborn enough author in the face of abundant and uniform textual evidence against it: " . . . if Marx found himself seriously at odds with Engels over the substance of *Anti-Dühring,* why did he not dissociate himself from it? . . . Even if Engels's story about reading the manuscript to Marx were untrue, or if Marx were not listening, it seems perverse to imagine that he ignored the content of the work altogether. Perhaps Marx felt it easier, in view of their long friendship, their role as leading socialists, and the usefulness of Engels's financial resources, to keep quiet and not to interfere in Engels's work. . . . It was possible for Marx to take the view that the first edition of *Anti-Dühring* would do more good than harm, since he detested Dühring's views and Engels picked on them without mercy."[12]

Darwin finally published his *Origin of Species* in 1859, Marx was delighted, though he did express some particular methodological reservations to Engels.) In the present passage Marx writes:

> Since the *real existence* of man and nature has become evident in practice, through sense experience, because man has thus become evident for man as the being of nature, and nature for man as the being of man, the question about an *alien* being, about a being above nature and man—a question which implies the admission of the unreality of nature and man—has become impossible in practice. *Atheism,* as the denial of this unreality, has no longer any meaning, for atheism is a *negation of God,* and postulates the *existence of man* through this negation; but socialism as socialism no longer stands in any need of such a mediation. It proceeds from the *theoretically and practically sensuous consciousness* of man and of nature as the *essence.* Socialism is man's *positive self-consciousness,* no longer mediated through the abolition of religion, just as *real life* is man's positive reality, no longer mediated through the abolition of private property, through *communism.* Communism is the position as the negation of the negation, and is hence the *actual* phase necessary for the next stage of historical development in the process of human emancipation and rehabilitation. *Communism* is the necessary form and the dynamic principle of the immediate future, but communism as such is not the goal of human development, the form of human society.[13]

It is interesting to contrast Marx's terminology here with the way later Marxism came to speak of a sequence from "capitalism" to "socialism" to "communism," using "socialism" and "communism" in senses which, at least at first blush, would seem to match (though in reverse) Marx's usage here of the terms "communism" and "socialism."

Not that the *1844 Manuscripts* are verbally consistent on this. Just a few pages before the last quoted passage belittling *communism,* we read, "Communism is the riddle of history solved, and it knows itself to be this solution."[14] But just what is the "communism" Marx was belittling? It seems to correspond to the "crude communism" described a few pages earlier still:

> Crude communism is only the culmination of this envy and of this levelling-down proceeding from the *preconceived* minimum. It has a *definite, limited* standard. How little this annulment of private property is really an appropriation is in fact proved by the abstract negation of the entire world of culture and civilization, the regression to the *unnatural* simplicity of the *poor* and crude man who has few needs and who has not only failed to go beyond private property, but has not yet even reached it.[15]

Perhaps some help in terminological unravelling can be found in Engels's Preface to the 1888 English edition of the *Communist Manifesto:*

> . . . when it was written, we could not have called it a *Socialist* Manifesto. By Socialists, in 1847, were understood, on the one hand, the adherents of the various Utopian systems: Owenites in England, Fourierists in France,

both of them already reduced to the position of mere sects, and gradually dying out; on the other hand, the most multifarious social quacks, who, by all manners of tinkering, professed to redress, without any danger to capital and profit, all sorts of social grievances, in both cases men outside the working-class movement, and looking rather to the "educated" classes for support. Whatever portion of the working class had become convinced of the insufficiency of mere political revolutions, and had proclaimed the necessity of a total social change, that portion then called itself Communist. It was a crude, rough-hewn, purely instinctive sort of Communism; still, it touched the cardinal point and was powerful enough amongst the working class to produce the Utopian Communism, in France, of Cabet, and in Germany, of Weitling. Thus, Socialism was, in 1847, a middle-class movement, Communism a working-class movement. Socialism was, on the Continent at least, "respectable"; Communism was the very opposite. And as our notion, from the very beginning, was that the "emancipation of the working class must be the act of the working class itself," there could be no doubt as to which of the two names we must take. Moreover, we have, ever since, been far from repudiating it.

It is easy to exaggerate the extent to which a change in the terminology used by a scientist and polemicist like Karl Marx will necessarily represent a substantive change in the man's opinions. But one point on which I think he did at least substantively recast his views after 1844 was in the area of ethical theory. In 1844 he followed Feuerbach in appealing to "human nature" as the ultimate standard for ethical evaluation. There is, of course, a very long tradition behind this appeal, stretching back to Aristotle and, especially, the Stoics, and most prominently seen today in traditional Roman Catholic moral teaching. Moralists appealing to "human nature" as their ethical touchstone need not agree on what *human nature* actually is. But they do all see it as somehow affording a standard of evaluation independent alike of supernatural revelation or of the personal feelings of the evaluator. Feuerbach considered that what specifically distinguished (and ennobled) the human race was an intellectual concern, going beyond all practicalities and the particularities of daily life, to universal truths in general and thus, when it came to human affairs, to the human *species* as a whole. A human is a "species being," he theorized, and, as such, ought to love humanity.

Marx too made much in 1844 of the "species being" character of the human essence. He accordingly denounced industrial capitalism for setting people, especially job-seeking workers, in hostile competition with one another, as well as for grossly *narrowing* the character of their work through the modern division of labor, and, in general, for keeping workers from engaging in *free, creative labor,* which he declared to be the human essence. I'm sure Marx *continued* to hold these social evils, with all his heart and soul, against the capitalist system. But did he continue to object to these hateful phenomena *on the grounds* that they were contrary to human nature or the human essence?

In Marx's *1844 Manuscripts* we read, for example:

The whole character of a species—its species-character—is contained in the character of its life activity; and free, conscious activity is man's species-character.[16]

Conscious life activity distinguishes man immediately from animal life activity. It is just because of this that he is a species-being. Or it is only because he is a species-being that he is a conscious being, i.e., that his own life is an object for him. Only because of that is his activity free activity. Estranged labor reverses this relationship, so that it is just because man is a conscious being that he makes his life activity, his *essential being,* a mere means to his *existence.*[17]

Some contemporary political theorists who give *lip service* to "human nature" as an ethical standard, in effect employ "is in conformity to human nature" as an alternative form of expression with the very same meaning as "is morally good." For them *conformity to human nature* cannot then provide a *reason* for calling anything "morally good." The Marx of the *1844 Manuscripts* was not like that. Rather, with Feuerbach and other *serious* exponents of the "human nature" ethics, he wanted to make the *de facto* truth about the human species, whatever it might be, an ethical standard for *judging* human life. But he gave this idea up, I think, for two reasons. In the first place, his studies led him to the conclusion, as he put it in *The Poverty of Philosophy* (1847), that "all history is nothing but a continuous transformation of human nature."[18] Already in his 1845 "Theses on Feuerbach" he had written in Thesis 6,

Feuerbach resolves the essence of religion into the essence of *man.* But the essence of man is no abstraction inherent in each single individual. In its reality it is the ensemble of the social relations.[19]

To say that human nature continuously changes over the course of history is not to deny that in some respects it stays the same. But equating the human essence with the changing ensemble of social relations surely precludes making that essence a normative standard for *judging* those social relations.

Marx's other reason, I believe, for giving up the appeal to *human nature* as the ethical standard for judging social life was the perception that, if coherent, such a standard could only be *conservative.* To make *de facto* human nature—in the end, simply the statistical norm—the ultimate basis for the ethical norm, is necessarily to end up endorsing as "natural" the existent status quo, while confining what can be condemned as "unnatural" to exceptional cases that deviate from its normal pattern.

Engels' thinking underwent an evolution similar to Marx's at this time, partly independently and partly under the influence of Marx. Here is a note Engels made later in 1845 upon a passage from Feuerbach's *Principles of the Philosophy of the Future (Philosophie der Zukunft).* Our quotation opens with part of an inner quotation from Feuerbach and then proceeds with Engels' comment upon it. (The second and fourth italicizations in the inner quotation are emphases added by Engels.)

"What my essence is, is my being. The fish is in the water, but its essence cannot be separated from this being. . . . It is only in human life that being is divorced from essence—*but only in exceptional, unfortunate cases.* . . . Only where your heart is, there *you are.* But all things—*apart from abnormal cases*—like to be in the place where they are, and like to be what they are."

A fine panegyric upon the existing state of things! Apart from abnormal cases, a few exceptional cases, you like to work from your seventh year as a door-keeper in a coal-mine, remaining alone in the dark for fourteen hours a day, and because it is your being therefore it is also your essence. . . . It is your "essence" to be subservient to a branch of labor.[20]

Feuerbach's "fish in the water" makes a reappearance in 1846 in the following passage in the *German Ideology* (Marx and Engels still permit themselves here a sarcastic reference, using "scare quotes," to the political project of bringing human "existence" into line with the human "essence"):

As an example of Feuerbach's acceptance and at the same time misunderstanding of existing reality, which he still shares with our opponents, we recall the passage in the *Philosophie der Zukunft* where he develops the view that the being of a thing or a man is at the same time its or his essence, that the determinate conditions of existence, the mode of life and activity of an animal or human individual are those in which its 'essence' feels itself satisfied. Here every exception is expressly conceived as an unhappy chance, as an abnormality which cannot be altered. Thus if millions of proletarians feel by no means contented with their living conditions, if their "being" does not in the least correspond to their "essence," then, according to the passage quoted, this is an unavoidable misfortune, which must be borne quietly. These millions of proletarians or communists, however, think quite differently and will prove this in time, when they bring their "being" into harmony with their "essence" in a practical way, by means of a revolution. Feuerbach, therefore, never speaks of the world of man in such cases, but always takes refuge in external nature, and moreover in *nature* which has not yet been subdued by men. But every new invention, every advance made by industry, detaches another piece from this domain, so that the ground which produces examples illustrating such Feuerbachian propositions is steadily shrinking. The "essence" of the fish is its "being," water—to go no further than this one proposition. The "essence" of the freshwater fish is the water of a river. But the latter ceases to be the "essence" of the fish and is no longer a suitable medium of existence as soon as the river is made to serve industry, as soon as it is polluted by dyes and other waste products and navigated by steamboats, or as soon as its water is diverted into canals where simple drainage can deprive the fish of its medium of existence.[21]

The final *German Ideology* quotation we need to consider here is from an attack on the moralizing "true socialist," Hermann Semmig. The extract opens with a quotation from Semmig's article, "Communism, Socialism, Humanism," and continues with a comment by the authors of the *German Ideology* (the italicizations within the inner quotes have been added by Marx and Engels):

"Relying entirely on the *moral core* of mankind, *socialism"* decrees that "the union of the sexes *is and should be* merely the highest intensification of love; *for* only what is natural is true and what is true is moral."

The reason why "the union, etc., etc. is and should be," can be applied to everything. For example, "socialism, relying entirely on the *moral core"* of the apes, might just as well decree that the masturbation which occurs naturally among them "is, and should be, merely the highest intensification of" self- "love; *for* only what is natural is true and what is true is moral."

It would be hard to say by what standard socialism judges what is "natural."[22]

Forty-seven years after first publishing his important early work, *The Condition of the Working-Class in England* (1845), Engels wrote a new preface for the first British edition of the book (1892), which included the following paragraph, in effect on the subject of philosophical "humanism":

It will be hardly necessary to point out that the general theoretical standpoint of this book—philosophical, economical, political—does not exactly coincide with my standpoint of today. Modern international Socialism, since fully developed as a science, chiefly and almost exclusively through the efforts of Marx, did not as yet exist in 1844. My book represents one of the phases of its embryonic development; and as the human embryo, in its early stages, still reproduces the gill-arches of our fish-ancestors, so this book exhibits everywhere the traces of the descent of modern Socialism from one of its ancestors, German philosophy. Thus great stress is laid on the dictum that Communism is not a mere party doctrine of the working class, but a theory compassing the emancipation of society at large, including the capitalist class, from its present narrow conditions. This is true enough in the abstract, but absolutely useless, and somtimes worse, in practice. So long as the wealthy classes not only do not feel the want of any emancipation, but strenuously oppose the self-emancipation of the working class, so long the social revolution will have to be prepared and fought out by the working class alone. The French bourgeois of 1789, too, declared the emancipation of the bourgeoisie to be the emancipation of the whole human race; but the nobility and clergy would not see it; the proposition—though for the time being, with respect to feudalism, an abstract historical truth—soon became a mere sentimentalism, and disappeared from view altogether in the fire of the revolutionary struggle. And today, the very people who, from the "impartiality" of their superior standpoint, preach to the workers a Socialism soaring high above their class interests and class struggles, and tending to reconcile in a higher humanity the interests of both the contending classes—these people are either neophytes, who have still to learn a great deal, or they are the worst enemies of the workers—wolves in sheep's clothing.

Notes

1. Frederick Engels, *Ludwig Feuerbach and the End of Classical German Philosophy* (Moscow, 1969), I.

2. Karl Marx, Frederick Engels, *Collected Works* (New York: 1976), vol. 5, 107.

3. *Collected Works*, vol. 6, 512.

4. Ibid., 511

5. *Collected Works*, vol. 5, 468.

6. Ibid., 456.

7. Ibid., 457.

8. Ibid., 457.

9. *Collected Works* (New York: 1975), vol. 3, 336.

10. Engels, *Ludwig Feuerbach and the End of Classical German Philosophy*, I.

11. *Collected Works*, vol. 3, 328.

12. Terrel Carver, *Marx and Engels: The Intellectual Relationship* (Bloomington, Ind., 1983), 129–131.

13. *Collected Works*, vol. 3, 305–306.

14. Ibid., 296–297.

15. Ibid., 295.

16. Ibid., 276.

17. Ibid.

18. *Collected Works*, vol. 6, 192.

19. *Collected Works*, vol. 5, 4.

20. Ibid., 13.

21. Ibid., 58–59.

22. Ibid., 463.

11

Marxism, Humanism, and Ecology

James Lawler and Zaid Orudjev

The ecological crisis has called into question fundamental assumptions of traditional humanism. Insistence that respect for the *human* individual be considered the highest moral and political norm is increasingly criticized as a form of "speciesism"—analogous to racism and sexism. Humanist arrogance is blamed for the disregard and exploitative approach to nature which has brought the world to the brink of ecological disaster. Of course such a disaster would be a disaster for humanity, as well as for nature itself. But as long as mankind is concerned primarily with human welfare, it is argued, and adopts a purely utilitarian attitude to nature, then so long will the problem of ecology be with us. Instead of regarding the natural world as a mine of resources—perhaps more limited than we had once imagined and so in need of a more cautious management strategy—what is required, according to some ecologists, is a fundamentally new idea of nature as having value in itself. Humanism should be replaced by some kind of naturalism. If necessary, human interests should take second place to the interests of those species whose claim to the earth preceded ours. The morality to which we should aspire is not one requiring careful use of nature, but one which demands a progressive withdrawal from nature, a suspicion and skepticism regarding all interventions in nature. We in the developed countries of the world should be willing to accept a decline in standards of living, already bloated to excessive proportions. If the rest of the world follows our present example there can only be ecological calamity.

Such criticisms are equally addressed to Marxist humanism with its conception of the human essence as an ensemble of distinctly *social* relations, arising from the transformation of nature and progressively evolving with the expansion of human productive forces. Moreover, the most casual empirical reference to the ecological catastrophes afflicting the socialist, or formerly socialist, world appears to confirm the belief that no "socialism" which stresses the all-importance of society and social productivity is capable of solving the problem of humanity's relation to nature. Here we will briefly sketch the elements of a response to such "antihumanist" criticisms as far as these can give us an occasion for describing the distinctive nature of Marxist humanism.

Humanism consists in the conviction that the spiritual and practical activity of individuals and states should be guided by the interests of the *individual* human being. The Egyptian pyramids, constructed on the bones of thousands of people, are a testimony to the achievements of human culture, but not a reflection of humanism. Nor should humanism be identified with concern for the general or abstract interests of humanity or "progress," regarded as a long-term goal to which concrete human individuals can be sacrificed. Against such abstract humanism, Marx and Engels defended "real humanism": *"Real humanism* has no more dangerous enemy in Germany than *spiritualism* or *speculative idealism,* which substitutes *'self-consciousness'* or the *'spirit'* for the *real individual man. . . ."*[1]

Respect for the individual, materially existing human being had become a cultural ideal with the Renaissance. In the philosophy of Kant respect for the individual human being as an "end and not only as a means" is taken to be the central imperative of morality. The problem, however, had always been the practical realization of this norm, not merely in the occasional actions of individuals but on a broad social scale. The ideal of justice, Kant held, requires that the honest person should also be a happy one, whose natural as well as personal needs are satisfied. Rejecting the subordination of individuals to precarious future outcomes, Kant held that a truly humanist morality could only be realized by God. Hegel was quick to point out the contradictoriness of such a position which in the name of humanism replaces human by divine activity. In the passage cited above, Marx and Engels likewise criticize Hegel's spiritualism and the speculative character of his notion of the rational state as the final agent of humanization. Marxism replaces the powerless moral imperative of Kant and the speculative political conception of Hegel with an account of social-historical laws of human development that both explain the emergence of humanism as an ideal as well as indicate the social-historical processes that tend to bring about its realization.

In his draft program for the First Congress of the Communist League in London, written in 1847, Engels proposed humanism as the goal of the Communist movement. To the question, "What is the aim of the Communists?" he replied, "To organize society in such a way that every member of it can develop and use all his capabilities and powers in complete freedom and without thereby infringing the basic conditions of this society." Such a goal is ultimately to be achieved by the elimination of private property and its replacement by the "community of property," communism. Communism is based on two points: "Firstly, on the mass of productive forces and means of subsistence resulting from the development of industry, agriculture, trade and colonisation, and on the possibility inherent in machinery, chemical and other resources of their infinite extension. Secondly, on the fact that in the consciousness or feeling of every individual there exist certain irrefutable basic principles which, being the result of the whole of historical development, require no proof. . . . For example, every individual strives to be happy. The happiness of the individual is inseparable from the happiness of all, etc."[2] The second point here is clearly the widespread recognition of humanist ideals, which have achieved the status of general social norms. But how should these norms be realized in reality? The community of property is to be accomplished "by enlightening and uniting the proletariat," inasmuch as while other subordinate and exploited classes freed themselves from oppression by becoming privileged classes in their turn, the proletariat can free itself only through changes which result in freeing all of humanity. Such liberation is not to be accomplished "at one stroke" but "gradually," since the "development of the masses cannot be ordered by decree." And "the first, fundamental step for the introduction of the community of property is the political liberation of the proletariat through a democratic constitution." The path of enlightenment and unity is preferable to revolution, but "the development of the proletariat in almost all countries of the world is forcibly repressed by the possessing classes and . . . thus a revolution is being forcibly worked for by the opponents of communism."[3] The particular circumstances of the modern proletariat, whose very existence is conditioned by the tremendous expansion of the productive capacity of humanity, push it in the direction of achieving ideals of humanism—a society in which, in the words of the *Manifesto,* "the free development of each is the condition for the free development of all."[4]

But if this is evidently humanism, is it not also a flagrant example of the attitude to nature which is responsible for the ecological crisis? Can we any longer boast of the "infinite extension" of the productive exploitation of natural resources? To reply to these questions it is necessary to examine further the Marxist conception of the human being. To the acknowledgment of humanistic goals, Marxism adds not only a specific conception of the way to realize these goals, but also a theoretical approach to the study of human history which offers an explanation of the emergence of humanist ideals and the conditions for their realization. In this theoretical approach we can distinguish both general methodological principles and definite social-historical conceptions. Central to the dialectical methodology of Marxism is a recognition that its concepts are not fixed and eternal, but evolving and historically specific. This is a crucial point, since formulations offered in the nineteenth century should not be understood as dogmas to be defended by identifying those aspects of contemporary life that confirm them, or to be refuted by stressing novel conditions. It is methodology that enables Marxists to enrich and develop the conceptions of Marx in the dialectical spirit of Marx and Engels themselves.

Three principles of dialectical method can be distinguished in our context. The first is that in the study of any developing process, only knowledge of the mature stage of that process makes it possible to grasp its essential features. If we knew nothing about the butterfly, what would be our conception of that species which appeared only in the form of the caterpillar? It is in this spirit that Marx wrote, in his discussion of the nature of scientific method: "The anatomy of man is a key to the anatomy of the ape."[5] Since human existence is itself a late result of biological evolution, of natural history, the study of the human being can give us a deeper understanding of nature than were we to treat prehuman nature as a self-contained totality. However, this principle is not so easily applied, since it assumes that we can have adequate knowledge of the human being. But human history is itself an incomplete process, and we cannot say that mankind has reached its mature state. Indeed the ecological crisis is one striking indication that humanity has not yet reached its own state of maturity.

The second principle of dialectical methodology refers to the fact that in developmental processes the emergence of a qualitatively new structure occurs first in a simple or primitive form within the conditions of the previous state of affairs which made it possible. But then, as the new system develops more fully, it tends to subordinate its preceding conditions to its own specific laws of development. Conditions that previously were the cause of the new system tend to become the effect of that system once it has reached its independent level of development. For example, the existence of trees presupposes the existence of soil, but in the course of its development, the tree contributes to the enrichment and transformation of its soil. The emergence of capitalism depends on the accumulation of money, on the one hand, and workers without their own means of production, on the other. These conditions were caused by processes occurring in the history of feudalism. As capitalism develops, however, it reproduces and expands the existence of such necessary conditions which originally owed their existence to other causes. Human life, likewise, presupposes a state of development of nonhuman nature. Primitive humanity depended on the availability of plants and animals, as well as other natural factors such as a temperate climate, which owed their existence to preexisting natural causes. But as human society develops, agriculture and herding replace food-gathering and hunting, and, with the aid of fire, artificial temperatures replace natural ones.

Is such active intervention in nature the beginning of its "destruction"? Primitive peoples, who regarded nature as something sacred and saw themselves as parts of nature, engaged in an *extensive* mode of appropriating natural resources. Given the natural process of population increase in early human societies, such a mode of appropriation would soon have stripped the environment bare of accessible natural resources. However, the development of human society beyond the most primitive mode of production corresponds to the *intensive* development of the productive forces. The cultivation of agricultural and animal resources tends to preserve nature, rather than to exhaust it, even as nature itself becomes increasingly "humanized." Nature is thereby conserved, not by being left to itself, but by its transition to a form that is increasingly mediated by human activity. Such development has not been without its own ecological downside. For example, as a result of the extensive development of early forms of agriculture, deforestation has often had ruinous ecological consequences which translated into famine for the human being. However, we should not say that early agricultural and herding societies represented the mature development of human society. The path of the further intensive development of agriculture has overcome the dire predictions in the nineteenth century of Malthus, who was the first to raise the problem of ecology in clear form.

A third principle of dialectical method is the principle of dialectical contradiction. New systems emerge as a result of interconnected oppositions within the previous conditions. Because of conflicts between the organism and its environment, new species emerge which are better adapted to their surroundings. Dialectical contradictions, unlike the contradictions of formal logic, involve intermediary connections between the polar elements. A definite "ecological niche" mediates the relation between the organism and the larger environment. This mediating environment includes contributions not only from the environment, but also from the organism itself. Species evolve through the mediation of new means of acting on the environment, new organs of adaptation. In arid conditions, plants acquire extensive circulatory systems. More developed animal species emerge with complex means of acting on their environments, such as the speed, agility, power, and intelligence of the tiger, armed with tooth and claw. Such highly developed species in turn tend to constitute environments to which other animal and plant species must adapt. But in prehuman nature such subordination of earlier conditions to newly emerging species is only an embryonic tendency. In the contradiction between environment and organism, it is the environment which is the predominantly active side, the relatively independent element, to which the organism must adapt or perish.

With such principles in mind, we can turn directly to the question of the human species, and the social-historical conceptions of Marxism which underlie its theory of humanism. For the human species owes its existence to a qualitatively new form of mediation between the organism and its environment. Unlike other species, human organisms are distinguished by the fact that they purposefully interpose between themselves and their natural environment objects of their own fashioning. While the earliest humanoids used the raw materials of nature, sticks and stones and spontaneously occurring fire, the modern human species emerged in the course of the active shaping of tools, as well as the elaboration of artificial systems of signs as mediating factors of human intelligence which become increasingly central to human activity. The interposition of an ever more complex chain of artificially created, externally existing mediating links between the human organism and the natural environment leads to the formation of a "second nature," a humanized nature to which the resources of the "first nature" tend to become subordinated. While the animal species adapts to an independently existing environment, the human species exists in an environment increasingly of its own making. While biological evolution takes the form of the emergence of new biological organs of adaptation, and hence the emergence of new species, human evolution involves the development of the powers of the human species itself, through the creation of new inorganic means of production and communication existing outside of the individual body, together with new forms of social organization.

In the course of human evolution, it is the nature and character of such intermediary links between the human being and the natural environment that comes to determine the historically specific nature of definite human individuals. A crucial element in the system of connecting factors between the individual and nature is the other human being, i.e., the social system of relations between human beings. Relations between the human individual and nature are therefore mediated by the relations existing between human beings. It is the nature of such relations, Marxism insists, that provides the "key" to understanding and to solving the contradiction between humanity and nature.

The causes of the ecological crisis can be seen in the growing complexity of the intermediary factors that simultaneously unite human beings to nature, but in increasingly complex ways, and separate them from it. When wealth can be indefinitely accumulated by individuals in the form of money, and the competitive pursuit of profit by a minority drives the productive system, all earlier natural limits to productive activity are destroyed—until the very existence of the natural world is placed in jeopardy. As long as exploitative relations exist between human beings, as long as the majority of human beings are motivated primarily by immediate biological needs while the wealth produced by human labor is not subordinated to the well-being of each individual, as long as distinctively human needs—above all the need for creative labor—are felt and satisfied only by a fortunate minority, then one cannot say that humanity has reached the point of having become truly human. Human society still evolves according to the main rule of nature: adaptation to the environment for the sake of survival. But in this case the environment is the human environment, which nevertheless evolves independently of people like the blind forces of nature.[6]

The conception of humanism advocated by Marxists today must take into account new developments of the twentieth century. In the nineteenth century at the time of Marx's writings, the proletariat, the class of workers that does not possess its own means of production, was only a minority of the population even in the advanced countries, while the majority consisted of the "petty bourgeoisie," workers who work with their own tools, land, or shops. With the growth of capitalist industry, coinciding with the development of the proletarian class, the accompanying ruin of the petty bourgeois majority gave birth to non-Marxist, "petty-bourgeois socialism." The hallmark of such socialism is its insistence on complete equality for all members of society, irrespective of the level of the productive forces. Its humanism is therefore an "abstract humanism," denying the concrete individual with his or her differences in abilities, needs, and activities. To maintain an abstract standard of equality in the complexities of practical life, and in defiance of the institutions of social and economic life that evolved over previous centuries, petty-bourgeois socialism requires the strengthening of the state-bureaucratic apparatus—in the name of equality and "man."

For Marxism, by contrast, it is primarily the inequality between the wealth and power possessed by ever smaller elite groups in control of giant enterprises and the rest of society that blocks progress towards a society based on real humanism. Moreover, according to Marxist socialism, which builds on the accomplishments of the market economy and capitalism, socialism is a transitional society from capitalism to communism, and therefore involves features of both systems. Petty-bourgeois socialism, on the contrary, takes a radically negative attitude to capitalism, and to the past heritage of mankind more generally. In backward countries in the twentieth century, with large petty-bourgeois populations, and confronting all the difficulties of cultural survival in a world already dominated by the developed capitalist countries, petty-bourgeois socialism, which often takes on Marxist clothing and uses Marxist terminology, has had a strong appeal. Socialism, so understood, is regarded more as an *alternative* to capitalism, than as a system which overcomes its eventual limits while building on its achievements. The victory of petty-bourgeois socialism in the Soviet Union took place in the late twenties, when the "compromises" of Lenin's New Economic Policy were ended, and the country embarked on the creation of the command-administrative economic system, which imposed "pure Marxism," i.e., petty-bourgeois socialism, by force where necessary.

Ecological catastrophes in the Soviet Union have been connected with the inner dynamics of the command-administrative system for which competition among bureaucracies for state allocations overshadowed the real needs and opinions of the individual human being. This result has discredited the idea of socialism in the eyes of many who seek a solution to the global crisis of the environment. And yet this crisis points out more and more clearly the need for world-wide limits to be placed on forms of economic development for which profits for capitalists or privileges for bureaucrats provide the main motives for economic life. The additional crisis of poverty in the third world intertwines with the ecological crisis. Only the intensive technologies available to developed countries (but often not used by them) can avoid the ecological damage caused by the cruder methods of production that are more accessible to poorer countries. More than ever before it is evident that the relation between mankind and nature is mediated by relations among human beings—even for the preservation of wilderness. Only by creating a truly human society, in which the needs of the concrete individual take priority, will mankind find its true path to nature. This cannot be a nature left to itself, but neither is it a nature to be exploited for narrowly conceived human ends. Rather, it is becoming more and more evident that mankind, as the highest product of nature and nature's way of becoming conscious of itself, must take responsibility for the earth. Practical implementation of such responsibility presupposes the emergence of a mature human society, and the transition to a form of human life in which, in the words of Marx who postulated the unity of naturalism and humanism, the productive activities of people are governed by the laws of beauty.[7]

Notes

1. Karl Marx, Frederick Engels, *Collected Works,* vol. 4 (New York, 1975), 7.
2. Karl Marx, Frederick Engels, *Collected Works,* vol. 6 (Moscow, 1976), 96.
3. Ibid., 101–102.
4. Ibid., 506.

5. Karl Marx, Frederick Engels, *Collected Works,* vol. 28 (New York), 42.

6. Frederick Engels, *Ludwig Feuerbach and the Outcome of Classical German Philosophy* (New York, 1970), 48.

7. Karl Marx, Frederick Engels, *Collected Works*, vol. 3 (New York, 1976), 277.

12

Zarathustra and Enlightenment Humanism

David Goicoechea

Whatever I create and however much I love it—soon I have to oppose it and my love: thus will my will have it.

And you too, enlightened man, are only a path and footstep of my will: truly, my will to power walks with the feet of your will to truth.[1]

Between 1650 and 1850 there was an interplay of four modern, intellectual attitudes: rationalism, enlightenment humanism, romanticism, and historicism. Enlightenment humanism flourished from 1750 to 1800. It was conceived from the seed of the new empirical sciences. It was born as a new aesthetics, a new ethics, and a new politics. It flowered forth in the American and French revolutions. Men like Locke, Voltaire, and the Encyclopedists conceived of it. Men like Benjamin Franklin and Thomas Jefferson worked it out. Men like Immanuel Kant saw it through to its demise. Kant's three critiques were within its spirit. His *Religion Within the Limits of Reason Alone* was already beyond it. Effective religion as ground of aesthetics and ethics was seen as exceeding the limits of reason. Enlightenment humanism trusted that man as a rational animal could so cultivate his reason that he could bring about progress for all humans. "Liberty, Fraternity, Equality" was its goal. Equal opportunity was sought for all.

Nietzsche's *Thus Spoke Zarathustra* can be read as the paradigm postmodernist assessment of enlightenment humanism. To focus upon enlightenment humanism in *Zarathustra* is to focus upon the lion. Zarathustra tells us that his drama is one of spirit becoming camel and then lion and finally child. The camel is the symbol of Christian Platonism. The lion is the symbol of enlightenment humanism. The child is the symbol of postmodern Dionysianism. But the story of the lion is complex. To understand the fundamental attitude of enlightenment humanism in *Zarathustra* we must rhetorically, poetically, and philosophically consider: (1) what the lion is, (2) how the lion came into being, (3) how the lion lived, (4) how the lion died, and (5) how the child was born out of the death of the lion.

In *Ecce Homo* Nietzsche tells us that his Zarathustra refers to the ancient Persian Zoroaster, who first set up the opposition between light and dark, between good and evil. What we see in *Thus Spoke Zarathustra* is that Zarathustra himself goes through three metamorphoses. As the Prologue begins we are told that he had come up to the mountain cave at the age of thirty. Now at the age of forty he is ready to go back down to the people to give them his new wisdom. Up at the cave between thirty and forty he had gone through a metamorphosis. He had become the lion. Throughout Part 1 he speaks as the lion. Parts 2, 3, and 4 reveal the detail of his transition from lion to child. Throughout the four books we get several flashbacks about his having become and been the camel. So Zarathustra is a personification of western man and of each man during his camel-like stage of Christian Platonism, his lion-like stage of enlightenment humanism, and his child-like stage of postmodern Dionysianism.

We begin to see what the lion of the enlightenment is from the very first pages of the Prologue. As Zarathustra goes down from the mountain peaks into the forest he meets the old, holy man. He says that he is going to the people out of love. He is going to give them a gift. As we proceed we shall see that the drama of Zarathustra is primarily a conflict of loves. The camel has the fundamental attitude which orders life around love of God and love of neighbor. "Love the absolute absolutely and the relative relatively" is the ideal of Christian Platonism. The lion has acquired a new fundamental attitude. His ideal is the gift giving love. The enlightenment humanist seeks to love all men and secure for them justice and peace upon earth. The fundamental attitude of the child will be a new love, the love of eternal recurrence, the *amor fati*.

In the first chapter of Part 1, "On The Three Metamorphoses," Zarathustra reveals two more essential attributes of the lion of the enlightenment, that the humanist secures autonomy and becomes a no sayer. We read:

But in the loneliest desert the second metamorphosis occurs: the spirit here becomes a lion; it wants to capture freedom and become lord in its own desert.

It seeks here its ultimate lord: it will be an enemy to him and to its ultimate God, it will struggle for victory with the great dragon.

What is the great dragon which the spirit no longer wants to call lord and God? The great dragon is called "Thou shalt." But the spirit of the lion "I will". . . .

To create freedom for itself and a sacred no even to duty: the lion is needed for that, my brothers.[2]

The lion is the beast of prey that wins his free autonomy, that says no and I will. The lion is a revolutionary spirit that destroys the old morality and the old religion in order that new values might be created.

But there is a fourth essential attribute that must be made explicit. It is the spirit of free inquiry in which the lion by operating within the limits of reason alone is free from any authority. Zarathustra calls this his will to truth. The enlightenment man limits his suppositions to that which is bounded by conceivability. Thus the lion's is an active spirit which (1) is based on the gift-giving love, which (2) says no to the traditional value hierarchy, which (3) is autonomous, and which (4) operates within the limits of reason alone. It frees itself from the tradition with the double negativity of its no saying and its limiting inquiry to reason alone. It frees itself for equality and justice with the double positivity of its gift-giving love and its autonomy.

Zarathustra explains this fourfold essence of enlightenment humanism throughout Part 1 as he presents the lion's criticism of the camel. This criticism provides a genetic account of how the lion came into existence. The criticism of the camel and therefore the birth of the lion centers around the phenomenon of resentment. Resentment is an attitude toward suffering made up of impotence, brooding, a reversal of the value hierarchy, and a creation of the rewarder-punisher God. The Jews were a little people living between the great superpowers. The Egyptians, the Babylonians, etc. would take turns molesting them and reducing them to slavery. That was their suffering. They often felt helpless and impotent to do anything about it. They brooded at their wailing wall and performed the sour grapes trick. They turned physical strength and beauty and health into vice. They turned their own littleness and weakness into virtue. They called it humility, meekness, justice. They saw God as a judge who would punish their enemies and reward their obedience. The Christians had the same resentment. They were martyred and chased around the catacombs. They were fed to the lions. They too turned their littleness and their weakness into virtue. Poverty, chastity, obedience became the core of the Christian attitude. The wealth, health, pride, and strength of the enemy was seen as vicious. They thought of their judgmental God as punishing their enemy with eternal torment. They thought of him as rewarding them with eternal bliss. Throughout Part 1 the lion roars against this value reversal of Christian Platonism. The free inquiry, autonomy, no saying, and gift-giving love of the lion arises out of saying no to the impotence, brooding, value reversing, and rewarder-punisher God of the camel. Resentment is shown as a poison root whose finest fruit is Christian compassion.

Zarathustra begins to reveal the genesis of the lion by criticizing the value reversal of the camel. The lion's roar is directed against the chairs of virtue, the afterworldlings, and the despisers of the body. The Christian Platonist's virtue is mocked insofar as it makes possible a good night's sleep. If such complacency is the goal of life, then Christian virtue makes sense. The afterworldlings know, love, and serve God in this vale of tears that they might be happy with him throughout eternity. The lion sees such an attitude as one of revenge against this life and the earth. The despisers of the body from within the framework of their Platonic, Augustinian, Cartesian hierarchy make the body far less important than the soul. They despise matter and its time and space in favor of the spiritual and its eternity. But the lion takes a new attitude toward the great opposition of being and becoming, of truth and appearance, of good and evil, etc. He argues that their traditional hierarchical relation is a value reversal. He argues that they are related dialectically instead of hierarchically. Just as you cannot have an inside without an outside, so does the implicit need the explicit, so does spirit need nature. It is the lion's task to translate spirit back into nature, to reclaim the proper valuing of the physical. The enlightenment humanist's no saying arises out of a criticism of the Christian Platonist's value reversal which is hierarchical and revengeful.

Throughout Part 1 there are not only direct assaults of the lion upon the camel. There are also many chapters treating traditional themes which reveal a possible threefold attitude toward them. Attitudes toward war, friendship, women, chastity, death, marriage, and children are clarified in their camel-like, their lion-like, and their child-like dimensions. These rhetorical chapters each reveal the passive camel, the active lion, and the receptive child in their relation to friendship, chastity, death, etc. These important aspects of life can each be approached with an attitude of impotent brooding. Zarathustra explains, for example, how a negative, brooding attitude can be taken toward marriage. Someone might want to marry because he or she wants to get out of the loneliness and misery of his present life. Zarathustra asks, "Do the animal and necessity speak from your desire? Or isolation? Or disharmony with yourself?"[3] Then he asks of the one who desires marriage, "Are you the victor, the self conqueror, the ruler of your senses, the lord of your virtues?"[4] Such a lion of autonomy is far more fit for marriage than the brooding camel. The camel is introverted in his misery. The lion is extroverted in his powerful control. These fundamental attitudes touch each aspect of one's life. One can approach them as a brooding camel. But one should approach them as an autonomous lion. That is the message of Zarathustra as he gives his wisdom to the people of the town of The Pied Cow throughout Part 1.

In Part 2, chapter 20, "Of Redemption," Zarathustra explains the root of resentment's impotence. It has to do with the line of time and time's 'It was.' In this very important chapter in which he first explores the relation between resentment, will to power, and love of eternal recurrence he writes:

> 'It was': that is what the will's teeth-gnashing and most lonely affliction is called. Powerless against that which has been done, the will is an angry spectator of all things past.[5]

Most of all this 'It was' refers to 'the fall.' The camel in his faith accepts the notion of the fall. He gets down on his knees and accepts the burden of guilt. 'The fall' is both Platonic and Christian. It is seen as the source of all suffering. Against it man is believed to be impotent. He needs to be redeemed and saved by grace. But the lion wants to redeem man from his redeemer. The enlightenment humanist thinks that man can lift himself up by reason alone. This begins when the power of the 'It was' is denied and emphasis is put rather upon the free possibilities of the future. The lion with his representational thinking believes that he can represent time as a line of progress without any necessitating past. The lion replaces the myth of the fall with the myth of progress. By saying no to the value reversal and the impotent brooding in which it is based the lion comes to birth as a no saying, autonomous spirit of free inquiry. He has redeemed himself from times 'It was.'

However, the enlightenment humanist does not see himself primarily as a no sayer. It is true that he never says or does anything without prefacing it with: "There is no God and man is not fallen." But according to Zarathustra the reason for the lion's contempt is his love. Because the lion has a higher idea of love than the camel, the lion has to say no to the camel's value reversal and to the camel's God. The camel sees God as perfect love. Zarathustra's arguments against God's existence all center around the notion of perfection and perfect love. The old pope who retired from service when God died says to Zarathustra:

> Whoever honors him as a god of love does not think highly enough of love itself. Did this god not also want to be judge? But the lover loves beyond reward and punishment.[6]

To the lion's mind the love that gives gifts is more truly love than the love that rewards and punishes. Zarathustra ends Part 1 in praise of the gift-giving love. The gift-giving love is like the walking staff which his disciples give him as Zarathustra is about to leave them. The staff has a gold orb on top that is encircled by a serpent. Gold is a rare and mellow value, like the gift-giving love. The snake loves the earth. He caresses it with his belly at all times. The gift giving attitude arose as a criticism of the judging attitude of the camel.

However, Zarathustra as the lion does not end Part 1 with only a praise of the gift-giving love. He is departing. He says that he shall return. But he says:

> With another love I shall then love you.[7]

The quotation at the beginning of Part 2 repeats these prophetic words. A new love is on the horizon. The rest of the book will tell us of the shortcomings of enlightenment humanism and how man can further overcome himself.

We can further understand the enlightenment humanism stage of Zarathustra's life by seeing how he lived as the lion. In brief, he lived as a bridge between camel and child. His dramatic career consisted of words and of works. He dispensed his words of wisdom in order to give honesty and humor to the lower man. He performed the works of love to give them a more healthy and hardy life. But slowly a silence began to well up within his words that made him doubt his words. Slowly a play began to flicker about his work that suggested a new speech and a new love. Soon after the enlightenment humanist began his new life as the autonomous, gift-giving lover who said no from within the limits of reason alone, strange symptomatic troubles began to afflict him. A tension began to grip him. His love became aware of its contempt; his wisdom of its folly; his will to power of a certain acceptance of fate; his enlightenment of a foreboding darkness. Zarathustra who was to be a healer became ill. He became aware of his weariness and shamelessness, his nausea and pity. Zarathustra, the lion, who lived as the bridge and the wanderer became the practioneer of creative illness.

In *Ecce Homo* as Nietzsche tells us about his *Zarathustra* he points out the special place of "The Night Song." After finishing Part 1 in northern Italy he went to Rome in the late fall. "The Night Song" was the first chapter that he wrote after Part 1 even though it appears in the middle of Part 2. It is a lament that poetically introduces his criticism of enlightenment humanism. It sings of the contradictions within the lion's life. It is an 'ennightenment' song about enlightenment. It resonates with the original Zoroaster's binary opposition between light and darkness. Zarathustra, the lion of enlightenment humanism, begins to purr after all of his roaring. The song reads in part:

> It is night: only now do all songs of lovers awaken.
> And my soul too is the song of a lover . . .
> Light am I: ah, that I were night!
> But this is my solitude that I am girded round with light.
> Ah, that I were dark and obscure!
> how I would suck at the breasts of light . . .
> I do not know the joy of the receiver; and I have often dreamed that stealing
> must be more blessed than receiving . . .
> My joy in giving died in giving, my virtue grew weary
> of itself through its abundance!
> The danger for him who always gives, is that he may lose his shame; the
> hand and heart of him who distributes grow callous through sheer distributing.[8]

Such became the life of the enlightenment lion. Like a sun king from behind the great, golden orb of his shaggy mane he roared out the message of the noonday light. But in his feelings he longed for the darkness of midnight. From the pompous heights of his moral pretentions he proclaimed his prohibitions. But he wanted the songs of the night. He began to feel his autonomy as a lonely solitude, his free inquiry within the limits of reason alone as a calculating coldness, his no saying as a weariness, his gift-giving love as a callous shamelessness that lacked the joys of receiving. By day he uprightly roared out the nay saying of his moral indignation. By night he longed for the yea saying of the cat on the prowl. He lived as a bridge alright; as a cold, callous, calculating, cacophonous means to an end, who was never an end in himself. He was a momentary footpath for wanderers. But at night he wished that he too could be a wanderer rather than one of those cold little stars up there all by itself.

The lion lived in the tension of the light and the dark, of proclaiming enlightenment but seeking 'ennightenment.' He died as his contradictions were unmasked. He lived by unmasking the resentment of the camel. He died when his own resentment was unmasked. In Part 1, chapter 1, "On The Three Metamorphoses," Zarathustra says:

To create new values—even the lion is incapable of that: but to create itself
freedom for new creation—that the might of the lion can do.[9]

Zarathustra here states that at bottom the lion of modernism retains the values
of the camel of antiquity. Hegel with his dialectics of progress by reason
is basically the same as Augustine with his hierarchy of ascent by grace. The
lion still says the no of resentment and not yet the yes of creation. Thus
Zarathustra continues:

But tell me, my brothers, what can the child do that even the lion cannot?
Why must the preying lion still become a child?
    The child is innocence and forgetfulness, a new beginning, a sport, a
self-propelling wheel, a first motion, a sacred Yes.
    Yes, a sacred Yes is needed, my brothers, for the sport of creation:[10]

The lion of the enlightenment died because it became evident that its no saying
was born of resentment and was not creative. Enlightenment no saying is
as much a nihilism as the Christian Platonist's denial of the earth. After his
poetic criticism of enlightenment Zarathustra spells the resentment out more
clearly in his rhetorical chapter on "The Tarantula."
    In Part 2, chapter 7, he shows how equality and justice, the great passwords
of the enlightenment, are rooted in revenge. Zarathustra is not opposed to
'liberté' but he is very opposed to 'egalité.' He says:

You preachers of equality! You are tarantulas and dealers in hidden revenge-
fulness! . . .
    That the world may become full of the storms of our revenge, let precisely
that be called justice by us. . . .
    Justice speaks thus to me: 'men are not equal.'[11]

Zarathustra thinks it is evident that humans are not equal in talent or
opportunity and that they never will be. Those who preach equality are taking
revenge on the higher man. They want to pull down all to the lowest common
denominator. The enlightenment humanist claims that inequality is unjust.
But such a judgment already begins to reveal the violent revenge of the lion.
    Does all this imply nihilism? The camel is an earth denier. The lion is
a camel denier. Both are no sayers. Neither can change man's situation. They
might invent atomic power, but it implies the atomic bomb. Sartre's *Devil
and the Good Lord* which is written in a Nietzschean spirit shows how the
lion with his gift-giving love can do more evil than the camel in his neigh-
boring love.
    Zarathustra is not a nihilist. His dramatic words and works show that
the life-affirming child can be born out of the death of the lion. The birth
of the child further reveals Zarathustra's attitude toward enlightenment
humanism. By understanding the child's sacred yes, we can better understand
the lion's no.
    The death of the lion has to do with the shortcomings of the gift-giving
love. Poetically we have seen that gift giving lacks the joy of receiving. The

one who only gives gifts becomes a cold, callous, calculating, and cacophonous star of solitude. Rhetorically, we have seen that the gift giver who wants equality and justice for all remains vengeful in his heart. Zarathustra also reveals philosophically why the lion must die that the child might be born. His philosophy centers around the concepts of will to power, resentment, and the eternal recurrence of the same. In a word, Zarathustra, the personification of the will to power, discovers that the receptive love of eternal recurrence is higher than the gift-giving love. The will to power is the life force insofar as it strives for higher life. The story of the demise of the lion and the birth of the child is told in two important chapters. Part 3, chapter 2, "The Vision and the Riddle," and Part 3, chapter 13, The "Convalescent," show us Zarathustra, the lion, becoming ill because of the snake bite. He goes into a coma for seven days out of nausea at the thought of eternal recurrence, which would mean the impossibility of the myth of progress. But he convalesces and arises as the child, saying yes even to eternal recurrence. Throughout *Zarathustra* there is an epistemological, metaphysical, ethical, and religious explanation of this transition away from enlightenment humanism and toward the love of eternal recurrence.

In the chapter on "The Despisers of the Body" Zarathustra shows what is wrong with the epistemology that wants to remain within the limits of reason alone. The representational ego, he claims, is just a tool and a toy of the great reason.[12] By the great reason Nietzsche is referring to what Freud will develop as the unconscious and Scheler as the realm of the heart. As Shakespeare might say, "There is more in our world than our philosophies will ever know." But Nietzsche's philosophy aims at dealing with that excess of perspectives which we know through emotional cognition. The styles of Zarathustra, the dramatic narrative with its personifications and 'animalifications,' its metaphor and metonomy, its typology and parody, extend knowledge beyond the limits of reason alone. We can know the shortcomings of the gift-giving love though our feeling as Zarathustra shows in *The Night Song*. We can hear the possibilities of the love of eternal recurrence as Zarathustra does when as a convalescent he hears the hurdy-gurdy song of the animals.[13]

The metaphysics of rugged individualism or autonomy is also overcome throughout the text of Zarathustra. The Dionysian metaphysics stresses the unity of life. In keeping with the Romantic criticism of enlightenment autonomy, Zarathustra would agree that, "No man is an island. We are all part of the main." Zarathustra stresses not only our unity with one another, but with all of nature. We are rooted in our land, our food, and our blood. The lion does not have autonomy from all of this. The cold solitude of enlightenment metaphysics is as false as the limited calculus of its epistemology. As Zarathustra convalesced he discovered his unity with nature and with all men. The child is aware of his dependence. He does not live in the hubristic illusion of autonomy. The child's metaphysics sees the one within the many rather than each isolated individual.

The child's ethics which goes beyond the ethics of good and evil is an overcoming of the cacophonous no saying of the enlightenment lion. The child says yes to all, even the small and the evil. The love of eternal recurrence is an unconditional love of all. Life is such that whatever is will return again and again. There is no progress. But that is fine. We need not say no to the camel and the lion. We can say yes to them. That is the will to power's highest way of loving, The *amor fati* does not imply the violent judgment that wants to change the camel and the lion. All that can change is our own attitude. When we say yes rather than no the camel and the lion within us are being transformed into the child. That is the highest work of love which the will to power can perform. Since we are all united, the child's love of eternal recurrence is a love that changes the world just by receiving it as it is.

But the child's yes saying is not only a playful and creative yes saying. It is also yes and amen saying. It is the saying of a sacred yes. Zarathustra is the most reverent of all atheists. His lion-like atheism is only a clearing of the way for the reverence of his Dionysian joy. The yes and amen saying of Zarathustra, the child, is his simple prayer of praise and thanksgiving. The new speech and new love of the child no longer give with the callous hand. They have become as tender as the feet of doves. The will to power reaches out to higher life by accepting all of life. Zarathustra has gone beyond the ancient hierarchy of the opposites and the modern dialectic of the opposites which demeaned becoming, appearance, the temporal, and evil in favor of being, truth, eternity, and the good. He now affirms all in his creative affirmation of the opposites. He says yes to the littleness of the camel as well as to the greatness of the lion. He says, "Let them return again and again." He says that because he loves 'ennightenment' as much as enlightenment. In the night he can graciously and joyously receive all.

Notes

1. Friedrich Nietzsche, *Thus Spoke Zarathustra,* trans. R. J. Hollingdale (New York, 1969), 138.
2. Ibid., 54.
3. Ibid., 95.
4. Ibid., 95.
5. Ibid., 161.
6. Ibid., 273.
7. Ibid., 103.
8. Ibid., 129.
9. Ibid., 55.
10. Ibid., 55.
11. Ibid., 123.
12. Ibid., 62,
13. Ibid., 234.

13

Heidegger: What Is Called Humanism?

Richard S. G. Brown

Heidegger's answer to the question on humanism stems from a series of reflections on the essence of action. In the "Letter on Humanism," Heidegger begins with the claim that "We are still far from pondering the essence of action (*Handeln*) decisively enough." (193)[1] To answer this question, Heidegger sets out to demonstrate that it is thinking, albeit a particular kind of thinking, which is essential to action, or more specifically, that thinking must be understood to be the genuinely human activity. However, to reach this conclusion, Heidegger has to establish the relationship between Being, which is the element of human thinking understood as action, and the essence of man as "ek-sistence."

"But whence and how is the essence of man determined?" (200) In asking this question, Heidegger seeks what he calls "the humanity of man, the *humanitas* of *homo*." (200) He wonders whether or not, in our modern, technological times, we are "really on the right track toward the essence of man." (203) Through a typically circuitous route, we discover that, for Heidegger, and properly for humanism as well, "Ek-sistence identifies the determination of what man is in the destiny of truth." (207)

Having sketched the route that Heidegger takes in order to answer the question on humanism, and even knowing in advance that the question itself is posed explicitly as a question concerning the essence of human action, we must still ask along with Heidegger, whether we can "obtain from such knowledge directives that can be readily applied to our active lives?" (236)[2] It is to be expected that this is precisely the question which should be addressed by anything deserving of the name "humanism." However, in the "Letter," Heidegger attacks traditional humanism in order to establish that thinking is the only genuinely human activity and, therefore, it might be equally expected that thinking would present us with the requisite directives that are applicable to our active lives. It is necessary to see just how thinking, in Heidegger's idiosyncratic sense of the term, serves as the essence of action before we can ask whether or not Heidegger can legitimately invest it with the status of the standard measure of human activity.

HEIDEGGER'S HISTORY OF HUMANISM

According to Heidegger's history of humanism, *"Humanitas,* explicitly so called, was first considered and striven for in the age of the Roman republic." (200) The metaphysical tradition from which all humanism(s) stems, however, dates from the time of Plato and Aristotle even though the first humanism to have explicitly used the term dates from the Roman period. "We encounter the first humanism in Rome: it therefore remains in essence a specifically Roman phenomenon which emerges from the encounter of Roman civilization with the culture of late Greek civilization." (201) In tracing the development of this tradition, Heidegger claims that humanism was the Roman adoption of Greek *paideia* and consequently packed within the term was an implicit distinction between the cultured and educated who followed the Greek *paideia* and the barbarians who did not. *"Homo humanus* was opposed to *homo barbarus."* (200) Though "humanism" begins in Rome, Heidegger considers that the "same" humanism could be said to have passed from the Romans through the Middle Ages, the Renaissance, and the eighteenth century (though explicitly excluding Hölderlin) and became the basis of such apparently diverse philosophies as Marxism, Christianity, and Sartrean existentialism. Heidegger's point is that "however different these forms of humanism may be" (201) or may appear to be, "they nonetheless all agree in this, that the *humanitas* of *homo humanus* is determined with regard to an already established interpretation of nature, history, world, and the ground of the world, that is, of beings as a whole." (202) What is *the* interpretation that Heidegger believes all humanism(s) share? Simply put, every traditional or historical kind of humanism has "presupposed the most universal essence of man to be obvious. Man is considered to be an *animal rationale."* (202) Whether Roman, Christian, Sartrean, or Marxist humanism, all of the superficial differences in form and expression among them virtually collapse given the underlying similarity in their singular view that man is, in essence, nothing but an *animal rationale.*

Heidegger's central objection to traditional humanism is not that its interpretation of man's essence is incorrect but rather that the interpretation itself, and therefore humanism, is thoroughly permeated by and impregnated with metaphysics and on account of this connection must fall prey to all of the criticisms and objections that Heidegger has against the metaphysical tradition.[3]

> Every humanism is either grounded in a metaphysics or is itself made to be the ground of one. Every determination of the essence of man that already presupposes an interpretation of man without asking the truth of Being, whether knowingly or not, is metaphysical. The result is that what is peculiar to all metaphysics, specifically with respect to the way the essence of

man is determined, is that it is "humanistic." Accordingly, every humanism remains metaphysical. In defining the humanity of man humanism not only does not ask about the relation of Being to the essence of man; because of its metaphysical origin humanism even impedes the question by neither recognizing nor understanding it. (202)

According to Heidegger, metaphysical humanism, in spite of its intentions to the contrary, actually forsakes man and the *humanus* in *homo* when it believes that it can adequately define man's essence in terms of *animalitas*. This interpretation, according to Heidegger, neglects and disregards man's essential *humanitas*. "Expelled from the truth of Being, man everywhere circles round himself as the *animal rationale.*" (221) Under the rubric of humanism and therefore under the sway of metaphysics, the human being, forgetful of Being, has striven to achieve his essential end as *he* views it (as world view or *Weltanschauung*) and therefore as he misunderstands it. In accepting man's essence as the rational animal, metaphysical humanism fails to recognize man's true or genuine essence as ek-sistence and what this entails, for Heidegger, in terms of man's primordial relationship with Being. In other words, it is Heidegger's contention that metaphysics fails to think the ontological difference between Being and beings and that it preoccupies itself exclusively with beings to the exclusion of Being to their mutual detriment.

> Humanism, therefore, in the more strict historiographical sense, is nothing but a moral-aesthetic anthropology. . . . It designates that philosophical interpretation of man which explains and evaluates whatever is, in its entirety, from the standpoint of man and in relation to man.[4]

This forgetfulness of Being and consequently, this preoccupation with human beings, permeates and characterizes all humanism. Insofar as humanism is, and remains, insensitive to the ontological difference between Being and beings, it is, and remains, metaphysical. Indeed, Heidegger declares, "the essence of humanism is metaphysical." (224)

HEIDEGGER'S CRITIQUE OF METAPHYSICAL HUMANISM

Heidegger's central thesis in the "Letter" is that *"humanus"* in the word "humanism" should be grounded in *humanitas,* that is, the genuine essence of man rather than in *animalitas*. On his account, man is something "more" than merely a rational animal. Heidegger explains that the "more" in this instance means "more originally and therefore more essentially in terms of his essence." (221) Even though metaphysical humanism explicitly and consciously desires that "man become free for his humanity and find his worth in it," (201) Heidegger claims humanism not only fails to set the work and dignity of man as *animalitas* high enough but, paradoxically it seems, it sets the value and worth of human beings too high when it remains oblivious to Being. "Even the highest determinations of the essence of man in humanism still do not realize the proper dignity of man." (210) Even the existential understanding of man as lord or tyrant of beings, Heidegger contends, falls well below man's true dignity and worth. In a nutshell, metaphysical humanism fails precisely because it is not humanistic enough.

> Humanism is opposed because it does not set the *humanitas* of man high enough; (210) . . . the essence of man is too little heeded and not thought in its origin . . . .(203)

What then, in Heidegger's view, is the genuine essence of man which would give to him a dignity and worth even greater than that of lord or tyrant of beings? Heidegger maintains that man's essence is his ek-sistence (205) and, as ek-sistence, the "counter-throw [*Gegenwurf*] of Being." (221) Much more than a lordly tyrant of beings, man should be understood to be an impoverished "shepherd of Being." (221)

THE ESSENCE OF MAN AS EK-SISTENCE

Heidegger holds that the essence of man is his ek-sistence with the term "ek-sistence" indicating that man, and properly man alone, stands in the lighting or clearing of Being and reciprocally stands out as man into the truth of Being. In Heidegger's etymological terms, the lighting or clearing of Being belongs to the there (*Da*) of the human being as there-being (*Da-sein*) who sustains in care the lighting of Being.[5] Insofar as *Dasein* is essentially care (*Sorge*), man must be regarded as the shepherd or the guardian (*Hirt*) of Being. The truly dignified, albeit impoverished, dignity of man lies exclusively in his role as guardian because it highlights man's care for Being. As Heidegger says, man "gains the essential poverty of the shepherd, whose dignity consists in being called by Being itself into the preservation of Being's truth." (221) Only *Dasein* has the essence or way to be of ek-sistence. Only man's particular way to be is "an ecstatic inherence in the truth of Being" (205) which is derived "existentially-ecstatically from the essence of the truth of Being." (212) It is as a "fateful sending" (207) of Being that *Dasein* is understood to be "thrown" from Being and, at the same time, the "counter-throw" of Being.

> Man is, and is man, insofar as he is the ek-sisting one. He stands out into the openness of Being. Being itself, which as the throw has projected the essence of man into 'care', is as this openness. Thrown in such fashion, man stands 'in' the openness of Being. (228–229)

LANGUAGE IS THE HOUSE OF BEING

One of Heidegger's best known announcements is that "Language is the house of Being." (193) However, it is important to understand exactly in what sense language is both the *house* of Being and the house *of Being?* Heidegger asserts that language is the house of Being because language "comes to pass *from*

Being and is pervaded by Being." (213, emphasis mine) In fact, language is thought to be the "lighting-concealing advent of Being itself." (206) Insofar as man alone ek-sists or stands out in the lighting of the truth of Being, man alone is able to dwell in and to guard the house of Being.

> Because plants and animals are lodged in their respective environments but are never placed freely in the lighting of Being which alone is "world", they lack language. (206)

To dwell in the truth of Being by means of language is the essence of man's being-in-the-world for "language is at once the house of Being and the home of human beings." (239) "Ek-sistence thoughtfully dwells in the house of Being." (239) Being-in-the-world furnishes man with the feeling (*Befind-lichkeit*) of being at home in the world and it is *Dasein's* nearness to Being or, more accurately, Being's nearness to *Dasein*, which Heidegger identifies as the "homeland" (*Heimat*); the "homeland of this historical dwelling is nearness to Being." (218)

However, what about the homelessness of modern man recognized, for example, by such thinkers as Nietzsche? Heidegger contends that man in the modern, technological age is no longer at home in the world and that this feeling of homelessness "is coming to be the destiny of the world." (219)[6] The homelessness which modern man experiences is a result of man, in the throes of metaphysics and nihilism, having abandoned Being for the sake of beings. Homelessness simply follows as a manifestation of man's forget-fulness of Being in the wake of metaphysics.[7]

In the "Letter," Heidegger bemoans what he understands to be the "dev-astation" (198) and the "downfall of language" (199) in our technological age which he judges to be "a threat to the essence of humanity" (198) and therefore to humanism in his proper or more appropriate understanding of the term. In our modern, unthinking age, human beings are uprooted and not at home because their language has become technological and bankrupt within the forgetfulness of Being. Consequently, Heidegger looks forward to some future time, the "essential future (*Wesenszukunft*) for historical mankind" (204), to-ward the "thinking that is to come" (*das künftige Denken*, 210) when thinking and poetry can again free language from philosophical concepts, logic (though not *logos*), metaphysics, technology, and even grammar into what Heidegger regards as a more original or primordial context within which man once again can be at home in the world, dwelling in the house of Being. *"Everything depends upon this alone,* that the truth of Being come to language and that thinking attain to this language." (223, emphasis mine) It is thinking that builds upon, although it does not itself build, the house of Being.

HEIDEGGER'S THOUGHTS ON THINKING

Heidegger endeavors in the "Letter" to initiate the return of thinking to its rightful and original element, namely, Being (*Sein*) by first pondering the essence of action *vis-à-vis* the essence of *homo humanus* as ek-sistence and then by relating them in turn to the ground of Being through language and through man's essential activity of thinking.

Heidegger declares that Being is the element of thinking. If there is no thinking apart from this element, then thinking can only be the thinking of Being. "Said plainly, thinking is the thinking of Being." (196) For Heidegger, this amounts to a circular definition (which is no disadvantage) insofar as any thinking which is not the thinking of Being is automatically disqualified as thinking *simpliciter*. However, when man no longer thinks the element of Being, he ushers in, at the same time, the beginning of metaphysics, and therefore of metaphysical humanism, nihilism, and technology as well.[8] "Being, as the element of thinking, is abandoned by the technical interpretation of thinking." (195) Metaphysics, in its forgetfulness of Being, conflates the onto-logical difference and collapses Being (*Sein*) into beings (*Seiende*). According to Heidegger, it is thinking, and only thinking, which can relate Being to the essence of man as ek-sistence. Only in thinking, understood as the original and primordial activity of the human being, does Being come to language. Being manifests itself through language.

Once Heidegger discloses that "Thinking *acts* insofar as it thinks" (193, emphasis mine), he comes full circle to the place from which his thinking began in the "Letter": the question of the essence of action. Heidegger claims that it is Being itself which presides over thinking and consequently over the essence of humanity as well. It is important to note that, for Heidegger, thinking "lets itself be claimed by Being so that it can say the truth of Being." (194) Insofar as thinking belongs to Being, it should listen to Being (196) but, at the same time, it most often does not. But Heidegger insists that even the fact that listening (or mis-listening?) has not taken place, witness the advent of metaphysics and technology, "lies in the destiny of Being." (210) It is also the reason behind the Heideggerian enterprise of destroying the tradition or overcoming metaphysics and, at the same time and in the same fashion, the entire tradition of humanism which accompanies it. It is Heidegger's hope that in the future, man as ek-sistence will again think the truth of Being but this hope too seems to lie in the very same destiny of Being.

> To think the truth of Being at the same time means to think the humanity of *homo humanus*. What counts is *humanitas* in the service of the truth of Being, but without humanism in the metaphysical sense." (231)

HEIDEGGER'S "ORIGINAL" HUMANISM

Heidegger asks, "But does such thinking—granted that there is something in a name—still allow itself to be described as humanism? Certainly not so far as humanism thinks metaphysically." (212) We have seen how Heidegger rejects any form of humanism which attempts to explain or to evaluate man from the exclusive and exhaustive standpoint of man as a particular kind of being or animal among beings. However, Heidegger does embrace one kind of "hu-manism" which understands itself from the standpoint of man's relationship to Being or, more accurately, from the standpoint of Being in its relationship to man. Heidegger can accept only a "humanism" which is sensitive to the ontological difference and therefore a "humanism" which has, in fact, surpassed or overcome metaphysics. If humanism *qua* metaphysics necessarily imports along with it the technical, theoretical, and therefore exacting rigor of philosophy as if it were science or if humanism necessarily entails the logic, grammar, physics, and rules of ethics which constitute its *Weltanschauung,* then Heidegger must reject it. For this reason, Heidegger doubts whether the term "humanism" can be restored or even ought to be retained as Beaufret assumes in his question.

> To restore a sense to it can only mean to redefine the meaning of the word. That requires that we first experience the essence of man more primordially; but it also demands that we show to what extent this essence in its own way becomes fateful. The essence of man lies in ek-sistence. That is what is essentially—that is, from Being itself—at issue here, insofar as Being appropriates man as ek-sisting for guardianship over the truth of Being into this truth itself. "Humanism" now means, in case we decide to retain the word, that the essence of man is essential for the truth of Being, specifically in such a way that the word does not pertain to man simply as such. So we are thinking a curious kind of "humanism." (224f.)[9]

Within the "Letter," Heidegger makes reference to both "original think-ing" (195) as well as an "original ethics" (235) understanding both expressions as part and parcel of his thinking concerning the essence of human action in its relationship to the essence of man as ek-sistence. It would therefore seem to follow that the most appropriate term for Heidegger's "curious kind of humanism" would be "original humanism" since the term "original" would have exactly the same meaning for Heidegger in each and every case.

The closest we come in the "Letter" to a *bona fide* definition of what Heidegger means by "original humanism" is undoubtedly the following: "For this is humanism: meditating and caring, that man be human and not inhu-mane, 'inhuman', that is, outside his essence." (200) This is not in itself an inadequate definition of "humanism," original or otherwise, but it is far from clear from what we have already gleaned about Heidegger's original human-ism that meditating and caring *about Being* not about beings can in itself prescribe or direct any realistic or practical kind of human interactivity or, for that matter, proscribe inhumane activity.

Heidegger himself raises the question of whether or not his thinking, which rejects metaphysical humanism outright, is not for that very reason condemned for being inhuman and inhumane. "Should we still keep the name 'humanism' for a 'humanism' that contradicts all previous humanism—although it in no way advocates the inhuman?" (225)

HEIDEGGER'S INHUMANISM?

It is both interesting and important to ask whether Heidegger's original hu-manism, which rejects metaphysical humanism, is therefore but "a glorifica-

tion of barbaric humanity." (225) It is also worth remembering that traditionally, the cultured and educated humanists were always distinguished from the
barbaric. If Heidegger's original humanism by his own admission contradicts
all previous humanism, it would seem only logical to regard it as barbaric
and therefore an inhumanism. In a similar fashion, logic also seems to dictate
that Heidegger's rejection of metaphysical humanism in favor of original
humanism is therefore not only an "affirmation of inhumanity" (225) but an
endorsement for a godless irrationalism which, in short, denies any transcendence or value. Is Heidegger's original humanism not simply an "irresponsible and destructive nihilism?" (226) Heidegger's answer is anything but
a simple no, arguing that his obvious "opposition to 'humanism' in no way
implies a defense of the inhuman but rather opens other vistas." (227)[10]

Nevertheless, such thinking should not be understood to be indifferent,
illogical, or immoral. Why not? What is Heidegger's line of reasoning which
permits him to reject humanism, on the one hand, but nevertheless not be
forced to accept inhumanism on the other?

HEIDEGGER'S TRANSCENDENTAL ARGUMENT

In the *Critique of Pure Reason,* Kant argues that the hallmark of transcendental thought is that it precedes empirical truth (as well as falsehood) and
makes it possible.[11] In a similar fashion, Heidegger argues that there is something more fundamental, primordial, or original about the human being as
ek-sistence than metaphysical humanism could understand. According to
Heidegger, Being is thought to be prior to everything else, if not in any strictly temporal or logical sense, then at least in a conceptual sense. Heidegger
claims that metaphysics actually conceals the truth both of Being and of *Dasein's* essential relationship to the truth of Being. Thinking therefore must
overcome metaphysics.

> Thinking does not overcome metaphysics by climbing still higher, surmounting
> it, transcending it somehow or other; thinking overcomes metaphysics by
> climbing back down into the nearness of the nearest (231). . . . the thinking
> that thinks from the question concerning the truth of Being questions more
> primordially than metaphysics can. (230)

Heidegger appears to adopt a transcendental argument when he says that:
". . . the task of thinking what is still principally to be thought and, as Being
is prior to all beings, is their guarantor and their truth." (232) Using this
form of argument, Heidegger demonstrates how metaphysical questions, as
well as metaphysical labels, are derived from the nonmetaphysical truth of
Being. For example, what we understand by the word "God" depends on
a more fundamental, primordial, or original question, namely, the essence
of divinity. However, the question of the essence of divinity cannot be answered
without recourse to the more fundamental question concerning the essence
of the holy. However, this is not thinking's bottom line. The most fundamental

and primordial question to ask (and hopefully to answer) has to do with the truth of Being. Thinking therefore precedes such philosophical and metaphysical distinctions as theism and atheism, ethics and ontology (236), theory and practice (236, 240) and in doing so, grounds them or makes them possible. Such primordial or original thinking of the truth of Being, Heidegger says, "comes to pass before" metaphysics and insofar as it serves as the guarantor of such concepts, they themselves do not, and cannot, apply to original thinking. The transcendental truth of Being, it seems, precedes metaphysical truth (as well as falsehood) and makes it possible. For this reason, Heidegger will not permit such philosophical distinctions as subject-object, possible-actual, theoretical-practical, or essence-existence to apply to his "original humanism."

> The questionable essence of humanism has likewise compelled us to think the essence of man more primordially. With regard to this more essential *humanitas* of *homo humanus* there arises the possiblilty of restoring to the word 'humanism' a historical sense that is older than its oldest meaning chronologically reckoned. (224)

THREE FLAWS

If we accept Heidegger's reasons for proclaiming that his original humanism, even though it is an explicit rejection of metaphysical humanism, is not *ipso facto* inhuman or inhumane (many would not be so generous), it is still possible, and necessary, to identify three flaws which may puncture Heidegger's case concerning the merits of an original humanism.

The most telling as well as the most widespread of the three is that Heidegger's original humanism is riddled with the kind of vagueness and arbitrariness which could easily precipitate into inhumanism. This follows, in effect, from the "transcendental" thinking which ranks and reveres the "law of Being" over both the laws of logic and the rules of human praxis. Heidegger makes no bones about this ranking. "The fittingness of the saying of Being, as of the destiny of truth, is the first law of thinking—not the rules of logic which can become rules only on the basis of the law of Being." (241) Indeed, as if it were not clear enough already: "More essential for instituting rules is that man find his way to his abode in the truth of Being. This abode first yields the experience of something we can hold on to." (239) The question is, hold onto what exactly? What is there to get a grip on?[12]

Heidegger claims in the "Letter" that ". . . there is a thinking more rigorous than the conceptual." (235) This rigorous thinking can only be thinking about Being. Heidegger places the human activity of thinking and poetry against conceptual, metaphysical, and technical thinking. The difficulty with Heidegger's thinking, however, is not just that the realm of thinking is closed to metaphysics and therefore suspiciously immune to critical inspection but, more importantly, Heidegger claims that his original humanism constitutes the "original ethics" and therefore should precede and ground all human activity and practice. Although Heidegger says that his thinking has no result, it is nevertheless a deed (*Tun*). But a deed that also surpasses all *"praxis."* (239) It is far from being a comforting thought that the alleged ground of human praxis is poetically and metaphorically voiced in such terms as silence, mystery, the nameless, and simplicity with access, if any access at all, only to a sensitive few. And it must also be remembered that, for Heidegger, man's access to the thought of Being as the ground of praxis is itself determined or ruled by Being.

In the "Letter," Heidegger elucidates that "Being remains mysterious . . . ." (212)[13] Heidegger also describes such thinking as "simple." He informs us, for example, that thinking "gathers language into simple saying . . . as clouds are the clouds of the sky." (242) However, the alleged, or even acknowledged, simplicity of such original thinking does not make it easier to understand what the rule or law of Being is or how, for that matter, any directives for human activity might, or might not, be disclosed in accordance with it. "What is strange in the thinking of Being is its simplicity. Precisely this keeps us from it." (240) "Through its simple essence the thinking of Being makes itself unrecognizable to us." (240) It is difficult not to believe that thinking which is simple to be thought (222) and a task of simple inquiry (227) is not "prey to arbitrariness." (240) But how can Heidegger claim that such thinking is not arbitrary? If it is not arbitrary, "Whence does thinking take its measure? What law governs its deed?" (240) Against what standard does Heidegger measure the truth of Being or even the value of the truth disclosed to man by Being?

The perceived adequacy or inadequacy of Heidegger's answer may depend on whether the reader of the "Letter" is conceptually or poetically bent. Heidegger's answer is modest: "Speaking lets the simplicity of the manifold of thinking's dimensions rule." (195)[14] Heidegger claims that the human being is subordinate to the call or rule of Being and must therefore prepare and await Being's claim. Davidson argues that if this is Heidegger's solution to the question of humanism, it dissolves into Being's indifference toward, if not suppression of, the human being. Being's claim on man can be and has been misunderstood (by Heidegger himself it seems) and can therefore just as easily lead man astray towards inhumanity than toward the essence of man as *humanitas* and care. Davidson therefore rightly charges Heidegger's thinking with arbitrariness. "When the realm of arbitrariness joins with the suppression of the human, we can be pushed to the point of no return, facing the brink of an abyss."[15]

In the same vein, Bernstein does not put much faith, or positive philosophical value, on Heidegger's answer to the question of humanism, namely, that we may one day hope to answer the silent call of Being.

But I want to argue that such a response to the question of humanism is not only totally inadequate, but is itself extremely dangerous—dangerous because it seduces us into thinking that all human activity (other than the activity of thinking) reduces itself (flattens out) into *Gestell,* manipulation, control, will to will, nihilism; dangerous because it virtually closes off the space for attending to the type of thinking and acting that can foster human solidarity and community.[16]

The second flaw to explore is that a good case can be made for regarding Heidegger's original humanism as pessimistic. There is nothing wrong with pessimism *per se* (although a pessimistic humanism would be a strange beast). The difficulty is that Heidegger's original humanism rests squarely on his hope in some future thinking of the truth of Being. If it turns out that there is very little reason for Heidegger or anyone else to be hopeful that such thinking will ever, in fact, occur, it would deflate that hope which is already precarious enough.

If a pessimist is an optimist with experience, then it is probably fair to say that Heidegger's attitude about the possibility of becoming free from metaphysics, nihilism, and technicity and therefore free for thinking the truth of Being begins on an optimistic note in *Being and Time* (1927) and then hits a high, though very sour, note in the "Rectorship Address" of 1933. By the time of the "Letter" (1947), however, Heidegger can only say that "Being is still waiting for the time when it will become thought-provoking to man." (203) "Before he speaks man must first let himself be claimed again by Being, taking the risk that under this claim he will seldom have much to say." (199; cf. 223) Finally comes the now famous statement from Heidegger's *Der Spiegel* interview (1966).

> Only a god can save us. The only possibility available to us is that by thinking and poetizing we prepare a readiness for the appearance of a god, or for the absence of a god in [our] decline, insofar as in view of the absent god we are in a state of decline.[17]

Bernstein laments that "it is *almost* as if Heidegger has completely 'given up' on the *humanitas* of *homo humanus,* despairing of even the possibility that man can come into the clearing of Being . . . ."[18] Rorty's explanation for Heidegger's increasingly pessimistic thinking is because Heidegger decided that since the Nazis didn't work out, only a god can save us now.[19] It can only be conjectured whether or not Heidegger's pessimistic turn was occasioned by his (un)timely realization that the National Socialist Movement was not so much the cure for nihilism as it was nihilism itself in disguise.[20]

The third flaw with Heidegger's original humanism is that it is prejudiced in favor of the German and Greek languages and therefore parochial and narrow minded.[21] If we extend Heidegger's announcement that language is the house of Being, are we to understand that all languages are different houses in the same neighborhood or simply different rooms within one and the same house? Heidegger states quite clearly, albeit unconvincingly, that "I am thinking of the special inner kinship between the German language and the language of the Greeks and their thought. This is something that the French confirm for me again and again today. When they begin to think, they speak German. They assure [me] that they do not succeed with their own language."[22] It is simply prejudice within a global village to believe that the Greek and German languages are attuned in some privileged way to the truth of Being while English, French, Chinese, Japanese, or Sanskrit are not.

Notes

1. Martin Heidegger, "Letter on Humanism," in *Basic Writings,* trans. David
Farrell Krell (New York, 1977), 189–242. All page references to "Letter on Humanism"
are internalized.

2. Martin Heidegger, " 'Only a God Can Save Us': The *Spiegel* Interview (1966),"
trans. by William J. Richardson in *Martin Heidegger: The Man and the Thinker,*
ed. Thomas Sheehan (Chicago, 1981), 45–75.

3. Heidegger will eventually argue that ". . . even what we attribute to man
as *animalitas* on the basis of the comparison with 'beast' is itself grounded in the
essence of ek-sistence." (204) In "The Age of the World Picture" (written in 1938),
Heidegger says that "What is decisive is that man himself takes this viewpoint as
produced by himself, maintains it voluntarily as that taken by himself, and as the
basis of a possible development of humanity." Martin Heidegger, "The Age of the
World Picture," *The Question Concerning Technology and Other Essays,* trans. William Lovett (New York, 1977), 132. In "Plato's Doctrine of Truth," published in 1947
as a companion piece to the "Letter," Heidegger says that "The beginning of metaphysics in Plato's thinking is at the same time the beginning of 'Humanism:' This
word ought to be thought of essentially here and therefore in its broadest meaning.
Hereafter then 'Humanism' means the process bound up with the beginning, unfolding, and end of metaphysics so that man, after various considerations, but always
knowingly, moves into a position in the midst of beings without becoming the highest
being." Martin Heidegger, "Plato's Doctrine of Truth," trans. by John Barlow, in
Philosophy in the Twentieth Century, ed. W. Barrett and H. Aiken (New York, 1962),
269. Magnus relates humanism to the epistemological or Platonic concept of truth
which ". . . makes truth dependent upon man, explicitly or implicitly, in his dealings
with beings." Bernd Magnus, *Heidegger's Metahistory of Philosophy: 'Amor Fati',
Being and Truth* (The Hague, 1970), 77.

4. Heidegger, "The Age of the World Picture," 133.

5. Bernstein complains that ". . . it is not the authentic care and solicitude of
other human beings that is his [Heidegger's] major concern [in his later writings],
but the care of Being and Language itself." Richard J. Bernstein, "Heidegger on
Humanism," *Praxis International* 5 (1985): 106. Although Bernstein's observation is
correct, his complaint would be misplaced if authentic care and solicitude for other
human beings followed from the care human beings have for Being.

6. Compare *Heimat* (home or homeland), *Geheimnis* (mystery), and *Unheim-
lickeit* (uncanniness or the feeling of not being "at home").

7. According to Heidegger, ". . . technicity increasingly dislodges man and
uproots him from the earth." (*Spiegel,* 56) In the interview, Heidegger cites Rene
Char: "This poet, who certainly is open to no suspicion of sentimentality or of glorifying
the idyllic, said to me that the uprooting of man that is now taking place is the
end [of everything human], unless thinking and poetizing once again regain [their]
non-violent power." (*Spiegel,* 56) For Heidegger, who might actually be suspected
of sentimentality, ". . . everything essential and of great magnitude has arisen only
out of the fact that man had a home and was rooted in a tradition." (*Spiegel,* 57)

8. "What emerges in Heidegger's writings after *Sein and Zeit* is a reiterated
series of hidden identities: philosophy = metaphysics = humanism = nihilism =
enframing . . .". Bernstein, "Heidegger on Humanism," 101.

9. ". . . Heidegger's thought is anti-humanist, better prehumanist . . . ." "Since
the humanisms of the tradition are intrinsically correlative with the metaphysics that
is thus surpassed, the conception of man as ek-sistence is in effect the surpassing

of humanism, but inasmuch as it discerns man's true value, is it not by that very fact a humanism of a higher kind? Whether or not the word be retained is a matter of indifference." William J. Richardson, *Heidegger: Through Phenomenology to Thought* (The Hague, 1967), 531 and 552.

10. Heidegger says, "To think against 'logic' does not mean to break a lance for the illogical but simply to trace in thought the *logos* and its essence which appeared in the dawn of thinking, that is, to exert ourselves for the first time for preparing for such reflection. Of what value are even far-reaching systems of logic to us if, without really knowing what they are doing, they recoil before the task of simply inquiring into the essence of *logos*?" (227) With the alteration of a few words, the paragraph could be changed into Heidegger's argument as to why his antihumanism does not entail inhumanism. "To think against 'humanism' does not mean to break a lance for the inhuman but simply to trace in thought the *humanitas* of *homo humanus* and its essence which appeared in the dawn of thinking, that is, to exert ourselves for the first time for preparing for such reflection. Of what value are even far-reaching humanisms to us if, without really knowing what they are doing, they recoil before the task of simply inquiring into the essence of *humanitas*?" (My parallel passage following Heidegger at 227.)

11. Kant argues that "All our knowledge falls within the bounds of possible experience, and just in this universal relation to possible experience consists that *transcendental truth which precedes all empirical truth and makes it possible*" (B 185, emphasis mine). Immanuel Kant, *Critique of Pure Reason,* trans. Norman Kemp Smith (New York, 1965), 186. Compare: "Rather, as clearing, the 'beyond' of Being precedes both thinking and Being in such a way as to make possible the very presence of thinking and Being to one another." John Sallis, "Echoes: Philosophy and Non-Philosophy after Heidegger" in *Philosophy and Non-Philosophy After Merleau-Ponty,* ed. Hugh J. Silverman (New York, 1988), 101.

12. I find a parallel between Heidegger's thinking here and passages in the first book of Wordsworth's "The Prelude" when the ten-year-old poet steals "the bird which was the captive of another's toil" and later steals a boat. In both instances, Nature (with the capital N) "speaks" to the poet. Can rules for directing human action stand on this?

13. Heidegger himself announced that mysticism was "the mere counterimage of metaphysics." See Martin Heidegger, *Nietzsche: The Will to Power as Knowledge and as Metaphysics,* trans. Joan Stambaugh, David Farrell Krell, and Frank A. Capuzzi (New York, 1987), 182. Why does Heidegger push in this particular direction? ". . . there has been a great deal of evidence that Heidegger gladly acknowledged to visitors the closeness of his thinking to the Taoist tradition and to Zen Buddhism." Otto Poeggeler, "West-East Dialogue: Heidegger and Lao-tzu" in *Heidegger and the Asian Tradition,* ed. Graham Parkes (Honolulu, 1987), 49.

14. Steiner would have Heidegger go one step further than poetry and art and wonders why Heidegger did not make a case for music. "Music is almost wholly absent from Heidegger's considerations. I have suggested that this is a drawback, for it is music which might best have instanced two of Heidegger's foremost propositions: the fact that meaning can be plain and compelling but untranslatable into another code: and the extreme difficulty we may encounter in seeking to locate the source of expressive existence, the kernel of existential energy and intelligible occurrence, in a phenomenon, in a structure which, unmistakably, *is* right there in front of us. But if music is missing, the visual arts have a distinctive function in Heideggerian ontology." George Steiner, *Heidegger* (Glasgow, 1978), 126.

15. Arnold I. Davidson, "Questions Concerning Heidegger: Opening the Debate," a symposium on Heidegger and Nazism, intro and ed. by Arnold I. Davidson, *Critical Inquiry* 15 (1989): 423.

16. Bernstein, *"Heidegger on Humanism,"* 102. He continues, "I fail to see how for all its metaphoric power, Heidegger's 'poetic' remarks about dwelling, *ethos,* and letting be, provide any determinate orientation or guidance for how we are to live our lives in 'authentic community'—or what such an 'authentic community' even means. (ibid., 106) He adds, ". . . a 'higher' or more 'primordial' sense of humanism that doesn't help to provide any orientation towards our *praxis* comes very close to being empty. Not only is it empty, but it is also dangerous because it can mystify the *content* of such repetition." (108) Rorty's criticism of Heidegger is basically the same. "Heidegger was the greatest theoretical imagination of his time (outside the natural sciences); he achieved the sublimity he attempted. But this does not prevent his being entirely useless to people who do not share his associations." Richard Rorty, *Contingency, Irony, and Solidarity* (Cambridge, 1989), 118.

17. *Spiegel,* 57. "We cannot bring him [god] forth by our thinking. At best we can awaken a readiness to wait [for him]." (57) ". . . I know nothing about how this thought has an 'effect.' It may be, too, that the way of thought today may lead one to remain silent in order to protect this thought from becoming cheapened within a year. It may also be that it needs 300 years in order to have an 'effect.'" (*Spiegel,* 60)

18. Bernstein, "Heidegger on Humanism," 99.

19. Ibid., 102.

20. Rorty, *Contingency, Irony, and Solidarity,* says, "On the general question of the relation between Heidegger's thought and his Nazism, I am not persuaded that there is much to be said except that one of the century's most original thinkers happened to be a pretty nasty character." Having already called Heidegger a "Schwarzwald redneck" (111), Rorty goes on to say that ". . . as a philosopher of our public life, as a commentator on twentieth-century technology and politics, he is resentful, petty, squint-eyed, obsessive—and, at his occasional worst (as in his praise of Hitler after the Jews had been kicked out of the universities), cruel." (120)

21. Otto Poeggeler, for example, says that "the English language still remained one which Heidegger scarcely understood, and for which he had little respect." Otto Poeggeler, "West-East Dialogue: Heidegger and Lao-tzu," 49. Compare: ". . . insofar as Heidegger tries to take over the ancient Greek experience of Being as the true past, that Greek experience becomes the criterion and the fore-project underlying all interpretation of Being. But the situation is not so simple when the problem concerns the ontological horizon of meanings itself, since the ontological horizon of meanings has already been transmitted in some form or another from the past, before meeting with the past clearly and thematically. Gadamer calls this transmitted horizon of meanings 'prejudice' (*Vormeinung*)." Kohei Mizoguchi, "An Interpretation of Heidegger's Bremen Lectures: Towards a Dialogue with His Later Thought" in *Heidegger and the Asian Tradition,* ed. Graham Parkes (Honolulu, 1987), 195.

22. *Spiegel,* 62.

14

What Now Little Man?

Comedy, Tragedy, and the Politics of Antihumanism

Samuel Ajzenstat

To raise the question of humanism is to ask what it is, if anything, that gives value to human life. The search for anything like a single answer to this question may offend our pluralist biases as well as strain our credibility. But even if we allow a variety of detailed answers, they will divide, I believe, into two broad categories and it is these that I should like to explore in this essay. The two humanisms I have in mind can be labelled the humanism of the ordinary and the humanism of the extraordinary. The upshot of the first is to see the value of life in the natural gratifications that make for comfort and ease—being warm, well-fed, healthy, sexually satisfied, and surrounded by friends. The upshot of the second is to see the first as soporific and dehumanizing, as, in the words of Nietzsche's Zarathustra, "poverty and filth and wretched contentment."[1]

These two accounts of the value of human life are so opposed to each other that it would seem we must choose one or the other and that the crucial battle over the status of the human is between them. What I wish to suggest is that though they really do contradict each other, the holding of either without the other is a distortion of the human, a distortion typical of modernity because we lack the understanding of how to hold both of them together. To attempt to embrace them within a Hegelian synthesis would itself be a typically modern evasion of the radical duality that these two humanisms point to in our experience. Our age is not comfortable with duality and so, I would argue, not comfortable with the human. Some sort of duality seems to me worth defending. What kind of duality it is and what other kinds it might lead us to is what I wish to explore in this essay. Such a discussion must, I think, begin phenomenologically by identifying the surface dualities of which we are directly conscious but must move from there in the direction of metaphysics. For sooner or later we must face the question whether our direct, obvious consciousness is or is not a false consciousness, whether there may not be after all a unity at the heart of the dualities we experience. This question cannot, I think, be approached within a purely descriptive perspective. But, except for some tentative suggestions, I shall largely remain at the descriptive level.

Much of the force of Nietzsche's writings is to pit these two conceptions of the human against each other. If we accept that the extraordinary moment can only be the moment in which one's "wretched contentment" comes to an end, it would seem to follow that until we turn away from the pursuit of ordinary gratifications we must lose the "greatest experience" since this lies in "the hour in which your happiness, too, arouses your disgust."[2] For Nietzsche this is the tragic moment. And we are denied it as long as we take it as something that we must run away from. "One will see that the problem is that of the meaning of suffering: whether a Christian meaning or a tragic meaning."[3] Like others, Christian and otherwise, since, Nietzsche finds that Biblical religion excludes tragedy. Some, on the other hand—Simone Weil seems to be an example—respond by casting Christianity in a strongly Nietzschean mold. To be in a position to see beyond these alternatives we must come to grips with the question of the relation between the ordinary and the extraordinary, the humanism of contentment and the humanism of suffering. What does the tragic view of life tell us about the relation between contentment and suffering? Do the great tragedies see happiness as the enemy of the human?

Much of the Nietzschean case has to be acknowledged. Nor do we need to stay within a Nietzschean context to see this. Despite the fact that many different definitions have been given of tragedy and of the tragedies of different periods over the centuries, there is no dispute about the fundamental aspect that comes to be called the paradox of tragedy: that it lifts us up, exalts us, satisfies us deeply by showing us terrible pain, suffered or inflicted. The earliest of our great tragedians puts this so naively as to be charming. In *Prometheus Bound* the chorus interrupts Prometheus as he is about to tell Io of the suffering she has yet to endure:

Not yet: Give me too a share of pleasure. First let us question her concerning her sickness, and let her tell us of her desperate fortunes.

And they are anxious for Prometheus to tell her of sufferings she does not yet know about: "For sufferers it is sweet to know beforehand clearly the pain that still remains for them."[4]

There is no end of theories as to why it is a sweet pleasure to hear the tale of one's own or of others' sickness, desperation, pain, and suffering. Instead of canvassing any of them directly I should like to approach the question of the nature of tragedy from a different direction. Most of the theories will agree that the spectacle of suffering is sweet and some will add the further consideration, with Nietzsche, that in some way or another tragedy shows a human being entering a plane of being that is higher just because normal comforts and restraints no longer exist. That a boundary line is crossed from normal to abnormal existence is surely the case with all tragedies. What is not always clear is that the transition should bring one to a higher human state. Much as one may wish to believe in the heightened self-awareness that comes with the pain of confronting the force that opposes one's being, it is not easy to think of Othello or Macbeth or Lear as being finer human beings for having moved into the darkness unless we are convinced that the truth is darkness so that these characters are coming face to face with the truth and taking us vicariously with them. Nevertheless, if we take it that something like the Nietzschean perspective is true, that crossing the boundary line out of the normal world is the making of us, whatever it may cost us and others, we might be tempted to draw a Nietzschean conclusion: that the highest human being will be the one who sets out to conquer the merely human in himself, crossing the boundary by an act of will into a territory where protection is no longer available. But this seems to me to be the point at which the Nietzschean perspective fails. The tragic hero never steps over the line voluntarily. He does not do whatever he does with the intention of being left out in the cold and the dark beyond the pale. If he did he would be an unintelligible monster rather than a tragic hero.

Once we see this, it is possible to move towards a different conception of tragedy. The teaching of tragedy is that we are obligated to run away from just those experiences which would be the exalting of us, the raising of us to a higher level of being. It is true that at some point the tragic hero may cease to try to get back over the boundary line into normal life. But, especially in Greek tragedy, the hero's adventures will almost always be counterpointed by another set of characters: often the chorus; in *Hippolytus,* Phaedra's nurse; in the *Agamemnon,* the watchman and the herald, who are resolute not for death but for mediocrity: "may the eye inescapable of the mighty Gods not look on me."[5]

When I first began to read Greek tragedy, I had a romantic's certainty that the playwrights meant us to despise these characters. They were intended, I believed, simply to make the nobility of the suffering hero stand out all the more brightly. I cannot prove that this is not so. But it now seems worthwhile to me to try to see them differently. They do bring the hero into brilliant relief. But they are also there to remind us that it is our business as human beings to struggle as hard as we can to fend off the conditions in which we could be lifted up to nobility and heroic greatness.

This theme, which I am arguing is an essential part of tragedy, seems to constitute the whole of comedy. Comedy has often enough been seen as an appeal to our cruelty, our desire to see our fellow man ridiculed. This aspect of it is not easy to square with the happy endings that accompany the ridicule. But both fit together nicely if we can think that the fundamental teaching of comedy, if it has one, is the sweetness of the merely human. This is especially evident in Greek comedy. To bring it out and to raise some difficulties about it I want to glance briefly at *The Clouds* of Aristophanes.

The Clouds is especially interesting for our purposes for an apparently paradoxical feature of it. In this play Aristophanes uses the figure of Socrates—whether fairly or unfairly is not my present concern—to depict scientific enlightenment as bringing destructive social, political, and moral consequences. The crux of his case is that the scientific approach to man is reductionist. The upshot of the wisdom which Pheidippides learns inside Socrates' think-tank and which he uses to justify beating his father is this:

> Look to Nature for a sanction. Observe the roosters, for instance, and what
> do you see?
>
> A society
> Whose pecking-order envisages a permanent state of open warfare between
> fathers and sons. And how do roosters differ from men, except for the trifling
> fact that human society is based upon law and rooster society isn't?[6]

Our law, by which we differ from roosters, is to be understood through that aspect of ourselves which we share with the roosters, our natural desires. And nature is no more moral in us than it is in roosters, since the laws of Zeus have suffered the same fate as the laws of man when thunder and lightning are shown to be merely the effects of a physical vortex. Among the results that Aristophanes identifies are the collapse of contractual obligation and of familial piety, the rejection of shame over adultery and incest. We should expect that against all this he will look for a way to reassert the special value of the human.

Paradoxically, however, what Aristophanes offers as an antidote to this reductionism is a reductionism of his own. For the human beings that he shows us are little more than roosters. Here, as everywhere else, Aristophanes is at pains to depict the essential human activity not indeed as passing laws but as passing wind, farting, burping, crapping, and fornicating. What sort of humanism is that?

To understand what Aristophanes is doing in this play we have to see that he is aware of a crucial irony in scientific enlightenment. As Aristophanes depicts scientific reductionism, it does not arise from a desire to lower man but to raise him. Science is the attempt to use our minds to scale the heights and attests to the human confidence that it is our high calling to live in the truth and through it achieve a sort of immortality. This, of course, is why when we first meet Socrates in this play he is swinging in a basket suspended from the ceiling:

> SOCRATES. Why are you calling me, ephemeral one?
> STREPSIADES. First, I beseech you, tell me what you're doing.
> SOC. I tread on air and contemplate the sun.
> STREP. Then you look down on the gods from a perch and not from
> the earth?—if that's what you're doing.
> SOC.   Precisely, you see
> only by being suspended aloft, by dangling my mind in the heavens and
> mingling my rare thought with the ethereal air, could I ever achieve strict
> scientific accuracy in my survey of the vast empyrean. Had I pursued my
> inquiries from down there on the ground, my data would be worthless. The

earth, you see, pulls down to itself the moisture from the thought.
The same thing happens also to water cress.[7]

Underlying Aristophanes' critique of science is thus the claim that the attempt to lift man above the human ends up by lowering him below the human. "As Socrates was investigating the courses and revolutions of the moon and was gaping upwards, a lizard (it was night) crapped on him from the roof."[8] To fight the lowering of man thus requires a fight against the lifting of man. If he is not to be crapped on, he must not gaze upwards and must keep his mouth shut.

The idea that reaching high brings us low, that "pride goeth before destruction" (Prov. 16:18), that it is the poor in spirit that are blessed, is, of course, one of the commonplaces of our religious tradition. But I would guess that many people would find Aristophanes' blunt way of putting it crass and disgusting in its apparent contempt for any idealism. This feeling has to be taken seriously. It is a clue to an ultimate narrowness of vision in Aristophanes and in comedy in general. But it is also, I think, from another point of view a clue to an incompleteness of vision in ourselves.

By allowing the ordinary to reassert its claims, comedy sets us the main problem with which humanism has to cope. Is the value of the human to be found in something that resides in even the most mediocre specimens of the race and is it with us even in our moments of crass and complacent gratification or is it to be found in the rare specimens who experience the falling away of those gratifications? In what seems to be a Nietzschean perspective it is all too easy to say that if comedy chooses the former of these two humanisms, tragedy chooses the latter. But I have already suggested that this is not the case, that if we take Greek tragedy as our example, it is possible to see tragedy as the meeting place of the humanism of the ordinary and the humanism of the extraordinary.

This is one way of understanding what Plato means at the end of *The Symposium* when he has Socrates attempt to convince Agathon and Aristophanes "that the same man might be capable of writing both comedy and tragedy—that the tragic poet might be a comedian as well."[9] To see what Plato means by this we must see why it is an appropriate issue to introduce at the end of *The Symposium* and this appears when we see the fundamental issue of the dialogue, the aspect of love that comes to the fore, as the relation between the ordinary and the extraordinary in human life. Here, as in *The Clouds,* Aristophanes is the great spokesman for the ordinary. In *The Clouds* Strepsiades is cured of his desire to pass beyond the normally accepted practices of his society when his son Pheidippides claims the right, on the basis of his new-found scientific enlightenment, to beat his mother, Strepsiades' wife. Earlier in the play Strepsiades has blamed his financial woes on his wife and her family. Furthermore, he has been taught in the play that contractual obligations are merely conventional and are of no force to bind the enlightened. What, then, at last binds him to his wife? The answer is in his description of his marriage early in the play:

> I was a rustic, she from the town:
> classy, luxurious, aristocratic.
> Well, so we got married and we clambered into bed—
> I smelling of new wine, fig crates, wool, abundance,
> she in turn of perfume, saffron, kisses with the tongue,
> luxury, high prices, gourmandizing, goddess Lechery
> and every little elf, imp and sprite of Intercourse.[10]

The bond that brings Strepsiades back to responsible membership in the community with its ordinary decency and piety would seem to be the sexual bond. And this is, of course, exactly what Plato has him arguing in *The Symposium*. The function of sex is to be a substitute for the storming of the heavens, making us content to live on the earth. Against this defense of the ordinary, Plato sets a group of men who, whether or not they are deceiving themselves, take homosexual love as the symbol of transcendence of the merely physical or natural. The earthly love, Aphrodite Pandemos, as Pausanius tell us, "governs the passions of the vulgar" and specially defines heterosexual relations. "Whoever they may love, their desires are of the body rather than of the soul . . . they make a point of courting the shallowest people . . . looking forward to the mere act of fruition and careless whether it be a worthy or unworthy consummation."[11] For Pausanius as for Aristophanes the issue is between a love that escapes the body and a love that is bound by the body.

It may seem that the Socrates we know would have to affirm the attempt to escape from the body, even if he doubts that the difference between homosexuality and heterosexuality is the crucial one. If so, then he is certainly concerned to deny the essential feature of Aristophanes' speech. Why then, at the very end, should he pay such high respects to comedy as to suggest that the tragedian must somehow be capable of it, as if the tragic gift cannot exist without the comic one, as if, in fact the transcending of the normal human condition cannot be of value unless it contains that affirming of the normal human condition that comedy attests to? This question brings us to the brink of a crucial difference not only between Nietzsche and Plato but between Nietzsche and the tragic tradition on which he claims to draw and also perhaps between modernity and the ancient tradition generally.

To show that there are characters in tragedy who affirm the comic perspective is not yet to show that there is a unified perspective that embraces both the comic and the tragic attitudes. One cannot after all simultaneously seek the extraordinary and run away from it, embrace the pain and suffering of life and try, at all costs, to avoid it. One must live either tragically or comically. Or can one?

The great problem on which I think modern humanism, and modern philosophy generally, has foundered, is the problem of integrating the ordinary and the extraordinary. This is the problem that lies below the surface, for example, when Rousseau, having attacked in his *First Discourse,* in an almost Aristophanean manner, the craving for distinction that powers and is in turn powered by the development of the arts and sciences, then attempts in the last two books of the *Emile* to provide his ordinary hero with a sphere of high, romantic idealism capable of inspiring instead of destroying a fundamentally simple, mediocre life. It is also present in Kant's attempts to integrate freedom and determinism, noumenal and phenomenal existence, autonomy and heteronomy. But without looking at these cases in detail, I shall try to see in a simpler way, in terms of simpler examples, why these attempts fail.

Critics of modernity often speak as if the fundamental character of modern philosophy is to have taken the side of the ordinary against the extraordinary as against the ancients who made the opposite choice. What I have said about Plato suggests that I regard this as a mistaken view. This sort of critique of modernity is itself impregnated with a characteristically modern set of attitudes so that to try to see why it is a misunderstanding can help to show what modernity really is and what it is, if anything, that we have lost. In clarifying the modern the status of the concept of tragedy is crucial because the salient issue is our attitude towards pain. For many of the critics the characteristic modern attitude towards pain, the characteristic modern ethic, is to be found in utilitarianism. Leaving aside the issue of positive pleasure, it is at the very heart of utilitarian philosophy to see the fundamental ethical goal as the alleviation or elimination of pain. To those for whom the tragic spirit involves the joyful embrace of pain, the crucial alternative is not utility vs. duty (as might appear to be the case in Nietzsche). For those who see it this way, including Nietzsche himself, Nietzsche can be said to have a profounder understanding than Kant of what our most crucial ethical choices come down to. Kant is sometimes lampooned, as in Schiller's famous little verse, as believing that I can't be doing my duty unless it hurts. Against this Kant's defenders argue that he did not see pain as a positive requirement for duty but only as a sign of the fact that duty could not be identified with inclination and would show its distinctness most clearly on those occasions, probably the typical, on which the two were in conflict. For Kant pain remains a negative thing and is not a part of that *summum bonum* in which duty and happiness coexist. But it is possible to turn this defense of Kant into a criticism by arguing that pain must be seen as a positive thing because the moment it disappears the clash of forces has disappeared and with it our consciousness of ourselves since we know ourselves only in the clash of forces. Once the step is taken of making pain a positive thing the concepts of duty and reason can be dispensed with on the grounds that universals are not needed to lift us out of our merely natural circumstances; that is already done for us by sheer arbitrary will runnng up against the forces that surround it. Pain marks any exertion of will and any exertion of will is a transcendence. Kant's quarrel with utilitarianism is thus seen as not being ultimate. For neither is tragic. But modernity focuses on this quarrel because modernity is not tragic either. By reasserting the tragic and the primacy of pain Nietzsche defends the modern and ushers in the postmodern. But in doing so he is seen (incorrectly, I have suggested) as reviving the ancient wisdom of the Dionysian.

Not every critique of modernity along these lines sees Nietzsche as the antidote. What is common to most such critiques is the sense that for moderns the primary ethical imperative is the gratification of arbitrary desire: our control of nature through technology thus really means nature's control of us since it gives us over entirely into the power of naturally felt inclinations. Even Kantian rationality is seen as a cover for the technological mentality. Our virtues, as Nietzsche put it, make it easier for us to sleep. The modern is the triumph of complacency and, once again, "wretched contentment." The comic spirit, in this view, has triumphed.

Those critics of the modern who see the arbitrary will as leading ultimately to conformity and complacency must turn away from Nietzsche, even if they can on occasion quote him to their own ends. But they do not turn away from him for precisely the right reason. What needs to be brought out in what I have just said is that Nietzsche like Kant stands for duty and against inclination. The identification of pain rather than reason as the human capacity by which we transcend mere gratification does not mark a fundamental cleavage in the modern mentality. What is distinctive of the modern is an obsession with duty, that which we ought to do though the heavens may fall. Thus for Nietzsche the will to power is not an arbitrary, relativistic self-indulgence but an absolute calling every bit as imperious as the categorical imperative and meant to accomplish exactly the same goal. With very few exceptions, modernity has been a quest to live in the spiritual alone, from Descartes through Nietzsche right up to Jonathan Livingston Seagull who discovers his own divinity through the recognition that his spatio-temporally bound body is mere illusion. There is no solid agreement on how we are to cash out our pure spirituality. Technology, for example, means so much to many of us not because we are crass materialists but because through our stereos and films, VCRs and contraceptives we fancy that we can stop the seeping away of the future into the past and experience a limitless present. Not all of these attitudes are tragic because not all of them seek transcendence through pain. But they are closer to it than to the comic victory of the ordinary. When modernity is described in this way we can see that it is not the comic spirit that has triumphed at all. The contempt for "wretched contentment" which Zarathustra gives voice to is right in the mainstream of modernity and Nietzsche is one of our great absolutists, idealists and perfectionists.

In this perspective, modernity is the defeat of the comic spirit. I said above, however, that this profile applied with very few exceptions. The main exception, I think, is utilitarianism which is the closest we are able to come to acknowledging the importance of the comic. But I have already said that our way of asserting the comic is as impaired as our way, under the guidance of Nietzsche, of seeing the tragic. It remains to speak of what holds the two perceptions together as modernity is unable to do.

What I have been saying about modernity will be seen to be in some respects just the opposite of what Alasdair MacIntyre says in *After Virtue*. Most human virtues, I have been suggesting, are what it is reasonable for us to hope never to be called upon to display, just as duty is what it is reasonable to hope will never be demanded of us. But I can take a leaf from MacIntyre's book by arguing that in the modern world attitudes exist in a fragmented state alongside one another and in apparent contradiction because a world view that ties them together no longer seems available. What is it then, that ties together the comic and the tragic view, so much so that both, as we have seen, must be present in the great tragedies?

The answer is, after all, rather simple. I expressed the problem by asking how can we seek the meaning of our lives in running away from what we at the same time know gives our lives their ultimate meaning. How can it be "authentic" to try to escape from "authenticity." The answer, of course, lies in our knowledge or belief that we will not be able to escape. And this in turn rests on the faith that the universe is under the control of a force that can see to it that we run up against authenticating experiences, however hard we run in the other direction. The recognition that we reach the heights in confronting danger is sane just so long as we leave it in the hands of powers beyond us to arrange that confrontation. When we continue to believe in the importance of the confrontation but no longer believe in the powers, we are left in the impossible, insane position of having to manufacture the dangers for ourselves. Or to put it slightly differently, when we stop believing in the torturing deity beyond us we will be forced either to stop believing in the value of the torture or to start torturing ourselves. These two alternatives define the two one-sided humanisms with which I began this paper. Neither is fully acceptable. To torture ourselves is merely to reduce suffering to a sadomasochistic game that no one ultimately should be able to take seriously. To see suffering in this way can only drive us back to the other alternative which is to see no value in it. But to stop believing in the value of suffering is, as Nietzsche well knew, one-sidedly though he may have known it, to stop believing in the value of life, to grow to hate life and finally to struggle only to obliterate it. It is not a mistake to see human beings as called to seek pleasure and avoid pain. It is only a mistake to think they can succeed. And in the moment when the sane, human, all-too-human project fails, utilitarianism, for all its fundamental truth, has nothing helpful to say to us. And neither, in that moment, has the ethic of rational duty. At that moment it is the ethic of tragedy that speaks to us. But only while we retain our commitment to comedy.

Something of what it means practically to hold comedy and tragedy in tension with each other will be clearer if I explain what I meant by including in my title the phrase "the politics of antihumanism." The two humanisms that I began with and tried to show were one-sided and inadequate both demonstrate a tendency to call themselves as much antihumanisms as humanisms, the first because it wishes to show man as integrated into nature, the second because it wishes to show the human as valuable only in the light of its ability to transcend itself. But both of these are antihumanisms in another sense. Each tends to suggest the dispensibility of certain kinds of human beings. For the humanism that understands itself as naturalism and understands nature simply as the comic struggle to overcome pain, lives in which pain cannot be overcome are likely to come to seem worse than useless. The desire to eliminate suffering slides all too easily into the desire to eliminate the sufferer. For this the second humanism, with its high valuation of suffering as one of the principal modes of reaching beyond the merely biological, can provide an antidote. But for this second sort of humanism or antihumanism, as we know from Nietzsche, there is a tendency to regard the human who does not suffer or does not want to suffer as worthless, as all-too-human. At the bottom of this lies a valuation of sheer consciousness so high as to make simple membership of the species no more than a potentiality with no meaning at all until it passes into a higher state. To me it seems truer that we should be eternally torn between a commitment to the biological species as such and a commitment to its most transcendently conscious specimens. I cannot prove either of these two commitments. But I think it may be after all that pain achieves its highest value when it teaches us both commitments at once and makes it impossible for us to find complacent rest in either. Without tragedy, comedy is complacency. Without the complacency of comedy, tragedy itself becomes complacent. But each with the help of the other remains reluctant and ironic.

The commitment to comedy gives tragedy a poignancy and meaning beyond simply reluctance and irony. Much of what I have been saying can be summed up by an image that every philosophy student knows, Plato's image of the release from the cave. " 'And if,' I said, 'someone dragged him away from there by force along the rough, steep, upward way and didn't let him go before he had dragged him out into the light of the sun, wouldn't he be distressed and annoyed at being so dragged?' "[12] Plato does not here seem to be explicitly speaking of pain and suffering, except incidentally. Nevertheless, the image he presents, as we all know, evokes the sense that crossing the boundary between the ordinary and the extraordinary is not something we can undertake willingly. In this sense I think it can be helpful to think of Plato as in part meditating here on the tragic sense, even though the parable of the cave culminates with an experience of the good and the beautiful rather than the horrible that we are used to associating with tragedy. It is helpful for a number of reasons. If we take it as a guide, it suggests in however mysterious a way that there is a good and a beautiful available only to those who are forcibly uprooted from the ordinary and the normal. The torturing deity, whatever it is, takes on the look of a kind god. At the same time Plato shows no contempt for those who wish to stay chained in their seats in the theatre of images; everyone wishes to. The difference between Plato's picture and the one I have tried to present lies in his suggestion that the life of the cave is ultimately illusory. If this is so, then I find myself urged by a different view of the tragic, grounded in the Old Testament, to take sides against Plato and argue that the unreality of the cave does something to dissipate the full paradox of tragedy. But that is not what I principally want to draw attention to by mentioning the cave. It is rather that in Plato's story, there is, even if ambiguously, even if one is irrevocably changed, a way back over the boundary line into something like an ordinary life. The modern sense of tragedy, to which I have alluded in a few places above, is, I think, that there is no way back. Does a return to the normal, a "comic" reassertion of the rights of the ordinary, violate the genuinely tragic spirit?

We know that in Greek tragedy it does not. The heroes of Greek tragedy, or many of them—Prometheus, Orestes, Philoctetes, perhaps even Oedipus (men more often than women)—are not only dragged out of normalcy; like the hero of Plato's cave they are dragged back in. It is perhaps only in Euripides that the comic ceases to reassert itself. There is probably no need to come down hard on one side or the other as long as it can be allowed that the tragedy which permits a recrossing of the boundary line (which is what is meant by a "happy ending") is at least as tragic as one that does not.

The problem of happy endings is a more complicated one than might be thought, but I cannot give this paper a happy ending without briefly alluding to it. I promised at the beginning to defend a kind of dualism or better duality against a monist conception of reality. The duality I have defended has not been, at least not so far, one of body and mind, flesh and spirit, but one of comedy and tragedy. I have characterized modernity as a rejection of duality and have argued that this rejection produces intolerable monisms, a monism of the comic posing as a humanism in which nevertheless human life is merely stupid and a monism of the tragic which also poses as a humanism but exhorts us to increase suffering rather than to strive to alleviate it. Against this I have argued for a tragic vision which is dualistic because it sees life as a tension between two quite different forces, one that pulls towards normalcy and the other that pulls away from it. I have suggested that for the tragic vision this tension is ineradicable in the sense that one of these forces will not fully triumph over the other. If this is so then there is a sense in which it really does not matter if there is a happy ending or not; it will not eradicate the tension. The hero who returns to the normal will carry his abnormality with him and will not cease to feel its presence.

That may be all there is to be said about it. But I am reluctant to leave it at that. I have identified the tragic spirit with tension, a tendency to see life as a tension. But to get at the real tension we must put one more twist into the argument. Simply to see life as a tension, a duality, is ultimately to embrace a sort of Manichaeism, a vision of the world as an endless clash between good and evil. In this view the universe is the scene not of a cosmic tragedy but merely of a melodrama. But I have already argued that the ordinary and the extraordinary are both aspects of the good. And this suggests that underneath the duality there is unity or harmony. However, simply to opt for an ultimate unity or harmony is to risk losing the tragic sense altogether, replacing a tension by a synthesis. To retain the tragic insight we have to retain the sense of tension. But this does not mean we must give up entirely the sense of an ultimate oneness, even if not between the forces we experience tearing us apart. It means rather that the tragic tension, fully understood, is between our tendency to believe in the ultimacy of the tension and our tendency to believe in the ultimacy of the harmony. The happy ending is not at bottom something that is made out of the tensions of the earlier acts. In spite of the temporal flow of the events of the tragic the happy ending bears witness to a mode of being that exists alongside the sufferings. Each is as true as the other. Neither eradicates the reality of the other. Something of this can be found in Hegel's account of tragedy with its emphasis on the collision of opposite and equal rights as well as in the wonderful slogan in which he speaks of "the union of union and non-union." What I am reluctant to accept in Hegel is the suggestion that the ultimate union is a synthesis of the union and disunion that we experience in tension with each other. But the question of whether what is ultimate in the universe has the tensions of our existence as its contents or whether it transcends them altogether brings us to the borderline between tragedy and theology. And over that boundary, as over any other, we should hesitate to step until we are dragged.

Notes

1. *Thus Spake Zarathustra*, "Zarathustra's Prologue," section 3. The translation is from *The Portable Nietzsche*, ed. Walter Kaufmann (New York, 1954), 125. See also the passage on sleep, in Part 1, "On the Teachers of Virtue," 140–142.

2. Ibid.

3. *The Will to Power*, trans. Walter Kaufmann and R. J. Hollingdale (New York, 1968), no. 1052.

4. Aeschylus, *Prometheus Bound,* lines 631, 698, trans. David Grene in *Greek Tragedies*, ed. David Grene and Richard Lattimore, vol. 1 (Chicago, 1960).

5. Ibid., lines 902–904.

6. Aristophanes, *The Clouds,* trans. William Arrowsmith (New York, 1962), 124.

7. Aristophanes, *The Clouds*, combining Arrowsmith's translation, p. 33, with the translation of Thomas G. and Grace Starry West in Plato and Aristophanes, *Four Texts on Socrates* (Ithaca, 1984), lines 223–227.

8. Ibid., West translation, lines 171–3 slightly amended.

9. Plato, *Symposium, 223d,* trans. Michael Joyce in *The Collected Dialogues of Plato*, ed. Edith Hamilton and Huntington Cairns (Princeton, 1969).

10. Aristophanes, *The Clouds,* combining Arrowsmith, p. 20, and West, lines 47–52.

11. Plato, *Symposium* 181b. See Hamilton and Cairns, *The Collected Dialogues of Plato*, note 9.

12. Plato, *The Republic,* 515e, trans. Allan Bloom (New York, 1968).

15

Foucault and the Question of Humanism
Charles E. Scott

Since the words *human being* mean earthly being or the one who is of the earth and since the *human* in our day inevitably has a connotation of spirituality, I begin with the notation that we are discussing our historical earthly spirituality when we discuss humanism. The questions of both morality and transcendence also cannot be avoided when we examine humanism and when we take that word to mean human nature or disposition. If we understand the word *humanism* to refer to the study of the humanities, our disciplines of literature, history, philosophy, religion, and the languages, we are nonetheless thrown into the question of who we are in our studies of our expressions and modes of expression and who we are as we relate to ourselves by means of these disciplines. A certain devotion to human interests and ideals is also usually meant by the word when it is used in our academic context. We are convinced for the most part that we are well served in our society by teaching and learning the canons that structure our traditions of self-understanding. Without knowing how we have come to ourselves, how we have found ourselves in our arts and disciplines, we know that we shall be ignorant and mentally impoverished.

Knowing these things as academics we also know that we lack agreement on what constitutes us as humans. Our collective body of humanistic knowledge does not contain agreement on such beliefs as that we are defined by a relation to God, that we are essentially volitional subjects, that we embody an ultimate purpose for life, that we have a definitive origin, that we are essentially rational, that we have a transtemporal nature, or that we have a nature at all. I shall begin by noting that these disagreements constitute our humanity in our humanistic tradition and that they tell us something about ourselves, our earthliness, and our mortality. The best evidence about ourselves is found in the heated controversies whereby we assert and defend one body of humanistic knowledge and belief over against other humanistic knowledges and beliefs. Both our modern desire to be one kind of thing in our earthliness and not many, contradictory things, and the impossibility of fulfilling that destiny are manifest.

I want to highlight the structures of disagreement that constitute humanism and our humanity in that broad tradition. The rediscovery of the texts of our western antiquity and the growing sense of the historicity of our being are major aspects of humanism. Not an agreement on who we are as human beings, but a continuing contest over who we are in the context of texts and historical finitude appears to be definitive of this tradition. I shall bring Foucault's thought into the discussion by focusing on the way in which his genealogical approach functions. The importance of traditional texts, practices, and institutions is a given for his work. Foucault is a part of humanism in this sense, but he departs from it by allowing his thought to be moved and formed by the gaps and fissures of the humanistic tradition rather than by an effort to achieve theoretical superiority on the questions of human nature and destiny. His way of thinking is as important as the content of his genealogical accounts, and until his readers see how Foucault thinks, they probably will confuse genealogical thought with theoretical or metaphysical thought. By that confusion, Foucault's encounter with humanism will be blurred, if not completely missed.

I shall discuss the ethos of genealogy in order to intensify Foucault's movement through and beyond humanistic discipline. The aspect that is most important for us is the recoiling, self-overcoming movements of this thought. In that movement both the claims of humanism and the way humanistic knowledge are constituted come into question.

The framework of my discussion is set by the possibility that human flourishing is retarded by our efforts to be definitive about ourselves and is enhanced when humanism in its several meanings is held in question. The question of my remarks is found in the claim that humanism is true to itself when it overcomes its own meanings by the movements of uncertainty and self-contradiction that constitute it. If humanistic thinking attempts to be universal in its intelligence and piety, it denies its own temporality and becomes demonic regarding itself. As it overcomes itself and moves into nonhumanistic thought and attitudes, as it loses its authority regarding itself, it, by that movement, understands its own earthliness. It is earthly as it comes to its unspeakableness regarding itself. Otherwise the voluble disciplines that constitute it and give it voice, infatuated as they always are with their words, rhythms, and learning, constitute a passing moment in human history that accomplishes no more than an enjoyment of overlooking its own passing.

GENEALOGY'S ETHOS

An ethos—in the case of genealogy, a living movement of thought—takes place in Foucault's discourse although it is not one that leads to an ethics. This movement of thought is characterized by recoils in which distances and divisions of traditional humanistic formations recoil in Foucault's thought in a way that displaces the structures and desires of self-relation. Foucault's thought recoils on itself, for example, in a way that prevents itself from becoming a basis for specific ethical programs. It comprises a recoiling movement that keeps both totalizing claims about ourselves and ethics as such in question. We shall see how this recoiling occurs in three examples whereby we will be in a position to see that humanism as a way of knowing and living is put in question.

Recoiling Knowledges

Characteristically Foucault's genealogies produce knowledge that falls back on its own inheritance and by this return recoils away from the powers that have ordered things and protected themselves in the given, inherited discourse. The recoil may occur under the exposing force of the genealogical study as in the case of *The Order of Things* in which the study pushes itself back to the largely subverted and overlooked events and disruptions that have led to the attraction and viability of genealogical knowledge. In this case the mutations and disruptions that have been traditionally ignored and that are major forces in forming the structures of knowledge under investigation are given considerable power in ordering and forming Foucault's discourse. His genealogical recoil, in the sense of falling back, involves returning to the lineage of his own work, uncovering the nonsystematic interruptions in systemic knowledge, showing that these interruptions are motivations toward genealogy within nongenealogical methodologies and epistemological orders, and recasting the formation and succession of these methodologies and epistemological orders in terms of the mutations and disruptions that they have systematically ignored. His genealogical knowledge falls back on its own lineage by the force of factors in the lineage that have been excluded from their own self-interpretations.

There is a second kind of recoil in *The Order of Things*. In it the knowledge developed by the genealogical study has the effect of coiling again the various discursive and epistemic strands that make up its lineage and forming a springing, self-overcoming movement whereby the truth of this knowledge is put in question. This recoiling movement includes an appropriation by the genealogical knowledge of its place in the lineage of discourse-specific regularities that order and define the knowledges that it studies. It finds itself to be composed of the elements that it is also putting in question. It arises, for example, out of both the ruptures of the modern subject of knowledge and the regularities of knowledge that define this disruption. This kind of recoiling movement, in the sense of coiling again in a springing movement, emphasizes in Foucault's genealogical knowledge both the regional and mutational formations that constitute it and the space of dissociation that characterizes it. Foucault's genealogical knowledge is thus always in a position to critique, mock, parody, and ironize itself. The possibility of parody according to Foucault, for example, arises from "the unreality" that helps to produce our images and interpretations of the past—the projections that arise from the confederations of meanings and sense in a specific discourse, the projections of historical continuity, for example, or the ideal of sufficient explanatory accounts of historical events.

As the projective "unreality" that makes genealogy possible in our heritage comes to be "enjoyed" in a genealogical study, the genealogy becomes susceptible to the parody that it exercises on the subject of analysis. It finds satisfaction in the instability of its own certainties, and this satisfactory instability, as we shall see, is the significant part of its recoil from the orders and practices that it uncovers and that play a role in the uncovering process. In the context of *Discipline/Punish,* for example, genealogical knowledge recognizes itself in and speaks out of a lineage in which a combination of constraint, control, and punishment are ingredients in the lineage that produces this disciplinary, genealogical knowledge. But Foucault's knowledge coils itself in a spring-like suspicion (an aspect of its satisfaction in its own instability) in its process of seeing and recognizing its lineage and has the effect of releasing itself from the grip of its own concepts. Its paradox is its uncertain certainty, its releasing the discipline of its accomplishment at its limits, and making part of its discipline a cultivation of the instability that will overcome its own procedures and certainties. This release occurs in part as the confinement of discipline is opened out to other options in the genealogical discourse of the disciplinary heritage. Instead of recoiling into a defensive posture or into a posited originary presence or experience, it is a recoiling motion that embodies no more than the tension of its spring out beyond its established territory. In the case of *Discipline/Punish,* one is driven toward a kind of knowledge that, in its disclosure of the concealing, punishing heritage of discipline, is ill at ease with its own discipline and is left with the questionableness of its own knowledge. This recoil is made in part by the torsion of the concealing and uncovering that go on in Foucault's genealogy.

A third type of recoiling that is typical in Foucault's thought, and one that combines with the springing motion, is exemplified in volume one of *The History of Sexuality.* Foucault finds that sexual repression is a major force in our modern discourse of sexual liberation. This is a discourse that he names 'sexuality.' Instead of pleasure of bodies, sexuality inscribes shame of bodily pleasure in the name of sexual liberation. This genealogy, which is found particularly in the discourse of psychoanalysis and its many progeny, is a part of the lineage of fear and repression in the name of liberation, and it comes to be known genealogically in this lineage as part of this lineage. This genealogical knowledge recoils, in the sense of winces, before its own history and coils itself again in a springing movement away from its own 'sexuality' in the direction of pleasures that it as a discourse does not know how to embody. This recoiling is made by the forces of wincing, revealing, recognizing, releasing, and constraining, all of which occur in Foucault's discourse.

In *The Order of Things, Discipline/Punish,* and *The History of Sexuality* we can say preliminarily that genealogical knowledge recoils on itself and from itself without the benefit of origins or essences in a springing movement that is like self-overcoming rather than like movements of self-establishment, continuous repetition, or disciplined self-nurturence.

The Reader's Recoil

We have noted that Foucault's thought takes place in the movement of his discourse. Reading it and thinking through it involve one in a process distinct from that of standing outside of the movement and observing it from within a different configuration of ordering powers. The recoiling, self-overcoming process is not a law or principle of self-presentation or self-realization. It is not like a principle that gives unity or order or telos to the discourse. 'Self-overcoming' names in part the effect of nonsystematizable random aspects that move through a systematic discourse or a tradition that has several noncompatible strands. These random aspects have the effect of recoiling our universalizing and categorizing ideas back on themselves as they reveal the lineage of those ideas in its heterogeneous and arbitrary formations. The absence of extradiscursive law, for example, in the western formation of laws that are taken to be universal—that kind of instability—has a recoiling force when it is thematized within our common orders of concepts and principles. It is the force of recoil in thinking with organizing principles which in their work show that they themselves are taken to be necessary, but are necessary only in the discourses that they unify. Self-overcoming in this context is found in the effect of the known random and unstable necessities, the torsion of laws that have their authority by virtue of given lineage and that order all random things within their jurisdiction as though they derive their force from outside their heritage.

In Foucault's case, knowing is in tension with categories, logics, and exchanges that form his knowledge. His knowledge is anarchic in the sense that no thought of primal origin, foundation, or continuing presence structures the word patterns. This means that as one follows his thinking in the text one undergoes the transformation of the metaphysical patterns and habits of thought that are in the text, and, as we shall see, subtle physical transformations also take place that may occasion a hostile recoil on the part of the reader in the sense of shrinking back, wincing, or quailing in relation to the transformational processes. This process is, of course, distinct from the rebound of self-overcoming in his text. It is a movement away from self-overcoming, and this kind of recoil is often all the more powerful because it is unconscious.

The interaction of rebound in the text and shrinking from the text in reading it create a strange situation of reading. One may exercise a shrinking violence regarding the text by unconsciously and systematically eliminating the work's own self-overcoming as one interprets it. This reaction is evident in some discussions of Foucault which reinscribe a metaphysical context or problematic like that of the necessity of a constructive concept of subjectivity, an implicit ethics, or a hidden humanism. Others read him as a historicist or a historical relativist by ignoring the fact that the meaning of these orientations derives from a way of thinking that polarizes transcendental and temporal reality, a polarization that is problematized and largely eliminated in his thought. Those who interpret him as a structuralist, for example, overlook the metaphysical concept of structure that characterizes structuralism, as well as its self-enclosed calculus of interpretation, and eliminate the self-overcoming recoils that move his thought away from a structuralist orientation.

These ways of reading Foucault have in common a reassociation of metaphysical patterns and ideas that are destabilized in Foucault's thought. There is a shrinking recoil in these interpretations in the face of the self-overcoming that rebounds in and away from its own lineage and forces itself away from its regional center. It repeatedly falls away from the definitive interests and affections of traditional language, and this falling away in the discourse both addresses and repels a reader's inherited discourse of world order. This engagement is like a death experience. As one undergoes the quiet passing away of a scheme of definitive linkages, a pervasive quailing recoils one back to familiar ground and motivates commentaries that recapitulate a discourse's metaphysical basis for life and hope. This recoiling then becomes a movement in the reader, paradoxically, and a phenomenon by which one may understand the turning point of Foucault's thought into a metaphysic that his thought has overcome. A genealogy of this manner of perverting Foucault makes possible a reentry into the self-overcoming that is carried negatively in the reaction.

Genealogy as Effective History and Curative Science

In his discussion of Nietzsche's genealogy Foucault outlines a way of writing history that "introduces discontinuity into our very being as it divides our emotions, dramatizes our instincts, multiplies our body, and sets it against itself.

> 'Effective' history denies itself the reassuring stability of life and nature, and it will not permit itself to be transported by a voiceless obstinancy toward a millennial ending.[1]
>
> Knowledge is allowed to create its own genealogy in an act of cognition; and 'Wirkliche Historie' composes a genealogy of history as the *vertical projection of its position.*[2]

As a history projects its position vertically, so that its seams, traumas, and mutational influences become apparent, like layers of sedimentation, its process is "curative."[3] The formation of the patterns of knowing that give it its perspective are apparent, not hidden to it, and the effects of all the constrained factors—such as posited necessary causes, continuing presence, or transcendent laws of formation—these effects lose their power to organize blindly the linkages, multiplicity, and disruptions of things. It is the epistemic demand for constant and transcendent elements, elements that are found in the layered sedimentation, that give an aura of pathology to the traditional discourses when they are known in the perspective of their discontinuous, broken, and serially repeated associations. In that sense genealogy is "curative" as it comes to know the fragments and random associations that function as though they were expressions or disclosures of nonfragmented, continuous foundations or presence. The genealogy recoils on these claims and procedures within the genealogy.

If we stopped at this point we would appear to have a version of enlightenment discourse. Genealogy would appear to shed light on certain metaphysical assumptions and concepts by virtue of the discontinuity that characterizes them and to cure us of our illusion in the presence of certain overlooked facts in our lineage. But the effect of this kind of history is to show that the genealogical approach is itself an outgrowth of a series of epistemic and institutional patterns and practices which fail to appropriate their own generative, discursive life. The curative aspect is not found in an elimination of a false discourse by a true one, but in a knowledge that finds itself repeating and departing from the inheritances that it describes. The genealogical description is not from outside of a given lineage, but from within it in the perspective of its exclusions, borders, unreconciled orders, unreconciled differences, and strategies of repression. This recoil in the lineage and away from it takes place in forces embodied in both a disciplined wincing that develops the given discourse from the perspective of one or more aspects of the discourse before other of its aspects, and a coiling again in the form of genealogical knowledge which rebounds away from its own authoritative repetition. In this recoiling process the stoppage by self-maintaining and self-repeating centers of power of generative, exposing language, and the emergence of options that come on the verge of disclosed dangers and failures, are cured. The genealogical discourse is opened by its exposure of its lineage to its own dissent and to its own overcoming, its own lack of continuing presence in the form of a transdiscursive subjectivity or regulation, and to its own dangers. It is open to whatever emerges as other than genealogy as the lineage of genealogy dies away by the recoiling force of its own knowledge. This type of genealogy is not based on an insistence to be true or on a will to power, but occurs in the force of its self-overcoming recoil. It is composed by the conflicts and coalitions within western thought and practice; it organizes its lineage by the forces of those coalitions and not by the validity of its principles.

We may summarize the elements of genealogical ethos in the following way: 1. Foucault's genealogy is implicated in what it comes to know and is epistemically involved in what it exposes. The disruptions in a given lineage provide a discursive basis for his genealogy's disruptive, curative aspect as he thinks in the perspective of what is excluded from the discourse's organizing forces. 2. The coiling again movement includes a torsion and a springing counterplay of these elements by: (a) making public a lineage's uses of power; (b) uncovering those uses of power in structures of oppression and exclusion that play a role in the genealogy's own knowledge; (c) giving disciplined attention to nonsystematizable randomness; (d) giving focus to accidental formations and universalized values and ideas and the absence of transcendent regulations in the formation of laws that are taken to be 'natural,' transcendent, and universal; and (e) elaborating the discourse-specificity of the principles, rules, and regulations that are regionally necessary in a given genealogy. 3. The movement of Foucault's thought is not ordered by a will to truth, a will to universal knowledge, or the concept of a self finding itself in self-expression. These elements are present in Foucault's discourse, but within a recoiling movement that mitigates their ordering power. 4. The wincing recoil in Foucault's thought is an effect of the interplay of traditionally peripheral and outcast forces, which have nontraditional organizing power in his work, with the central organizing forces in the tradition whose organizing power is weakened when their oppressive limitations are exposed. 5. The conflicts that are encouraged in his genealogies among the various ordering powers are empowered and maintained by the prominence he gives to their divisions and nonsystematizable differences. By maintaining the conflicts without reconciliation by means of systematization or self-constitution on the basis of selected, ideal values, the force of the conflicts tend to engender options that go beyond the conflicts without resolving them. Neither reconciliation nor harmony plays significant ordering roles in his discourse. 6. A negative or hostile recoil by the reader in the presence of the self-overcoming movement in Foucault's thought is usually a movement of thought that eliminates the self-overcoming of its own lineage and that reinstitutes a self-maintaining, authoritative structure of thought.

This ethos involves an embodiment of thinking and speaking that does not reconstitute an emphasis on identity and selfhood. In it one is not inclined to reconstitite a *definitive* self. Rather, this discourse is on its own terms always optional. One can move in it and then move out of it either by its own self-overcoming force or by the force of a change of direction and orientation or by one's insertion of oneself into a very different discourse. The fear and suspicion that Foucault's genealogies arouse are not only a matter of one's having a different and valued perspective. One may become a different body in thinking through Foucault and undergo the emergence of different tastes, desires, and expectations. In that changing body a person knows that in this shift his/her other embodiments are optional identities, that identity enjoys no transcendental regulation, that one is a discursive body amidst many discourses and subdiscourses. One may move out of Foucault's ethos—on its terms one can always move out of it—perhaps rather more markedly than Aphrodite the morning after an evening's bout, but not so marked as to have lost something essential, not so marked as to have fallen or risen by the standards of a self that seeks fulfillment of an already given nature. The embodiment of Foucault's ethos includes knowledge of the optional manner of selfhood and identity. One is in a movement of self-overcoming in which the necessities of *this* movement bear witness to the dangers that one has learned to dread and attempted to prevent. In this ethos one has felt a desire to expose those dangers, including the danger of definitive selfhood, and of the best values and selves he/she knows. One also feels and knows the temporality of the desire to expose, the discursive quality of constituting actions, the continuous, mutational quality of discourses, the unprotected standing of values in this discourse, and the vague horizon that promises only options, experiments, and the loss of who one insists on being: an ethos without an ethics. Selves develop who are doubtful of selfhood because of the tendency to totalization that is found in the activity of self-constituting actions. Lineages are found to recoil in themselves by virtue of the divisions that define them. And one finds no complete prescriptions in all of this because the self-overcoming movement arises from the dangers, ignorance, totalizations, repressions, and conflicts that define the lineage of our possibility of being a self at all. Prescriptiveness, selfhood, and the ecstasy of insight are as much in question as are the limits of representation, the authority of the professional, and the powers that subvert human life in an effort to govern it well. The question of ethics is part of the curative effect of genealogy. Our thoughts and practices are not 'cured' by becoming better persons, but by exposing the dangers of the desire to be better. *This* embodiment, in contrast to self-constitution and the subjectivation that it makes inevitable, is a body of self-overcoming, one that makes knowledge in this movement and is an ethos of recoil in a lineage that has injured human beings by making them self-constituting selves.

If space permitted our next step would be to consider Foucault's specific accounts of the formation of the human self and the values that proliferate in the tradition of humanism. For now we can say that his manner of thought does not advance or produce the ideas that characterize humanism, nor does it refute them. It puts them in question as Foucault finds in his own lineage the forces of recoil and self-overcoming that the lineage has suppressed. This suppression appears to be constitutive of its authority and indicative of its limits. By thinking in its limits and proliferating differences Foucault finds that the humanistic tradition has tended toward its self-surpassing as it has insisted on its right to establish its universal validity.

Notes

1. M. Foucault, *Language, Counter-Memory, Practice,* ed. Donald F.Bouchard (Ithaca, N.Y., 1980), 154.
2. Ibid., 157, emphasis added.
3. Ibid., 156.

PART THREE

THE ENIGMAS OF HUMANISM

16

Acting Human in Our Time
Zygmunt Adamczewski

The agents themselves have to consider what is suited to the circumstances on each occasion . . . .(*Nichomachean Ethics* II 2 1104)

Aristotle's foundation for the philosophical understanding of ethics consists of conduct that is distinctively human, i.e., conduct that is chosen as suitable by every agent on his or her own. Contemporary conceptions of what human beings should or would do are subject to confluent pressures, equally of ancient strength even though of modern appearance. On the one hand, the traditional dominance of reason, either theoretical or practical, appears with scientific facility to command human enactment as a process of rational mechanism: calculable, coded, categorical. On the other hand primeval motion by feeling, e.g., pleasure or pain, utilizing apparent progress such as in psychotherapy or biochemistry, appeals to human behavior treated as an emotional animalism: instant, ingenuous, irrepressible. In their confluence, both these contemporary pressures subject the human being to powers he can not possibly claim as his own, distorting his distinctive actuality as an agent. The question of conduct, which is suitable only when there is the choice of properly acting human, becomes more open than ever in our time.

The conception of reason in the theoretical sense develops from the Platonic grasp of Ideas which contain the immutable aspect of mutable transience, through the medieval adequation to the eternal truth of reality, into the Kantian pursuit of what is transcendent to experience. Throughout, the tendency is to go beyond the way entities immediately strike man's temporal awareness, toward some more "perfect" *order*. While some rationalists would question this, the claim of reason can be seen as that of abstraction from the fleeting, imperfect, unmanageable. Increasingly in modern times, reason comes to rely on and be identified with the procedures utilizing abstract entities, so that today "rational" cognition may be restricted to the adequate formulations of mathematical logic; and these in turn provide access to the calculable and computable—no longer by any means an essentially human prerogative.

But this is not the only line of development: practical reason was not invented by Kant. Particularly under the dominant weight of Judeo-Christian religion, rationality comes to influence man's *doing* as well as his knowing. This is a rather different rationality: not grounded in man, its sources are taken as divine. While man is granted reason, this power of his can be hardly compared to the supreme reason of the universe; consequently, much is rational that cannot be comprehended by man. Therein lies the directive source of everything that man can be commanded, prohibited, permitted—*to do.* With this tradition behind it, the Kantian practical reason can issue in imperatives. But there and elsewhere, the growth of secularizing disbelief gradually removes or veils the divine source, while reason remains as that which is to rule. And thus in modern times the "rational" becomes vested in rules and regulations, commandments, principles and codes of behavior. It does not primarily matter whether they issue still from religious belief or from political adherence, "racial" consciousness, social and institutional membership. They are there to put order into what could otherwise be disorderly.

With all the obvious differences in this sketch of the two lines of rational evolution, it is interesting to note their points of convergence. They both concern man's relation to entities abstractly transcending his individual existence. Correlative to this, they both represent his search for manageable order, even though it be alien. Again correspondingly, they both yield results which are "authoritative" in an impersonal and *unowned* mode of acceptance, which thus postulate a sameness for all individuals in question. Not coincidentally, this sameness has an atemporal character: the rational order both of knowing and of doing is postulated and asserted as unchanging, as valid beyond any man's place in history.

Most important in the convergence of these lines is how that comes to affect the existing human being. The configuration of reason for men of our time is novel: it is so on account of recent technical transformations. Technically applied, theoretical reason has produced mechanical models of calculation and computation far exceeding the powers of an individual man who therefore has to adapt himself to them, with pains. Machines can perform the orderly kind of "thinking" with much more speed and reliability than an ordinary individual. Nor is he in control and possession of them; if anyone is, it must be the "superior" nonindividual entities: governments or institutions, bodies political, commercial, academic, etc. At the same time, it must be noted, it is precisely such entities, inheriting the throne of divinity, that utilize the practical history of reason today in issuing rules, codes, prescriptions. The consequence is that man to be "rational" must on the one hand imitate the order of the machinery of knowledge and on the other hand behave obediently towards entities "greater" than himself. To do that which "is done" with efficiency and precision—this is the management of reason. Expected of the individual is *not responsible action but rather correct reaction to requirements, theoretical and practical;* he is less agent than re-agent. All this is very far from the Aristotelian vision of responsibility which considers for itself what is suited: the distance shows up the *abdication of conduct.*

It can still be said that this choice is open to the human being of our time: to live easily in the mechanical order of rational reactions. But the choice in this perspective becomes inconspicuous and forgettable, since it is the choice *not* to choose on one's own. In this restricted version of rationality—which is not described as unavoidable—man does not respond to the openness of being there, but reacts to closed prescriptive patterns of expectations. Where he knows the rules, as a unit of society, a party member, an employee, even as parent, he is expected to obey them; where the procedure is in doubt, he is expected to calculate the prospects and follow the logical results; least expected is that he should act in a unique manner of his "own." To put it drastically, the model is one of button-pushing with expected reactions to follow. Does such a *mechanism* exhaust the meaning of "rational life"? No, but in our time this is its closest context for a great many people, not excluding some who call themselves philosophers: the mechanism of codes, rules, calculations, results, and automatic reactions —not an equivalent of *human* conduct.

The other contemporary possibility in this design can be shown in polar opposition to the mechanism of reason: while this relies on expected reactions, the other moves with the unpredictable spontaneity of feeling. While the former requires restraint for the sake of order, the latter demands outlet at the risk of disorder: this is less tangible, less clear in history, and also less novel. Although its origins in thought are understandably ancient, yet its present sophistication is relatively recent. The main conceptual thread of this tendency can be seen in hedonism, a doctrine which, though it be vacuous, is difficult to eliminate especially in its appeal to immature minds. Yet in our time it would be an oversimplification to think here of a naive pursuit of pleasure, especially when taking into account the influence of psychoanalysis, sadomasochism, sex "education," as well as admixtures of cults, mystical, anarchist, "idealistic." It can amount to pursuit of pain, of violence, of desire or excitement, even of apathy. But what such contemporary "emotionalism" inherits from older hedonist aspirations is the yielding to immediacy of experience and a voluptuary demand of novelty. It is in this respect, too, opposed to a "rationalism" that depends on and seeks concreteness of experiential data shunning abstractions, thus even the calculated abstractions of Benthamic hedonism. While it often professes contempt for involvements of social machinery, like any other contemporary development it is not free from reliance on technical resources of society in their ability to stimulate and "expand" experience: cars, electronics, drugs are welcome instruments to secure immediately speed, fun, carelessness, danger, stimulation, with much ease.

Emotionalism is understood here as a *receptive* accumulation of experiential challenges with little regard for their further significance in existence. It asks for, and as soon as available, takes in immediate joy, immediate risk, immediate lust, and more naively and vaguely, immediate peace in the world, immediate change in power structure, immediate universal love. It is obviously though not exclusively attractive for the young, while the prospect of reactional mechanism is much more pertinent to older age. But their contrast must not be identified with a clash of generations: some people never outgrow juvenility and some court senility while growing up. The yielding to the emotional and sensational tones for the sake of concentrating the feeling that one is alive resembles the "aesthetic" pattern of existence, as visualized by Kierkegaard, and like it, is doomed to frequent frustration. While it lacks the mechanical perpetuity of rationalism, nevertheless because it draws on the immediate elemental sources of natural life, it has a capacity for each resuscitation, after failures, reawakening with fresh appeal; thus the transition from this to something "ethical" is in no way necessitated, as Kierkegaard tended to suggest. Rather, this is a matter for open choice, although once more it may be observed that the choice of feeling receptivity in its natural closeness and apparent obviousness is hardly perceptible, therefore very much in question: what is easier than accepting pleasure—why should there be any "choosing" of it?

What becomes of the human being in such passive yielding to the empirical flood brought by nature? It cannot be said that he renounces open discovery of being, but it can be claimed that he fails to avail himself of the possible human stance for it: active in an ecstatic grasp. In other words, man acquiesces here in a restriction to the nature of the *animal* he is, because feeling experience is by no means a human distinction: it is the right of animal awareness. This, while certainly not predeterminately closed, is not, either, "dis-closing" and self-founding as the human can become. Men who at all costs want to feel more alive are merely alive, no more. This is no negation of humanity, since that is animality, too. The model for living by accumulation of immediate experience will be ever more refined and rich, when adopted by humans; it remains for all that an animal model. When the operative mode is simply taking in whatever is there because it is there, pleasing, exciting, thrilling, then this lacks the strictly human possibility or power: to question how to be, to search for a self-stance in the world, to consider on one's own what is suited to that. With choice neglected, perhaps negligible, this means in its own terms *an abdication of conduct.*

If this be well understood, such a possibility of existence can be summarized under the heading of "passion." But when this term is mentioned, what is intended is not so much its driving, reaching, thrusting significance, as rather its primitive sense which contrasts it with "action": accepting, undergoing, receptivity. In the yielding mood which expands human animality, the prompting experiences are those of instinct, impulse, reflex; and these, while not disqualified as stimuli of action proper, do not form it as human action. Another etymological scope of "passion" is that of suffering; but again, not in its later connection with pain, which may be incidental, but in the older sense of subjection and even indifference. It is with these provisions that man's reliance on the manifold of empirical immediacy can be understood as "passional." And in this sense the human being, not fulfilling his possibilities as an ethical agent for conduct, can be regarded existentially as passive: yielding to what nature provides, he takes life and lets it merely give itself to him.

It may be noted at this point, however, that the earlier sketched contemporary contraction of "rationalism" which produces man as mechanical reagent also gives him a "passional" role. While it might have been confusing to allude to passion in the passages referring to rationalism, nonetheless in the present understanding this can apply. The man who automatically obeys and follows the commands and rules of impersonal reason can also be seen with regard to his possible existence as no more than undergoing it and subjected to it. This conclusion, if proper, may be interesting. At first, "rationalism" and "emotionalism" are generally understood as in polar contrast; but in their closer interpretation they turn out to be in a way cognate. The two possibilities sketched out are not meant for an alternation: a chosen way to be for man of our time need not pass through just these alternatives, although in the midst of present phenomena around the world, they constitute actual pressures upon him. Due to this fact, it is easy to fall into *rational mechanism or emotional animalism.* But ethically more in question is the choice *between* what these two have in common—viz., *passional subjectedness* —*and* some other way. The two pressuring possibilities can have a cognate relationship because both of them signify a passing off the other way to exist: conduct suiting a human agent.

In Aristotelian terms, one might be tempted to say that wherever there are two extremes requiring comparison, there is the ethically proper middle ground. This paraphrase is naturally, with regard to tradition, hazardous and questionable. The objection can instantly be raised that for Aristotle two extremes include an excess and a deficiency, and that he might have allowed for both with reference to feeling, also for a deficiency of reason, but certainly not an excess of it; indeed, that for him reason was to be found only in the golden middle. All this is historically undeniable, yet must be judged precisely with respect for history, i.e., history of ideas and conceptions. Aristotle, no more than anyone else, could have foreseen their future transformations. What reason amounted to for him already diverged from what it meant to Plato; and it can not be readily asserted that he would recognize his "reason" in the subsequent significations given to that word by Aquinas, Descartes, Spinoza, Hume, Kant, Hegel. Therefore, while anyone might criticize the foregoing characterization of "rationalism," it should be granted that this had to take into account factors present in our time, and not twenty-four centuries ago. *The origin of ethics in conduct,* recollected here from Aristotle, may have been found with his notion of rationality; it may not be, in the present, with what that notion has become. It appears that a definite shift has taken place across history: that which used to fulfill adequately the human "function," reason, has been dehumanized into abstraction, while the opposing aspect of concrete immediacy has been adapted, in particular technically, to such sophisticated human inclinations as to disguise its original animality. In consequence, the spontaneity of feeling may show in an attractive light, so as to be invoked as more naturally human than a universally ruling "mechanism of concepts and principles" (F. Nietzsche, *The Birth of Tragedy*, XV).

That this is very remote from the Aristotelian intentions need hardly be reiterated.

In our time, acting as human as possible is very visibly exposed to moving pressures that are not very contemporary at all. What is easily conceived as progress does not ease the chance for choosing conduct suitably owned by the agent, nor need this—if outstanding in nature—chance be taken with ease. Possibly, being human discloses itself as becoming ever more open to question.

17

Pyrrhonism and the Concept of a Common Human Nature in Eighteenth-Century Aesthetic Thought

Michael Cardy

The great sixteenth-century writer, Montaigne, was not a systematic philosopher but rather, as Bertrand Russell noted, the most characteristic figure of that "large and fruitful disorder" which epitomized intellectual life during the Renaissance.[1] In the "Apologie de Raimond Sebond," the longest of his essays, Montaigne set out to write a vindication of the orthodox fifteenth-century Spanish theologian, Raimondo Sebon. In the course of his discussion of Sebon, however, Montaigne completely undermined the foundations of the theologian's ideas. Sebon believed that faith was justifiable through reason. Montaigne cited a variety of examples from classical and modern philosophy to show that rational arguments applied to the same set of postulates had led thinkers to widely divergent conclusions. Human reason, therefore, could not be trusted. Montaigne expressed it thus:

> But the fact that there is no proposition to be found in human discourse that is not subject to debate and controversy, or that cannot be so, illustrates very well that our natural judgment does not grasp at all clearly what it does grasp. For my judgment cannot convince the judgment of my companion, which is a sign that I grasp what I do through some means other than through a natural power that exists in me and in all men.[2]

If reason, then, was such an unreliable tool for deriving sure knowledge about the world, simply because it led to differing conclusions among different men and women, by what means could such knowledge be acquired? Montaigne opted, experimentally, for sense perceptions. "All knowledge," he noted, "is acquired through the senses: they are our masters. . . . Learning begins through them and finds its resolution in them."[3] That conclusion, however, was entirely interim and, as Montaigne realized, in the essay he had already vitiated it. Significantly, it was in the course of a digression on human beauty that the capacity of the senses to generate accurate knowledge had been questioned:

> As for the beauty of the body, I would be pleased to know if we are in agreement about its description. It is likely that we scarcely know what our beauty in nature and in general is, since we give to our human beauty so many diverse forms. If there were some natural prescription for this, we would all recognize it in common, just like the heat of fire.[4]

But the senses do not provide a common response to beauty in the same way that we can all recognize heat. The same is true with respect to ugliness in nature. Just as one man's meat is another man's poison, so one man's beauty is another man's ugliness. Definition of either escapes universally applicable criteria and becomes a matter of individual taste. Montaigne seemed to have arrived at a position held by the Pyrrhonists of antiquity, according to which neither reason nor sense perception could afford any accurate knowledge about the world upon which all men and women could agree, with the exception of purely biological responses to phenomena such as heat. Thus, says Montaigne, man "cannot escape the fact that the senses are the sovereign masters of knowledge; but they are uncertain and falsifiable in all circumstances."[5] Hence the famous *Que sais-je?* of Montaigne.

The skepticism of the Pyrrhonists over all matters, even about the existence of existence itself, might well seem to be Montaigne's final despairing position. In the "Apologie" there are in fact a considerable number of references to the Pyrrhonists of antiquity, but almost all of them are hostile and unflattering. Montaigne thus castigates the philosophical tradition that best seems to support his arguments. Clearly the Pyrrhonist position is inimical to any form of religious belief, since it states that we can believe nothing afforded either by our mind or our sense perceptions. The only solution, for Montaigne, was to postulate the existence of God, belief in whose existence resolved all intellectual dilemmas, since the mysteries of His Divinity transcend even the most sublime efforts of puny human beings. Montaigne, in all humility and sincerity, bowed before the superior, incomprehensible, and transcendent nature of God: "It is no wonder that our natural earthly capacities cannot conceive of that supernatural and celestial knowledge; let us bring to it nothing more than obedience and humility."[6] Having set out to prove the rational nature of religious belief, Montaigne was only saved from the extremely unpalatable conclusions to which his arguments might be thought in all logic to have led him by his deeply felt faith. However, in the "Apologie" Montaigne had raised a warning signal. He had given notice to his successors that, when treating of aesthetic matters, they had better tread gingerly, since the apparently anodyne field of aesthetic ideas could easily become very dangerous territory indeed. Through his serious flirtation with Pyrrhonism, Montaigne seemed to have cut away the ground upon which firm statements about any matter of importance could be made.

In the seventeenth century, few thinkers accepted Montaigne's challenge directly. Descartes' attempt to restore order out of chaos could only be made by postulating a principle of reason which the Pyrrhonist position seemed already to have cut away. Pascal, addressing himself to the *libertins* who looked back to Montaigne as a precursor justifying their attitudes, engaged in an implicit dialogue with Montaigne and in particular with the latter's apparent advocacy of the relativity of all human judgments. Thus, Montaigne had said in the "Apologie": "What truth is confined within those mountains, which is falsehood in the world beyond them",[7] which a terse sentence of Pascal echoes and reformulates in the following manner: "Truth on this side of the Pyrenees, falsehood on the other."[8] That statement is not just an expression of Pascal's Jansenist gallicanism; it was, more importantly, a very puzzling problem that required solution, since Pascal could never have condoned complacent acceptance of moral and spiritual relativism. Pascal did not solve the problem, despite the intellectual *brio* of the *Pensées,* but at least he saw the necessity of elaborating a universally acceptable psychology of human beings if Christianity was ever to be vindicated as the one true religion that responded to all the needs of mankind.

Contemporaneously, the intervention of Hobbes into the intellectual debates of the century did not assist those who sought to extrapolate order from the potential chaos triggered by Montaigne's thought. Hobbes depicted human beings as limited by their own egocentricity and, in their relationships, activated by self-interest and fear. He considered that moral judgments were made in terms of individual human urges, were thus relative, and could be tested against no sure, absolute criteria. It appeared, then, that whether one started from ethics or aesthetics, the same conclusion was reached: there existed no certain basis for making judgments. In both fields, the quirks of the individual were paramount. No action, no taste, was more valid than, or preferable to, any other. All judgments were relative.

What sparked the serious reconsideration of aesthetic matters in France and led to the abundance of treatises, essays, and discourses on questions such as beauty, genius, and taste identifiable in eighteenth-century bibliography was the Quarrel of the Ancients and the Moderns, which took place in the last fifteen years or so of the seventeenth century and was rekindled in the second decade of the eighteenth.[9] Parallel quarrels also occurred in England and Italy. To rehearse the arguments of both sides in the Quarrel would far exceed the bounds of the present paper; for the purposes of this text, what matters is that some very eminent names among the French intelligentsia—men and women who shared more or less the same education, values, and prejudices—could not agree about a number of basic aesthetic questions. In particular, there existed serious division over what constituted beauty in literary discourse and how it was to be detected. It is worthwhile noting, in passing, that in the seventeenth and eighteenth centuries, beauty in art was conceived of primarily in terms of literature, with architecture and the visual arts rather behind and music nowhere in sight, at least until around 1750. It is also worthy of remark that British aesthetic thinkers of the age were more inclined than their French counterparts to draw their examples from the beauty of the natural world.

Given the cosmopolitanism of the eighteenth century and the rapid movement of ideas from one national culture to another, it is futile to approach
the aesthetic ideas of the period in anything other than a comparative perspective. This study is largely, though not exclusively, concerned with four
texts: J. P. de Crousaz, *Traité du beau* (1715); Francis Hutcheson, *An Inquiry into the Original of our Ideas of Beauty and Virtue* (1725); the *père*
André, *Essai sur le beau* (1741); and Diderot, article "Beau" in *Encyclopédie*
II (1752).[10] The thinkers in question will be considered in groups of two in
chronological order. Given the dangers implicit in the Pyrrhonist argument
as set out by Montaigne, the crucial questions these thinkers had to face were:
(i) Has beauty an objective, absolute existence or is its existence dependent
on the subjective perception of a sentient being? (ii) If the latter, how can
relativity of judgment be avoided in aesthetics and, by extension, in ethics too?

Both Crousaz and Hutcheson were Calvinists and thus had a strong
incentive to affirm the existence of absolutes. However, they both decided
that beauty depended for its existence on human perception. Crousaz expressed it thus: "Our hearts pay homage to it (= beauty) without consulting
the ideas of our minds, and it seems that it triumphs over us without requiring us to help in its victory."[11] Hutcheson claimed that "beauty, like other
names of sensible ideas, properly denotes the perception of some mind."[12]
Despite his use of the word *mind,* Hutcheson considered the apprehension
of beauty sudden and intuitive, entirely beyond the capability of logical analysis: "The pleasure does not arise from any principles, proportions, causes,
or of the usefulness of the object, but strikes us first with the idea of beauty;
nor does the most accurate knowledge increase this pleasure of beauty."[13]

Crousaz and Hutcheson held different views of perceptions, however.
Crousaz divided perceptions into two categories, those acquired through *ideas*
and those acquired through *feelings.* Each category had its own area of action:
"Ideas preoccupy our minds, feelings interest our hearts; ideas amuse us, they
exercise our attention, but feelings dominate and overwhelm us."[14] Since feelings had this overriding power, we could not be master of them. But the
mind, too, was capable of apprehending beauty in its own right. There were
thus two kinds of apprehensions of beauty, those of *ideas* and those of *feelings.* While Crousaz readily conceded the intuitive responses of the latter,
it was the former which afforded more certain value judgments. Moreover,
in man's perfect state before the Fall, the two sorts of perceptions would
have coincided and thus provided the same aesthetic and moral judgments.
For Crousaz, the mind was the source of the truth of our judgments while
the heart lay at the basis of the quirks of taste. Crousaz clearly saw the immediacy of aesthetic responses and yet he clung tenaciously to an intellectual
principle of beauty, which could be interpreted as God working aesthetically
through human beings. It was his means of avoiding subjectivism and relativity in aesthetics.

Hutcheson, certainly influenced by Locke and Addison, was far less
suspicious than Crousaz of the pleasure principle in aesthetics. Moreover, he
adhered to an optimistic view of the world and humanity characteristic of
early British deism. He believed in a benevolent creation formed by a "Great

Architect" who had so fashioned human beings that the universe was pleasant to them. The pleasure experienced before the beauty of the world differed little from one person to the next; indeed, how could it be otherwise when the potentiality for feeling aesthetic pleasure was an innate faculty bestowed by a just God on His creatures, just as He had conferred upon them a "moral sense," which was the source of all virtue and of their capacity to detect it. Because he did not distrust pleasure and feeling, Hutcheson claimed that the judgments afforded by the senses were no different from those that would have been reached by reason: "The pleasant sensations generally arise from those objects which calm reason would have recommended had we understood their use."[15] By postulating a faculty of aesthetic response germane to a sixth sense and combining it with his optimistic view of creation, Hutcheson eliminated the need to discuss aspects of beauty based upon different kinds of perceptions.

However different their emphasis, then, Hutcheson and Crousaz agreed that beauty is dependent upon human perception and that its apprehension was sudden and intuitive. This was the main tradition of aesthetic ideas in the eighteenth century. The père André and Diderot in the article "Beau" lie outside that tradition, for they both sought and believed they had found a definition of beauty independent of human perception. André was a very rare bird in eighteenth-century French thought: he was a Platonist. Moreover, he quite overtly identified his adversaries as the "modern Pyrrhonists," whom he does not name but who were almost certainly Montaigne and perhaps Pierre Bayle. He attacked them because they "consider beauty . . . as a question of pure taste and pure feeling."[16] Since he himself found the essence of beauty to reside in the preference of human beings for "regularity, order, proportion, symmetry" to their opposites, André asked rhetorically of the Pyrrhonists: "Would not even the slightest attention to our basic ideas have convinced them that regularity, order, proportion, symmetry are essentially preferable to irregularity, disorder, and disproportion?"[17] André wrote that there existed "an essential beauty . . . independent of any institution, even the divine one."[18] Unfortunately, he was unable to define any of his terms clearly nor did he distinguish his essential beauty, which appears to be ideal or absolute, from other categories of beauty which he attempted to establish. He could not demonstrate, either, in what way his essential beauty was independent of God.

Given père André's manifest confusion over aesthetic ideas, it comes as a surprise to read Diderot's assessment of his essay as "the most logical, extensive, and best-argued system I know."[19] But André was the only one of the modern theorists to postulate the existence of objective beauty beyond any consideration of human perception. Diderot, too, wished to establish an essential beauty of the same kind. He prefaced his definition of beauty with an analysis of the sensual and intellectual bases of the growth of certain ideas such as order, relationships, proportion, connections, arrangement, and symmetry which begin to develop at birth. Through consideration of these ideas in a large number of cases, the human mind quickly proceeds to generalization so that they and their opposites become abstract ideas which are as much a part of human experience as the ideas of length, breadth, depth, quantity, and number. Given this, then, what quality is indispensable to any imaginable account of beauty? Diderot claimed that it was that of *relationships:* "I call *beauty* outside myself everything that has within it the capacity to awaken in my understanding the idea of relationships; and *beauty* with respect to myself everything which does in fact awaken that idea."[20] By the first part of that definition, Diderot hoped to establish an objective standard of beauty, which he called *real beauty,* as opposed to that contained in the second part, which he called *perceived beauty.* In Diderot's view, the façade of the Louvre, because of its capacity to awaken the idea of relationships, would always be beautiful, even if there were no human beings, or beings of a similar construction, to perceive its beauty. Thus *real beauty* is not dependent upon an actual perception, as Crousaz and Hutcheson had suggested, only on a theoretical capacity to awaken the idea of relationships in the event of perception. The *perceived beauty* is the actual fulfillment of the first part of the definition, the human observer experiencing the idea of relationships. Diderot anticipated an objection which had to be confronted and which Montaigne, whom he greatly admired, would have been the first to raise: Why do judgments of beauty vary so greatly from one individual to another? He devoted much space to discussing the causes of the variability of judgment and listed twelve, among them differences in talent and environment and the inadequacy of language as a medium of description. It says much for the subtlety and range of Diderot's mind that his enumeration of these causes constitutes a formidable case against the objective existence of beauty as he had attempted to develop it. There were further weaknesses in Diderot's theory, notably his conception of *real beauty,* which has no connection with the tangible world until it is subject to human perception, and also his failure to define the idea of relationships, which in his view lent the theory universality.

In fact, the position on beauty adopted by Diderot in 1752, or more precisely in 1751 when he wrote the article "Beau," was a strange one for him. In 1749 he had published a work called the *Lettre sur les aveugles,* which is in many ways a key text in his intellectual development and which so outraged the authorities that they imprisoned him for three months in the Chateau de Vincennes. The work can be envisaged as an experiment in Lockean sensationalism, quite consciously so, as one of Diderot's statements indicates: "I have never doubted that the state of our organs and our senses has a great deal of influence on our metaphysics and our ethics, and that our most purely intellectual ideas . . . are very closely connected to the conformation of our bodies."[21] The *Lettre* exemplifies very well one of the salient features of eighteenth-century French thought—the flight from rational deduction into experimental induction—and marked a major step in Diderot's progress towards a position of philosophical materialism.

The *Lettre sur les aveugles* was based on wide reading on the topic of blindness and contains some astonishing ideas for the time. For example, Diderot was one of the first to understand the compensation factor in people deprived of a sense, namely that they enjoyed a heightened susceptibility in their remaining senses. Applying this idea to the sense of touch, he speculated on the possibility of reading through the fingers, thus anticipating the work of Louis Braille in the first half of the nineteenth century. But Diderot also used the case of the blind person to undermine the teleological proof of the existence of God, according to which we see God in the majesty of His creation and, in wonder and awe at the beauty of the universe, we recognize and worship the Supreme Being. The blind person could not see the universe and was therefore unlikely to believe in God. Above all, Diderot claimed that the imagination, the aesthetic values, the metaphysics, and the ethics of blind persons differed necessarily from those of the sighted. In short, Diderot was using the case of blindness to contest the universal applicability of Christianity. Consideration of the topic led him to a position in which he seemed to be advancing the relativity of all human values. And that position was a long way from the postulate of the existence of an objective beauty independent of human perception that appeared in the article "Beau" written two years later. How can one explain the apparent *volte-face?*

It would be easy to suppose that Diderot, chastened by his experience of prison, decided to publish nothing that might seem to question the absolute values upon which French society of the time was ostensibly based. It is certainly true that all the more subversive texts he subsequently wrote circulated in manuscript only and did not appear in his lifetime. There is another reason, however. By the early 1750s Diderot had conceived the ambition of writing a science of man that would combine philosophy, psychology and, as he later realized was necessary, physiology. He never wrote the work but pieces of it are to be found in texts like the *Pensées sur l'interprétation de la nature* and the *Rêve de d'Alembert,* together with the documents that are annexed to it, while a very large chunk of it was incorporated into the *Traité de physiologie,* which was left unfinished at his death. It is arguable that, between 1749 and 1751, Diderot realized that the *Lettre sur les aveugles,* apart from leading him to prison, was also leading him to a Pyrrhonist position. The great work he envisaged was perforce postulated on the existence of a human nature common to all and amenable if not to definition then at least to analysis and partial description. Pyrrhonism, by calling into question the universality of the idea of human nature, threatened to vitiate every single statement in the work Diderot proposed to write. Hence the position adopted in the article "Beau" can be envisaged as a holding operation, a statement pro tem., which at least had the merit of affirming absolute values while Diderot set about writing his science of man, a science that would of course have to include a consideration of ethical values too.

Diderot did not solve the philosophical problems posed by Pyrrhonism, but he subsequently used his method of experimental induction to show that the nature of the individual was in a constant state of flux and that human nature as a whole, far from being amenable to fixed definition, was constantly changing. In the *Rêve de d'Alembert* (1769) Diderot prefigures a theory of evolution, including natural selection, which he worked out through his favorite method of dialogue. Biology therefore seemed to provide a way to sidestep metaphysics. Since nature, according to Diderot, is in a constant state of change, human beings, in order to survive, have to adapt and change also.

It might be assumed that Crousaz and Hutcheson, André and Diderot, all failed in their enterprise, whether they postulated an objective beauty or not. In one way or another, they all contorted themselves into knots in their confrontation with aesthetic questions, either in Crousaz's special and unconvincing theory of different kinds of perceptions or Diderot's assumption of an objective beauty for his own philosophical purposes. Moreover, the first three thinkers all had God as a backstop, since they shared a theocentric view of the universe. We should recall, though, that Montaigne too had had recourse to God in order to get the fly out of the flybottle. They were all, willy-nilly, confronting the Pyrrhonist position and they failed to counter it.

In another, though subsidiary, discourse, they were a good deal more successful. This was their treatment of the motif of the beauty to be found in ugliness. Plainly, not every object in the natural world is beautiful; some we would categorize, without thinking, as ugly. It is around the early years of the eighteenth century that taste in respect of certain natural phenomena, mountains for example, began to change. It was noted that the natural world, in certain forms and moods, could inspire terror or awe in the beholder and that these emotions, in some obscure way, were pleasurable. This feeling was well analyzed by Addison when speaking of the pleasure afforded by "the sight of what is great, uncommon, or beautiful." He noted that while ". . . the horror or loathsomeness of an object may overbear the pleasure which results from its greatness, novelty, or beauty, . . . there still will be . . . a mixture of delight in the very disgust it gives us."[22] This idea, that aesthetic pleasure was frequently mixed, passed rapidly into France and was applied to human spectacles by the abbé Dubos in his *Réflexions critiques* (1719). Speaking of the pleasure experienced by the Romans at the spectacle of gladiatorial combats, Dubos remarked: ". . . there exists in the cruellest spectacles a kind of attraction which makes them enjoyable to the most humane peoples."[23] Not long after Dubos, Hutcheson too noted the beauty in ugliness as well as the kind of ambivalent emotion we derive from it:

> There are horrors raised by some objects which are only the effect of fear for ourselves, or compassion towards others . . . for we find that most of those objects which excite horror at first, when experience or reason has removed the fear, may become the occasions of pleasure, as ravenous beasts, a tempestuous sea, a craggy precipice, a dark, shady valley.[24]

Similar feelings were often experienced in the presence of ruins, envisaged as so rooted in their landscapes that they formed an integral part of them. The traveller Dupaty, around the middle of the century, reacted thus to the ruins of Paestum: "Let me derive from this solitude, from this desert, from these ruins, a sort of horror which enchants me."[25] An enchanting horror. That is exactly the feeling Addison, Dubos, and Hutcheson had described and that Edmund Burke subjected to a more sustained analysis in his *Philosophical Enquiry* of 1759. Burke made the feeling a separate aesthetic category, which he termed the *sublime*. His basic definition is as follows: "Whatever is fitted in any sort to excite the ideas of pain and danger, that is to say, whatever is in any sort terrible, or is conversant about terrible objects, is a source of the sublime."[26] Like Dupaty, Burke used oxymoron to summarize the feeling in a nutshell: he called it a *delightful horror.*

In parallel with this reflection on the beauty to be found in ugliness is another idea, less original, which has its roots in antiquity: the ability of the artistic creator to transform ugliness in nature into artistic beauty. Both Crousaz and Hutcheson subscribed to this view. Thus Crousaz: "The representations of the most hideous and hateful things can nonetheless be beautiful too, for example, the depiction of a monster, a murder or a barbarous act."[27] And Hutcheson:

> To obtain comparative (= artistic) beauty alone, it is not necessary that there be any beauty in the original . . . the deformities of old age in a picture, the rudest rocks or mountains in a landscape, if well represented, shall have abundant beauty though perhaps not so great as if the original were absolutely beautiful and as well represented.[28]

Significantly, Hutcheson contradicts himself immediately by adding: ". . . nay, perhaps the novelty may make us prefer the representation of irregularity." Hutcheson's afterthought, by underlining the originality of new insights on nature and their artistic expression, anticipates the future of aesthetic thought in the century and points the way towards a solution of the Pyrrhonist dilemma, at least in the realm of aesthetics. The novelty and irregularity of which he spoke were echoed in Diderot's comment on the sublime in a letter written to his mistress, Sophie Volland, in 1762:

> Great effects arise in all cases out of voluptuous ideas mingled with terrifying ones; for example, beautiful half-naked women offering us a delicious potion in the bleeding skulls of our enemies. That is the model of all things sublime. It is then that the soul opens itself to pleasure and shudders with horror. These mixed sensations fix the soul in a posture that is completely strange; it is the very essence of the sublime to penetrate us in a manner that is entirely out of the ordinary.[29]

The juxtaposition here of *pleasure* and *horror* indicates the understanding of one of the most important eighteenth-century figures that aesthetic sensations were a good deal more complex than had hitherto been thought. The passage from Diderot's letter, indeed the whole discourse on the beauty to be created out of ugliness, anticipates the sense of *strangeness* characteristic of much modern art.

The close links between aesthetics and ethics have already been noted. The thinkers under consideration clearly struggled so hard to place aesthetics on a firm footing because they feared the consequences for moral philosophy if they did not do so. The consequences of failure may be illustrated briefly by a passing reference to Sade. Sade almost certainly reflected upon Rousseau's belief that conscience or intuition, the inner voice of man's true nature, constituted the principle tool of morality and came to the conclusion, as Rousseau effectively did, that everything that was natural was good. In a horrendous travesty of Rousseau's proposition, Sade in his novels depicted characters fulfilling themselves as individuals by inflicting disgusting cruelty on helpless victims in a sexual context and, moreover, providing a seemingly logical justification for their outrageous conduct. One passage from *Justine,* the words of the diabolical Dom Clément to Thérèse, will suffice to illustrate this point:

> Doubtless the most absurd thing in the world, my dear Thérèse . . . is to seek to argue about men's tastes, to oppose, blame or punish them, if they do not conform either to the laws of the country one lives in or to social conventions. Really, men will never understand that there exists no sort of tastes, however odd or criminal one may suppose them to be, which do not depend upon the sort of organization we have received from nature. Once that is accepted, I ask you, what right has any man to dare demand of another to reform his tastes or to model them on the social order? What right have the laws, which are made for man's happiness, to dare to treat with severity the man who cannot correct himself or who could only do so at the expense of that happiness which the laws are supposed to safeguard? But even if one desired to change one's taste, is that possible? Do we have the capacity to remake ourselves? Can we become other than we are?[30]

What Sade was doing here, and the point is central to the message of his novels, was extrapolate the unthinkable from the Pyrrhonist position and justify the rights of self-fulfillment for those who proved themselves fit to enjoy them, regardless of the cost of those rights to others. The fact that such an affirmation of moral anarchy required victims for its achievement, that some human beings had to be sacrificed for the gratification of others, concerned Sade not at all. In the passage quoted Sade based his arguments on matters of *taste.* The link with aesthetics is immediately apparent. The moral anarchy so feared by the aesthetic thinkers was thus, in some sense, embodied by the moral philosophy of Sade.

The ideas of Sade have had little future. In well-regulated societies, the force of law is used to discourage people from committing the kind of atrocities depicted in Sade's novels and the application of the law is justified by the pragmatic argument that an individual's rights cease when they begin to infringe upon the rights of others. We judge actions primarily by their effects on others; we apply utilitarian, experimental criteria to the formulation of ethical judgments. Such an approach to moral philosophy is doubtless as old as Aristotle, and it seems to work.[31] Nonetheless, Sades teaches us that, for our own peace of mind, we had better separate ethics and aesthetics. This is, in effect, what has happened since the end of the eighteenth century. It is now rare to find mainly ethical criteria applied to the assessment of artistic questions. In short, the Pyrrhonist approach is anathema in ethics, but acceptable in aesthetics.

This paper deals with the last concerted effort that was made to establish the science of beauty on firm foundations, together with some of the problems the thinkers concerned had to face and some of the reasons for their failure, though that failure was surely limited and accompanied by some gains. By pointing to the beauty to be found in, or created out of, ugliness, the thinkers in question helped to stimulate a reawakening to the immense resources of inspiration still available to the artist, thus counteracting a sense prevalent at the end of the seventeenth century, in France at least, that nature had been in some way exhausted by the great thinkers, scientists, and artists of the previous age. The very serious problems raised by the Pyrrhonist challenge were either absorbed into a theocentric view of the universe, sidestepped, or diverted into productive channels by the application of the method of experimental induction. It can come as no surprise, therefore, that parallel with the eighteenth-century discourse on beauty there occurred a reflection on taste, the principal features of which would require another paper as long as this one just to outline.[32]

Pyrrhonism in its aesthetic mode is doubtless harmless enough. If the nature of each individual is more imminent than immanent, then *homo aestheticus* is in a constant state of flux. The growth of individualism since the end of the eighteenth century has ensured the abandonment of any concept of a traditional culture and exalted the primacy of relativism in aesthetics. In no genre now does art possess common postulates nor does the public apply common criteria in assessing it. A modern liberal society can certainly absorb the critical disarray engendered by such a situation. The case is otherwise when the relativism bred by Pyrrhonist discourse is applied to moral philosophy. As soon as personal morality is characterized solely as a matter of individual taste, as Sade described it at the end of the eighteenth century, any action can be justified and anarchy is likely to ensue. What the thinkers studied in this paper tried to do was to shore up a crumbling philosophical position and to reaffirm a faith in humanity that seemed to be threatened by the moral nihilism so easily engendered by the Pyrrhonist discourse.

Notes

1. Bertrand Russell, *A History of Western Philosophy* (London, 1961), 18.

2. Montaigne, *Essais,* ed. Maurice Rat (Paris, 1962), vol. 1, 631. All translations from the French are my own.

3. Ibid., 661.

4. Ibid., 533.

5. Ibid., 667.

6. Ibid., 554.

7. Ibid., 651.

8. Pascal, *Oeuvres Complètes,* ed. Jacques Chevalier (Paris, 1954), 1149. In context, Pascal was discussing the relativity of human justice, but he was aware of the dangers of Pyrrhonism for Christian apologetics.

9. See Hippolyte Rigault, *Histoire de la Querelle des Anciens et des Modernes* (Paris, 1856) and Hubert Gillot, *La Querelle des Anciens et des Modernes en France* (Nancy, 1914). These two books have not been superseded and remain indispensable for any study of the Quarrel in France.

10. The editions used are: J. P. de Crousaz, *Traité du beau* (Amsterdam, 1715); Francis Hutcheson, *An Inquiry into the Original of our Ideas of Beauty and Virtue,* 3rd ed., corrected (London, 1729); J. André, *Essai sur le beau,* nouvelle édition, augmentée de six discours (Paris, 1810); Diderot, article "Beau," *Encyclopédie,* vol. 2, ed. J. Lough et J. Proust in *Oeuvres Complètes* (Paris, 1975-) vol. 6, pp. 135–

234   *The Enigmas of Humanism*

171. Useful material on aesthetic ideas in eighteenth-century France is to be found in T. M. Mustoxidi, *Histoire de l'esthétique française 1700–1900* (Paris, 1920) and Raymond Bayer, *Histoire de l'esthétique* (Paris, 1961). See also the chapter on "Beauty, Genius and Taste" in Michael Cardy, *The Literary Doctrines of Jean-François Marmontel,* Studies on Voltaire and the Eighteenth Century 210 (Oxford, 1982), 20–55. The texts under review, and many others, are there envisaged in a rather different perspective.

11. Crousaz, *Traité,* 63. The only recent full-length study of Crousaz is Jacqueline E. De La Harpe, *Jean-Pierre de Crousaz et le conflit des idées au Siècle des Lumières* (Geneva, 1955).

12. Hutcheson, *Inquiry,* 14. Still worth reading on Hutcheson is W. R. Scott, *Francis Hutcheson: His Life, Teaching and Position in the History of Philosophy* (Cambridge, 1900).

13. Hutcheson, *Inquiry,* 11.

14. Crousaz, *Traité,* 8.

15. Hutcheson, *Inquiry,* 37.

16. André, *Essai,* 101.

17. Ibid., 23.

18. Ibid., 19.

19. Diderot, *Oeuvres Complètes,* vol. 6, 147.

20. Ibid., 156. The most comprehensive book on Diderot's aesthetic ideas is Jacques Chouillet, *La Formation des idées esthétiques de Diderot, 1745–1763* (Paris, 1973). There are many incisive comments on the topic in Lester G. Crocker, *Two Diderot Studies: Ethics and Esthetics* (Baltimore, 1952).

21. Diderot, *Lettre sur les aveugles* in *Oeuvres Complètes,* ed. J. Assézat et M. Tourneux (Paris, 1875–1877), vol. 1, 288.

22. Steele, Addison and others, *The Spectator,* ed. Donald F. Bond (Oxford, 1965), vol. 3, 540.

23. J. -B. Dubos, *Réflexions critiques sur la poésie et sur la peinture,* 6e édition (Paris, 1755), vol. 1, 21.

24. Hutcheson, *Inquiry,* 72.

25. Quoted by Roland Mortier, *La Poétique des ruines en France* (Geneva, 1974), 150.

26. Edmund Burke, *A Philosophical Enquiry into the Origin of our Ideas of the Sublime and Beautiful,* 2nd ed. (London, 1759), 58.

27. Crousaz, *Traité,* 45.

28. Hutcheson, *Inquiry,* 39–40.

29. Diderot, *Correspondance,* ed. G. Roth et J. Varloot (Paris, 1960–1967), vol. 4, 196.

30. Sade, *Oeuvres Complètes* (Paris, 1962–1964), vol. 3, 199.

31. I am simplifying here, of course. I realize that we take into account people's intentions when judging their actions, also that we do not blame them for actions the consequences of which they could not have foreseen.

32. There is a considerable bibliography on the subject of taste as an aesthetic faculty. A good starting point for the study of French discourse on the topic is J.-B. Barrère, *L'Idée de goût de Pascal à Valéry* (Paris, 1972).

18

The Human Person in American Pragmatism

Richard P. Francis

I begin by clarifying the meaning of Pragmatism as it applies to all of its devotees, giving its common features. While there was some slight European interest, Pragmatism has always been called "American," in the "United States" sense of American. It is considered to be the indigenous philosophy of the United States, something more or less original in the world's several millenia of intellectual history, if that is possible. Nevertheless, this school or movement originated and flourished in the United States at the turn of the twentieth century and genuinely occupied scholars throughout the first half of this century. Right now it is not fashionable for anyone to call himself or herself a Pragmatist even though W. V. O. Quine is sometimes called the last Pragmatist and Richard Rorty contributes to the movement.[1] But then labels are eschewed by most modern scholars.

In the United States, historically, serious philosophy developed as Puritanism, Republicanism, Transcendentalism, Idealism, and last of all, Pragmatism. While all of the other movements had close European determinants, only Pragmatism was relatively free from such influences, not being an adaptation or variation of European philosophy. It more naturally represents the American spirit and way of life.[2] The term "Pragmatism" is a translation from the Greek for whatever is "practical" or a "practicalism." So our native-born philosophy is one of practice, rather than one of contemplation or speculation; one of action, of doing, rather than one of deep or irrelevant thinking.

The United States is a new nation, with a background of practical pioneering and settling the wilderness. Just before and at the turn of the century, rapid industrialization, capitalism, and the market forces were culturally fundamental, so that appropriately the "cash value" of ideas came into play. While not altogether abandoning the traditional past, correctly enough, Pragmatism emphasized far more the rich possibilities of the future. Ideas were never abstractions, but always plans-for-action, something "to do," carrying practical future consequences. Working ideas set up certain habits of action in the happy expectation of changing, reconstructing, or civilizing the world. Except for this energetic, busy kind of philosophy, how else could the United States in such a relatively short time become the most powerful country in the world?

As did the early settlers, the Pragmatists believed in a powerful, plastic, resilient nature. For human beings that nature is always changing as they themselves are changing, caught up individually and socially in an adventurous, hazardous, ongoing experience. "Experience" is a fundamental term as an active, interacting, undergoing, undertaking, and reconstructing of life's events. In a tough, perilous world of nature, optimism prevails in that human experience can be zestful, anticipating and shaping the future in a regularly meliorating, benevolent fashion. The promise of the future encourages confidence, hard work, ambition, efficiency, and striving for success. The American way is usually successful and victory laden, with a drive to win. An almost therapeutic freshness drives the people from project to project, from problems to resolutions, from traditional encrustations to testing novelties, from fear to adventure. The Pragmatists accordingly view the tenuous, impermanent world as a "pressure boiler" that needs to be tamed, conquered, and even exploited for its promise. Failures do occur, of course, which are good reasons to try and try again until some modicum of success is reached, however lasting or short-lived it is.

The Pragmatists typically rebel against metaphysics as constructing useless, abstract explanatory systems, logically removed from ordinary, day-to-day, piecemeal, concrete, individual experiences. Yet they all fit into some kind of empiricism that stresses and values concrete, real experience as the locus of action and thought, always with contingent, tentative, unfinished results. Observable experience is the matrix of learning and action which gives concrete meanings to ideas and serves as the source for continuing growth in understanding and in shaping things. All concrete experiences are interconnected with others in a basic network of forces constantly shaping and reshaping themselves. Each individual existent, including human beings, is actively engaged in an ongoing practical way in order to survive and to maintain itself. Human beings are usually never simply passive observers of nature but are empirically imbedded in an ongoing, complex nature, engaged continuously and strenuously in learning-by-doing, to make sense of things, or to solve problems. Within experience, replete with possibilities, the human organism is energized "to do something." Within empiricism, as a type of metaphysics, the Pragmatists insist that Pragmatism is not so much a philosophy, as it is a method, not so much a system of ideas, as a way of doing things.

In fact, in all cases the Pragmatic method is the method of getting practical results, of checking on and of manipulating things to produce improvement, or problem resolution and tension reduction. Even our intelligence is meant to be something practical in checking the results of our ideas to see if our ideas do in fact make any significant difference in our concrete lives. Useful ideas that do improve things approximate the truth, or validation, or warranty of those ideas. Human intelligence is more geared to problem-solving than to anything else. It emerges out of the powerful, complex forces of nature only under conditions of stress and is meant to resolve that stress and to ameliorate the circumstances. The essential and exclusive reason for the existence of our intelligence is to deal with stress in our transacting and interacting with diverse problematic environments including the physical and social environment.

Because they respected the real, undisputed progress that modern science makes in human life, the Pragmatists all agreed to the central importance of the fact and method of science as crucial to and as the stereotype of the Pragmatic method. The method of Pragmatism is the method of science because science solves problems beneficially and improves the human condition. The Pragmatic method is the scientific method. In writings such as "How to Make our Ideas Clear" and *How We Think,* as well as in the *Quest for Certainty,* and in *Logic: The Theory of Inquiry,* repeatedly the scientific method is established as the only worthwhile method that succeeds.[3]

This method begins with a "felt need," a doubt, or uncertainty, a dispute, a crisis, a problem however minor or major, and follows with our clarifying the problem configuration, to see what belongs and what does not. Then various hypotheses (or ideas as plans for action) are considered to resolve the problem, and one hypothesis is selected to test it, to see if it works out in this concrete problem situation as a verifiction in fact of the chosen hypothesis. This problem resolution improves that experience. Or, if there is no improvement, or if matters are worse, then we are back at step one of sensing a need and starting the process all over again. Human beings then are problem solvers, buttressed by science.

All of the Pragmatists, correlative with their empiricism, were naturalists and unabashedly espoused the evolutionary teachings of Charles Darwin.[4] All life is strife. In the struggle for existence, the more adaptable forms of life emerge through the process of natural selection and rejection, whereas the less capable are destroyed. Insofar as individual human life exists, it does so only because it has gained the ability to adapt over countless generations. It continues to survive and to maintain a lifestyle only insofar as it possesses the adapting ability to deal with relentless conflicts between the individual human organism and all of the threatening environments. Happily or not, human nature can only survive, adapt, and emerge, given the sifting strains of natural selection. In fact, according to pure Darwinism, it is the species, and not the individual of the species, that survives. So any individual life is subordinated to the reproductive survival of the species. Hence, the individual is less important and certainly less powerful than the species or group. Also, historically, species themselves go out of existence in strife-filled competition with other species that prove to be stronger in nature's constant, brutal evolutionary contest.

According to evolutionary Pragmatism, there is no special value to human nature's emergence, because we are simply thrust forward in a deadly battle for survival among competing natural forces. The reason why we exist at all is simply but importantly that we, compared to other organisms and species, have learned to adapt in the struggle for existence. As long as we keep adapting in perilously threatening environments, as a process in the process of nature, we shall prevail. Once we individually or collectively lose our adapting ability, we shall perish and nature will continue without us. Thus, human nature is only an episode, even a passing episode, in the vast intersecting, powerful forces of nature. Apparently this is not a case for sorrow or for joy, but as long as we adapt, we can still reflect a kind of good fortune or optimism for our survival and for our great abilities as human beings.

More correctly and distinctively, human nature emerges whenever a part of nature becomes disturbed or problematic. Generally nature tends towards equilibrium or balance. When some intersecting forces threaten or challenge that equilibrium, part of nature becomes self-reflective. This reflection of nature upon itself is the emergence of intelligence and correspondingly of human nature. Importantly, human nature comes into existence then as the intelligent problem-solver. Human nature persists prominently during critical problem solving phases of nature. Correlatively, after problems are solved, human nature and intelligence become less distinct and more latent in an overall more harmonious nature. Our special adapting ability to solve problems generates and preserves us, and also essentially defines us. Reputedly, while nature tends towards a balance of competing forces, human nature even causes crises or problems in order to assure in practice our emergent, adapting power to survive. Therein intelligent human beings use the method of science, as noted earlier, by starting with a "felt need," etc. Evidently, the method of science in managing and manipulating nature historically is the most useful so far for human survival and success. It gives us some control over our environment even as the environment fashions us.

Indeed, even when thinking or acting intelligently, we never leave nature, but are constantly immersed in natural forces with the beckoning opportunity to take charge to a degree and to steer nature according to our ideas. Our formulation of ideas, as plans of action, thus immersed in nature, takes charge somewhat and gives some direction to the evolutionary process of nature. Human intelligence can and does manipulate the intersections of nature by using the energy stimulated by problems, by remaining always in transacting and interacting contact with the environment. We can never leave this by abstraction. Our very ideas are a redistribution of evolutionary, natural processes, functioning however competently, completely immersed in nature, including both physical and social nature. The nearest we come to abstraction is in the formulating and comparing of hypotheses, but even this is all an expenditure of natural energy. Still, we give some direction thereby to the evolutionary process.

Since all existence is change or process, anything stable or appearing permanent, such as individual human beings, is illusory. Concrete individuals are experiencing a rate of change so slow as to appear stable. Human beings are always changing with no really permanent or stable aspect or part, even though at times we may appear to be stable or enduring. Everything is part of the larger natural processes that are relentlessly changing. Thus, everything, including human nature and experience, is always changing. There exists no permanent essences of any kind, including none of humankind. Everything is in a constant reorgnization by interacting and transacting with something. Human nature too is part and parcel of the inexorable network of interactions with environments. We serve as that function of change that becomes reflective (intelligent) from time to time. Yet all of that always changes. Basically, all that exists is change, and the interactions and complexity or diversity of change. Specific individuals are explained as different levels in the complexity of changes displayed in nature's transactions. Accordingly, human existence, life, and all experience, including the intellectual, are contingent, tentative, developing aspects of change. Any semblance of the truth of anything existing would be in whatever continues to survive in the everlasting contest.

The human individual represents a survivor. Yet, while American Pragmatist philosophy respects the individual, the social is a more important category of existence. The individual person correctly is intrinsically constituted by and in his or her social relationships with others. The self, as primarily social, is continuously forged in transactions with others and emerges in a developmental process within society. The individual is a social creation, wherein the individual is integrated within the community, and has no meaning or even existence outside of it. Nature reaches a significant, definitive level of complexity, which is society, which is always more powerful than the individual.

All of the classical Pragmatists, namely Charles Saunders Peirce, John Dewey, and William James, subscribed to everything thus far presented. Overall, Peirce, the first Pragmatist, worked with a theory of meanings and of belief, by insisting that the best way to clarify the meaning of a concept was to discover its practical consequences. He devoted himself mainly to logic. For James, Pragmatism was also a way to clarify ideas that therapeutically worked out especially with sentiment or temperament playing an important part. For Dewey, Pragmatism also was a workable theory about the effectiveness of knowledge wherein ideas are always instruments to manipulate or control results.[5]

To keep within the limits of this paper, I shall now confine myself further to John Dewey's philosophy about the human person, which is especially consistent with everything said previously. Dewey was the consummate humanist. In his prolific 93-year lifetime, writing over 800 pieces, he was acknowledged as the most influential American philosopher during the first half of our century.[6] He declared that the distinctive office, problems, and subject matter of philosophy grow out of the stresses and strains in community life with its changes. He explained that the ultimate subject matter of philosophy is human experience and its problems.[7]

Accordingly, Dewey's concept of the person is functional, in that a person is what a person does. A person and his experience are the same. We exist for the most part in precarious conditions having survived, up to this point, the evolutionary dangers of natural selection. We have adapted by created habits that succeed however temporarily. The person is a biological organism that becomes intelligent in encountering and solving problems. As an intelligent problem solver the person is able to pass from the immediate, precognitive instinctive life of nature to the cognitive level which often ends in some ameliorating condition. More broadly, we experience transactions that are for us chemical, biological, and the more typically human kind. We are more clearly defined as organisms in transactions with our environments.[8] The transactions define us as part of an ongoing, developing, changing nature. So much are we defined as a function of interactional nature, that Dewey preferred to depersonalize us by substituting, for example, "it thinks" rather than "I think" for the intelligent process.[9] The English language forbids this, but Dewey would have eliminated all personal nouns and pronouns and used only verbs to convey all existence as action.

Pragmatically, we are what we do; we are our experience that includes our instincts, cognitions, emotions, and decisions. On the one hand, we are passive, that is, experiencing whatever happens to us, whatever we undergo. On the other hand, Dewey places greater value upon our active experience, our decisive, intelligent manipulation or control of our surroundings or environments. Within this manipulation, our intelligence is sharpened, and, really importantly, we create our ethical values within our intelligent transactions. Value (or good) is whatever improves our experience, ameliorates it, whatever works beneficially. Disvalue (or evil) is whatever exacerbates or makes our experience worse. Our human action creates good (what works) and evil (what does not work). Values thus are good ideas that beneficially work out in our active experience. Disvalues are evils, or bad ideas that do not benefit us or that cause us harm. We act morally correctly by solving problems well, or badly by failing that task. We produce our own good or evil.

Our ideas are instruments for action that cumulatively benefit or harm us and our corresponding environment as well. We actively give moral tone to experience by decidedly creating values, that is, ideas that work. Our passivity, of course, keeps us going, but our activity qualitatively makes the difference between merely suffering through something or doing something good about something. This active value production is always future oriented by our anticipating good results and by trying not to make matters worse. Value production, or ethics, zestfully orients us towards shaping future possibilities, by anticipating good and not bad results.

With ethics being primarily, energetically future oriented, Dewey paid less attention to past experience or to traditional backward matters. This is contrary to the usual empiricism, but past traditions for him were relevant only if they still worked out in shaping the future. Traditions that do not work will fall by their own weakness given the usual natural pressures. Our habits that fit the traditions of family, school, church, business, etc. are adjusting for us only insofar as they are useful or practical. Their weakness encourages us to strike out afresh in new directions to create better results. Moral habits usually work out better for the individual and his community over the long range so that traditions may certainly be useful.

Morals cannot be separated from human nature, from our concrete and social mixture. Abstract ethical codes, like anything theoretical, Dewey discards. Mankind is the only resource for values without any theological originator or enforcer of ethical codes. Since the individual and society are the same or equivalent, a moral person directly reflects a moral society as a moral society impacts directly upon the person. In this light, ethics works through our regular social habits and endeavors as in business, civic life, and all associations. Morality is social.[10]

Human nature, Dewey teaches, is not comprised of body and soul, or matter and mind. In a changing context, the explanation is always functional, and not about essences. As noted earlier, we *are* what we *do,* being creatures of instinct and habit, as organisms transacting with enriching and threatening environments. Whenever our habits do not function well enough, or break down, we feel a need to do something about that. Hence, our organized, cognitive process begins to deal with any dysfunction, or disruption of nature. In intelligently resolving the issue, we create new habits to help us with the future.[11]

It appears that, within the strict regimentation of nature, the human organism cannot be free. Dewey complains that the traditional notion of free will separates moral activity from nature and from our public life. For him, free will is nonsense unless we turn to the actual concrete details in the struggle for freedom of thought, speech, assembly, creed, etc. This is free will functioning in the open-air world and not in some private inner consciousness. Curiously, while denying any inner freedom hidden within the person, he also denies any strict deterministic, environmental, evolutionary law completely regulating the person. Predictably he locates human freedom in the *interaction* of the "elements of human nature" and our natural and social environments. Only in that interaction can our desire and choice count for something.[12] He acknowledges that compared with outside forces we are frail, but our intelligence is the key to freedom by our study and foresight that are socially and scientifically buttressed. Freedom refers to variability, initiative, innovation, departure from routine, and experimentation. The crux of freedom is in foreseeing future consequences and in controlling future possibilities. Rather than our will, knowledge and intelligence comprise our freedom. And what really actualizes our freedom is our future foresight, in refining and expanding present activity, by our desire, deliberation, and choice.

While, for good reasons, Dewey greatly emphasized intelligence, he did not neglect aesthetics or religion which are refinements of the human condition. In his *Art as Experience,* he extolled emotive or aesthetic events as that aspect of experience that is final, complete, consummatory, or intransitive.[13] Aesthetic events, while not necessarily manipulated, are concrete and particular (not theoretical), valued in themselves, to be captured and enjoyed for themselves as "peak" events. The person can naturally enjoy these events ranging from a color-flushed sunset to a pleasing style of life.

For all practical purposes, religious experience is the same as the aesthetic, except for its deeper intensity. In his writing *A Common Faith,* Dewey explained that religious experience adjusts the many aspects of our lives into an active, more enduring harmony, by our sensing a wholeness with nature, by sensing the possibilities of nature as a fertile resource for ideals grounded in nature's possibilities, and by realizing that the conjunction of what is real with the ideal is a useful meaning of the word "God."[14] God is useful as the conjunction of the real and the ideal, as the unity of all ideal ends. For Dewey, God does not preexist but functions like a practical idea encouraging realistic ideals in human experience. Dewey himself admitted to "being religious" but denied "having a religion" which he found useless.

All told then, human nature is explained, in strictly humanistic terms, as a changing, always busy, episodic, biological, transient organism that solves problems intelligently along scientific lines, creates values in morally competing facts and ideas, is socially significant, interactionally free, aesthetically capable, and religiously encouraged.

My exposition of Pragmatic human nature has been faithful, but it is not necessarily sympathetic, especially to Dewey's philosophy, for the following reasons. Pragmatists placed uncritical confidence in the scientific method expecting that science can do only good and not harm. Unquestionably, scientific technological ventures have advanced and improved modern life. Science has also produced incalculable harm as in the Nazi holocaust, in the abortion industry, in world wars, in highway accidents, in international terrorism, in computer-driven stock market crashes, in industrial environmental pollution, in nuclear war, etc. Science always needs a code of ethics and a broader metaphysics to guide it, which the Pragmatists reject.

In rejecting abstract codes of ethics, they invite behavioral chaos by not having moral expectations in standards, principles, or norms. Pragmatism allows for moral and social chaos because the individual creates his own ethics. We know the destruction of the family by sexual laxity and promiscuity, the high divorce rates, millions of pregnant teenagers, increasing one-parent homes below the poverty level, drug abuse, street crime, the horrors decimating mankind by the rampant AIDS epidemic, etc. People are confused, alienated, and depressed because they do not know how to act, as the Pragmatists encourage ethics "on the run" in a constantly changing world.

Furthermore, because human nature is defined as a rate of natural change, as a function rather than as an essence, there is no basic difference between human beings or pigs or trees, etc. There is no way of knowing what we are, if we are defined only in behavioral terms that cannot distinguish between us and anything else. What we are and how we act must be different so that each kind of being can behave within its own kind of potential. Also, to define the human individual to be the same as society makes little sense, because society is a collection of individuals with each individual retaining his or her own identity. "Society" is a grammatical fiction.

An exaggerated importance is placed on intelligence as the problem solver. While that is useful, no real case is made for compassion, caring, or love in human relationships, which may have to supplement, or even to a degree, overcome intelligence. Moreover, a complete devotion to Darwinism extolls power and force in the life-threatening arena of constant peril. This tells us that we are powerful animals, predators upon the weak. Here intelligence can only be the use of force, of destructive energy.

Within scientific determinism, freedom of the will is correctly rejected. Then market-place freedom is contrived as our intelligent interaction with future possibilities, which violates empiricism. Empiricism requires past experience to determine everything, but the Pragmatists want to be empiricists with a future, a real contradiction.

Nor is it clear how our aesthetics and religion come out of biological evolution. Nevertheless, in Pragmatism's world *only* of evolutionary change or process, their kind of complete or intransitive aesthetic and religious events are impossible. And because God is useful as the unity of all ideals, which cannot ever be realized, God is also made impossible, even though they would like us to use him.

Notes

1. Ernest Gellner, "The Last Pragmatist: The Philosophy of W. V. O. Quine," *Times Literary Supplement,* 25 July 1975, 848; Richard Rorty, *Consequences of Pragmatism* (Minneapolis, 1982).

2. Roy Wood Sellars, *Reflections on American Philosophy,* in *American Philosophy: A Historical Anthology,* ed. Barbara MacKinnon (Albany, 1985), 157.

3. Charles S. Peirce, "How to Make Our Ideas Clear," *Popular Science Monthly* 12 (Jan. 1878): 286–302; John Dewey, *Logic: The Theory of Inquiry* (Carbondale, 1986), 106–122; John Dewey, *How We Think* (New York, 1933); John Dewey, *The Quest for Certainty* (New York, 1929).

4. John Dewey, *The Influence of Darwinism on Philosophy and Other Essays in Contemporary Thought* (New York, 1910).

5. Richard P. Francis, "Ultimate Constants in the Metaphysics of John Dewey" (Masters thesis, University of Colorado, 1955); also, "The Doctrine of Natural Selection in John Dewey's Value Theory" (Ph.D. dissertation, University of Notre Dame, 1964).

6. David Sidorsky, *John Dewey: The Essential Writings* (New York, 1977), vii.

7. John Dewey, *Reconstruction in Philosophy* (New York, 1920); also *Experience and Nature* (New York, 1929).

8. MacKinnon, *American Philosophy,* 260.

9. John Dewey, *Human Nature and Conduct* (New York, 1957), 287.

10. Ibid., 278–86.

11. John Dewey, "The Unit of Behavior" in *Philosophy and Civilization* (New York, 1934), 233–48.

12. John Dewey, *Human Nature and Conduct,* 278.

13. John Dewey, *Art as Experience* (New York, 1958 reprint).

14. John Dewey, *A Common Faith* (New Haven, 1934).

19

Sartre and the Humanism of Spontaneity

Monica C. Hornyansky

I think it may well be that Sartrean humanism is the most thoroughgoing and the most intense of the humanisms being examined in this collection. This is not to say that it is the wisest or the most comprehensive; but rather that it is the most specialized as a humanism and nothing else—a philosophy of the human individual in all possible detail, circumstance, and association.

First, let me try to make my title clear. It centers on the word "spontaneity," because I think this word captures the ultimate goal of Sartre's thought, as well as its crucial starting point.

"Spontaneity" has two shades of meaning. The first describes a kind of being which arises, without any very clear origin or necessary foundation, "of itself," or *sua sponte*. This is in accordance with what Sartre thought of as the peculiar modal nature of human existence, as contingent. While contingency is at the core of *all* being for Sartre, it is especially significant for human being, because only humans, as far as we know, feel the lack of some kind of ground for their existence, some ultimate truth which founds it and gives it the blessing of necessity and justification. Indeed, if we try to fit ourselves to any definition of necessary being, in terms of perfection of being, we immediately perceive our inadequacy. Only a God could be necessary in these ways; yet, as everyone knows, Sartre argued that God himself could be only contingent, since the concept of a self-caused being is contradictory.

In the first place, then, human spontaneity is the spontaneity of a being capable of willing but conceiving of himself or herself as unwilled, the merest upsurge of consciousness in a largely unconscious world. However, I think, looking into the history of the world, that this meaning of spontaneity—"of its own accord"—is in fact secondary, a weakening of its primary meaning, which is derived from *sponsum,* a pledge, or promise. This more original meaning is the one which guarantees the peculiarly moral nature of Sartre's humanism. For what impresses him is the desire of human spontaneity, in itself unaccounted for, to give an account of itself, to the point that its attitude to its own existence is that such an account is *required*. The result of this is that the spontaneity of consciousness, able to imagine what is not, and fearful of pervasive contingency, spins fantasies of good and evil, salvation and damnation, which take leave of this world and translate themselves into another. The question to which Sartre addressed himself was how to bring this imagination to heel so that it answers to, becomes responsible to, the real needs of men and women in *this* world, rather than the dubious conditions of personal salvation beyond it. The aim of Sartre's specifically atheistic humanism was to reabsorb the meaning of good and evil, virtue and vice into the person and into the community, rather than father them on a transcendent sphere, and thus to redirect the human fund of aspiration and resolve towards the coherence and significance of everyday existence.

The etymological connection between *spon*taneity and re*spons*ibility is an expression of these existential facts of human life, the contingent emergence of consciousness and the imaginative response of that consciousness to its situation—a varying individual pledging of the self to a willed and constructed existence. This is what gives human existence its moral character. Sartre's philosophical humanism in its first expression in *Being and Nothingness* and its further development in the *Critique of Dialectical Reason* is the working out through various concepts of the implications of this emergence of responsibility out of spontaneity, the distinction which bears the weight of our moral being, without transcendence, but equally without reduction. The rest of this paper will be devoted to trying to show how this project differentiates Sartre's from other humanist thought, via, first, Heidegger's criticism of it, in answer to Sartre's 1945 lecture, *Existentialism Is a Humanism.*

Heidegger objects that Sartre's humanism, based on his description of the human being as an ontologically isolated consciousness in the face of a nonconscious universe, ignores the relational nature of human existence as being-in-the-world, a relationship which enfolds and illumines Being through language and thought. What he decries is Sartre's so-called Cartesian starting-point, because it perpetuates an outdated dualism, and hence a recidivist subjectivity, which isolates human reality from its setting, an example of what Heidegger calls "the modern metaphysics of subjectivity".[1] A correct phenomenological description of human reality would show, Heidegger thinks, that in enfolding Being in language and thus in the light of truth, at least at the ontological level of description, the duality of subject and object is properly transcended and laid to rest. But Sartre's insistence on the ontological primacy of the subjective individual leads the way inevitably, after the first few pages of *Being and Nothingness,* to a trivially ontic level of description; it is man as unique individual upon whom Sartre expends all his considerable powers of syncretic system-building, while for Heidegger:

The sentence "Man ek-sists" . . . responds to the question concerning man's "essence." We are accustomed to posing this question with equal impropriety whether we ask what man is or who he is. For in the *Who?* or *What?*

we are already on the lookout for something like a person or an object. But the personal no less than the objective misses and mis-construes the essential unfolding of ek-sistence in the history of Being.[2]

Sartre's humanism then is clearly on a different level of description from Heidegger's thought. While Heidegger wants to show how human being in its most general phenomenological description as being-in-the-world is an expression or mouthpiece of Being itself, Sartre wants to show how each unique individual makes his own life in conjunction with other unique individuals; and in addition, how this—his moral purpose—can be carried out in the most authentic way through action. Now although Sartre *would* say that the intellectual and the artist *act* in their thoughts and writings— in their *words,* that is—I think he would be far from agreeing with Heidegger that words or thoughts or thanks in the face of Being are the *essence* of man. Heidegger seems to have thought that there is intuitive wisdom in the first structures of metaphor by which human reflection lifted itself clear of matter and of things, into the upper air of thought and concept, and he called this process "poetry." In such words as "thinking" and "understanding," for example, we figure forth the processes of reflection as praise or the building of a structure; this intuitive figuring or clearing of the truth about our Being, and thence about Being itself, makes of language a kind of transcendence in immanence. As a quick (as it were) woodcut impression of the difference between these views of language and existence, one might imagine Heidegger in his country retreat looking out beyond the forest to a further vista—Being itself—and *rightly* regarding Sartre as mewed in his city café, or wowing them in the lecture hall, largely in oblivion of Being, rather than enfolding it in speech. There is a kind of idealism in Heidegger's adulation of language as originally poetic, rather than expository, which is very far from Sartre's more matter-of-fact view of this distinction. For Sartre, language is either, as prose, an evolving instrument variably translucent, through which we aim rather successfully at reality, or, as poetry, a virtual *matter* of words whose euphony and ambiguity the poet molds to his own creative sense. He also valued such ambiguities philosophically, as an instrument of thought. But language was not, for him, I believe, a pipeline to Being itself, a view of language, more-over, that can go risibly wrong in the hands of any other but a knowledge-able polyglot.

Sartre's humanism, then, is not properly general, in Heidegger's view. It remains on the ontic level of the description of beings, because it cannot escape from an individualist subjectivity which ignores the philosophic task and duty of questioning Being in its most profound sense. It can develop in no other direction than the description of the individual *qua* individual. Further, Heidegger says, as merely another contender for the low ground of beings, Sartre cannot challenge Marxist or scientific humanism. Sartre's area of action or argument, philosophically speaking, has shrunk from the open upland of ontology and a renewed metaphysics, to the pitiful exercise yard of the psychological, the political, even perhaps of idle talk.

Can this criticism be satisfactorily answered? I believe it is true to say first that Sartre's thought does have the limitations of an extreme civility: that is, it is the thought of a mind fully satisfied by immanent human relationships. The man was "allergic to chlorophyll"; like Socrates strolling outside the walls of Athens, he might say: "Trees and countryside have no desire to teach me anything; it's only the men of the city that do." Any philosophy, then, like Heidegger's, which steps outside the human sphere and attempts to see it in a larger perspective is bound to find Sartre's thought dismayingly man-centered. On the other hand, Sartre's thought does have the advantages of its specialization. Heidegger thought of his phenomenological description of *Dasein* as aiming through *Dasein* to Being itself, "the transcendens pure and simple." Although this "transcendens" contains, as Heidegger says, the "possibility and the necessity of the most complete individuation," he makes being-towards-death the node of individuation, tracing from it, in broad outline, the conditions of human existence. For Sartre, however, the most important questions about human being concern this very process of individuation— this is his area of specialization, as it were, to the exclusion of "transcendens" in Heidegger's sense. The most important question for existence is to understand how the unique individual human comes to be, in order to be able to make an altered self come to be, if such a change, or conversion, were desirable. The intricacies of this evolution of the individual personality from Sartre's Cartesian starting point into a dialectical relationship with others, the attempt to show how such a starting point can be the ontological foundation of the manifold associations of human community, form the subject matter of all of Sartre's later work. This grand design of his thought was perhaps not yet obvious in 1947 when Heidegger wrote the *Letter on Humanism;* consequently his criticism, although right on the money in the respect I have outlined, misses the development of Sartre's thought which lifted it out of a sclerosed Cartesian duality and set it on a path which was then hard to foresee.

This development was his attempt, in the *Critique of Dialectical Reason,* to reconcile his conviction that the individual is an originator of action with economic determinism. Heidegger had reproached Sartre with not recognizing the importance of the historical in Being, and therefore being unable to enter into a productive dialogue with Marxism, but Sartre himself realized that he had overstated the case for the individual freedom which consciousness makes possible, and in particular had not distinguished among the various elements which make up the tapestry of events, the many ways in which the interplay of motive, environment, goal, and circumstance results in straitened personal choice and creativity. His desire to tackle the description of historical events, in order more fully to understand the unique individual and his function in them, first seems to have become a central preoccupation in the *Notebooks for a Morality,* the abortive work immediately following *Being and Nothingness,* and, according to Ronald Aronson, it seems to have become a matter of urgency following his falling-out with Merleau-Ponty over his (Sartre's) tolerance for Stalinist policies. However, a few years before this, Sartre had made clear his reasons for rejecting both Marxist and scientific humanism, in his essay *Materialism and Revolution.*

Sartre's objection to both of these alternative humanisms is the same:

that they regard the individual as subject primarily to external causation, whether biological, social, or economic. Now at the beginning of this paper, I said that I thought Sartre's humanism was one of the most thoroughgoing and intense, and this is the place to show that this is so. The distinguishing mark which signals this is that others tend to locate the ultimate springs, urges, shapings, and limits of human action outside of human consciousness—in external nature, or in a human nature interpreted in biological terms, not inherently different from the terms in which one would describe any other animal. But Sartre, without denying in any way that human being *is* biogical, i.e., a natural evolutionary emergence, *would* nevertheless point out that the ability to judge the self in light of the past, and in the anticipation of a desired future which can be vividly imagined, means that human affairs, human history, and the existence of the individual as far as it is willed, is sufficiently exempted from natural causation to require a different kind of description from that used for other life-forms. Human action is *elicited* by a vision of the future rather than *caused* by antecedent states of affairs. His objection to the Marxist view, that individuals are a product primarily of the physical environment and resulting social relations, is that it tends to diminish the importance of individual action in the setting of large material and economic change. Sartre wanted to show that this is wrong by working out ways of comprehending history—correctly, he thought—as the consequence of individual decision and aspiration working like a yeast in the material emergence of events. The description of the being who inhabits a *human* world, therefore, requires concepts, and modes of description, which consistently exhibit this difference in the way in which the emergence of historical change, unlike natural process, is understood. What I want to do now, then, is to touch on some of these concepts and modes of description, as illustrating these aspects of Sartre's humanism, in which the uniqueness of the individual is regarded as the principal focus of interest, and the principal source of the significance of human existence. I mean here to distinguish this kind of philosophical interest from, for example, the Greek interest in permanent reality and the truth which corresponds to it as that which ought to interest a thinker, or Kant's primary interest in setting the bounds of philosophical knowledge and method. For Sartre all that was most interesting in philosophy was linked to the primary question, what accounts for the peculiar complexity of the human person?

Sartre objected to materialism of any stripe because, even here, he thought, it was dishonest to claim to be able to eliminate the observer and/or the actor from the description of the world. While Heidegger had reproached him with being incorrigibly "subjective," Sartre in turn reproaches materialist thought with a spurious claim to objectivity:

> We know that a Kantian may make assertions about nature since according to him reason constitutes experience. But the materialist does not admit that the world is the product of our constituting activity: quite the reverse, it is we who are the product of the universe. Why then should we consider that the real is rational since we have not made it, and we reflect, from day to day, only a miniscule portion of it? The success of science, strictly speaking, could make us think that this rationality is *probable,* but it could

also be a matter of a regional, statistical rationality; it could hold for a certain order of size and crumble above or below that limit. . . . [Thus it seems that] by a dialectical movement which one might foresee, materialist rationality passes over into irrationality and destroys itself: if the psychic fact is conditioned rigorously by biology and biological fact in its turn by the physical state of the world, one sees perfectly well that human consciousness can express the universe as an effect expresses its cause, but not in the way a thought expresses its object.[3]

A fortiori, then, scientific thought has the wrong aims and the wrong ideal of itself to be a model for the description of human relations, developments, and action. The difference between the description of scientific law and human description is just the difference between being able to describe relations that are, on the one hand, statistically, generally, or cyclically predictable, and on the other hand the unidimensional sequence of events in human history, where the requirements of predictability leave out what chiefly makes history: the characters, aims, desires, opinions, and acts of individuals. *People are not concepts, as Kierkegaard pointed out; now, in the twentieth century, we have to add that neither are they "forces."* What they do cannot be explained without bringing in such ideas as judgment, hope, intention, plan, strategy, tactic; these elements of agency are the vital other strand which together with natural and contingent fact weaves the grand dialectic of history, and a proper understanding of it. And as Sartre said in his final conversations with Simone de Beauvoir, try as he might, he had been unable to find any way to *materialize* this contribution of individual human consciousness to historical events.

The upshot of this is that if you agree with Sartre that human agency, both as individual and as collective, requires different principles of explanation, description, and prediction from natural events, then you may be a humanist of the Sartrean kind. The two modes of human description which he established were what he called "comprehension" for the individual and "dialectical reason" for collective action in political, economic, and bureaucratic relations. Here enters, for example, the important distinction for existentialist humanism between *states,* as antecedently caused, and *situations.* States are pure results of external impacts and minglings: the elements are separable, their combination can be analyzed into these constituent parts. In human affairs, however, characterized by the mingling of the contingent event and the intentional act, decision results in something inherently synthetic and novel—what he called, after Jaspers, a "situation"—rather than the mixture as before. Another important defining category for comprehension of the unique individual is the identification of his "project," that is, the vision of his future which informs the human present of the individual. For Sartre, the individual is a complex singularity who can be understood only synthetically, through a sympathetic attempt to grasp his perspective on the world. The contribution that philosophy can make to this is to increase and conceptualize the gamut of self-knowledge, first through a basic ontological self-understanding, and second through concepts of existential psychoanalysis, such as "states" and "situations." These were the two levels of self-comprehension—that is, the ontological and the existential—described in *Being and Nothingness.*

Corresponding to the understanding of the situational interplay of consciousness and contingent givens in the individual is the concept of "dialectical reason," a synthetic understanding of events and institutions, in the larger public human arena. Here the equivalent to the elements of consciousness and facticity on the individual level, are what Sartre called *praxis* and the *practico-inert,* which are discussed in *The Critique of Dialectical Reason.* Praxis is the multifarious intentional activity of communal life; but it often results in the "practico-inert," a clumsy term for an obstinate problem in human affairs, the fact that our best intentions go wrong, and result in inhumane institutions, laws, and objects, which are hard to avoid, correct, or undo. The human world is always in a state of incipient arrest and frustration because our ideas cannot, as it were, fly; they are expressed in matter, in routine, in failing imagination, in the mass; they hang around to haunt us in forms we did not foresee. Think of plastic, think of program selling, think of the Senate, think of the law's delay, think of the banality of evil. Dialectical reason in reflecting and reflecting upon the historical interplay of praxis and practico-inert is intended as the means of bringing this mix of intention and accident back into control by seeing it whole, or "totalizing" it, to use Sartre's term, and thence achieving at least the preliminaries necessary to amend it. Only in enunciating what is learnt by this process, as, for example, Parkinson's Law or the Peter Principle, can we tame the institutional monsters we produce, and ascribe them to the ultimate initiator and intended beneficiary, the individual human person.

It is by means of such concepts as these—praxis and practico-inert, state and situation—that Sartre would always identify human history as other than natural evolution; and consequently distinguish between scientific reason which understands by analyzing its objects into its component elements, and dialectical reason, which understands synthetically by assuming a purposeful and therefore unified phenomenon.

Sartre's humanist existentialism then is not a *vague* position. It is not a materialist humanism for he was always, as far as any such metaphysical view is concerned, an agnostic; and equally, the absence of a transcendent category from his thought is not the consequence of a metaphysical position, but a purely experiential conclusion. His thought occupies the ground between materialism and idealism, that of existence, and consequently the full spectrum of human experience; and it commands a precise method of phenomenological description which he worked out in mind-numbing detail in his later works, both philosophical and biographical. Although it remained rooted in his first ontological description of the human individual as unique, it developed a theory of history and therefore of the social consequences of the ontological ground. If one were to try to place it in the philosophical tradition—an enterprise that I have been thinking about in the light of Allan Bloom's book *The Closing of the American Mind*—I think I would certainly see Sartre in the train of those Enlightenment philosophers who tried, and not unsuccessfully, to substitute the nexus "reason and freedom" as the foundation of human worth, in place of the possession of an immortal soul under God's ordinance. Sartre enters the dialogue specifically in the wake, in the order of time, of Darwin and Nietzsche, and in the order of thought, of Kierkegaard and Bergson. By this I mean that his response to the materialisms of the twentieth century is a reprise of the response of Kant and Hegel to Enlightenment empiricism, and heavily derivative from their arguments. Because of Nietzsche and Darwin, however, the issue of exactly what human self-consciousness and human intelligence amount to, as a claim to the exclusive possession of moral sensibility, and therefore superiority to the rest of the natural world, reaches crisis proportions not only in the history of thought, but in history itself. For this reason, Sartre's elaborations on the relations among human consciousness, individual action, and historical change constitute his claim to be taken seriously as a twentieth-century contribution to the humanist tradition in philosophy. From what I have said, I hope it is clear that he uses that philosophic tradition to perform the Socratic function of moral commentary in the public and political arenas, a course that has opened him to accusations of fellow-travelling and intellectual dishonesty. Leaving these aside, however, I would prefer to point out the weakness of his position, very much in passing I'm afraid, from a more theoretical point of view. My reservations about Sartre's thought as a humanist do not so much concern his activities within political movements which in the end turned out to be incompatible with the theoretical foundations of his thought. He recognized all that himself. Rather, I would return to his extraordinary kinship with Socrates in his focus on the relations among self-knowledge, human excellence, and social good. Like Socrates', his temperament was the temperament of a city man, and for all city dwellers, the question of how people behave towards one another is the most important. For the foundational thinker—that is, one for whom the truth about the circumstances of human life must be the foundation of action in the absence of religious conviction—the recourse to custom, or to transcendence, are both equally closed. In addition, for such a mind nature, or the cosmos, or at its most grandiose, the idea of Being, also lack any legislative force. He cannot, therefore, place his theory of man, or the individual, in a larger context, as the axiom from which he deduces his theorems. Socrates died physically for this fault, although in other ways, interestingly enough, he seems to be as lively as ever. And Sartre, I would like to contend, was still in business at roughly the same stand a couple of thousand years later, trying to show what moral responsibility is, and to work out a method for understanding and therefore being able to undertake it. Leaving our relation to transcendence obscure is now less dangerous to the individual thinker than it was to Socrates. I believe, however, that in the modern era concentration on the purely human sphere is a danger, perhaps of a more amorphous kind, and one which may not be easily remediable in the Sartrean framework. Sartre's right to an important place in the evolution of the humanist tradition *may,* for this reason, be correspondingly open to dispute.

Notes

1. M. Heidegger, "Letter on Humanism" in *Basic Writings* (London, 1977), 199.
2. Ibid., 207.
3. Sartre, "Materialism and Revolution," in *Situations, III,* trans. Monica C. Hornyansky (Paris, 1949), 142–43.

20

The Humanistic Implications of Liberation Theology: Juan Luis Segundo and Karl Marx

Marsha A. Hewitt

The central problem posed by humanism for Christianity, succinctly stated, is how to reconcile human autonomy and subjective agency with belief in an external, supernatural agency that somehow governs reality. This implies the further problem of locating the historical subject: human beings, God, or some combined divine/human activity. How are human beings to understand themselves and their relation to the world: in terms of obedience to the dictates of an external divine force, explained and transmitted through Scripture, tradition, and an ecclesiastical teaching authority, or might human beings view themselves as responsible subjects of their own lives, as the producers of history? Expressed in this way, humanism and theology appear as irreconcilable opposites operating with quite different epistemologies and ontologies, which give rise to competing truth claims. Nonetheless, various efforts have been made by Christian thinkers to allow for a humanism that allows for the full realization of human potential, that holds that openness to others means openness to God, and that the kingdom announced by Jesus has to do with the humanization of the world. Such interpretations of the Gospel are central and highly emphasized in the social justice themes of contemporary theology, such as political theology, feminist, and black liberation theology, etc. These theologies have strong humanist implications that are often left unelaborated, rarely drawn to their inevitable conclusions.

Any effort to integrate humanist thought and theology is highly problematic, since humanism[1] is generally understood as the negation of the natural/ supernatural dichotomy, perhaps agnostic at best. One of the common principles of humanist philosophies is a rejection of the supernaturalist conceptions of the universe, along with a supernatural source of ethical values, understanding that there is no ethical meaning independent of human experience. There appears to be little (if any) common ground between humanism and theology, especially when the latter is defined in traditional, classical terms, as the science of faith and the explication of divine revelation. Humanist theories and theology operate with different categories of truth, and with different methodologies; humanism focuses upon the human being and human experience in the world, whereas theology traditionally focuses upon God and the salvation of the individual soul. This description of the basic difference between humanism and theology, although highly schematic and general, is basically correct, in spite of the many instances of dialogue and confrontation between theology and humanism.

This essay will draw out some of the humanist dimensions of the liberation theology of Latin America, as it developed from the late sixties to the early eighties in the work of a particular theologian, whose thought can be read in a socialist humanist key. Socialist humanism derives from a reading of Marx which focuses on the anthropological, ethical, social, and political themes in his thought that have been denied by various currents of twentieth century "Marxisms," especially Leninism and Stalinism. These "humanist" themes in Marx have been elaborated in particular by the *Praxis* philosophers, a group of mainly Yugoslav sociologists and philosophers who in the sixties and seventies published the internationally known journal *Praxis*. The kind of socialist humanism developed by this group has found its way indirectly into liberation theology, as will be discussed below.

Liberation theology also manifests strong intellectual affinities with critical theory, especially as it was worked out by the "early" Frankfurt school.[2] Many of the preoccupations of critical theory—the relationships between theory and practice, the meaning of changing historical circumstances and the possibility of social transformation, the necessity of articulating class consciousness, the need to develop a materially based critique of domination—are central to liberation theology as well. Both liberation theology and critical theory approach these and other questions through a reformulation of the central theories of Marx and Hegel. The pervasive influence of Marx on liberation theology has opened it toward both critical theory and socialist humanism at the same time. In this paper I will attempt to explore briefly both these dimensions of liberation theology by focusing on the use of Marx by Juan Luis Segundo.

I will suggest that the social theory of Marx (via the twentieth-century interpretations mentioned) constitutes the primary mediation of liberation theology's implicit humanist dimensions. Liberation theology points toward a form of socialist humanism which recognizes the necessity of the total transformation of the individual and society within history, so that questions of personal salvation, for example, become absorbed into what is perceived as the more fundamental questions of social, political liberation. I will also identify some of the difficulties which arise when theology attempts to incorporate and appropriate some basic categories and concepts of Marxian social theory. Segundo certainly tries to appropriate Marx partly from the perspective of a socialist humanism that is closest to the *Praxist* group. He draws on the work of Erich Fromm, an associate of both the *Praxis* intellectuals and the Frankfurt school, and who has developed the concept of socialist humanism through his interpretation of Marx. In Segundo's work we may see the depth of Marx's influence on the theology of liberation,[3] along with the more problematic aspects of trying to integrate theological and social categories of analysis into each other. Before moving on to this aspect of the discussion, it is necessary first to outline very briefly some of those features of socialist humanism that can be traced in liberation theology.

One of the foundational principles common to socialist humanism and liberation theology is the consciousness of the need for the total liberation of human beings from all forms of alienation.[4] Although necessary, economic and political emancipation are only partial aspects of human liberation; the economic and political prosperity achieved in modern capitalism cannot form an adequate basis for a humanistic society, in the sense of a humane society in and through which the human being may actualize his or her potential as human. Society must become community, in the sense of a community of ends, which holds the human being as the highest value of all. In theological terms, this is understood as the *koinonia,* the diaconal and charismatic community in which the variety of gifts of all individuals is put in the service of the whole people of God, which dwells in one Spirit.[5] The Christian view of communal sharing of the community of goods finds its biblical and theological expression in the Christian notion of the *koinonia* (I Cor: 12) and the Eucharist.[6]

Both socialist humanism and liberation theology agree that a socialist transformation of the world is a complex and responsible task which involves much more than a change in external circumstances alone, but includes a radical change in human being's internal, alienated nature and values and ideals. According to one group of Columbian priests, "We are led to direct our efforts and actions toward the building of a Socialist type of society that allows us to eliminate all forms of man's exploitation of his fellow man" and in the words of Argentinian Priests of the Third World, this will be a "Latin American socialism that will promote the advent of the New Man."[7] In this regard, the Christian concept of *Metanoia* or conversion provides an adequate understanding of inner transformation but mediated through a socialist political praxis. It is held in socialist humanism that social change is impossible without moral and spiritual transformation at the same time.[8] The socialist humanist principle that a human being only realizes one's "universal activity" as a social being is not antithetical to much contemporary theology (including liberation theology) which sees the locus of one's encounter with God in one's openness to others in mutual service within the people of God.

According to Erich Fromm, love is "crucial" to Marx's sense of human relationship with the world; Marx equated love with all that which is life and immediate, sensuous experience. "Let us assume . . . man to be man, and his relation to the world to be a human one. Then love can only be exchanged for love, trust for trust, etc. . . . it is love which teaches man to truly believe in the world of objects outside him. . . ."[9] Jesus understood that only through love can human beings relate to each other, and the world, in a genuinely human way. One realized one's orientation to God through one's actions toward others.

For both liberation theology and socialist humanism, ontological questions are intimately connected with anthropological questions. One of the most compelling appeals of Marx for liberation theology is summed up in the following quotation from Gajo Petrović:

> Marx's philosophy . . . is neither "pure" ontology, nor "pure" epistemology, anthropology, ethics, social and political philosophy, etc.; its essence is in a continuous relationship, a continuous "interplay" between the most general, "most abstract" questions of ontology and anthropology, and "the most ordinary" questions of everyday life.[10]

In my view, it is this realization that allows a theologian like Segundo to open an extended dialogue with Marx because he realizes that Marx's thought does not need to be taken as a global anathema that is the utter negation of all aspects of Christian thought. Segundo also realizes about theology what Marx realized about philosophy in his famous 'Thesis Eleven,' and which is expressed by Gajo Petrović in this way: "Unless it is to remain abstract theorizing, philosophy [read: theology] cannot disregard the phenomenon of man's self-alienation; it cannot abstain from criticizing inhuman, exploiting society, or keep aloof from the struggle for a really human, socialist [humanist] society."[11]

Thus one of the overriding concerns of the *Praxis* philosophers appears in an interpretation of Marx as concerned with the question of what a human being is and what are the authentic, unalienated relations between human beings in a transformed world.[12] While the preoccupation with questions of human essence and the possibilities of individual/inner and social/external transformation are integral to both socialist humanism and liberation theology, it nonetheless remains to be seen whether or not socialist humanism and theology are finally integratable, without important and far-reaching transformations within theology itself. To pursue this, we must turn to the conversation between Segundo and Marx.

Before doing this, one final thing must be said. Most of the major liberation theologians explicitly acknowledge a strong commitment to socialist politics which they see as the only means by which a total transformation of society can occur. This socialism is no Marxist-Leninist or Stalinist mutation, but one which is both relevant to the specific conditions of Latin America and which includes the concept of a "new man," an idea which they derive directly from Ché Guevara. It is a socialism that while faithful to the "central intuitions of Marx," is "beyond all dogmatism."[13] "The liberation of our continent means more than overcoming economic, social, and political dependence. It means, in a deeper sense, to see the becoming of mankind as a process of the emancipation of man in history."[14] In order to determine what are those "central intuitions of Marx" and how they contribute to the creation of the "new man" (i.e., socialist man), I now turn to Segundo.

Most liberation theologians attempt to distance themselves from Marx as much as possible, or tend toward vagueness in relation to Marx, which is curious, since liberation theology in its present form would not be possible without Marx. Through a confrontation with Marx that is sympathetic and which consciously recognizes the importance of Marx for "contemporary theology, particularly . . . the most imaginative and creative brands of it,"[15] Segundo has begun to push theology beyond its limits as classical theology, and toward a critical theory of society whose basic interest is the full emancipation or dealienation of the human being, along lines similar to those of socialist humanism. Segundo analyzes Christianity as a cultural phenomenon (or ideology) which *also* is capable of expressing the contradictions of society as a whole, including those forces that negate the status quo.

In order to develop this approach to Christianity, Segundo turns to Marx, in an effort to appropriate some of Marx's insights. In so doing, Segundo brings Christian theology to the threshold of its own self-negation as theology, since the central focus of theology decisively shifts from God and revelation to society, politics, and history. Marcuse's description of the transition from Hegel's social theory is helpful, in analogous fashion, to understanding what Segundo might represent in a parallel development in the area of theology:

"Hegel's system brings to a close the entire epoch in modern philosophy that had begun with Descartes and had embodied the basic ideas of modern society . . . [Hegel] recognized the social and political order men had achieved as the basis on which reason had to be realized. His system brought philosophy to the threshold of its negation and thus constituted the sole link between the old and the new form of critical theory, between philosophy and social theory."[16]

The shift of emphasis from theology to critical theory that can be detected in Segundo's work is in part based upon a "ruthless criticism" of the existing social order, the aim of which is to expose the nature of class society and alienation in all its existing forms, and also to restore the human being to the central focus of action, i.e., as an end in him- or herself. In like fashion with Marx, Segundo also attempts to construct a theory which is itself a concrete, practical activity with an emancipatory intent. In part, Segundo is trying to resolve, in Christian theology, the present dichotomy between theory and practice, overcoming the reification of theory that is manifested in empty speculation, and of practice as unreflective activity. Segundo also rejects the reification of Marx's thought in the form of Stalinist ideology, and instead searches for points of intersection between what may be generally called Marxian and Christian anthropology.

Part of the purpose of this essay is to situate liberation theology in its proper intellectual context, which is to say, the theoretical mediations of Marx and critical social theory. In this way the humanist dimensions of liberation theology may be explicated. It is Segundo who at present is the theologian whose work goes farthest in an explicitly humanist direction.[17] To examine the relationship between liberation theology and the humanist themes in Marx and critical theory is not to deny or ignore the theological roots of it and the crucial impact of Vatican II; indeed, liberation theology views itself as the true heir of Vatican II. However, a consideration of the larger theological influences on liberation theology must remain beyond the scope of this essay. The most fascinating and problematic feature of Segundo's development of liberation theology is the extent to which he tries to integrate Marx, since in so doing Segundo effects a shift from one order of truth claims to a quite different one. Part of this shift includes recasting the focus of history in terms of the struggle for total emancipation of the human being in society and history and the kind of practical transformation necessary to achieve this goal.

The methodological basis of all liberation theology is history and concrete reality, and as such, liberation theology cannot be said to derive from any preceding theology. Liberation theology thus does not exist as a mere branch of theology, but rather self-consciously strives to replace all hitherto existing theology.[18] Furthermore, if liberation theology continues to develop along the path that theologians like Segundo have laid out for it, then it clearly threatens not only to replace theology, but to effect the negation of theology altogether. Because of his overriding preoccupation with social analysis and transformation, Segundo must try to integrate the categories and language of the social sciences into his thought, since strictly theological categories of analysis are inadequate as such to confront society and transform it. Segundo is thus often caught in certain theoretical contradictions; he realizes, for instance, that theology cannot exist any longer in terms of a separate realm of discourse and epistemology, and yet he tries to remain a theologian.[19] He also attempts to formulate an ideology-critique of all existent Christian theology, which leads him to use theology against itself, so that he can come up with a transformed/ transformative critical theology that will be by its nature liberatory.

Segundo seems entirely aware that the real enemy of religion and of the individual as historical subject is capitalism. The irony is that if Christianity can in any way be a countervailing force capable of at least undermining the various forms of alienation and dehumanization produced by capitalism, then it must turn to Marx. This irony is compounded by the fact that in its efforts to integrate Marx and religion, Christian theology threatens to bring about its own dissolution from within. This is not to deny the possibility of a transformed, reconstructed religious consciousness which acts as a humanizing force in society. Segundo draws back from pursuing this line of thought and instead tries to demonstrate that Marx and Christianity are not mutually exclusive theories.

Segundo does not confront the whole corpus of Marx's work, but rather attempts an integration of those "proper" and "positive" element of Marx's thought into his own theology.[20] Like other liberation theologians, Segundo finds in Marx the social analysis required to expose the nature of social reality in Latin America. In this way he can be read as engaging in a Christian-Marxist dialogue; but a theologized Marx is quite something else, and it is when his dialogue passes over into an attempted synthesis that Segundo becomes entangled in major problems that are very difficult to solve.

The most explicit and accessible points of contact between Marx and Segundo are readily apparent if one compares, for example, Marx's *Theses on Feuerbach*[21] and almost any of Segundo's statements about his own theological method which has to do with social and political analysis. In Thesis II, Marx defines the "question of objective truth" as a "practical question," not a theoretical one, in which theory is "isolated" from practice. He emphasizes the concrete, "this-sidedness" of thought wherein theory and praxis are linked in the practical, critical activity of human consciousness which itself is engaged in the process of social change and liberation. Marx understands the real task of theory is to bring about a dynamic unity between subject and object, so that theory's grasp of societal contradictions does not merely name the concrete historical situation, but rather acts as a force within it to initiate concrete social change. This applies to the way in which Segundo conceives of theology when he writes that:

> The most progressive theology in Latin America is more interested in *being liberative* than in *talking about liberation*. In other words, liberation deals not so much with content as with the method used to theologize in the face of our real-life situation.[22]

In Thesis VI, Marx defines "the human essence" as "no abstraction," but "in its reality it is the ensemble of the social relations." Marx negates the concept of the ideal, abstract human individual who embodies "human essence" apart from concrete activity, in order to affirm human beings as conditioned by their material context and concrete life conditions, which are deeply bound up with the material forces of production and the social relationships to which they give rise. Segundo does not dwell upon the abstraction of individual man or address the question of "human essence" in any sustained fashion. He too is concerned with human beings in the context of their material conditions and social relations, which comes through when he writes of the "proletariat" and his "own historical commitment"[23] for the liberation of the proletariat (i.e., all the poor and oppressed in Latin America). Segundo's main interest is practical, involving the transformation of society on the concrete and material level, which is evident in his whole approach, for example, to Jesus as a man whose main concern was for the well-being, both spiritual *and* material, of human beings.

Segundo is fully aware of the fact that his theology is thoroughly contingent upon and conditioned by the "realm of human options and biases" and that it is "intimately bound up with the psychological, social, or political status quo."[24] For him, theology exists within a given cultural milieu, is inevitably mediated by it, and if it is to be relevant to that context, it cannot remain within its own immanent system. Thus any major changes in theological thought and method in any given period must be seen, at least in part, as a response to that specific cultural and historical situation.

Some of the problems of Segundo's specific cultural context, to which he attempts to respond, involve the revolutionary activity of various guerrilla groups and the severe government and military repression characteristic of authoritarian and/or military regimes. It becomes apparent in Segundo's work that the traditional discourse of Christianity, its *logos* about God expressed through the language of symbol and representation, is no longer adequate to address the "structural, systematic" injustice[25] of Latin America. Segundo's aim is to transform theology into a praxis of liberation, whose aim is structural transformation and widespread changes within the society. Thus the specific symbolic language of theology must dissolve as a separate form of discourse, giving way to the discourse of politics, since it is in the political realm, not the theological, that Segundo sees changes occurring. This is why Segundo cites the Peruvian theologian, Gustavo Gutierrez, who declares that theology is necessarily the "second step," and is *a posteriori* to politics. Segundo quotes Gutierrez, who defines politics in this way:

> Human reason has become political reason. For the contemporary historical consciousness, things political are not only those which one attends to during the free time afforded by his private life; nor are they even a well-defined area of human existence. . . . It is the sphere for the exercise of a critical freedom which is won through history. It is the universal determinant and the collective arena for human fulfillment. . . . Nothing lies outside the political sphere understood in this way. Everything has a political color. . . . Personal relationships themselves acquire an ever-increasing political dimension. Men enter into relationships among themselves through political means.[26]

This view of politics as a fundamental human dimension implies that all human activity, including thought, belongs to the practical sphere of human existence, so that human beings must look for truth and its verification in their concrete practice. This is contrary to most theological reasoning, which grounds truth in God and revelation. If one accepts Marx's assertion that existence is prior to consciousness, then knowledge is not a matter of discovering the ultimate, fixed truth that is meant to explain reality. Rather, knowledge is understood as an open-ended, partial, historically embedded process which, *per definitionem,* will never yield or reveal any final truth, since it does not exist. Such an approach to reality focuses upon the possibilities yet to be realized in history and anticipates social and political alternatives whereby those possibilities might be actualized. The task of critical social theory is to negate the existent, in all its unfreedom and consequent human alienation. A critical theoretical perspective on social reality rejects the mere factuality of the existent in order to discover the possibilities for a more authentic, unalienated, and genuinely socialized humanity, in which the needs of the individual and community are interdependent, and self-consciously understood as such. To borrow Herbert Marcuse's language, negation of the existent is positive, because it has a liberating function in its "Great refusal to accept the rules of a game in which the dice are loaded," and in its ability to make the absent present "because the greater part of the truth is that which is absent."[27] The negation of the existent also means the negation of the social order, so that negation is "political negation" which may find expression in nonpolitical language, since "the entire dimension of politics becomes an integral part of the status quo."[28]

The logic of Segundo's thought accords with Marcuse's view of the relation between theory and practice, and the primary place of politics. If Segundo is approached from the perspective of these features of critical theory, then his own theoretical method and intent become clearer and more coherent. Certainly it cannot be said that Segundo is completely unfamiliar with the central tenets of critical theory, and he refers to the work of Marcuse. This is hardly surprising, especially when one considers that critical social theory has had an irrevocable impact on contemporary theology in general:

> Lack of conformity with, or negation of, existing reality, then, has come to form an intrinsic feature of theology just as it has come to form an intrinsic feature of knowledge in the school of dialectical thinking—and the Frankfurt School especially.[29]

Segundo would have fared better in his use of Marx if he had tried to develop the critical theoretical dimensions of his thought as well as his affinity with socialist humanism. Segundo's attempt at recasting aspects of Marx is in line with critical theory, and yet the way he uses Marx is problematic. His reading of Marx is too often selective and eclectic, and at times he lapses into a selection of passages from Marx and integrates them into his own thought. Thus Segundo moves in and out of a polemical dialogue with Marx, imposing on the text certain interpretations and conclusions that are highly questionable. This is partly due to the fact that Segundo has not yet been able to transcend strictly theological discourse to the extent needed in the kind of dialogue he is engaged in with Marx. Segundo questions the strict "materialism" of Marx's theory of social relations (without defining what "materialism" is, as he comprehends the term) concluding that by "material" Marx recognized and accepted both material *and* spiritual dimensions as implied in the relations of material production and their consequent social relations. He writes:

> The term 'mode of production' is much less *materialistic* than is often assumed by both its advocates and its opponents. As Marx repeatedly stressed, the mode of production—or, the concrete economic structure—does not just take in the organization of the means of production: i.e., its more quantitative and hence 'materialist' aspect. It also takes in the 'human relations' generated by the type of production in question and by the appropriation of the means of production. And in these relations between human beings, effected in and through work, are included many elements which we could rightly call 'spiritual' and which are not nebulous idealizations. The concrete is complex. It is material and spiritual, even for historical materialism—or at least for the materialism of Marxism's founders.[30]

Although Marx's concept of the relations of material production and social relations is indeed complex and multidimensional, he does not use the term "spiritual" to describe them. Consider this passage from his *Preface to A Contribution to the Critique of Political Economy*:

> In the social production of their life, men enter into definite relations that are indispensable and independent of their will, relations of production which correspond to a definite stage of development of their material productive

forces. The sum total of these relations of production constitutes the economic structure of society, the real foundation, on which rises a legal and political superstructure and to which correspond definite forms of social consciousness. The mode of production of material life conditions the social, political, and intellectual life process in general. It is not the consciousness of men that determines their being, but, on the contrary, their social being that determines their consciousness.[31]

Human beings, then, for Marx, cannot be divorced from the material conditions of concrete existence, and concrete existence includes all social relations and intellectual life "up to [their] furthest forms."[32] Consciousness is "conscious existence, and the existence of men is their actual life-process."[33] Consciousness relates to the material, the practical, and not the spiritual, which Marx gives no legitimate credence to as a category in any case. Segundo may well attribute a spiritual dimension to human experience, but Marx does not, and cannot be read to do so. Spiritual implies an abstract hypostatization of human relations apart from the concrete, practical context in which people live and act. As such, "spiritual" can be understood as a form of alienated consciousness. I would not deny that what Marx means by all social relations "up to [their] furthest forms" is understood by Segundo as "spiritual," but this demonstrates Segundo's efforts to translate Marx (at least sometimes) into theological language. The problems which arise from this effort show the limitations of traditional theological language, and point toward the need to develop a language that articulates a religious consciousness of social reality not dissimilar to the socialist humanism outlined above.

For Marx, "spirit" has more to do with Hegelian philosophy, which he rejects as sheer abstraction. In applying the term "spiritual" to Marx's material concept of history, Segundo simply engages in a reductionism of Marx's understanding of the complex interconnection between the productive forces of society, the relations of production, and social relations. Yet Segundo's understanding of spirit resonates with the Hegelian notion of *Geist,* which is exactly what Marx so vehemently criticized in Hegel's philosophy. Segundo writes:

> The spirit . . . is concrete. And consciousness, its organ or product *par excellence,* must return to the concrete in order to construct its practical projects. . . . Theoretical praxis which seeks to transform the world is precisely the activity of the spirit geared toward the creation of a new world. Hence 'materialism' cannot be an alternative to the spirit and its functions.[34]

This is not Marx, but rather echoes of Hegel, and it is surprising that Segundo even tries to elaborate upon Marx's material conception of history by a superimposition of a Hegelian philosophy of history and does not realize it. This particular passage shows that Segundo has actually turned Marx upside down, which is perfectly understandable if his intention is to insert the notion of spirit into Marx. But in that case, Segundo would do better to pursue this line of thought vis-à-vis Hegel, and not Marx.

In fact, Segundo might have fewer theoretical problems altogether if he had chosen to open a dialogue with Hegel, since Segundo's theory finally cannot disassociate itself from relying on an absolute 'something' as a conditioning or guiding element in his own approach to history and human praxis. Even though Segundo's theological method begins with and emphasizes the primacy of practical action of human beings in their concrete environment, he remains disturbed by the problem of relativity, and it is this concern which drives him toward Hegel. He asks:

> How and from where can there arise an *absolute* that will put order into all that relativity in praxis? . . . Action cannot be structured without something unconditioned that subjects everything else to unity. That unconditioned need not be a God or a metaphysical entity, but it has to be a value.[35]

Here Segundo introduces an abstract category that implies a dialectical relation between an absolute, unconditioned value—which could be God, a metaphysical entity, or Absolute Spirit—and historical contingency and change. Again, this approach to the question of relativity and history reveals a closer proximity with Hegel than with Marx, and touches directly upon the question of the subject of history. However, Segundo distances himself from Hegel, dismissing him on the charge that Hegel's "idealism" is "characterized by a valuational indifference on the part of the philosopher [and the dialectic itself]."[36] While Segundo roundly criticizes Hegel, he does not enter into a serious analysis of Hegel's philosophy. Segundo's charge against idealism, then, turns out not to be the issue but rather that Hegel's philosophy is not partisan, which is really what Segundo means by valuational; that is, it lacks a specific commitment to a particular social, historical group:

> Neither the lord nor the bondsman, the skeptic or the stoic, incarnate a value or get any preference. If there is any value in Hegel's dialectic, it is to be located in the opposition itself, not in either one of the antagonists. Values are conveyed by the process of opposition only.[37]

Segundo rejects Hegelian dialectics on the grounds that it posits the wrong category as the "unconditional" of human history and praxis. Yet for Hegel, the unfolding of reason and freedom through the process of history, transcends the players of history, be they individuals or social groups. For Hegel, the dialectic of history is initiated by Absolute Spirit, the ultimate aim of which is the absolute identification of subject and object, and as such, history inevitably unfolds toward the Good. Segundo prefers an engaged value as the motivating historical force. Methodologically and formally speaking, there seems to be little difference here between Segundo and Hegel. Thus, as Hegel did not sever philosophy from metaphysics, neither can Segundo sever theology from metaphysics, although he thinks he does. However, Segundo insists upon his greater affinity with Marx, who "brought dialectic back down to realism, to 'real human beings.' "[38] The separation that Segundo insists upon between Hegel and Marx is more apparent than real, since for both thinkers concrete human action is key to historical change. Where Hegel and Marx differ concerns the locus of historical agency, the identification of the subject of history, which for Marx is clearly and unequivocally human beings in and through their concrete activity. But Segundo accounts for Marx's methodology, i.e., his material conception of history in which the human being is the only subject, as actually resting upon a deeper moral judgment which is that of the just cause of the proletariat. Here Segundo treads on dangerous ground, by obscuring the decisive difference between Marx and Hegel as located in their opposing conceptions of historical subjectivity. When Segundo rejects Hegel's dialectical method on the grounds of it being valueless, he misses the crucial point, thus reducing Hegel to a kind of dilettante. He does not recognize that his location of value as the unconditioned absolute of human praxis and history raises serious questions about the historical subject in his own theory, questions which take him far away from Marx. One wonders how Segundo can claim to dissociate himself from Hegel on the point of the subject of history, and why he does so, and then identify with Marx who clearly rejected any such notion of an "absolute" or unconditioned element as the dynamic motive force of human history. While Segundo's appropriation of Marx's social philosophy and even important elements of his anthropology threaten to push Segundo's theology beyond its own boundaries, Segundo cannot quite seem to take the final step. However close he professes to be to Marx, Segundo remains caught within what can only be called the idealist Hegelian framework. He cannot take, as it were, the final step into an unambiguous humanism. And yet, it is partly his interpretation of the humanism he sees in Marx that leads him so very close, to concluding with Marx, that the root of man, is man.

To reject Hegel on the grounds of his dialectics, dismissing the importance of dialectics in general, is also far from Marx. In volume 1 of *Capital,* Marx writes:

> My dialectic method is not only different from the Hegelian, but is its direct opposite. To Hegel, the life-process of the human brain, i.e., the process of thinking, which, under the name of "the Idea," he even transforms into an independent subject, is the demiurgos of the real world, and the real world is only the external, phenomenal form of "the Idea." With me, on the contrary, the ideal is nothing else than the material world reflected by the human mind, and translated into forms of thought.[39]

The decisive difference between Marx and Hegel lies within the location of the historical subject, not in the dialectical method per se. Segundo slides over this point because his central interest is to show that Marx's theory rests upon an anthropological faith in a value, and he refers to Marx's realist "relocation of the dialectic" which,

> inevitably entails the accentuation of some *predialectical "faith."* . . . It is not the dialectic that leads Marx to place himself on the side of the proletariat. . . . Marx's position is not one of opportunism abetted by predictions which the dialectic makes possible. . . . His option is an effort to change the world by establishing values.[40]

Marx's "relocation of the dialectic" has nothing to do with values or simply taking sides. Segundo cannot legitimately reduce Marx's insistence on human beings as historical subject to a partisan preference for one historical group over another, based upon an abstract value. This is to read Marx as a moralist, which he was not. Moreover, Segundo's rejection of the dialectical method on the grounds of the absence of values makes no sense. Marx's method is also dialectical, and he inherited it from Hegel, and it has nothing to do with values in the sense Segundo means. Marx acknowledges how he had "openly avowed" himself as "the pupil of that mighty thinker" (Hegel) from whom he inherited the general theory of the dialectic, while disagreeing with Hegel about its location:

> The mystification which dialectic suffers in Hegel's hands, by no means prevents him from being the first to present its general form of working in a comprehensive and conscious manner. With him it is standing on its head. It must be turned right side up again, if you would discover the rational kernel within the mystical shell.[41]

Marx stresses the importance of negation in dialectics, another element taken from Hegel, with its power for "breaking up" the "existing state of things," "because it regards every historically developed social form as in fluid movement, and therefore takes into account its transient nature not less than its momentary existence; because it lets nothing impose upon it, and is in its essence critical and revolutionary."[42] Like Hegel, Marx also understands dialectics as negative dialectics, which Segundo for some reason repudiates only in Hegel, whom he dismisses as using "the negation of the negation" as an irritating "manner of speech, *ad nauseam*."[43] Segundo unfortunately interprets Hegel's conception of negation in a literal, vulgar way:

> Unlike a small child, an adult human being knows that a chair is not really the negation of a table, ever. Nor is the canine carcass the negation of the dog . . . mere differences are not negations. . . . *Only if I want to sit down,* and deliberate where to sit down, *can* the chair become metaphorically the 'negation' of the table, and vice versa.[44]

There is no point to debate with Segundo about Hegel's concept of negation, and its importance for the overcoming of alienation, for example, since Segundo offers a simple caricature of Hegel in the above quoted paragraph, and seems to show no interest in a serious discussion of this point. My aim is, however, to show that his disagreement with Hegel and his siding with Marx on the issue of dialectics as a question primarily of values is misplaced and unnecessary. There is no reason for Segundo to dismiss Hegel, before even entering into a serious evaluation of his philosophy. This whole confusing discussion in Segundo about Marx, Hegel, and dialectics is finally irrelevant to Segundo's real purpose, which is to try to show that Marx's theory is grounded in a "pre-dialectical" values-structure. At some point Segundo drops the term 'materialism' in favor of 'realism,' so that Marx's critique of Hegel is understood as a "*realist* reworking of Hegel's dialectic."[45] What Segundo does not realize is that when he rejects the notion of Absolute Spirit as the motive force of history, he in fact obliterates God, and hence his theory can no longer be understood as theological but some form of humanism. Stated in other words, the notion of Absolute Spirit is the notion of God raised to the level of philosophy or thought—the articulation of the universal essence, as it were, of that which is grasped in religion and theology as God. If Segundo is to develop his thought in accordance with itself, he must abandon God, and opt for humanity as the unalloyed subject of history. In this way, Segundo would transcend theology and move his analysis into a humanist theory of man's being in society.

However, these issues shift to a level of secondary importance, and his central focus moves to a discussion of the meaning of faith and values:

> Neither historical materialism nor dialectical materialism can claim to deter-
> mine the value (the 'ought-to-be') possessed in and of themselves by premises
> which are, by definition, *self-validating*—i.e., which belong to the realm of
> meaning.[46]

For Segundo, faith, and the values which proceed from it, are beyond the boundaries of theoretical methodology.[47] Values constitute therefore an absolute, unconditioned, and fixed transcendental truth which grounds and mediates both theoretical and practical methodology. Segundo thus undermines his own theoretical consistency by reverting back to theological, ahistorical categories as foundations of history. While insisting on humanity as subject of history (but remaining confused on this point), he then suddenly abandons humanity as the proper subject of history.

It is precisely here that Segundo reveals the idealist and transcendental strain within his thought. But this becomes extremely problematic as he consistently tries to impose this view on Marx, asserting that Marx's "realist dialectic" is itself grounded in a "particular conception of meaning and value," and even further that "only those who share this meaning and values structure can use Marx's method of cognition and action in a logical, effective way."[48] One wonders if this is a purely descriptive or moralistic statement. It seems to imply that the underlying motivation of Marx and anyone else concerned with the abolition of class society and the liberation of the proletariat (and all humanity) necessarily arises from an abstract principle or value concerning the just cause of an oppressed humanity. Segundo thus turns Marx into a utopian socialist, never confronting Marx's repeated attacks on utopian socialism from the perspective of a scientific, materialistic analysis of the concrete laws and mechanism of history.

Despite these problems, Segundo remains very close to critical theory as well as to those groups of thinkers who have attempted to read Marx by way of a socialist humanism. These writers, along with critical theorists, are two important examples of efforts to reclaim Marx from distortions derived from mechanistic and deterministic interpretations that have so unfortunately reified Marx's thought through Leninist and Stalinist ideologies. Segundo acknowledges that he reads Marx's thought in a humanist key, turning to Erich Fromm to support his position that Marx was a humanist: "It must be noted that labor and capital were not at all for Marx only economic categories; they were anthropological categories, imbued with a *value judgment* which is rooted in his humanistic position."[49] (Segundo's italics). Segundo's actual discussion about Marx's humanism is brief and mostly descriptive, and he acknowledges the existence of the large body of literature on the subject, with its controversial debate. Segundo does not delve into this debate, however, but concedes that Marx does indeed have a concept of a human being which is "partially derived from Hegel,"[50] and that Marx does profess, "The essence of the human being," which Segundo immediately labels as a *"transcendent datum* par excellence."[51] Segundo proceeds to assert that such a humanism has nothing to do with science, and that its "premises" are based upon an idea of "essence" which is self-evident. Like socialist humanist interpreters of Marx, Segundo also understands Marx's anthropological themes as raising questions about Being in general, about man's "essence" and the possible transcendence of his alienation.[52]

There is another point that must be raised with regard to Segundo's interpretation of Marx, and that is his assertion that Marx's "materialism" is not incompatible with belief in God. Segundo states that all Marx's theory does is to criticize or "combat religion in one of its historical forms,"[53] although he does not explain what he means by this or which historical form he has in mind. Segundo tries to demonstrate that there is no intrinsic connection between Marx's thought and atheism:

> There is no more of a relationship between atheism and a materialism consistent with the thought of Marx (be there one Marx or two) than there is between atheism and historical materialism, or atheism and dialectical materialism.[54]

Although Segundo is partly correct, this assertion is misleading if one looks to the writings of Marx himself, who clearly rejected not only religion and theology as forms of ideology, but also the notion of God itself, although not strictly from the point of view of an atheist. In the *Economic and Philosophical Manuscripts (1844),* Marx writes:

> A *being* only considers himself independent when he stands on his own feet; and he only stands on his own feet when he owes his *existence* to himself. A man who lives by the grace of another regards himself as a dependent being. But I live completely by the grace of another if I owe him not only the sustenance of my life, but if he has, moreover, *created* my *life*—if he is the *source* of my life.[55]

Marx continues this passage to nullify the doctrine of Creation, citing the *"Generatio aequivoca* [as] the only practical refutation of the theory of creation" of the world; he then rejects the doctrine of the creation of Man, even physically by any force other than human: "even physically man owes his existence to man . . . by which *man* repeats himself in procreation, thus always remaining the subject."[56] Marx goes on to undermine the very question of atheism as a legitimate question, claiming that it is not an issue for socialist man: "Since for the socialist man the *entire so-called history of the world* is nothing but the begetting of man through human labor," so that man has:

> The visible, irrefutable proof of his *birth* through himself, of his *process of coming-to-be*. Since the *real existence* of man and nature has become practical, sensuous, and perceptible . . . the question about an *alien* being, about a being above nature and man . . . has become impossible in practice. Atheism has no longer any meaning, for atheism is a *negation of God,* and postulates the *existence of man* through this negation; but socialism as socialism no longer stands in any need of such a mediation. It proceeds from the *practically* and theoretically sensuous *positive self-consciousness* no longer mediated through the annulment of religion.[57]

Segundo refers to the first part of this quotation as Marx's "reason" for atheism.[58] It is not clear what Segundo means by this, or why he even raises it. Marx is not promoting atheism, because atheism is the negation of theism, and as such accepts the question of the existence or nonexistence of God to be legitimate. Marx does not accept the theist/atheist dichotomy to be relevant because it still formulates or mediates the question of concrete human existence in relation to a Creator, thus obscuring the fact of historical human subjectivity. Marx's humanism is unambiguous: if the root of man is man himself, there is no need to even think about God; socialist man, free of the alienation produced by class society and reflected in religion, one of its ideological forms, understands himself as his own "root" or essence. "Socialism is man's *positive self-consciousness* no longer mediated through the annulment of religion," wrote Marx, and Segundo does not see the full meaning of this statement partly because of the ambiguity of the humanist strains in his own thought. Segundo simply wants to declare that Marxism and atheism are not mutually exclusive, in order to remove the ultimate barrier between Christianity and Marx. Here again, it is necessary to show that Segundo displays a tendency to reduce or simplify Marx at certain points in order not only to build his own position, but to try to enlist Marx's support for it by his analysis and interpretation of the texts of Marx. For Segundo "Marx's work" is not "an ontology loaded with the transcendent datum that transcendent data do not exist at all."[59] If by "transcendent data" Segundo means God, then he would be hard pressed to show that there is any text in Marx that even allows the possibility of the existence of God. It there were, then theology (i.e., *logos* about God) would have to be seen as a legitimate activity for Marx. But for him, theology is nothing more that "philosophy's spot of infection."[60] But Segundo drops the matter, content with his unfounded assertion that Marx's thought does not necessarily imply denial of the existence of God. Again, this view is more compatible with Hegelian philosophy rather than with Marx.

In *The Liberation of Theology,* Segundo tried to construct a critical, materialist methodology of liberation theology, mediated through Marx. Segundo began his approach to theology by placing man as the center of human history so that the focus of his theology would be man in his concrete, material context, and whose purpose would be to change the structures of society for the liberation of Latin Americans. However, man as center, in the methodological sense, does not necessarily imply man as the sole subject of history. This is a highly important distinction. For Marx, man is clearly and unequivocally the subject of history, while for Segundo, he is the center or focus of history; however, subject and center (or focus) are not the same. Man as center implies that God remains the historical subject, working out his divine plan through humanity.

While Segundo's attempted appropriation of Marx is riddled with problems and contradictions, his work represents the most interesting and even promising efforts in contemporary Christianity to come to grips with Marx in a creative way. What Segundo strives to do is to overcome metaphysics in order to liberate theology from a sterile, ineffective ahistoricism, which often functions as an ideology of domination, and to render it a meaningful and fully historical, practical force for social transformation. In doing so, Segundo inevitably seeks to restore the human being, with all its potential for developing into its full humanity, as the main reality and end of history and society. Segundo's insistence on the affirmation of the human as an absolute value in itself distinguishes him from both classical theology and those forms of socialist, Marxist ideologies that prevail throughout Latin America. Segundo must confront the existence of significant and numerous revolutionary groups whose versions of Marxism, deriving from Lenin, Stalin, or Mao, allow little room not only for Christianity, but for a view of humanity as an end in itself. These ideologies reproduce, in a different form, the dehumanizing, instrumental rationality of capitalism as identified and analyzed by early Frankfurt school thinkers such as Max Horkheimer and later, by Jürgen Habermas. What Segundo is trying to do is to explore and develop the potential of Christianity to mount an effective critique and opposition of the social order that will lead to a genuinely liberatory political praxis for social change along with the overcoming of all alienation that blocks the realization of human potential in a humane world. To do this he must bring Christianity into serious and close association with Marx, which takes Segundo out of the realm of theology and into the formulation of a socialist humanist theory of society, which in liberation theology is still in its beginning stages. This may also be the beginning of a transformed consciousness which will act as a critical, prophetic voice and which will seek to restore the inherent value of human beings as ends, in a society which understands itself as a Kingdom of ends. This kind of religious consciousness was perhaps intimated by Horkheimer when he said, "a politics which, even highly reflected, does not preserve a theological moment in itself is . . . mere business."[61] In the work of Juan Luis Segundo, and in liberation theology in general, that effort to preserve that "theological moment" in politics is now taking place.

Notes

1. By "humanism," I mean an understanding of human beings as subjects of history, in the sense that history develops as a consequence of human activities. How-

ever, I do not wish to confuse human agency with an abstract notion of "humanity," which obscures concrete human beings and their historicality. The kind of "humanism" implied by liberation theology, as I interpret it, acknowledges human beings as historical actors, who produce and make history.

2. By "early" Frankfurt school, I refer mainly to writers like Max Horkheimer, Theodor Adorno, Herbert Marcuse, and Erich Fromm, whose interest was to rehabilitate Marx from the mechanistic reductionisms and reifications of Leninist and Stalinist ideologies. Although these writers had critical attitudes to what was called 'Marxist humanism', they were concerned with questions of historical agency, human freedom, and social transformation in a way that inspired the socialist humanism of the *Praxis* philosophers.

3. Although Segundo is not the only liberation theologian to address the issue of Marx's humanism (see also Jose Miranda, *Marx Against the Marxists,* Maryknoll, N.Y. 1980, ch. 5) he may be said to have profoundly absorbed certain aspects of Marxian thought that sets him apart from other liberation theologians who either refer to Marx as providing them with a "tool" of social analysis, or who try to show Marx's "latent" Christianity. For a fuller discussion of the depth of Marx's influence on Segundo, see my *From Theology to Social Theory: Juan Luis Segundo and the Theology of Liberation* (New York, 1990).

4. J. L. Segundo, "Capitalism Versus Socialism: Crux Theologica," in *Frontiers of Theology in Latin America,* ed. Rosino Gibellini, trans. John Drury (Maryknoll, N.Y., 1979), 240–259. Also, Zagorka Pesić-Golubović, "Socialism and Humanism," *Praxis, Revue Philosophique Edition Internationale,* Zagreb, 4 (1965): 520–535.

5. See, for example, Hans Küng's discussion of the early Christian concepts of service and gifts, the diaconal and charismatic structure of Christian communities in *The Church* (Garden City, N.Y., 1967), 495–502.

6. See Gustavo Gutierrez's discussion of the Eucharist in *A Theology of Liberation,* trans. and ed. Sister Caridad Inda and John Eagleson (Maryknoll, N.Y., 1973), 264.

7. Ibid., 111.

8. Zagorka Pesić-Golubović, "Socialism and Humanism," 524.

9. Erich Fromm, "Marx's Contribution to the Knowledge of Man," *Praxis, Revue Philosophique Edition Internationale,* Zagreb, 1/2 (1969): 60.

10. Gajo Petrović, "Philosophy and Socialism," *Praxis* 4 (1967): 548.

11. Ibid., 554.

12. Ibid., 554.

13. Gustavo Gutierrez, *A Theology of Liberation,* 90.

14. Ibid., 91.

15. Juan Luis Segundo, *The Liberation of Theology,* trans. John Drury (Maryknoll, N.Y., 1976), 13.

16. Herbert Marcuse, *Reason and Revolution: Hegel and the Rise of Social Theory* (Boston, 1969), 252–253.

17. For example, Segundo's *The Humanist Christology of Paul* suggests that the most appropriate way of understanding Paul's Christology is in an "*anthropological* or existential key" which allows Segundo to develop what he sees as the social and political justice dimension of Paul's thought. This approach to Paul's Christology is consistent with Segundo's own "antichristology," which emphasizes the humanity of Jesus and the human-centered values he lived by. This line of argumentation leads Segundo to conclude that "In itself, the resurrection is irrelevant" to one's opting to live as Jesus did (*The Humanist Christology of Paul,* ed. and trans., John Drury, Maryknoll, N.Y., 1986, 10 & 81). Also see *The Historical Jesus of the Synoptics* for Segundo's full argument.

18. Juan Luis Segundo, "The Shift Within Latin American Theology," lecture given at Regis College, Toronto, March 22, 1983.

19. Juan Luis Segundo, *Theology and the Church: A Response to Cardinal Ratzinger and a Warning to the Whole Church,* trans. John W. Wiercksmeier (Minneapolis, 1985), 40.

20. Juan Luis Segundo, *Faith and Ideologies,* trans. John Drury (Maryknoll, N.Y., 1984), 300.

21. Karl Marx, *Theses on Feuerbach,* in *The Marx-Engels Reader,* ed. Robert C. Tucker (New York, 1978).

22. Juan Luis Segundo, *The Liberation of Theology,* 9.

23. Ibid., 14.

24. Ibid., 13.

25. Juan Luis Segundo, *Faith and Ideologies,* 278.

26. Quoted in Juan Luis Segundo, *The Liberation of Theology,* 71.

27. Herbert Marcuse, "A Note on the Dialectic," in *The Essential Frankfurt School Reader,* ed. Andrew Arato and Eike Gebhardt (New York, 1982), 448.

28. Ibid., 449.

29. Alfredo Fierro, *The Militant Gospel,* trans. John Drury (Maryknoll, N.Y., 1977), 108.

30. Juan Luis Segundo, *Faith and Ideologies,* 180.

31. Karl Marx, *Preface to a Contribution to the Critique of Political Economy,* in *The Marx-Engels Reader,* 4.

32. Karl Marx, *The German Ideology,* in *The Marx-Engels Reader,* 154.

33. Ibid., 154.

34. Juan Luis Segundo, *Faith and Ideologies,* 180.

35. Ibid., 184.

36. Ibid., 234.

37. Ibid., 234.

38. Ibid., 234.

39. Karl Marx, *Capital: A Critique of Political Economy,* vol. 1, trans. Samuel Moore and Edward Aveling, ed. Frederick Engels (New York, 1967), 19.

40. Juan Luis Segundo, *Faith and Ideologies,* 234–235.

41. Karl Marx, *Capital,* vol. 1, 20.

42. Ibid., 20.

43. Juan Luis Segundo, *Faith and Ideologies,* 210.

44. Ibid., 210.

45. Ibid., 235.

46. Ibid., 225.

47. Ibid., 225.

48. Ibid., 236.

49. Ibid., 239.

50. Ibid., 240.

51. Ibid., 240.

52. Gajo Petrović, "Philosophy and Socialism," 548.

53. Juan Luis Segundo, *Faith and Ideologies,* 241.

54. Ibid., 241.

55 Karl Marx, *Economic and Philosophical Manuscripts (1844),* in *The Marx-Engels Reader,* 91.

56. Ibid., 92.

57. Ibid., 92–93.

58. Juan Luis Segundo, *Faith and Ideologies,* 247, n. 41.

59. Ibid., 241.

60. Karl Marx, *Economic and Philosophical Manuscripts (1844)*, 70.

61. Quoted in Charles Davis, *Theology and Political Society* (Cambridge, 1980), 133.

21

The Modern Spirit and the Paradox of Humanism

Kenneth Dorter

HISTORICAL CONSCIOUSNESS

The fact that we are aware of the correlation between historical change and ways of thinking already distinguishes our thinking from that of the ancients, and thus our ability to question the nature of modernity is itself a clue to the nature of what is distinctive about our age. People have always been aware of racial differences and differences of language and custom, but the idea of a culture that defines a national spirit without being reducible to supposed biological differences of race is peculiar to modernity. The Greeks distinguished *hoi nun* (people now) from *hoi palai* (people in the past), but they never supposed that the age itself might be ascribed a determinate character different from that of other ages. Even the superiority of the heroic age was due to the heroes' semidivinity, not to a difference in historical culture. Accordingly, one cannot imagine Plato, Aristotle, Aurelius, Plotinus, or even Lucretius, with his anthropological interest, asking about the nature of "the modern temper." In the same way the Romans saw themselves as culturally continuous with the Greeks and tended to imitate Greek culture without any apparent self-consciousness. Even Vergil, for all his sensitivity to history, portrays the Roman traditions as little more than Trojan traditions transplanted into Italy. This attitude is evident also in the Greek and Roman approach to the writing of history, which was event-oriented rather than anything like the history of nations that is pursued today.

The medievals, too, although always aware of the decisiveness by which revelation separated them from the Greco-Roman world, in many respects saw themselves as philosophically continuous with it and regarded the advent of revelation as a difference between enlightenment and lack of enlightenment rather than between two different tempers. When Augustine divides history into six epochs, for example, paralleling the six days of creation, they are divided not in terms of the rise of different cultures or civilizations, as we would do today, but rather by landmark events or figures: the flood, Abraham, David, the Babylonian exile, and Jesus.

If we think of the classical Greek conception of philosophy as a vertical relationship connecting the thinker more or less successfully with a higher reality, we today would add a horizontal axis representing our historical relationship with the specific tradition within which we always find ourselves, and in terms of which both our questions and answers about the nature of reality must be posed. Even if we conceive of the truth with which philosophy is concerned as in some sense timeless, it is always conceived within a current world in terms of concepts that are never given in an objectively neutral way. Only to the extent that philosophy understands what is distinctive in its age, therefore, can its own significance become clear to itself.

Even granted that our historical consciousness effectively distinguishes us from previous ages, this gives us no indication whether that consciousness is the foundation of our character or merely a symptom of it. Other characteristics have been proposed with equal plausibility as the defining feature of our age: the strict empiricism of modern science, the transformation of natural science into mathematics, the advent of technology, and the replacement of theism with humanism, for example. It is not immediately evident which, if any of these, is fundamental and which derivative, and how, if at all, they are to be related to one another.

Although any proposed starting point for modern historical consciousness will be somewhat arbitrary, owning to the bonds of influence by which any thinker is attached to his predecessors, there is some justification for focusing on the end of the seventeenth century as the time at which some important implications of the modern attitude began to emerge. From the time of Augustine's *City of God* to Jacques Bossuet's *Discourse on Universal History* in 1681, world history, although no longer simply anecdotal, was conceived as subordinate to theology. Pierre Bayle, however, provided it for the first time with an autonomous foundation, by applying to it the positivistic methods of empirical science.[1] Subsequently, the scientific model was further adapted to history in an attempt to discover not only objective historical facts but also the principles and laws that govern history as the laws of nature govern the physical world. On this basis Vico not only distinguishes common principles governing the life cycles of all cultures but also comes to appreciate the specific *character* of various cultures.[2] In the second half of the century, not only were the empirical method and the goal of the discovery of governing laws extrapolated from natural science to the study of history, but so too was the concept of progress. The character of political and cultural history, like that of science and technology, was to be understood in terms of perennial improvement.

The primary evidence for historical progress is the "advancement of learning" displayed by the cumulative character of science, together with the progressive innovations of technology. Once knowledge was identified with power, and our increasing power over nature was displayed in terms of technological capability, there was concrete evidence for the improvement of scientific knowledge, and it was inevitable that the interpretation of history in general as progress would suggest itself. The progressive view of history was born, accordingly, at the same time that modern technology began to take shape in the industrial revolution. (The very term "technology" appears to have been born in the eighteenth century.) Thus Turgot[3] and to a greater degree Condorcet[4] argue that history represents the progress of humanity generally (not just in the sphere of knowledge and technical ability) toward greater and greater perfection.

It is sometimes claimed that the idea of progress originates not with technology but with Christianity. In his important and provocative book, *Meaning in History,* Karl Löwith argues that the idea of progress arises from a misappropriation of the Medieval concept of eschatology. Following Comte, he distinguishes two strands within the concept of progress, (1) the belief that the present is superior to the past, and (2) the belief that the future will be a similar improvement over the present, and he claims that both of these originate with Christianity. On the first point he accepts Comte's view that

> [t]he first dawning sense of human progress was inspired by Christianity. By proclaiming the superiority of the law of Jesus over that of Moses, it gave rise to the idea of a fundamental historical progression toward fulfillment, from a less to a more perfect state.[5]

On the second, he argues that although the idea of a *future* progress is ruled out by the Christian belief that it itself represents the final stage of history, Christianity nevertheless provides the *model* for this further extension of the concept of progress, in terms of its belief in providence and eschatology. Thus, the enlightenment's

> law of progressive evolution replaces the function of providential government, perverting the secret provision by providence into a scientific provision by [in Comte's words] a *prevision rationelle.*[6]

Where Löwith disagrees with Comte is in his belief that Comte greatly underestimates the *extent* to which the concept of progress is a "secularization" of Christian beliefs, and as a result of which the concept's very legitimacy is in question.

Comte's (and Löwith's) claims that the sense of human progress begins with Christianity is mistaken, for a certain conception of progress is evident in ancient Greece as early as the sixth century B.C., in Xenophanes' remark that, "By no means did the gods reveal all things to mortals from the beginning, but, by seeking, mortals find out better in time,"[7] and it was not uncommon for the Greeks to regard civilization as a gradual emergence from barbarism. Löwith's second claim, that the idea of future progress too is transferred from Christianity, underestimates the *independent* evidence for the belief in progress afforded by technology. Löwith himself notes that:

> The first satisfactory view of general progress was proposed by . . . Pascal.
> He viewed the entire succession of man through the whole course of ages
> as *"one* man always subsisting and incessantly learning."[8]

The fact that Pascal was "a great Christian believer . . . [as well as] a great
scientist"[9] does not show that his perception, as a scientist, of progress in
learning was influenced by his Christian beliefs. Moreover, as Hans Blumenberg points out,

> Eschatology may have been, for a shorter or a longer moment of history,
> an aggregate of hopes; but when the time had come for the emergence of
> the idea of progress, it was more nearly an aggregate of terror and dread.
> . . . It is impossible to see how one expectation could ever result from the
> other, unless perhaps we were to represent the disappointment of the tran-
> scendent expectation as an agent of the immanent one. But then the time
> when the idea of progress first emerged and impressed itself on history would
> have to be moved forward by considerably more than a millennium."[10]

But if the view that the present is an improvement over the past dates
back to ancient Greece, this seems as hard to reconcile with the more usual
claim—which I accept—that the concept of progress is new in the eighteenth
century, as with Löwith's claim that it originates in Christianity. It is somewhat misleading to speak of "the concept" of progress at all, since writers
differed in their judgment about which kinds of values (e.g., theoretical
knowledge, control over nature, moral wisdom, political stability, material
prosperity, etc.) were definitive of the character of a civilization, and, therefore, what the measure of progress should be. Nevertheless, there is an important general difference between the ancient and modern conceptions, corresponding to Comte's distinction between the past and future components
of the concept.

Although there was no lack of recognition in the ancient world that
civilization arose from relatively primitive origins, and that future generations
would continue to make new discoveries, there seems to have been no sense
that these would dramatically alter the nature of civilization. To use a metaphor often employed in relation to the idea of progress, the Greek attitude
seems to have been analogous to the recognition that, as mature adults, we
have progressed from childhood by means of what experience has taught us,
and that we will undoubtedly continue to learn from experience. But it is
one thing to believe this, and quite another matter to believe that our future
discoveries will lead to a new metamorphosis that is as different from adulthood as adulthood is from childhood.

It is precisely the view that the future will be as much of an improvement over the present as the present is over the past—that in the future people will not only know things that we do not but that this knowledge will
change the nature of civilization so as to improve the happiness of human
existence—that is revolutionary in Turgot and Condorcet. Only when knowledge has been identified with power, and thus with the power to better the
conditions of existence, does this further step follow. The view that the future

holds great changes in the order of things as a result of our efforts is virtually without precedent, and in this understanding of the present as having its meaning in a creative relationship towards the future and away from the past, modern historical consciousness first becomes manifest. Our historical consciousness has undergone various transformations as the naive faith in progress began to wane or be modified, but its source, like that of modern science, lies in man's sense of his power to change the world essentially. Unlike the medieval philosophy of history, modern historical consciousness begins with a concern for the projects not of God but of humanity.

The link between our historical consciousness and the rise of modern science and technology is only one way in which the importance of the latter phenomena can be illustrated. In fact, if one traces back the development of virtually any characteristic associated with the modern age, they all tend to converge at the advent of modern science and technology. Heidegger's conception of the "homelessness" of modern man, and Marx's quite different conception of modern alienation, are both rooted, at least in part, in modern technology, while for Nietzsche the nihilism characteristic of the present age results from the death of God at the hands of modern science (and indeed science replaces Christianity as the repository of the "ascetic ideal"). Similarly, for Spengler science and technology are primary manifestations of what he calls the Faustian spirit of Western culture. Let us pursue the question of modernity, therefore, by turning our attention to the relationship between modern science and technology.

SCIENCE AND TECHNOLOGY

The radically different approaches to science by Descartes and Bacon are jointly representative of the unexpected harmony of the mathematical and the empirical that is to be found in modern science. "Unexpected" not only because, in classical traditions other than astronomy, empiricism and mathematics had been antagonists rather than allies (even Francis Bacon, for all the prescience of his confidence in the future of modern science and technology, did not foresee the mathematical character that these disciplines would have to have in order to achieve their success); but also because in one sense at least they are opposed in their very nature.

This can be seen from the diametric opposition in the way that each, in its modern scientific form, departs from the Greek version of science. Despite the seemingly self-evident character that empirical experimentation has since acquired, it was never employed by ancient science, which operated instead on a belief that rational models based on thoughtful observation would be sufficient for understanding nature. Experimentation proceeds rather from a skepticism about the ability of human reason to arrive at the truth of things by means of its own devices alone, and therefore demands that reason be constantly called to account in the world of sense experience by the creation and observation of physical representations of its theories. Empirical science would therefore see the ancients as overly rationalistic and insufficiently empirical. Mathematical science, on the other hand, would fault them for relying too much on merely general observations undisciplined by precise measurement and mathematical models—for being, in other words, too empirical and not sufficiently rational.

The analogue among the ancients of these divergent tendencies between empirical and mathematical approaches was the fact that, on one hand, except for astronomy the ancient physical sciences took little interest in mathematics—and this held true regardless of whether one looks at the Presocratic, Aristotelian, or atomistic versions of science—while on the other hand, the mathematical traditions like those of Plato and Pythagoras had no more regard for the claim of sense experience to provide us with knowledge of the nature of reality than the empiricists did for that of mathematics. But modern science not only combines these two inimical traditions; it can even claim to be at once more empirical than Greek science, because of its development of controlled experiment, and more mathematical as well, because of its development of mathematical techniques and models capable of representing natural processes with incomparable thoroughness and precision. In that case it might be tempting to give a Hegelian interpretation and suggest that modern science represents a higher synthesis of the antithetical elements of ancient science. But that would be misleading, as we can see from the manner in which the union of these two elements was effected.

One basis of the union between empiricism and mathematics, already implicit in ancient astronomy, was explicitly formulated by Roger Bacon in his observation that while empiricism and experiment are necessary to science as a means of refining the information conveyed by the senses, mathematics becomes a necessary tool to compensate for the limited reach of empirical observation. Direct observation is not always possible, especially in astronomy, and it is necessary to develop, as a kind of *deuteros plous* or second-best way, mathematical models whose predictions can be stated quantitatively and thus measured against future observations. It was the confirmation of such predictions that earned mathematical astronomy the respect whereby Descartes could say that, of our two ideas of the size of the sun, the idea derived from mathematics—that the sun is much larger and farther away than the senses suggest—is more to be trusted than the one derived from the senses. A second basis of their union, which was advocated by da Vinci, Galileo, and Descartes, was the fact that mathematics alone could provide science with the kind of exactitude and therefore certainty that it now sought.

In both cases, the way in which mathematics was joined to empiricism seems to suggest that their union is by no means an equal partnership or synthesis but an appropriation of mathematical techniques by empiricism for use as a tool to expand the horizons and reliability of its investigations. Despite the mathematical nature of modern science, in an important sense the enterprise of science is shaped not by the mathematical temper but by the empirical one. The difference between them is not negligible, for it is a species of the perennial dispute between rationalism and empiricism. The primary measure of reality for empiricism is the concrete corporeal realm that can be physically observed; but one who takes mathematics as the surest guide to the nature of reality is led away from the concrete to the abstract, since numbers prescind from physical properties. If pure mathematics rather than empiricism is taken as the science of Being, then Being must be conceived as incorporeal, as intelligible to the mind but not visible to the senses.

In Aristotelian terms, pure mathematics regards the world in terms of formal causality and teleology—whether one takes teleology in the weaker sense that the reason for the being of the world is to be found in necessitating mathematical principles such as elegance or economy, or in the stronger sense in which the meaning of all things can be discerned through number mysticism. Thus for Plato and the Pythagoreans the mysteries of mathematics were clues to the mysteries of being. Empiricism, on the other hand, is concerned with the material and efficient causes of physical phenomena, abstracting almost entirely from teleology and usually construing the formal aspect of reality exclusively in nominalistic terms. Accordingly, in empirical science mathematics functions not as an *intrinsic* clue to the nature of reality, but only as an instrumental one, a field of techniques for measurement and calculation. Even the mathematical Descartes was so much part of this current that he regarded mathematics not as an avenue to wisdom in its own right, in nonphysical terms, but as a tool for understanding physical processes, and he disparaged teleological and formal explanations in favor of mechanistic ones.

There are always exceptions to such general tendencies. In the ancient world Thales, and astronomers and engineers generally, appreciated the empirical applications of mathematics; and in the tradition of modern science speculative (if not always mathematical) thinkers like Paracelsus, Boehme, Kepler, Leibniz, and Goethe are primarily concerned with developing a conception of the unity of the whole and turn to empiricism for the *completion* of their thought, for the data to give concrete shape to their overview, as opposed to the empiricists who turn to a theoretical point of view only because of the limited range of our senses. But the comparative rarity of such figures, and the fact that they are more common in the early stages of the development of modern science than in recent times, only attests to the near-uniformity with which the empirical rather than speculative attitude dominates modern science.

With the Greeks it was different because the attempt of the ancient natural philosophers to discover the ways of nature was more directed toward a synoptic understanding of the general workings of the world, the way in which the one cosmos is differentiated into the many phenomena, than in a precise knowledge of the mechanism of physical processes. Presumably this is why, in spite of their creativity and genius, the experimental method never seems to have occurred to them. Had their ambitions been the same as those of the modern era, the means to those ends would likely have occurred to them as well, but their ambitions were in fact very different.

Not only were the Presocratic nature philosophers more interested in the general scheme of things than in the precise working details; even the Epicureans' concern with the working details of nature was less because of any intrinsic importance that they attached to them than because these details enabled them to explain physical existence without reference to the gods, and thereby lent credence to their gospel that mankind should live according to "hedonistic" rather than theistic values. Epicurean hedonism included of course the enjoyment of knowledge for its own sake, but such knowledge was again conceived in terms of general principles rather than precisely measured details. Unlike modern science, Epicurean science was not a foundation for a continuous project but was meant instead to be a set of definitive answers. Aristotle too—who in contrast with Plato is often regarded as a champion of empiricism—was by modern standards more speculative than empirical and accorded less attention to efficient than to formal and teleological causality. Indeed, the greatest obstacle for modern science was the gaining of acceptance for the empirical method in the face of the authority of the Aristotelian system.

A major reason for this modern shift of interest from the speculative to the empirical seems to lie in the difference of character between the ancient and modern ages, specifically with regard to the modern ambition of mastering nature. For the Socratic tradition the value of knowledge was manifest in terms of excellence or virtue, which implies a view of a beneficent nature in which moral principles are objectively present. Francis Bacon was distinctively modern in identifying the value of knowledge instead with power. The collapse of the geocentric conception of the universe enhanced that attitude considerably (although the gradual erosion of Christian belief would have had the same effect independently, if less rapidly), for if the earth is not the center of the universe, it is less likely that the universe exists for the sake of humanity, and nature is not so easily conceived as necessarily moral or hospitable to humankind.[11] It may instead seem neutral with regard to human values, or, in view of the frequency of natural hardships, even inimical to our interests, a kind of Kronos eating its progeny. In that case it becomes important for humanity to take our destiny into our own hands, doing everything possible to change the course of nature in accordance with our needs. Nature is no longer perceived as a womb or kingdom but as a brute system of forces that must be made subject to the rational governance of humanity.

Significantly, the Greeks showed themselves not only less concerned than we are with the details of the workings of nature but also less concerned with any program for overmastering nature. In terms of the human motivations that Plato distinguishes in the *Republic,* Greek science might be said to have been primarily governed by reason (*to logistikon*) whereas in modern science reason must share the throne with ambition (*to thumoeidês*). This was not because the idea of mastering nature did not occur to the Greeks; Empedocles wrote:

> And you shall learn all the drugs for illness, and defenses against old age, since for you alone I will accomplish all this. You shall stop the force of the tireless winds which rush upon the earth with their blasts and destroy the crop lands; and again, if you wish, you shall make them return. You shall create from black thunder storms a seasonable drought for mankind, and again you shall create from summer droughts the tree-nourishing streams that flow from the sky. And you shall lead out of Hades the spirit of dead man.[12]

But this manifesto had only a fleeting influence because it was as atypical of the generality of the Greek attitude toward nature as modern analogues of the Pythagorean attitude are of our own. It has been quite different with modern science, which was at least implicitly technological from the outset.

Modern science took the radically empirical form that it did because implicit in its study of nature was the project of controlling it. For this reason it was not enough, as it was for the Greeks, to conceive nature on a model that enabled one to understand it merely in principle; rather, one had to understand it in precise detail.[13] Here mathematics is invaluable since, by quantifying the factors of nature, one could make them subject to precise measurement. Thus the qualitative science of the ancients gave way to the quantitative science of the moderns, and the fruits of this change are evident in the history of technology's career. The fact that the Greeks did not embark on a similar course, even though they were already aware, in the case of astronomy, of the benefits of applying mathematics to scientific empiricism, points to the difference between the general goals of their science and those of ours.

This is evident too in the difference between technology and *techne*. The Greeks were as appreciative of the benefits of *techne* as we are of the benefits of technology, and they seem to have regarded it as virtually definitive of human nature and indispensible to human survival, as the myth of Epimetheus and Prometheus attests.[14] Technology, however, is not merely a continuation of the gradual development of human *techne* from prehistoric toolmaking to Roman engineering (although it is certainly that as well) but represents an important change of attitude. If *techne* is the devising of teachable techniques for achieving *particular* goals, technology entails as well the *general* ambition to achieve as complete a control over nature as possible. It is driven, therefore, not by the *ad hoc* challenge of particular problems or needs, but by the general challenge of the present *de facto* limitations of human power. Its goal is not something particular but indefinite augmentation, i.e., the "progress" of human control.[15]

The spirit of mastery by which modern science differs from ancient science, and technology from techne, is not an accidental phenomenon triggered by a particular circumstance such as the collapse of the geocentric world-view. The Epicureans, among others in the classical world, did not have a geocentric world-view but were not thereby led to feel the need to "take matters into their own hands." The change is the result rather of a difference in the way the nature of humanity, and not just that of the cosmos, was conceived. Thus it is evident not only in the modern approaches to science and technics but also in the newly humanistic approach to the arts. Beginning with the Renaissance, art and beauty are no longer treated as subordinate to theology, as they had been in the middle ages; nor is art any longer conceived on the model of an *imitation* of reality, as it had been since classical times, but is now conceived also as an imposition of human-made form *onto* reality.[16]

THE WILL

Among the perennial "problems" by which philosophy continually defines our ways of interacting with the world, the most fundamental are those concerned with the nature of reality, knowledge, morality, political collectivity, beauty, art, immortality, and freedom of the will. All but the last have been continual displays of formulation, solution, refutation, and reformulation of various kinds dating back to the origins of philosophical thinking in ancient Greece. But freedom of the will alone was not regarded as fundamentally problematic by the ancients in the way it has been by subsequent ages and thus seems to lack something of the same timeless legitimacy as the others. Its historical emergence as a central problem in modern times is in fact connected with the values distinctive to our age, especially insofar as willfulness is fundamental to the conception of mastery.

As a brief look at ancient philosophy will show, the ancients were not unaware of the phenomenon of willing and its role in our behavior[17] (any more than they were unaware of the possibility of undertaking to control nature) or even of the problematic nature of "free" choice, but they did not attach to it an importance warranting special study. It was important not per se but in the service of other questions.

Socrates, for example, in maintaining that no one willingly does evil, implicitly held a rationalistic and deterministic view of the will, in which the act of willing is reduced to what follows from our conception of the nature of goodness and of how the latter is to be applied in particular situations; but these implications are never developed explicitly. It displays *to us* an attitude about the will, but the will itself never becomes the subject of thematic inquiry for him. In Plato, too, the will appears only indirectly, such as in the doctrine of the tripartite soul. The nature of our motivations, and the way they are grounded both in our native character and our subsequent experiences, are discussed in detail but the concept of willing per se remains implicit.

In Aristotle the problem of will appears explicitly, but is treated only as peripheral to the question of responsibility. It remains entirely subordinate to that question without ever becoming a problem in its own right. In the *Nicomachean Ethics,* for example, Aristotle writes,

> But suppose someone were to say that all men seek what appears good to them, and have no control over the appearance; but rather, the sort of person one is determines how the end appears to him. In that case, if each person is somehow responsible for his own character, he will also be responsible for how things appear to him. Otherwise no one is responsible for his own wrongdoing, but does these things through ignorance of the proper end, since he believes that these things will bring him the greatest good; and the aim taken for the end will not be chosen by the person himself, but he possesses it by nature, like vision, and by means of it he judges well and chooses what is truly good. He who has a good nature will be someone in whom this is well developed by nature. For he will have the greatest and finest possession, which cannot be acquired or learned from anyone else; and to be well and finely possessed of this by nature would

be the most perfect and true good nature. But if this is true, how will virtue
be any more voluntary than vice?[18]

Here the deterministic position is dismissed because it would lead to the
conclusion that virtue and vice are involuntary, and that people are not responsible for their actions; which Aristotle takes to be manifestly false since
otherwise our inclination to honor good people and condemn bad ones would
be inexplicable.[19] Once again, there is no thematic treatment of the nature
of willing. The issue is raised within the context of moral responsibility and
is resolved not by inquiry into the nature of willing itself but by the implications of something else, the nature of praising and blaming.[20] In other places
he discusses the problem of determinism in nature, but with reference to contingency rather than willing.[21]

Lucretius too (following Epicurus) refers to the will in passing, but no
more focuses on it than did the others:

> Again, if all motion is always one long chain, and new motion always arises
> out of the old in order invariable, and if the first beginnings do not make,
> by swerving, a beginning of motion such as to break the decrees of fate,
> that cause may not follow cause to infinity, whence comes this free will
> in living creatures all over the earth, whence, I say is this will wrested from
> the fates by which we proceed whither pleasure leads each, swerving also
> our motions not at fixed times and fixed places, but just where our mind
> has taken us?[22]

Willing, the power to originate motion spontaneously, is treated as something
given, taken for granted, whose presence may serve as evidence for one feature of the Epicurean atomic theory, but it is not treated as something
problematic which deserves special attention. So little concerned was he with
will *per se* that even the tension between the voluntaristic tone of the passage
and the deterministic implications of the phrase "whither pleasure leads each"
was evidently not felt by him.

Cicero considers the question in *De Fato,*[23] with special reference to
Epicurus and Chrysippus but, once again, offers no sustained investigation
of the nature of willing. His primary concern is the question of whether all
things happen by necessity or whether there are nonnecessary factors such
as contingency and free will, and he sees so little need to investigate the question of willing per se that he suggests that the Epicureans ought to have
rejected determinism without introducing the vexed doctrine of the "swerve,"
simply by *asserting* that there is a "voluntary motion of the mind."[24]

In Marcus Aurelius the concept of the will appears perhaps more frequently than in any other classical writer. On the one hand he frequently
reminds us of our own freedom to do what is right,[25] while on the other
hand he also counsels our indulgence for the shortcomings of others, on the
grounds that their behavior is determined by their character, over which they
have no control.[26] But there is, once again, no consideration of willing per
se. Certain characteristics are noted in order to strengthen our moral resolve,
but it is this morality, rather than the will, that is at issue. In his case as

well an evident (although resolvable) tension between the charitable belief in the helplessnes of our neighbors to overcome the defects of their character, together with the insistence on our own freedom and therefore responsibility, seems to go unnoticed.

The first philosopher to devote a thematic investigation to the nature of the will was Plotinus,[27] and in his case we must bear in mind the influence of early Christianity. Although never sympathetic to Christianity, he lived toward the end of the Patristic period and, according to Porphyry, the question about freedom of the will was one of the topics that arose at the conferences in which Plotinus participated, perhaps together with Christian acquaintances like Origen. But even so he several times insists that the importance of the question lies in its relevance not to humanity but to the divinity. The analysis of human freedom is important only insofar as it clarifies the concept of freedom so that we can see whether it applies to the god: "For thus we would presumably learn also whether it admits of extrapolation to gods, and still more to god, or whether it does not admit of extrapolation."[28] Even for Plotinus, then, the question of human freedom does not merit attention per se.

It is only with Christianity that the problem takes on important dimensions, and accordingly in the Middle Ages the situation changes considerably. Already with Augustine a book is written *On Freedom of the Will,* devoted specifically to human freedom. The question is not conceived along the lines the debate was subsequently to take, but theologically, in terms of such questions as humanity's responsibility for sin, and whether we choose freely despite God's prior knowledge of what our choice will be. However, the underlying issue is identical with that in the secular version of the problem:

EVODIUS. But I would nevertheless like to know, if I can, why that nature which God foreknows will not sin, does not sin; and why that other nature which God foreknows will sin, does so. For I no longer think it is because God's foreknowledge compels the latter to sin and the former not to. Yet if there were no cause, the rational creature could not be divided into three types: one that never sins, and one that always sins, and one in between, that sometimes sins and sometimes acts rightly. What cause made these three divisions? I will not accept the answer "the will," because I am asking for cause of the will itself. It is not without cause that, although all are of the same class, the first will never wills to sin, the second always wills to sin, and the last sometimes wills to sin and sometimes does not. I clearly understand that the threefold division is not without cause, but what the cause may be I do not know.

AUGUSTINE. Since the will is the cause of sin and you are asking for the cause of the will itself, if I can find the cause, won't you then ask what is the cause of the cause that I just revealed? Will there be any end to your questions, delays, and postponements, when you really should want no more than to know the root of the question? After all, what cause of the will could there be, except the will itself? It is either the will itself, and it is not possible to go back to the root of the will; or else it is not the will, and there is no sin.[29]

Here, for the first time, the will is treated as a fundamental phenomenon whose investigation is accorded the utmost importance, although the point at which Augustine terminates the inquiry is just where many later writers would begin it. After Augustine the question never ceased to be a central one in medieval theology,[30] and Aquinas devotes a 15-article question to it in *De Veritate,* as well as passages of the *Summas.* Subsequently the concept of the will became the very cornerstone of the philosophy of Duns Scotus.

It is no coincidence that it was also in the Middle Ages that the transition began from *techne* to technology, the physical manifestation of the new importance accorded to human willing. Inventions like the mechanical clock and the magnetic compass dramatically increased humanity's power over nature, and the printing press made possible the dissemination and comparison of information on a scale that was previously impossible. The magnetic compass enabled people to explore and measure the earth's surface as never before, and the mechanical clock had the unprecedented effect of reducing time to a series of uniform and measurable parts. Previously, in the age of the sundial, the measurement of time was subordinate to the rising and setting of the sun, and the period of daylight was divided into an equal number of hours whose length varied with the length of the day. (Sundials accordingly had variable calibrations, depending on the season.) With the invention of the clock, however, even the rising and setting of the sun became subordinate to the human measurement of time, insofar as the time at which they occurred could now be given a numerical value. In addition to making time uniformly measurable, without which modern technology would be impossible, the mechanical ingenuity of the clock served as a model for what could be accomplished by mechanics, and indeed as a paradigm by which human power could be assimilated to the powers of nature. It became customary in the age of mathematical physics to think of the universe as a mechanical system on the model of clockwork, and even the Argument from Design for the existence of God was formulated in terms of this analogy: the existence of the universe implies the existence of a creator in precisely the way that the existence of a watch implies the existence of a watchmaker.

The interest in the human will that first arose in the middle ages seems to have been originally prompted—as the context of the theological discussions suggests—by the Christian concern for the salvation of the individual soul. Whereas classical religion emphasized fate, the Christian tradition emphasizes individual freedom and responsibility. There is an essential link between giving increased prominence to the individual and increased attention to the phenomenon of the will, for will lies at the basis of individuality. Reason or intellect, which has traditionally been regarded as the other fundamental human faculty, is a manifestation not of our individual discreteness but of our community, for what is known by one intellect may in principle be perceived equally by every other: truth, as Augustine points out, may be beheld by all intellects simultaneously.[31] When the same object becomes the objective of several wills, however, often the fulfillment of one necessarily excludes fulfillment of the others. Thus we can all know the same things without conflict, but cannot always will the same things without conflict; the phenomenon of willing is by nature egocentric while that of intellect is, ideally,[32] disinterested and impersonal. Unlike intellect, will, as something goal-directed, manifests itself as power and thereby is in competition with other wills whose power is often directed toward goals incompatible with one's own.

INDIVIDUALITY

In view of the connection between willing and individuality, it is significant that just as the conception of willing was accorded only passing attention by the ancients, the importance that they attached to individuality was also slight by our standards. One finds in ancient literature none of the elaborate character studies so central to modern writing; it is distinguished rather by a stylized spareness. While there is no lack of assertive individuals in classical literature, they are never radically individuated in terms of unique personalities, subtle biographical character motivation, and other such factors that are expected of modern authors. Neither are they masters of their fate but are instead always subordinated to the gods and fates; the importance of piety is for this reason a recurrent theme in Homer and still, some 800 years later, in Virgil. What we would consider praiseworthy self-reliance is punished in classical literature as *hubris*. The themes of fate and piety are felt strongly not only in epic poetry but in the drama of Aeschylus and Sophocles as well, and the great heroes of their plays are not wholly differentiated individuals like the protagonists of modern literature, but archetypes of possibilities within the relationship between gods and humans, as in Euripides they are psychological archetypes. In the comedies they are merely caricatures.

In the visual arts, as well, the modern interest in the individual can be seen in the extent to which our art takes ordinary individuals and situations as its subject matter, rather than the heroic or religious ones typical of classical art. In music (abstracting from lyrics) no precise parallel is possible because of its nonrepresentational nature, but it too has become more highly individuated, as measured by the increasing tendency toward personal expression since the Middle Ages.[33] The relative unimportance of individuals as the subjects for works of art in the classical world is paralleled in the theories of art criticism of the time, which emphasize the formal characteristics of art works (beauty, imitation, etc.), and their psychological influence but not their significance as the self-expression of the artist.

It was in the Middle Ages that Christian theology replaced the concept of fate with that of free will, and thereby conferred upon humanity a sense of individual power and responsibility that had no precise equivalent previously,[34] and which became considerably more radical in the Renaissance as it progressively freed itself from the religious sense of subordination to God. By now the concern with the individual, which was the basis for that change, has become a major force in virtually all areas of human activity. Protestantism, with its emphasis on the individual, won over a large proportion of the members of the more paternalistic Roman Catholic church, while even Roman Catholics today are increasingly defiant of the church's authority. Under the influence of capitalism the effective agent of social distinctions has become wealth, which stems from individual initiative, rather than the status of birth assigned to us by "providence." Slavery, which had been taken virtually for granted by the ancient world (although not without dissenters), became progressively mitigated until it died out almost entirely as an institution in recent times. Now most Western countries have universal suffrage, recognizing the importance of the individual per se; and even where repressive dictatorships exist, they often feel obliged to hold regular "elections," even if only one candidate is listed. More recently the trend toward, first, limiting the death penalty to only the most serious of crimes and, next, eliminating it altogether, is likewise based on the attaching of such high value to the individual person per se that the destruction of an individual life takes on such moment as to be virtually unjustifiable.

One finds a similar shift of attitude in philosophy as well. For Socrates, Plato, Aristotle, the Stoics, and the Neoplatonists the person as individual is subordinated to the person as citizen or human being; and even the Epicureans, who begin from the standpoint of the private pleasures of the individual, urge ultimately an overcoming of the standpoint of personal interest to one of disinterestedness in order to escape the cycle of pleasure and pain.[35] In modern philosophy, by contrast, the spirit of individualism is evident in a number of often very different ways. The almost complete acceptance today of the nominalistic or conceptualistic interpretations of universals is one of the most dramatic testimonials to the elevation of the importance of individuals since the middle ages. A very different manifestation of this elevation is the fact that modern philosophy has largely turned from the "objective" standpoint of antiquity to a "subjective" standpoint, taking as its starting point not the question of the nature of the world (which animated ancient philosophy) but the question of what the individual thinking subject is capable of knowing. This is as true for the empiricism begun by Locke as for the rationalism and idealism begun by Descartes, and, like the importance attached to individuality generally, its roots too lie in the Middle Ages, as one can see from Augustine's introspective approach.

More recently this tendency in philosophy, as in politics and elsewhere, has developed into more radical forms. Whereas to a great extent the history of modern philosophy had been a continuous development of novel systems, since the time of Kierkegaard and Nietzsche philosophy has increasingly turned away from systematic thinking, toward various forms of skepticism, positivism, and relativism. For thought to be "systematic" once meant that it was rigorous and constructive; one now speaks instead of "system building," and regards such endeavors as pretentious and dogmatic, "constructionistic" rather than constructive. Systematic thinkers such as Whitehead have been rare in this century and their thought, however impressive, has not shaped the future course of philosophy. There is an increasing (although not universal) tendency to be so conscious of the finitude of our individuality as to find it difficult to impute to our insights more than an individual and therefore limited belief, or to suppose that they might be the basis of a model possessing universal validity. It is most characteristically evident in the case of existentialism's inclination toward literature, which conceives and communicates more in terms of particular individuals and situations than universal concepts, and pragmatism's attempt to read out of philosophy any objective referent for our concept of truth.

The fact that philosophers remain capable of insisting on their views shows that there are still limits to this tendency, but the matters on which such certainty is claimed are far more modest than they once were, and far fewer. On larger issues there is a degree of skepticism that is perhaps unmatched since the waning days of antiquity; and the claim that philosophy might still be a quest for wisdom in the traditional sense of the word can hardly be made anymore without a sense of defiance or embarrassment.

THE PARADOX OF HUMANISM

If the above observations show that there is a fundamental difference between the classical and modern ways of regarding the world, what is the significance of that difference? Logically we might regard the modern revision either as an improvement over the classical attitude, a degeneration from it, or a mere difference that is neither being better nor worse in any absolute sense. The first of these views, that modernity has progressed beyond antiquity, is by far the dominant view today, although it is no longer maintained as uncritically as it was in Hegel's and Comte's day. The contrary view, that modernity is a degeneration from antiquity, was common in the Renaissance, when the cultural and intellectual legacy of the Middle Ages was regarded as far inferior to that of ancient Greece, and it reached a special prominence around the turn of the eighteenth century in the controversy between "the Ancients and the Moderns." In the twentieth century advocates of the superiority of antiquity have been notable especially within the German tradition: Martin Heidegger, Hannah Arendt, Karl Löwith, and Leo Strauss, for example.

It is the third view that I would like to defend, however, the view that there is no absolute sense in which one age is superior to another; the advantages and disadvantages of each are different and can be weighed only in accordance with the priorities of the individual passing judgment. Any cultural value is incomplete, for it represents a choice,[36] and any choice admits incompatible alternatives. This can be seen where, inevitably, its incompleteness becomes evident, and its alternatives make themselves felt and paradoxes arise.

It is frequently said that the driving value of the Greeks was rationality and order. Although all such generalizations are simplifications, this characterization has much truth in it. But at the very height of Greek rationalism the irrational rises up within it, whether intellectually, in the form of skepticism, or spiritually in the form of the aberrant. The rise of skepticism, as evidenced by sophists like Protagoras and Gorgias, and later by skeptics like Diogenes and Pyrrho, was virtually contemporaneous with that of philosophy and, in the minds of anti-intellectuals like Aristophanes, was inseparable from it. The idea of the aberrant, on the other hand, meets with a paradoxical recognition at the very heart of the "intellectualism" of the Socratic school itself. Socrates, for example, frequently relies upon his famous *daimonion* with its inexplicable but infallible warnings;[37] and both Plato and Aristotle remark on the intrinsic connection between rational philosophy and madness.[38] Among the poets, the most rationalistic is Euripides, who was at the same time the one most obsessed with the phenomenon of ungovernable passion.[39]

In our time an analogous paradox exists. Given the importance that we attach to individuality, one would expect the present age to be a utopia of humanitarianism; and yet in the nineteenth century, the very heyday of humanistic progress, the term "dehumanize" first came into use. It was used with increasing frequency as the progress of technology accelerated, and today the phrase "dehumanizing technocracy," as a pejorative description of the present age, has become almost a cliché. Such an accusation is not without foundation, insofar as the individual is progressively more threatened by unemployment, mechanization, and invasion of privacy, as computer, robot, and information-gathering technology becomes more sophisticated and pervasive. On the one hand, one can hardly deny the enormous benefits that technology has bestowed upon our civilization, or that there are grounds for hope that eventually machines will free us for a rich and varied life like that of the former leisure classes. But on the other hand there are also grounds for concern that our dependence on technology will inevitably lead to a master-slave dialectic in which, in the absence of substantial individual responsibilities, our lives will become not so much enriched by leisure, as emptied by idleness.

The paradox of an individuality that might be so endangered in practice while so exalted in theory is an inevitable outcome of our humanistic values. Because we are natural beings, the attempt to subordinate nature to our will entails the subordination of our own being: if the products of our will are preferable to those of nature, then the artificial is esteemed above the natural,[40] and machines must eventually be esteemed above human beings. Thus the tool by which we hoped to achieve dominion becomes the instrument of our own effacement, and as the power of human technology over nature increases, the place of the individual within the world becomes more problematic. In replacing the products of nature with those of human devising, wherever machines could be devised to do the work of people, people found themselves without jobs. More and more, people have ceased to be directly productive as individuals and have become instead tenders of machines, for the most part unskilled, approximating as closely as possible mechanical functions themselves. Consequently, as a result of humanistic self-assertion, as a result of our attempt to subordinate nature to our will rather than being ourselves subordinate to nature, we once again find ourselves subordinated to nonhumanistic principles, this time more oppressive because they lead in the direction of the mechanical rather than the natural.

The relationship between human workers and machines is becoming reminiscent of the relationship between eclipsed civilizations, such as the North American Indians, and the conquering culture that displaced them. Workers' attempts in the midst of rising unemployment to preserve their jobs against competition from machines often result in the continued existence of anachronistic jobs maintained artificially by a kind of dispensation on the part of management under pressure from labor unions, just as Indian cultures maintain an anachronistic existence in North America not by force of their own vitality but by a grudging dispensation from the countries within which they have their enclaves. Now that machines have been designed increasingly to duplicate and improve upon human thought processes as well as our physical capabilities, the immanent ascendancy of machines as the dominant "life" form has been predicted both by the enthusiastic[41] and the appalled alike, although not without considerable dissent.[42]

Whether such forecasts are accurate or not, the fact that they should confront us at this point in our history is a result not of some contingency— whether regarded as fortunate or tragic—that might have been avoided, but of the compelling urge of the modern age to replace nature with human creation, that has been with us at least since the Renaissance. Indeed, it is unlikely that people who design such machines would be capable of resisting, against their every self-interest, the eventual temptation to design machines to replace themselves as well. We pursue technology not only for utilitarian reasons, but also as an *intrinsic* challenge, an end in itself, and therefore as an intrinsic value.

This emphasis on the paradoxical nature of the modern spirit, like the corresponding remarks about the rationalism of ancient Greece, is in no sense intended as a rejection of the legitimacy of these values. Only if there were an *absolute* set of values that did not suffer from incompleteness or, therefore, limitations, would the identification of limiting paradoxes within the ancient and modern cultures imply some sort of refutation. However, I suspect that Hegel is right in attributing to every age the germ of its own negation, and I would take issue with him only to the extent that he might take his own age to be an exception. I put these paradoxes forward not as refutations but as necessary consequences of the inevitable incompleteness of any set of cultural values, and thus as illustrations of the perspectival nature of historical ages.[43] As choices, albeit unconscious ones, any set of values must rule out valuable alternatives whose absence eventually makes itself felt.

Thus, at the limits of the Hellenic value of rationality arose sophistry, which led to the skepticism characteristic of much of Hellenistic and Roman philosophy. The withholding of assent that constitutes skepticism similarly led to its opposite in the medieval value of faith, which rejects skepticism without embracing rationalism: truth and certainty are attainable as an act of the will rather than of the intellect. And at the limits of faith arose the positive sciences pregnant with technology—verifiable knowledge as the counterpart to belief. So too, at the point where human brain power and the muscle power of humanity and its beasts are no longer adequate to accomplish our aspirations to mastery, a new kind of *artificial* brain and muscle power begins to develop, which increasingly threatens to become a rival as well as a tool.

The spirit of an age is an intersection of the timeless that is common to all ages, and the timely. Thus Plato and Aristotle concerned themselves not only with the timeless questions of the nature of reality, truth, goodness, and beauty, but also with questions whose immediacy for them differentiated their age from other ages for which such questions would be of less vital concern—questions such as how reason could be vindicated from sophistry, and how virtue could be vindicated from amoral mythology. Similarly the medievals could not avoid the problem of the conflict between reason and faith, and the tension between grace and freedom. In the same way the issues with which modern and contemporary philosophy deals are not the result of a linear "progress" in which philosophy continually improves itself, but the result of altering choices, shifting perspectives, in which advances in one area are balanced by sacrifices in another.

Notes

An early version of this paper was presented at the XVIIth World Congress of Philosophy in Montreal, 1983. I would like to thank Robert Kane for valuable comments on a previous draft.

1. *Historical and Critical Dictionary* (1695-7).
2. *The New Science* (1725).
3. *Discourse on the Advantages that the Establishment of Christianity has Provided for the Human Race,* and *Discourse on the Successive Progress of the Human Spirit* (1750).
4. *Sketch of a Historical View of the Progress of the Human Spirit* (1793).
5. Karl Löwith, *Meaning in History* (Chicago, 1949), 73.
6. Ibid., 83.
7. Fragment 18.
8. Löwith, *Meaning in History,* 74.
9. Ibid.
10. *The Legitimacy of the Modern Age* (Cambridge, Mass., 1983), 31. See also Morris Ginsberg, "Progress in the Modern Era" in *Dictionary of the History of Ideas,* ed. P. Wiener (New York, 1973), 635.
11. E.A. Burtt's *The Metaphysical Foundations of Modern Physical Science* (London, 1959) is a classic documentation of this transformation and some of its consequences.
12. Fragment III.
13. It is presumably this difference that leads Werner Heisenberg to observe that "the statements of modern physics are in some way meant much more seriously than the statements of Greek philosophy." See *Physics and Philosophy* (New York, 1962), 74.
14. Plato and Aristotle refer to *techne* almost continually, and it was often honored in poetry as well. See, for example, Prometheus' speech at lines 436-71 of Aeschylus' *Prometheus Bound,* and the choral ode at lines 332-75 of Sophocles' *Antigone.*
15. Cf. Blumenberg, *The Legitimacy of the Modern Age,* 139: "the modern stage of human technicity can no longer be grasped entirely in terms of the syndrome of the anthropological structure of wants. The growth of the potency of technique is not only the continuation—not even the acceleration—of a process that runs through the whole history of humanity. On the contrary, the quantitative increase in technical achievements and expedients can only be grasped in relation to a new quality of

consciousness. In the growth of the technical sphere there lives, consciously facing an alienated reality, a will to extort from this reality a new 'humanity.' "

16. "This primacy of form in Renaissance life and thought is demonstrable in practically every intellectual field. Lyrical poetry leads the way by becoming the first and the most potent vehicle of the new will to form. In Dante's *Vita nuova* and in Petrarch's sonnets, the feeling for form is, as it were, advanced beyond the feeling for life. . . . The lyrical expression does not merely describe a complete inner reality that already has its own form; rather it discovers and creates this reality itself"— Ernst Cassirer, *The Individual and the Cosmos in Renaissance Philosophy*, trans. Mario Domandi (New York, 1964), 160.

17. Hobbes therefore goes too far when he writes that "the third way of bringing things to pass, distinct from *necessity* and *change*, namely, *freewill*, is a thing that never was mentioned among [the ancients]." See Thomas Hobbes, *The Questions Concerning Liberty, Necessity, and Chance*, vol. 5 of *The English Works of Thomas Hobbes*, ed. William Molesworth (Scientia Aalen, 1962), 1.

18. Aristotle, *Nicomachean Ethics* III. 5.1114a31–b13.

19. Ibid., 1113b23–1114a3.

20. Cf. Joseph Owens, C.Ss.R., *The Doctrine of Being in the Aristotelian 'Metaphysics'*, 2nd ed. (Toronto, 1963), 309: "Aristotle readily admits free will and what follows from it. But he does not allow it to form the subject of scientific consideration. In a word, Aristotle does not for an instant deny existence. He readily admits it in Being *per accidens*. But he does not seem even to suspect that it is an act worthy of any special consideration, or that it is capable of philosophical treatment."

21. Cf. *De Interpretatione* 9; *Physics* II. 5–6.

22. *De Rerum Natura* II. 251–60, trans. W.H.D. Rouse.

23. E.g., *De Fato* X–XI, XVII–XIX.

24. Ibid., XI.

25. E.g., *Meditations* IV. 3, V. 14, VIII. 29, X. 33.

26. Ibid., II. 1, IV. 6, IX. 42, XII. 16.

27. *Enneads* VI. 8.

28. Ibid., VI. 8.18–19.

29. III. 17, trans. Anna S. Benjamin.

30. Since boredom, as Schopenhauer pointed out, may be interpreted as a privation of willing, it is not surprising to read: "It seems that Casiano—in the fifth century of our era—was the first person to realize that one could be bored." Alfonso Sastre, "Seven Notes on *Waiting for Godot*," trans. Leonard C. Pronko in *A Casebook on "Waiting for Godot*," ed. Ruby Cohn (New York, 1967), 105. I would prefer to say, not that previously it was not realized that one could be bored, but that previously it was not believed that something like boredom was worthy of special attention.

31. Augustine, *On Freedom of the Will*, II. 7–14.

32. "Ideally" because will and intellect can be disengaged only in theory, and intellect is never entirely without its "arbitrary" point of view.

33. If one accepts Schopenhauer's claim that music is the only art form that directly expresses willing, then, because of the intimate connection between individuality and the will, the vastly increased importance of "absolute" music (music not in the service of lyrics, dance, or ritual) can be taken as another indication of the modern emphasis on the individual.

34. In *The Battle of the Books* Jonathan Swift aligns the medievals with the moderns, whereas we today tend to think of them as extensions of ancient philosophy; the present discussion lends credence to Swift's position. The medievals borrowed

their categories of organization from the ancients, but the substance of their thought was revolutionary in its implications. A personal testament like Augustine's *Confessions* would have been inconceivable in classical antiquity. Even Socrates' sketchy "autobiography" in the *Phaedo* is no more than an instantiation of the stages of the divided line.

35. Only in minor figures, such as Thrasymachus and kindred sophists, and the Cyrenaics Theodorus and Annicerus, does one perhaps find an egocentric individualism comparable to that of modern times; and that is one of the reasons that they are minor figures in ancient Greece. Like individuals of the modern period whose values correspond more with those of other ages, they testify to the constancy of human nature generally; but if we wish to discover the spirit of an age we must seek it in those who were taken as exemplary by their posterity, rather than in the more peripheral figures whose positions, although perhaps equally perennial, were never accorded a place of honor by the tradition of which they were part—and whose works, consequently, were hardly preserved.

36. For our purposes it is not necessary to take up the difficult question of how we may conceive the "making" of this choice. The classical treatment of the question is Hegel's discussion of the world-historical individual, in the Introduction to his *Lectures on the Philosophy of History,* Part II, section b) *(Die Mittel der Verwirklichung seiner Idee,* "The Means by which History Actualizes its Ideas"). Also see Freud's remarks on the "collective mind" in *Totem and Taboo,* trans. James Strachey (London, 1950), 1158–59 and context.

37. See especially *Apology* 31d; also 40a–c, 41d; *Euthydemus* 272e; *Euthyphro* 3b; *Phaedrus* 242b–c; and *Republic* VI. 496c. Compare Aristotle's claim that although "dreams cannot be sent by the god, . . . they are nevertheless 'daimonic,' for nature is daimonic although not a god" (*On Prophesy in Sleep* II. 463b13–15).

38. For Plato, philosophy, the "love of wisdom," is a species of the "erotic" genus of madness (*Phaedrus* 249d–252e). Aristotle, addressing the question physiologically, writes, "Why is it that all men who excel in philosophy, politics, poetry, or the arts are evidently melancholic, some to the extent of becoming afflicted with the malady of black bile, such as is told, in the stories of the heroes, about Heracles? . . . And many other heroes seem to have suffered in the same way as these. Recently there have been Empedocles, Plato, and Socrates, and many other famous men" (*Problems* XXX. 1. 953a10–28.).

39. E.g., *The Bacchae* and *Hippolytus.* The pioneering study of the limitations inherent in the Greek ideal of rationality was Nietzsche's *Birth of Tragedy.* For a more recent account see E.R. Dodds, *The Greeks and the Irrational* (Berkeley, 1951).

40. Leonardo da Vinci writes, "Oh investigator of things, do not praise yourself for your knowledge of things brought forth by nature in its normal course; rather enjoy knowing the aim and the end of those things designed by your mind" (*Le manuscrit de Leonard da Vinci,* ed. Ravaisson-Mollien, G fol. 47r. Cited in Cassirer, *The Individual and the Cosmos in Renaissance Philosophy,* 67).

41. E.g., Robert Jastrow, *The Enchanted Loom* (New York, 1981).

42. Certainly the history of technological overconfidence gives sufficient excuse to anyone who wishes to reject such a prediction. Anticipations of complete technological triumphs over nature have so far always proven premature, with nature proving intractable in unexpected ways. We seem no closer to solving the problems of hunger, disease, energy, and environmental pollution than ever, although the battlegrounds and weapons constantly change.

43. A prehistorical example of this is given by F. B. Jevons: "the domestication

[of animals] to which totemism inevitably leads (when there are any animals capable of domestication) is fatal to totemism" (*An Introduction to the History of Religion,* 2nd ed., 120; quoted in Freud, *Totem and Taboo,* 137).

22

The Inevitability of Humanism

Graeme Nicholson

The philosophical literature devoted to humanism since World War II has certainly given a new sense to this word. The Oxford English Dictionary, completed in 1928, recognized mainly three senses:

1. a moral one, signifying kindness and benevolence;
2. an antitheological one, the repudiation of the divine;
3. an intellectual one, the pursuit of philology and the humanities.

But Heidegger's publication of the "Letter on Humanism" in 1947 introduced questions that went far beyond all those frameworks. The letter sought to investigate whether the study of the human being had, in fact, been central and foundational in all past philosophy. It also sought to explore whether thinking should free itself from making man its center and its foundation. Thus, as a minimum, the question about humanism here concerned the constitution or architecture of the systems of western philosophy. But such an investigation would not only invoke the completed literary works of Aquinas or Kant or Marx: these works obviously betray the structure of western thinking itself, western science and existence.

The next decades saw further studies of humanism, particularly in France, that explored the place of the figure of man in all the sciences: political economy, the social sciences, the life sciences, and the historical and philological sciences. I shall draw in some arguments of Althusser and Foucault here to supplement Heidegger's commentary on the philosophers.

So evident is the tottering of humanism in our time and place that the word "man" has now become unusable: feminism has revealed that it had a spurious inclusiveness that reflected the false humanism of patriarchal society. As this word goes, so goes a certain picture or image or icon, the whole group of images or icons of man on the throne, man on the battlefield, man in the assembly. These images are broken more decisively by feminist critiques, I think, than by structuralist and poststructuralist intellectuals, but still the two have worked together for these two decades.

But is there then no word, no image, to take their place? Or are we left with an emptiness, the result of an iconoclasm too uncompromising? Can we exist without icons? Are we aniconic in fact? In recent decades, the word "human" has usually been an adjective but it was a perfectly good English substantive back in earlier centuries. It expressed most often the binary opposition to the divine, not a sex binarism. With the death of man might we anticipate the birth of the human? And might we receive the human image, picture or icon?

I would like my term "inevitability" to be understood in the sense of an argument, like those of Socrates in the dialogues. I shall seek to grapple with three authors here, and try to show how, despite their arguments for positions either nonhumanistic or antihumanistic, a deeper critical study will advance a humanistic argument that will prevail in each case. I am no Socrates, but the model of three short dialogues is the one I would like to follow.

First I shall examine Heidegger's "Letter on Humanism." I shall maintain that while it seeks to displace man from the center of thinking, his thinking is after all obliged to reinstate a human at the center. Next in Althusser, I show that his treatment of social formations or political economy seeks to omit the human being, but that his case fails at just that point. With Foucault, I show that while he erases the portrait, figure, or image of man, another picture appears to take its place.

THE "LETTER ON HUMANISM"

Our text is a letter, to Jean Beaufret, written in response to some questions Beaufret had posed him. Three of the questions are quoted in the text of Heidegger's reply: How can we give meaning again to the word "humanism"? How can one define the relation between ontology and a possible ethics? How to keep the element of adventure in research, without making it mere adventure? We must bear in mind that Beaufret's question about humanism is a postwar question, and surely we can grant that the question was right.

To give back a meaning to the word "humanism" presupposes that the word has lost its meaning. But this is to say that something has happened to man, not merely to the word, either that he has become inhuman, or that he is in a situation that threatens the loss of humanity, or even that he may be surpassing what is human. Humanism would be the viewpoint concerned that man remain human, or become human again. The difficulty Heidegger sees is to determine whether the notion of humanity, or the human essence, on which any humanism depends, can have any definitive meaning. This question is historical, because this notion had meaning in the past.

Heidegger makes his first commentary on the question: "I ask myself whether it is really necessary to hold on to the word 'humanism.' " The initial point made in answer to Beaufret's question is a reflection about titles and slogans in general, leading to several major paragraphs about the decay (*Veroedung*) of language. We see that Heidegger has generalized to a wide mode of discourse: All humanism is embedded, necessarily, in a particular mode of discourse, the metaphysical. And, speaking for myself, I do grant that humanism, however we understand it, has its roots deep in metaphysics. It is the particular case that brings the general case with it. Therefore my title "The Inevitability of Humanism" clearly implies further the inevitability of metaphysics. Neither has it ended, nor can it end.

Heidegger's initial discussion of humanism is historical, from the Romans through the Renaissance to the three contemporary forms, Marx, Christianity, and Sartre. He seeks to criticize each statement of it, not through distinct criticisms of each position but through an umbrella criticism of all, the generic criticism that they are all metaphysical. Thus humanism is intertwined with a still broader history: that of metaphysics. The criticism proceeds in the present case by showing how each humanism depends on a specific interpretation of being, nature, world, God, history, and so on. Some of these interpretations have proceeded from historical decisions about *humanitas*. In other cases, humanism proceeded from a metaphysical interpretation of the world.

Humanism in general would be the effort to bring man back into his essence: it is a concern that man be human, and so not inhuman. Hence this division of the essence, *human,* from the *inhuman* is presupposed. And thus the question arises how the essence *human* is determined.

But it is characteristic of modern humanism and modern metaphysics to put man at the center of things in an emphatic way: the *res cogitans* and transcendental philosophy in theoretical philosophy, and our welfare or our duty in practical philosophy. A figure like Sartre comes in here as the perfect illustration of a man-centered philosophy.

What Heidegger undertakes to do in the letter is to displace man from this position so central in thought's account of things—and so the estimate is correct that the letter either displaces or decenters man; and we are warranted too in saying "the subject." To fill this in further: again and again, Heidegger seeks to subordinate man to the truth of being, the manifestation of being, and so on. This results in the reinterpretation of a good number of human attributes.

In regard to *existence,* Heidegger repeats from *Being and Time* the sentence, "The essence of *Dasein* lies in its existence." But here he wants to spell the word *ek-sistence* (standing out) and he says:

> Man occurs essentially in such a way that he is the "there" [*das "Da"*], that is, the lighting of Being. The "Being" of the *Da,* and only it, has the fundamental character of ek-sistence, that is, of an ecstatic inherence in the truth of Being.[1]

Then on the *ego* he says in further elucidation:

But existence here is not the actuality of the *ego cogito*. Neither is it the actuality of subjects who act with and for each other and so become who they are. "Ek-sistence," in fundamental contrast to every *existentia* and "existence," is ecstatic dwelling in the nearness of Being. It is the guardianship, that is, the care for Being.[2]

With respect to *thinking* he says:

Assuming that in the future man will be able to think the truth of Being, he will think from ek-sistence. Man stands ek-sistingly in the destiny of Being.[3]

On *history* this remark follows immediately:

The ek-sistence of man is historical as such, but not only or primarily because so much happens to man and to things human in the course of time. Because it must think the ek-sistence of Da-sein, the thinking of *Being and Time* is essentially concerned that the historicity of Dasein be experienced.

And on *language* we read:

Being remains mysterious, the simple nearness of an unobtrusive governance. The nearness occurs essentially as language itself. But language is not mere speech, insofar as we represent the latter at best as the unity of phoneme (or written character), melody, rhythm, and meaning (or sense). We think of the phoneme and written character as a verbal body for language, of melody and rhythm as its soul, and whatever has to do with meaning as its mind. We usually think of language as corresponding to the essence of man represented as *animal rationale,* that is, as the unity of body-soul-mind. But just as ek-sistence—and through it the relation of the truth of Being to man—remains veiled in the humanitas of *homo animalis,* so does the metaphysical-animal explanation of language cover up the essence of language in the history of Being. According to this essence language is the house of Being which comes to pass from Being and is pervaded by Being. And so it is proper to think the essence of language from its correspondence to Being and indeed as this correspondence, that is, as the home of man's essence.

　　But man is not only a living creature who possesses language along with other capacities. Rather, language is the house of Being in which man ek-sists by dwelling, in that he belongs to the truth of Being, guarding it.[4]

Likewise, he reinterprets such notions as projection and personality in the light of the displacement of man, his subordination to the truth of Being, and the ek-static character of existence.

Now as to the very constitution of *Dasein* the question can still be asked: how different is it from Sartre's? Note that it is only rarely that Heidegger expresses a direct opposition to humanism:

Should we still keep the name "humanism" for a "humanism" that contradicts all previous humanism—although it in no way advocates the inhuman? And keep it just so that by sharing in the use of the name we might perhaps swim in the predominant currents, stifled in metaphysical subjectivism and submerged in oblivion of Being? Or should thinking, by means of open resistance to "humanism," risk a shock that could for the first time cause perplexity concerning the *humanitas* of *homo humanus* and its basis?[5]

But far more common is talk of revision or reinterpretation of humanism:

> The "*humanum*" in the word points to *humanitas,* the essence of man; the "-ism" indicates that the essence of man is meant to be taken essentially. This is the sense that the word "humanism" has as such. To restore a sense to it can only mean to redefine the meaning of the word. . . . "Humanism" now means, in case we decide to retain the word, that the essence of man is essential for the truth of Being, specifically in such a way that it is not man as such, man by himself, that really counts here [translation slightly modified].[6]

And if we consider this standing out, this ek-sistence, that is now made the very substance of man, we need to ask exactly *how* it differs from the negativity that Sartre made central to a being like ourselves, the *pour soi.* Yes, Heidegger locates the exister in the clearing of being and Sartre knew nothing of that. But they are not at odds over the constitution of the exister, the human.

This human figure shows up inevitably, I say, when Heidegger turns to address the second question posed by Beaufret: "What I have been trying to do is determine the relation of ontology to a possible ethics."[7] Heidegger wishes to escape the business of thinking up ethical principles. Indeed the abstractness of ethics must be a big part of what he hated in "philosophy," as he called it, but it is abundantly clear that Heidegger was far from being a skeptic about morals. The story he draws from the *Parts of Animals* telling about Heraclitus warming himself at the stove is undoubtedly a serious injunction from Heidegger about how to live. As a matter of fact, in invoking this story of an unpretentious thinker at home, he is also showing us his picture of himself—the peasant thinker up in the mountain hut. And what this story says most of all is the heart of the ethical. Heidegger's Germanizing of the Greek is so striking: *Auch hier nämlich wesen Götter an.* To put it into English: "Even this is a place where gods may choose to dwell." They dwell with humans!

ALTHUSSER: THEORETICAL ANTIHUMANISM

The guiding thesis for the book *For Marx* is that in 1845 Marx undertook an epistemological break. Prior to that his perspective had been humanistic. In the practical ideological sense, he sought to promote reforms and revolutions that would restore human dignity and community. And theoretically the focus of research was on man as a creature of need, community, production, and foresight. The break was the denial of man as the subject of theoretical research and the discovery of a new territory: the social formations and their articulation into their three layers: economic practice with its regularities, political practice, and ideological and theoretical practice. It is in keeping with such a break that Marxism would learn to understand itself as a theory that could only arise given that a certain state of affairs prevailed within the European economy, and likewise within the political and ideological practices. Mature Marxism is a self-situating theory that can analyze itself.

We should say more on this contrast. While the very youngest Marx had been a humanist, a liberal, and a Hegelian, he came subsequently under the influence of Feuerbach: this expressed itself perfectly, according to Althusser, in this remark from 1843:

> To be radical is to grasp things by the root; but for man the root is man himself.[8]

If we realize that in these years Marx's efforts had been very largely, first, to make a critique of religion, philosophy, and cultural life, and, secondly, to obtain journalistic freedom for radical thought, then we see the force of this humanism. All the cultural realities are reducible to human reality. And media of communication ought to respect the free occurrence of communication, not subject it to princely authority, which is in the last analysis of no convincing legitimation. It is this simple figure of man who joins the material reality of earth to the stars of the firmament, the superstructure of culture. For all practice and theory, man is his own subject.

When Marx turned against this thinking he also diagnosed it, according to Althusser:

> This problematic was neither vague nor loose; on the contrary, it was constituted by a coherent system of precise concepts tightly articulated together. When Marx confronted it, it implies the two complementary postulates he defined in the sixth thesis on Feuerbach:
> (1) that there is a universal essence of man;
> (2) that this essence is the real attribute of 'each single individual' who is its real subject.[9]

But to reject this was a radical theoretical break.

In 1845, Marx broke radically with every known theory that based history and politics on an essence of man. This unique rupture contained three indissociable elements.

(1) The formation of a theory of history and politics based on radically new concepts: the concepts of social formation, productive forces, relations of production, superstructure, ideologies, determination in the last instance by the economy, specific determination of the other levels, etc.

(2) A radical critique of the *theoretical* pretensions of every philosophical humanism.

(3) The definition of humanism as an *ideology*.

This new conception is completely rigorous as well, but it is a new rigor:

the essence criticized (2) is defined as an ideology (3), a category belonging to the new theory of society and history (1).

This rupture with every *philosophical* anthropology or humanism is no secondary detail; it is Marx's scientific discovery.

It means that Marx rejected the problematic of the earlier philosophy and adopted a new problematic in one and the same act. The earlier idealist ('bourgeois') philosophy depended in all its domains and arguments (its 'theory of knowledge', its conception of history, its political economy, its ethics, its aesthetics, etc.) on a problematic of *human nature* (or the essence of man). For centuries, this problematic had been transparency itself, and no one had thought of questioning it even in its internal modifications.[10]

In the new problematic the economic practice is understood according to the dialectic of the mode of production. The political practice is understood according to the possibilities for collective action given within a given conjuncture. These two layers do not matter so much here for my purposes, i.e., what exact views Althusser has about economic and political practice. At the third layer, the important duality appears between that which is ideological and that which is theoretical. Their common feature is to have been precipitated out of economic and political practice, though by no means in a simple determinism or epiphenomenalism. Theory only arrives in the midst of a prevailing ideology. An ideology grants to each of us the possibility of an ordered and organized conduct: it is our ultimate explanation of the world insofar as we undertake to act in it. Without a religion, or adherence to a political movement, or some world-picture, we could not act effectively. Theory, on the other hand, or science, makes the conscious correlation between economic practice, political practice, ideological practice, and itself. Materialist theory has always been partly present in ideologies, but only in fragments.

Humanism, e.g., the viewpoint of the young Marx, is an ideology: the hope and belief that men will benefit from humane reforms or revolutions. This belief Marx shared with most Christians, and most liberals. It gives guidance to many noble projects. However, theory, properly speaking, must expel this ideology from within itself. It conceals the actualities of the whole social formation, particularly by creating the illusion that men of good will could alleviate the condition of the proletariat through benign use of the levers of power.

Yet while Althusser absolutely denies that thesis, denouncing it as a theory, he maintains that the humanistic ideology plays a necessary role. His is only a *theoretical* antihumanism. Marxism must perpetuate humanistic ideology both before, during, and after the dictatorship of the proletariat.

> It is clear that *ideology (as a system of mass representations) is indispensable in any society if men are to be formed, transformed and equipped to respond to the demands of their conditions of existence.* If, as Marx said, history is a perpetual transformation of men's conditions of existence, and if this is equally true of a socialist society, then men must be ceaselessly transformed so as to adapt them to these conditions; if this 'adaptation' cannot be left to spontaneity but must be constantly assumed, dominated and con-

trolled, it is in ideology that this demand is expressed, that this distance is measured, that this contradiction is lived and that its resolution is 'activated'. It is in ideology that the classless society *lives* the inadequacy/adequacy of the relation between it and the world, it is in it and by it that it transforms men's 'consciousness', that is, their attitudes and behaviour so as to raise them to the level of their tasks and the conditions of their existence. [11]

This is not, he says, a Platonic theory of the noble lie. At most, it is a sober recognition of the dividing line between what is absolutely necessary for an adequate description of a social formation and what is not necessary.

But I should like to maintain that humanism cannot be relegated to the ideological domain, even given the broad and positive functions Althusser assigns to ideology. Rather, it is inevitably constitutive of the science of political economy and shows up in a number of sectors. I shall mention four of them.

1. Even if we do not think globally, even if we confine our attention to a single social formation, we cannot avoid noticing that armed conflict is always a possibility. War and peace are phenomena that have the highest relevance to any society: civil war, terrorism, revolutionary war, territorial war, world war.

2. Offenses against individuals and groups are a constant in human history; those short of war are the subject of legislation and judicial action: they are crimes.

3. People are born, die, get sick, seek health for themselves and others, and may or may not have the means to achieve health. Phenomena related to health and disease, of course, are nutrition, housing—in general, welfare.

4. It is our possibility to learn to read, to write, to acquire languages, mathematics, and sciences. Phenomena related to schooling are athletics, dance, opera, and music.

I have listed four classes of phenomena which I might call Defense, Justice, Health and Welfare, Education.

These are the key functions of a state, according to most political theories. Marxists generally comprehend them in the same way as everyone else—as political or state activities. They put them on the borderline between relations of production, on the one hand, and the ideological superstructure, on the other.

Anarchists (such as myself in earlier years) believed that these functions could be reabsorbed into the collective social life at a local level. Althusser, however, prefers simply to ignore them. Partly it is the evasive policies of Engels and Lenin that show up here: if we don't talk too much about Justice or Education, some day the state will wither away and the communist idea will take over. But there is more to it than that. These four state functions *cannot* be located in a level such as the "civil society" that Hegel talked about or the "social formations" that Althusser talks about. They are *state functions. And they are humanistic practices. They are undertaken by human agencies, and their effects are discernible only in human responses.*

FOUCAULT AND THE END OF MAN

I want to pinpoint the differences between Althusser and Foucault. The neo-orthodoxy of Althusser led him to write only for one audience. Foucault, by contrast, is wide open, will talk to everyone, and knows no orthodoxy. More centrally, Althusser wanted to talk about everything—his was a traditional type of Platonic philosophy in search of a lingo that would cover every phenomenon, and decree the non-being of whatever lay outside the discourse. Foucault, however, was a historian who contantly emphasized the limits of whatever topic he had. At times his writing seems encyclopedic but he fought against that tendency and was embarrassed by it and had no actual thrust to ontological prohibitions.

And yet if we look at *The Order of Things* and *The Archaeology of Knowledge,* it appears that Foucault is engaged in the practice of abolishing Man. What is going on here? The historian Foucault is drawing attention to a certain figure, that of Man, who has served to order and to guide all kinds of studies for the last two centuries: *homo faber, homo loquens,* and so on. But in the present conjuncture of scientific study, it is just this figure that stands in our way, blocking our access to that which requires study now. Each of our various discourses seems to lead us to some matter that calls for thought, and yet it is this human figure that stops us from taking the step that we need to take. We try to trace a theory of language or perception or the body back to some primordial, foundational, transcendental theory such as a phenomenology of lived experience.

> Modern thought has been unable to avoid searching for . . . a discourse whose tension would make it possible to analyze man as a subject, that is, as a locus of knowledge which has been empirically acquired but referred back as closely as possible to what makes it possible, and as a pure form immediately present to those contents; a discourse, in short, which in relation to quasi-aesthetics and quasi-dialectics would play the role of an analytic which would at the same time give them a foundation in a theory of the subject and perhaps enable them to articulate themselves in that third and intermediary term in which both the experience of the body and that of culture would be rooted. Such a complex, over-determined, and necessary role has been performed in modern thought by the analysis of actual experience. Actual experience is, in fact, both the space in which all empirical contents are given to experience and the original form that makes them possible in general and designates their primary roots.[12]

Earlier sciences, in the seventeenth and eighteenth centuries, and in the pre-Renaissance ages, had found other means for bringing the vast array of their materials into some tabular form, or some great code of being; but with the step into the nineteenth century, we were obliged to organize and unify the manifold through this organizing figure Man. The figure of Man, who could also be studied empirically, was also to play a grounding or transcendental function; and the philosophy that tried to encompass this duality in our own day was phenomenology.

The phenomenological project continually resolves itself, before our eyes, into a description—empirical despite itself—of actual experience, and into an ontology of the unthought that automatically short-circuits the primacy of the "I think."[13]

Ours have been times of human sciences arrayed around the three dimensions of this figure Man: labor, life, and language. History and political economy trace his works. We situate his life in the evolutionary arc. Philosophy, hermeneutics, and linguistics trace his expressions. But—

The human sciences are not, then, an analysis of what man is by nature; but rather an analysis that extends from what man is in his positivity (living, speaking, labouring being) to what enables this same being to know (or seek to know) what life is, in what the essence of labour and its laws consist, and in what way he is able to speak. The human sciences thus occupy the distance that separates (though not without connecting them) biology, economics, and philology from that which gives them possibility in the very being of man.[14]

These discourses, our own, are destined to pass over into a posthumanist discourse, and this organizing figure will have to yield place to new regularities.

Foucault's anticipation of this is far more deeply grounded than in some mere historicism or general theory of change. My paper cannot begin to examine all his reasons, and to get quickly through the issue I should like to say that I am in agreement with him. Let us just note one pervasive dilemma in all the versions of human science:

In any case, the unthought has accompanied man, mutely and uninterruptedly, since the nineteenth century. Since it was really never more than an insistent double, it has never been the object of reflection in an autonomous way; it has received the complementary form and the inverted name of that for which it was the Other and the shadow: in Hegelian phenomenology, it was the *An sich* as opposed to the *Für sich;* for Schopenhauer in the *Unbewusste;* for Marx it was alienated man; in Husserl's analyses it was the implicit, the inactual, the sedimented, the non-effected—in every case, the inexhaustible double that presents itself to reflection as the blurred projection of what man is in his truth.[15]

Whether or not we can predict the demise of man, let us hope with Foucault; let us seek to bring the effacement of that picture. But will a picture be restored?

The text of his book ends:

As the archaeology of our thought easily shows, man is an invention of recent date. And one perhaps nearing its end.

If those arrangements were to disappear as they appeared, if some event of which we can at the moment do no more than sense the possibility— without knowing either what its form will be or what it promises—were to cause them to crumble, as the ground of Classical thought did, at the end of the eighteenth century, then one can certainly wager that man would be erased, like a face drawn in sand at the edge of the sea.[16]

So Foucault.

Yet as the waves from the sea erase that face, I notice what sounds like a voice, or perhaps two voices or more. There are two voices, young, a woman's and a man's. The woman's voice is different from the man's and yet with different range and timbre there is a cadence the same for both. I think I can hear them across the waves of the sea that erases Foucault's Man. The two voices extend themselves towards each other, they seem to meet and tie in a knot. When one speaks, the other hears, and understands and responds. Though we cannot see them, we know that both are embodied—differently, yes, and yet in accordance. Now as we think, we listen to the two. I am extending my own voice by commentary, and my comment can let their voices be. We can all share in some understanding of the two lovers though it is my privilege as speaker to give voice to our understanding, to be subjective. Their dialogue and my monologue are indeed of one and the same vocal substance. Scholar, interpreter, commentator, spins out a monologue that can take on a ventriloquizing power; and that power is convincing. This dialogue from *Romeo and Juliet* will play again and again in many theaters, not so very differently from the way I read it out. By way of the voice we shall find a face and then the hands and the body. After the effacement of Foucault's man, there is a reappearance of some familiar humans.

> O gentle Romeo,
> If thou dost love, pronounce it faithfully:
> Or if thou think'st I am quickly won,
> I'll frown and be perverse and say thee nay,
> So thou wilt woo; but else, not for the world.
> In truth, fair Montague, I am too fond;
> And therefore thou mayst think my 'haviour light:
> But trust me, gentleman, I'll prove more true
> Than those that have more cunning to be strange.
> I should have been more strange, I must confess,
> But that thou overheard'st, ere I was ware,
> My true love's passion: therefore pardon me,
> And not impute this yielding to light love,
> Which the dark night hath so discovered.

ROMEO   Lady, by yonder blessed moon I swear,
            That tips with silver all these fruit-tree tops,—

JULIET   O, swear not by the moon, th'inconstant moon,
            That monthly changes in her circled orb,
            Lest that thy love prove likewise variable.

ROMEO   What shall I swear by?

JULIET   Do not swear at all;
            Or, if thou wilt, swear by thy gracious self,
            Which is the god of my idolatry,
            And I'll believe thee.

ROMEO	If my heart's dear love—
JULIET	Well, do not swear: although I joy in thee,
	I have no joy of this contract to-night:
	It is too rash, too unadvised, too sudden,
	Too like the lightning, which doth cease to be
	Ere one can say 'It lightens.' Sweet, good night!
	This bud of love, by summer's ripening breath,
	May prove a beauteous flower when next we meet.
	Good night, good night! as sweet repose and rest
	Come to thy heart as that within my breast!
ROMEO	O, wilt thou leave me so unsatisfied?
JULIET	What satisfaction canst thou have to-night?
ROMEO	The exchange of thy love's faithful vow for mine.
JULIET	I gave thee mine before thou didst request it
	And yet I would it were to give again.
ROMEO	Wouldst thou withdraw it? for what purpose, love?
JULIET	But to be frank, and give it thee again.
	And yet I wish but for the thing I have:
	My bounty is as boundless as the sea,
	My love as deep; the more I give to thee,
	The more I have, for both are infinite.
	I hear some noise within; dear love, adieu!
	Anon, good nurse! Sweet Montague, be true.
	Stay but a little, I will come again.
ROMEO	O blessed, blessed night! I am afeard,
	Being in night, all this is but a dream,
	Too flattering-sweet to be substantial.[17]

The voices and the figures are not the same as Foucault's man. They are not just the same as ourselves. Yet these figures are present in these voices in a commanding enough way to claim our attention. The humans are differentiated from the surrounding scene, gaining our attention in their ways. The human face and figure, while new in a certain way when the play is enacted in our own day and in the future, still have an aura about them that recalls many others that we know from our long history.

Inevitable—that in the thought of Heidegger, the human appears where the gods are pleased to dwell: in a kitchen. Inevitable—that despite the expulsions and repressions of Althusser's thought, the human appears as a subject of the state. Inevitable—with the disappearance of Foucault's Man, two lovers approach each other and approach us, by way of their voices. This humanism is inevitable in the future, and it will recall great images from our past.

Notes

I would like to thank Susan Woodard of Brock University for helping me in various ways with this paper.

1. "Letter on Humanism," trans. F. Capuzzi and J. G. Gray, in Heidegger, *Basic Writings,* ed. D. F. Krell (New York, 1977), 205.

2. Ibid., 222.

3. Ibid., 216

4. Ibid., 212–3

5. Ibid., 225.

6. Ibid., 224

7. Ibid., 231

8. *Preface to the Critique of Hegel's Philosophy of Right.*

9. *For Marx,* trans. B. Brewster (New York, 1970), 227–228.

10. Ibid., 227.

11. Ibid., 235.

12. M. Foucault, *The Order of Things* (New York, 1973), 320–321.

13. Ibid., 326.

14. Ibid., 353.

15. Ibid., 326–7.

16. Ibid., 387.

17. *Romeo and Juliet,* Act II, Scene 2.

23

Secular Humanism and Eupraxophy

Paul Kurtz

Humanism is what I have termed elsewhere a eupraxophy, literally, "good wisdom and practice in conduct."[1] But it is not unique; there have been other eupraxophies historically. In the Greek and Roman world, Epicureanism, Stoicism, and skepticism were eupraxophies. Each had a metaphysical world view, each made concrete ethical recommendations about how to achieve the good life, and each had epistemological theories. There have been many other kinds of eupraxophies: utilitarianism, Marxism, existentialism, pragmatism, perhaps even Confucianism and some forms of Buddhism; each contains various elements of eupraxophy. Some of these schools, however, are concerned primarily with *eupraxia* (that is, with good practice) and they deemphasize the *sophia*, the scientific and philosophic world view. Some, such as Marxism and utilitarianism, focus primarily on *social praxis*.

There are many variations of humanism: naturalistic, existential, Marxist, pragmatic, and liberal. We may ask, what is distinctive about the eupraxophy of modern-day secular humanism? I wish to propose a definition of humanism that is thoroughly secular. This definition is not arbitrary, since it classifies a set of propositions held by many scientists and philosophers who consider themselves to be humanists. Nonetheless, it involves a prescriptive recommendation about how to use the term *humanism*. Humanism includes at least four main characteristics: (1) it is a method of inquiry; (2) it presents a cosmic world view; (3) it contains a concrete set of ethical recommendations for the individual's life stance; and (4) it expresses a number of social and political ideals.

A METHOD OF INQUIRY

An essential characteristic of contemporary secular humanism is its commitment to a method of inquiry. This feature is so important that it may even be said to function as the basic principle of secular humanism. Questions concerning meaning and truth have been enduring ones in the history of philosophy, and they have come to the forefront since the growth of modern science. Epistemology is also pivotal to secular humanism.

Humanist epistemology may be defined first by what it opposes. It rejects the use of arbitrary authority to obfuscate meaning or to legislate truth. Throughout human history there have been persistent attempts by institutional authorities to do precisely that. The church and the state have been especially prone to define, codify, and enforce orthodoxy. The need for social order is such that humankind finds it useful or necessary to regulate conduct. Custom ensures some stability in social behavior and enables human beings to function with a clear understanding of expectations and of the acceptable parameters of civilized discourse and conduct. The rules of the game by which we live and work together are established—in constitutions, bylaws, contracts, laws, and regulations—and they enable us to fulfill our cooperative aims. It is one thing, however, to lay down the rules of conduct by law and to enforce them by sanction, leaving opportunities for them to be modified and revised in democratic societies. It is quite another to uphold unchanging orthodoxy of belief in the sciences, philosophy, literature, the arts, politics, morality, or religion and to seek to legislate acceptable modes of personal behavior. Here the appeal to authority is illegitimate, for it substitutes a conformist faith for intelligently grounded knowledge. Establishing orthodoxy in belief stifles discovery and blocks inquiry. Transmitting the fixed beliefs of an early age to future ones prevents bold new departures in thought. Even the most cherished beliefs so lovingly defended in time may become archaic; blatant falsehoods persist as prejudice encrusted by habits.

History is replete with pathetic attempts by past civilizations to enshrine their belief systems in perpetuity. Efforts to censor conflicting opinions have often led to violent social conflict. In worst-case scenarios such suppression degenerates into sheer tyranny over the human mind. Dictators, ecclesiastical princes, and vested oligarchs have tried to police the thoughts of everyone under their jurisdiction, using the Holy Inquisition, the Gestapo, or the NKVD to suppress dissent. In a weaker form, conformist pressures substitute public opinion or that of the leading authorities of the day for creative and independent inquiry. Abiding by conventional wisdom thus stifles new ideas. No one group can claim to have a monopoly of wisdom or virtue, and to proclaim one's fondest convictions as *obiter dicta* for everyone in the society is destined to fail. Even though power is the chief criterion for the perpetuation of a belief system, that is no guarantee of social stability, for the so-called authorities often disagree about truth. The reigning beliefs of one age may become the intransigent follies of the next. Thoughtless bigots wish to prevent any questioning of their revered articles of faith; they are fearful of change and challenge. Regrettably, all of the major religious orthodoxies historically have succumbed to the temptation to enforce their beliefs—when and where they had the power to do so—and to impose their practices upon the rest of society. Orthodoxies have allowed fanatic intolerance to prevail, and they have denied the right of those who disagree to voice their contrary faiths or dissenting opinions.

The same narrow mind-set appears in powerful political and economic elites, who fear any challenge to their privileged positions and thus seek to enforce by law what they consider to be the only legitimate system of belief. They strain to exclude outsiders who threaten their hegemony by declaring them political heretics or religious infidels.

In religion, orthodox belief systems are rooted in ancient dogmas held to be so sacred that they are immune to objective examination. The claims made in the name of God are shrouded in privileged revelations received from on high. The claims to divine authority are shielded from critical scrutiny by popes, cardinals, bishops, rabbis, mullahs, gurus, and other defenders of the faith. In politics and economics dissident minorities are excluded from the corridors of power. There is no forum available for them, no opportunity to participate in open inquiry. Thus the so-called Higher Truth, so protected from investigation, lies beyond contest. A similar closed syndrome can be found in philosophy or science when it is held to be immune to free enquiry. Thomism, Calvinism, and Marxist-Leninism were considerd official doctrines at various times in history by those who defended them in the name of an entrenched power elite. The same is true for Lysenkoism under Stalin or racist theories under the Nazis. In the battle for civil liberties in democratic societies political power has been wrested from repressive oligarchies. Unfortunately, the right to know has not been universally recognized as a basic human right in all societies, and there are wide areas—especially in religion and morality—that are still held to be immune to criticism.

The first principle of humanism is a commitment to free inquiry in every field of human endeavor. This means that any effort to prevent the free mind from exercising its right to pose questions and initiate inquiry is unwarranted.

But which methods of inquiry should be used? How do we evaluate truth claims? Philosophers have long debated the question "What is truth?" How we appraise knowledge claims depends on the subject matter under investigation, be it science, mathematics, philosophy, ethics, politics, economics, history, or the arts. Let it suffice for now to outline a minimal set of epistemological criteria that cuts across the various disciplines, without any lengthy explication in defense.[2] I will focus on skepticism, the scientific method, and critical intelligence.

Skepticism is a vital methodological principle of inquiry. I refer not to negative or nihilistic skepticism, which rejects the very possibility of attaining reliable knowledge, but positive, selective skepticism. This principle of skepticism implies that the reliability of a hypothesis, theory, or belief is a function of the grounds, evidence, or reasons by which it is supported. If a claim is not justified by objective validation or verification, we ought to be cautious in holding fast to it. The amount of supporting evidence will vary with the subject under scrutiny.

Probabilism points to the degree of certainty by which we are willing to ascertain truth claims. We should not attribute to any belief absolute infallibility. We should be prepared to admit that we may be mistaken. Beliefs should be taken as hypotheses: they are tentative or hypothetical depending upon the degree of evidence or the validity of the arguments used to support them.

Fallibilism is a principle which indicates that even when a claim is thought to be well supported, we should nonetheless be prepared to modify our beliefs if new evidence or arguments arise in the future which show either that we were in error or that our truths were only partial and limited. This applies in fields of formal knowledge, such as mathematics, as much as to experimental domains of inquiry. The skeptic should have an open mind about all questions and not seek to close responsible inquiry in any field. If after investigation there is insufficient evidence, the skeptic may say that the claim is unlikely, improbable, or false, or if further investigation is possible, he may wish to suspend judgment and admit that he does not know. Agnosticism, in this respect, is a meaningful option. We should be prepared to exercise doubt about a wide range of belief claims which we have little expectation at present of resolving. Skepticism is thus an essential method used in science, technology, philosophy, religion, politics, morality, and ordinary life.

But the question may be asked: *Which* method should be used to warrant beliefs? What are the criteria of confirmation and validity? Without attempting to resolve this question fully here, let me suggest the following criteria:

First, we should appeal to *experience* in all areas in which it is pertinent to do so. By this I mean observation, evidence, facts, data—preferably involving some intersubjective grounds that can be replicated or certified. Purely subjective or private paths to truth need not be arbitrarily rejected, but, on the other hand, they are not admissible to the body of knowledge unless they can be reliably corroborated by others. This empirical test is fundamental. But if we are to draw any inferences from it, then it must refer to experiential claims that are open to public scrutiny, not only in ascertaining whether they occurred but also in interpreting their likely causes.

Second, if an experience cannot be duplicated, there might be circumstantial evidence or at least *predictable* results by which we can evaluate its adequacy. In other words, our beliefs are forms of behavior, and they can be tested—at least in part—by their observed consequences. This is an experimental criterion used not only in laboratories but also in everyday life when we appraise beliefs not simply by what people say but by what they do.

Third, we use a *rational* test of deductive coherence, judging our theories or beliefs by relation to those we have already accepted as reliable. Hypotheses and theories cannot be viewed in isolation from other knowledge we believe to be true. They are logically consistent or inconsistent with it, and are judged by the criterion of validity. We can see this test at work not only in mathematical, logical, and formal systems but also in science and ordinary affairs when we test beliefs by their internal consistency.

The preceding criteria are used most explicitly in the sciences, where hypothetical-deductive methods prevail and where we formulate hypotheses and test them by their experimental adequacy and logical coherence. Science is not a method of knowing available only to an esoteric coterie of experts; similar standards of reasoning are employed in common everyday life when we are faced with problems and wish to resolve practical questions.

The terms *reason, rationality*, and *reasonableness* have sometimes been used to describe the general methodology that humanists have advocated:

that is, we should test truth claims objectively as far as we can, and if claims cannot pass the tests of reason (broadly conceived to include experience and rationality), we should either reject them or suspend judgment. We face an epistemological crisis today, for with the increasing specialization of knowledge, experts often restrict their use of objective methods of inquiry to their own fields of competency and are unwilling to extend reason to other areas of human knowledge. What is at issue here is whether we can apply the powers of reason so that they will have some influence on the totality of beliefs.

Perhaps the best terminology to describe objectivity in testing truth claims is *critical intelligence*. This means that we must use our powers of critical analysis and observation to evaluate carefully questions of belief. We first need to define what is at stake. Here clarity in meaning is essential. We need to be clear about what we wish to know and what is at issue. We need to ask: What alternative explanations are offered? We formulate hypotheses and develop beliefs that solve our puzzlement. The salient point is that only objective evidence and reasons will suffice to evaluate alternative hypotheses.

What is distinctive about humanism as a eupraxophy is that *it wishes to extend the methods of objective inquiry to all areas of life, including religious, philosophical, ethical, and political concerns that are often left unexamined.* There has been extensive research into specialized areas of scientific knowledge, particularly since technological discoveries have provided an enormous boon to human welfare; however, powerful forces have often distrusted and indeed prevented free inquiry into the foundations of social, moral, and religious systems. The crux of the matter is whether objective methods of inquiry can be applied to these vital areas of human concern. If critical intelligence were to supplant blind appeals to authority, custom, faith, or subjectivity, it could radically transform society. Free thought can be threatening to the privileged bastions of the status quo.

No doubt a basic point of contention between humanism and theism is precisely here: the application of scientific methods, rationalism, and critical intelligence to evaluate transcendental claims. The critics of humanism maintain that it excludes, almost by definition, claims to a transcendental realm. This, I submit, is not the case; for the humanist is willing to examine any responsible claim to truth. The burden of proof, however, rests with the believer to specify clearly the conditions under which his beliefs may be falsified. The humanist requests that whatever is under examination be carefully defined. God-talk is generally vague, ambiguous, even unintelligible. The humanist next wishes to know how the believer would justify its truth. If a meaningful claim is introduced, it needs to be corroborated. This means that private, mystical, or subjective claims to revelation or divine presence or mere declarations by ecclesiastical authorities that something is true are inadmissible unless they can be intersubjectively confirmed. We cannot exclude on a priori grounds any insights derived from literature, poetry, or the arts. These express enduring human interests. We only ask that they be analyzed carefully and tested objectively. Aesthetic experience is a rich part of human experience, and it may provide a wealth of insight and inspiration.

Any knowledge about the world drawn from these sources, however, requires careful evaluation.

The humanist is open to the subtle nuances of human experience, but he insists that we use our powers of critical judgment to appraise the claims to truth. In this sense, he draws upon the tested knowledge and the best available wisdom of the day. He will accept the claims of others—even if he has not personally scrutinized each of these claims—but only if he is assured that those claims have been warranted by objective methods, and that if he or someone else had the time, energy, and training he could scrutinize the procedures used to corroborate the findings. The methods of critical intelligence apply not only to descriptive truth claims, where we seek to describe and explain natural processes, but also to normative judgments, where we formulate eupraxic recommendations in the various domains of human action.

A COSMIC WORLD VIEW

Humanist eupraxophy does not simply assert a method of inquiry based upon the methods of science; it also seeks to use the sciences to interpret the cosmos and the place of the human species within it. The humanist thus attempts to make some kind of generalized sense of reality. Speculative metaphysics is in disrepute today, and rightly so if it seeks to derive universal principles about reality from purely intuitive or metaphorical methods. The primary source for obtaining knowledge about nature should be human experience. It is within the various disciplines of scientific research and scholarship that reliable hypotheses and theories are elaborated and tested. If this is the case, then any comprehensive view of nature must draw heavily upon the scientific understanding of the day. Since science is a rapidly expanding body of knowledge, there are ongoing modifications of principles, hypotheses, and theories. There may at times be fundamental shifts in outlook, in which long-standing paradigms are altered, as for example, the fundamental transformation of Newtonian science by relativity theory and quantum mechanics. We note also the basic changes that have occurred in genetics, biology, psychology, the social sciences, and other fields of research in the twentieth century. There are times when we build up and elaborate a body of knowledge by a process of accumulation and addition. At other times there may be radical disruptions: novel theories may be introduced and tested, and they may fundamentally alter the prevailing outlook. One must be prepared to change a cosmic perspective in the light of new data and theories. We must be tentative in our formulations and prepared to revise theories in the light of new discoveries.

Unfortunately, scientists in specialized disciplines are often unaware of developments in other fields, and they may be unwilling or unable to relate their findings to domains of knowledge outside their competence or to develop a cosmic view. This is where philosophy enters: the philosopher should interpret the knowedge of one discipline and relate it to other fields. Philosophy, by definition, is general, for it is concerned with finding common methods, principles, postulates, axioms, assumptions, concepts, and generalizations used in a wide range of fields. Here I refer to the philosophy of science and to the methods of analysis and generalization by which it interprets the various sciences.

The great philosophers have always attempted to do this. Aristotle's *Metaphysics* provided a critical interpretation of the key concepts and categories underlying our knowledge of nature. Similarly, Descartes, Leibniz, Hume, Kant, Russell, Dewey, Whitehead, and others reflected upon and attempted to interpret the sciences of their day. We need to do the same today, though it may be far more difficult than in previous ages because of the immense proliferation of the sciences; it is difficult for any one mind to sum up the enormous bodies of specialties in some sort of interrelated whole. If we cannot as yet succeed in this ambitious venture, at the very least we can try in a more modest way. Using physics, astronomy, and the natural sciences, we can develop some cosmologies that explain the expanding universe. Using biology and genetics we can try to interpret the evolution of life. We can use psychology to understand human behavior, and we can draw upon anthropology, sociology, and the other social sciences to develop appropriate theories about sociocultural phenomena. This is an ongoing quest. We do not have a comprehensive theory of the universe at present. Nonetheless we do have kaleidoscopic pictures of nature that are based on the sciences.

What does humanist eupraxophy tell us about the cosmos? Let us approach the question at first by negative definition, by indicating what is unlikely. There is insufficient evidence for the claim that there is a divine creator who has brought the universe into being by an act of will. The invoking of God as a cause of everything that is, is mere *postulation*, without sufficient evidence or proof. It is a leap outside nature. The concept of a transcendent supernatural being is unintelligible; the idea of a First Cause, itself uncaused, is contradictory. Even if the Big Bang theory in astronomy is useful in explaining the rapidly receding and expanding universe, this does not provide support for the claim that there was a Being who existed coterminous or antecedent to this explosion. The Big Bang may be the result of a random quantum fluctuation, not an intelligent plan.

To read into such a cosmological principle selective human qualities—intelligence, perfection, or personhood—is unwarranted. The universe does not manifest design; there is apparent regularity and order, but chance and conflict, chaos and disorder are also present. To describe the entire universe as *good* is an anthropomorphic rendering of nature to fit one's moral bias. If there is apparent good in the universe, there would also have to be apparent evil, at least from the standpoint of sentient beings, who at times devour one another in the struggle for survival or who encounter natural disasters that destroy them. If so, how can we reconcile evil with a provident deity? Theists are so overcome by the tragic character of human finitude that they are willing to project their deepest longings into a divine mind, and this enables them to transcend nothingness. For the theist the universe involves some teleological conception of salvation. Man, in some way, is at the center of creation; for God is endowed by man with human qualities, especially with a compassionate concern for our plight. God will save us if only we will devote ourselves completely to adoring Him, accept on the basis of faith that which passeth all human understanding, and obey His moral commandments as interpreted by His self-proclaimed emissaries on earth.

Much of the anthropomorphic character of the deity is derived from ancient texts held to be sacred and to have been revealed by God to specially appointed individuals. The Bible predicates the intervention of the Holy Ghost in history. Yet scientific and scholarly biblical criticism has made it abundantly clear that the Bible is a human document, a thousand-year-old record of the experiences of primitive nomadic and agricultural tribes living on the eastern shore of the Mediterranean. There is no evidence that Yahweh spoke to Abraham, Moses, Joseph, or any of the Old Testament prophets. The biblical accounts of their experiences are the records of Hebrew national existence, seeking to sustain itself by the myth of the "chosen people." These books have not been empirically validated; they express an ancient world view and the moral conceptions of a prescientific culture that invoked deities to sanctify its ideological aspirations.

The New Testament presents the incredible tale of Jesus, a man of whom we have very little historical knowledge. Obviously this is not an objective historical account. The "divinity" of Jesus has never been adequately demonstrated. Yet powerful churches have sought to inculcate the mythic story and to suppress dissent. The tale of Jesus' life and ministry expressed in the Four Gospels and the letters of Paul were written twenty to seventy years after his death. They are riddled with the contradictions implicit in an oral tradition. Defended by propagandists for a new mystery religion, the biblical accounts are hardly to be taken as dispassionate historical evidence for Jesus' divine origin. The tales of these so-called miracles and faith healings of Jesus are based on uncorroborated testimony by an unsophisticated people who were easily deceived. That the Jesus myth was elaborated by later generations and was eventually promulgated by powerful church institutions that dominated Europe for almost two millennia and still have inordinate influence on large sectors of the globe is evidence for the presence of a transcendental temptation within the human heart, which is ever ready to seize upon any shred of hope for an afterlife.

Similar skeptical criticism may be leveled against other supernatural religions. Islam is a religion based on the alleged revelations to Muhammad, received from on high through the archangel Gabriel, at first in caves north of Mecca and later in various other places. Careful reading of the literature about the origins of the Koran enables us to give alternative naturalistic explanations of Muhammad's ministry. He may have suffered from some form of epilepsy, which explains his trance states or swoons. He was able to convince others of his divine calling, and he used this ploy to achieve power. All of this is testimony to the gullibility of human beings and their willingness to abandon acceptable standards of rationality when they are confronted with claims to a Higher Truth. The same thing can be noted of the legions of saints, prophets, gurus, and shamans throughout history who have proclaimed divine revelations and have used their claims to delude and influence their followers.

Basic to the monotheistic approach is the belief in an afterlife. Is it possible for a "soul" to survive the death of the body? Jewish, Christian, and Muslim adherents fervently believe in the immortality of the soul, and Hindus, in its reincarnation from previous existences.

Unfortunately, the most resolute and objective investigations of claims of survival have shown them to be without empirical corroboration. Psychical researchers, parapsychologists, and paranormal investigators, for over a century, have produced reports of ghosts, spirits, apparitions, and poltergeists, but there is insufficient data to support the reality of discarnate existence, despite the legions of spiritualists, trance channelers, and past-life regressors who claim to be in touch with an unseen realm of spiritual reality. Although our fondest hopes and desires may *demand* life before birth or even after death, the evidence points in the other direction. Even if it could be proved that something briefly survives the death of the biological body, there is no evidence of an eternal state of existence or of a blessed union with God. The evidence for survival is based on wishful thinking and is totally inconclusive. Death seems to be the natural state of all life forms, even though modern medical science and technology are able to ward off disease and prolong life. Humanism is thus skeptical about the entire drama of the theistic universe: that God exists and that we can achieve salvation in an afterlife.

But what picture of the universe does humanism provide as a substitute? Perhaps not one that slakes the existential yearnings of the desperate soul, but one that is more in accordance with the world as uncovered by science. What we have today is an open-ended universe, perhaps ragged at the edges and with many gaps in our knowledge, but it is a picture supported by the best available evidence. At the present stage of human knowledge, the following general propositions seem true:

Objects or events within the universe have material explanations. All objects or events encountered have a physical character. Matter, mass, and energy may, however, be organized on various levels, ranging from the minutest microparticles on the subatomic level in fields of energy to gigantic objects such as planets, moons, comets, stars, quasars, and galaxies.

We encounter within the universe order and regularity on the one hand and chaos and random fluctuations on the other. Objects and events within the universe seem to be evolving. Change is an enduring trait of existing things. The cosmos as we presently understand it is something on the order of ten to twenty billion years old; it is expanding from what seems to have been a huge explosion. In any case, our planet is only one satellite of a minor star in the Milky Way, which is merely one galaxy among billions in the vast universe. What preceded the Big Bang, the physicists are not yet able to explain, and what will be the end of the universe—a whimper or a big crunch as matter implodes—is also difficult to say.

The universe is not, however, inanimate. There is some likelihood that organic life exists in other parts of the universe. The earliest known fossils uncovered on the earth are more than three billion years old. The most useful hypothesis to explain the diverse forms of life on our planet is that they evolved from common genetic material and split into diverse species. Evolution is a product of chance mutations, differential reproduction, and adaptation. The human species most likely evolved over a period of several million years, exhibiting processes that follow similar patterns in other species. Distinctive to human primates is the large cerebral cortex and the development of highly complex social systems in which tools are manipulated and signs and symbols function to enable linguistic communication. Genetics, biology, and psychology explain the emergence of human behavior and how and why we function the way we do. The social sciences are able to account for the development of the complex social institutions that help to satisfy basic human needs.

The study of culture demonstrates that individual members of the human species are physiochemical biological systems genetically predisposed to certain forms of behavior, yet able to learn; they are influenced by environmental factors and capable of adaptive behavior. There seems to be a creative component to all forms of organic life—this is especially true of the human species. The human organism is able to respond to stimuli not only by conditioned behavior but by expressing creative impulses and demonstrating cognitive awareness. Humans, as products of nature, are able to understand the causes and conditions of their behavior, and they are able to intervene in the processes of nature and change them by discovery and invention. Formerly, the course of human evolution was largely unconscious and blind. We can now redirect to some extent by conscious effort the evolution of the species. Human behavior may be modified by imaginative effort and ingenuity. Human beings manifest rational choice. They are able to solve the problems encountered in living and thus, in part, to determine their futures. This is the message of the humanist outlook.

A LIFE STANCE

Men and women are capable of free choice. How much and to what extent has been hotly debated by philosophers, theologians, and scientists. Clearly, our behavior is limited or determined by the conditions under which we act. There are physiochemical, genetic, sociological, and psychological causes at work. Yet, in spite of these causal factors, we are consciously aware and we are capable of some teleonomic and preferential choice. Cognition can selectively direct our behavior.

"What ought I to choose?" and "How ought I to live?" are questions constantly raised. Are there any norms that humanism can offer to guide our conduct? Can we discover any enduring ends or goals? Is there a good which we ought to seek? Are there ethical standards of right and wrong? Is there a distinct set of ethical values and principles that may be said to be humanistic?

These are large questions, and I can only sketch in outline form what I consider to be the ethics of humanism.[3] Its critics maintain that humanism lacks proper moral standards, that it is permissive, and that it allows subjective taste and caprice to prevail. Without belief in God, these critics assert, an ethic of responsibility is impossible.

These charges are unfounded. They emanate from an abysmal ignorance of the history of philosophical ethics, for philosophers have demonstrated the possibility of an autonomous ethic in which moral obligations emerge.

By arguing that ethics is autonomous, I simply mean that it is possible to make moral judgments of good, bad, right, and wrong independently of one's ultimate foundations; i.e., there is a fund of common moral decencies that can be developed in human experience. Yet humanist ethics does have foundations, and these are its eupraxophy, which in the last analysis completes it; for when questions of "ultimate" obligation or "ultimate" moral purpose arise the theist falls back on God, whereas the humanist is skeptical of that claim and places his ethics in a naturalistic evolutionary universe that is devoid of purpose. The humanist life stance thus has its grounding in nature and human nature.[4]

There are at least two alternative approachs to the moral life: (1) transcendental theistic systems of morality; (2) humanist ethics. Let me state simply that if God does not exist and the so-called "sacred" texts are not divinely inspired but are the expressions of human culture at certain historical periods, then appeals to transcendental ethics can hardly serve as guides for conduct. Interestingly, those systems which claim to deduce our moral obligations from a belief in God often promulgate contradictory codes of behavior, waging constant warfare about the legitimacy of rival priesthoods to interpret God's word properly. In any case, all systems of morality are humanly based; it is a question of which best serves the moral needs of humankind—theism or humanism.

What are the essential ingredients of the ethics of humanism? The humanist life stance has a clearly developed conception of what "good practice" and "right conduct" are. The ethics of humanism may be said to begin when men and women eat of the "God-forbidden fruit" of the tree of knowledge of good and evil. Critical ethical inquiry enables us to transcend unquestioned customs, blind faith, or doctrinaire authority and to discover ethical values and principles. Humanists maintain that a higher state of moral development is reached when we go beyond unthinking habits to ethical wisdom: This includes an appreciation of the standards of excellence and an awareness of ethical principles and one's moral responsibilities to others.

The starting point for humanism is a response to the question "What is the meaning of life?" The theist is mired in the salvation myth, which he believes gives meaning to his mortal existence, and he cannot comprehend how human beings can find life meaningful or behave responsibly without it.

The quest for transcendent meaning is a futile endeavor, however, for there is no evidence that nature has some mysterious divine reality locked away, which, once revealed, will relieve us of the need to make our own choices or direct our own destinies.

Life has no hidden singular meaning per se. The promises of priests and other religious leaders to provide a path is often merely a deception perpetrated on gullible souls who lack the courage to summon their own resources to live fully. The quest for the Holy Grail is an escape from facticity, contingency, and finitude.

Humanists begin with the realization that the universe is a vast, impersonal system, impervious to their interests and needs, yet regard it as full of wonderful challenges and opportunities that enable them to create their own life-worlds. They realize that death is the inevitable fate of all biological creatures, that the central value is to fulfill and enhance life itself—to eat of the bountiful fruit of the tree of life—and that to enjoy its succulent flavors and fragrance can be intrisically energizing and exciting.

To ask for *the* meaning of life, as if there were one magic key, makes no sense. Life is full of *plural meanings*; it can be abundant and overflowing with possibilities. The term *meaning* has significance only for sentient beings who are self-aware. The world of meaning is the field of nature and culture in which we discover things that are significant to us and in which we initiate our plans, actualize our projects, and create relationships that are of moral value.

Here then is the humanist life stance: humanists do not look upward to a heaven for a promise of divine deliverance. They have their feet planted squarely on Mother Earth, yet they have the Promethean fortitude to employ art, science, sympathy, reason, and education to create a better world for themselves and their fellow human beings.

From the standpoint of the individual, the summum bonum is worthwhile happiness. This is not a passive quest for release from the world, but the pursuit of an active life of adventure and fulfillment. There are so many opportunities for creative enjoyment that every moment can be viewed as precious; all fit together to make up a full and exuberant life which makes the world a better place.

A basic method for achieving the good life is the method of reason; we need to cultivate the capacity of critical intelligence in ethical inquiry and the knowledge of good and evil so that we can make sensible choices. For the humanist, practical wisdom is the ability to choose between alternatives after a process of deliberation, by appraising means and ends and estimating the costs and consequences of his choices for himself and others. For the theist ultimate virtues are obedience to God's commandments, faith in his deliverance, and some form of worship. For the humanist the three basic virtues are (1) *courage*—the determination to overcome and prevail in spite of adversity; (2) *reason*—the use of critical intelligence to solve human problems and to understand nature; and (3) *compassion*—the moral awareness of the needs of others.

Historically philosophers have recognized that happiness is a basic good of life, though they have long argued about its nature. Hedonists have maintained that happiness is the attainment of pleasure and the avoidance of pain; self-actualizers have said that it is the fulfillment of our potentialities. I submit that both ideas are involved in the good life, that we want enriched enjoyment *and* creative realization of our talents. If an individual is to achieve a state of happiness, he needs to develop a number of excellences.

I will only list these, without explication: the capacity for autonomous choice and freedom, creativity, intelligence, self-discipline, self-respect, high motivation, good will, an affirmative outlook, good health, the capacity to enjoy pleasure, and aesthetic appreciation.[5] Men and women do not live in isolation but fulfill their highest ideals in concert with others.

One also needs to develop an appreciation for what we may call "the common moral decencies." I submit that deeply rooted in our history as sociobiological beings are our potentialities for moral behavior. There are many ethical principles that reason can discover: (1) *integrity*—being truthful, keeping promises, being sincere and honest; (2) *trustworthiness*—fidelity, dependability; (3) *benevolence*—good will, absence of malice, consensual sexual relations, beneficence; and (4) *fairness*—gratitude, accountability, justice, tolerance, peacefulness, and cooperation. These principles are cross-cultural. They are widely recognized by human beings of different historical epochs and cultures. In particular, reflective ethical awareness demonstrates the fact that we have responsibilities to ourselves: to fulfill our talents and to develop self-respect and self-restraint. But we also have responsibilities to others, especially within the family: parents to children and children to parents; husbands to wives, and vice versa; and relatives to each other. We also have obligations that arise among friends. There are in addition moral duties that emerge within our circle of interaction within our communities. And last but not least, we have an obligation to the entire world community. I am only stating these ethical principles or moral decencies now, without any extended defense, but I submit that a person with a reflective and developed moral awareness can discover standards of excellence, decency, and responsibility.

The ethics of humanism stands in sharp contrast to theistic doctrines. The end of the good life is to realize the worthiness of life itself, to fulfill our dreams and aspirations, plans and projects here and now. It involves not only a concern for one's own life (some self-interest is not wicked but essential) and the fulfillment of one's own desires, needs, and interests, but also a concern for the well-being of others, an altruistic regard for the communities where one interacts. And it extends eventually to all within the planetary society.

Humanist ethics does not rest on arbitrary caprice but on reflective choice. Ethical principles and values are rational: they are relative to human interests and needs. But this does not mean that they are subjective, nor are they beyond the domain of skeptical critical inquiry. Our principles and values can be tested by their consequences in action.

What is vital in humanist eupraxophy is that humanists are not overwhelmed by the "tragic" character of the human condition; they must face death, sorrow, and suffering with courage. They have confidence in the ability of human beings to overcome alienation, solve the problems of living, and develop the capacity to share the goods of life and empathize with others. The theist has a degraded view of man, who, beset with original sin, is incapable of solving life's problems by himself and needs to look outside of the human realm for divine succor. The humanist accepts the fact that the human species has imperfections and limitations and that some things encountered in existence are beyond repair or redress. Yet even so, he believes the best posture is not to retreat into fear and trembling before injustice or the unknown forces of nature, but to exert his intelligence and courage to deal with these matters. It is only by a resolute appraisal of the human condition, based on reason and a cosmic world view, that the humanist's life stance seems most appropriate. He is unwilling to fall to his knees before the forces of nature but will stand on his own feet to battle evil and build a better life for himself and his fellow human beings. In other words, he expresses the highest heroic virtues of the Promethean spirit: audacity and nobility! And he has also developed moral sensibilities about the needs of others.

SOCIAL POLITY

Humanism is not concerned only with the life stance of the individual—however basic this is as an alternative to theism; it is also concerned with the achievement of the good society. The early Greek philosophers have discussed the nature of justice. For Plato justice can best be seen writ large in the state, but it is also seen in the life of the individual soul. Justice involves the principles of harmony, order, and reason. For Aristotle ethics and politics are related. He is concerned with the happiness of the individual, but the more comprehensive art is politics, for it deals with questions about the polity of governments and good constitutions. Historically the philosophers Machiavelli, Hobbes, Spinoza, Locke, Hume, Rousseau, Comte, Hegel, Dewey, and Russell have been vitally concerned with the nature of the just society.

Does humanism today have concrete recommendations for the social polity? Surely humanist eupraxophy must deal with the well-being of humanity on the larger scale, for if the ultimate good is life here and now, then this cannot be achieved by the solitary individual alone but only in concert with others within a larger sociocultural context. It is clear that eupraxophy does not simply delineate a theoretical intellectual position but also has something to say about social practice. Indeed, for Karl Marx social praxis was essential for humanism. Abstract atheism was insufficient in itself; one needed to move on to a positive program of social reform. The next stage in human history, he said, was communism, that is, the transformation of the class system and of the conditions of production. What was unique in Marx's thought was that philosophy was to go beyond the merely contemplative mode of understanding political and social philosophy to the practical implementation of its ideals. In this sense, Marxist philosophy was a eupraxophy. Regrettably, Marx's theories, which were grounded in Hegelian categories, seem to have submerged the individual before the dialectical processes of history; and the decisive forces on the historical stage were economic and social institutions. In Marx's and Engel's sociological interpretation of history, the forces and relationships of production are the foundation for social change; religious, political, moral, intellectual, scientific, and aesthetic factors were derivative and in the superstructure of society.

One can raise fundamental questions about whether Marx was a humanist and whether his humanism was betrayed by some latter-day Marxists who misinterpreted his writings. Surely Marx was a secular humanist in the sense that he rejected an idealistic-theist *Weltanschauung*. He was committed to a materialistic view of nature and denied the existence of divine salvation. He wished to use science (as he understood it) to reconstruct social conditions and to contribute to human progress. Moreover, he had a compassionate concern for ameliorating the life of the ordinary worker and emancipating him from alienated labor and oppression. The early Marx of the *Economic and Philosophic Manuscripts of 1844* seemed to express the highest humanistic values of freedom and creativity.[6] In this sense he is within the great tradition of historic humanist philosophy, an heir to the ideals of the Enlightenment, for he wished to use reason to solve social problems, and he had some confidence in the ability of man to do so.

There has been a deep split within contemporary humanist eupraxia between some forms of Marxism and liberalism. Many philosophers in Eastern Europe considered themselves to be Marxist-humanists, as distinct from Leninist-Stalinists. And there had been an irreconcilable rift in the West between democratic socialist parties and totalitarian communist ones. The central issue concerns democracy, for an indelible feature of humanism is its emphasis on *freedom*. The good society must seek to maximize freedom of choice and the autonomy of the individual as a basic value, and this cannot be sacrificed at the altar of the collective. This has been the first principle of classical liberalism—as expressed by Locke, Mill, and the Utilitarians— and it cannot be compromised. The pragmatic political philosophers John Dewey and Sidney Hook have attempted to accommodate both the individualism of liberalism and the sociality of Hegelian philosophy. The individual cannot live in isolation, for he interacts with others in society and culture. But what are the appropriate dimensions of individual freedom?

For the liberal democratic humanist it is first and foremost freedom of thought and conscience—philosophical, religious, intellectual, scientific, political, and moral freedom. This includes free speech, freedom of the press, the freedom to form voluntary associations and to pursue one's life style as one sees fit so long as one does not harm or limit the freedom of others. In specific terms, this means that the full range of civil liberties must be recognized by the just society, including the right to dissent and the legal right to oppose the policies of the government. This entails a commitment to political democracy: the right of the people to form political parties, to elect the officials of government, to determine the policies and programs of the state, to have some means to redress grievances, to be immune from arbitrary arrest and punishment, to be entitled to a fair trial and due process. Representative democracy bases its decisions on majority rule with the full protection of minority rights. Democracy also cherishes as basic values diversity, pluralism, creativity, and the uniqueness of individual citizens and groups in society. It is the compromise of these principles by some overzealous disciples of Marxism in the past, who were willing to use any means to achieve their ends—including revolutionary violence and state terror—that clearly demarcates totalitarian Marxism from democratic humanism. And it is for that reason clearly the case that Leninist-Stalinism is not a full humanism because it abandoned the central ethical value of individual freedom. Hopefully, Stalinism has given way and Lenin's heirs will become more democratic in their approach. Only time will tell.

Humanists can disagree about many things in the political and social sphere. Humanism is not a dogmatic creed. We cannot identify humanism with specific candidates or party platforms, in a particular period. Honest men and women often differ about what ought to be done. We can dispute about policies in the economic and political sphere: Should there be high or low interest rates or none? Should taxes be on consumption or income? How can we increase productivity and not despoil the environment? and so on. Humanists share with orthodox Christians and Jews any number of social ideals, and they may support common programs of political reform or stability. Humanists may differ among themselves on any number of concrete proposals. Such disagreement may be healthy; for there is not only one road to truth or virtue. We are all fallible. Humanism thus does not have a doctrinaire political platform on which it stands. Any effort to politicize humanism in a narrow sectarian way is unfortunate; one should not read political or economic conservatives out of the humanist fold. Nor should one ally humanism simply with socialism or free-market economic systems; the policies and programs that seem wise in one generation may give way to the experience of the next. The earlier identification of many idealistic humanists with left-wing socialism has been broken by the recognition that one should not compromise democratic freedoms or abandon incentive, which is so essential to expanding production. Many libertarians today, interested in defending freedom in the economic sphere, claim to be humanistic. Others believe that the wisest course of social polity is a mixture of welfare (socialist) and free-market (capitalist) policies.

Humanist eupraxia in regard to social polity thus should focus on the *basic values and principles* that all humanists share. What are some of the basic principles of humanist eupraxia as we enter the twenty-first century? The first commitment of the humanist, I submit, must be to the *method of intelligence* (as John Dewey argues in his definition of liberalism) as the most reliable way of solving social problems.[7] This means that social policies should be considered hypotheses based on the findings of the best empirical research of the day and tested by their consequences in action. The wisest and most sensible method of political governance and social change is by *democratic methods of persuasion.* Our ultimate reliance in a democracy must be on a fully informed citizenry as the chief source of power and decision making. The broader ideal here is the need to encourage widespread participation by the people in all the institutions of society in which they live, work together, and function. How this works out depends on the specific institutions. Here we are talking about political, economic, and social democracy.

If the methods of intelligence and democratic participation are to succeed, we need a well-educated and intelligent public. Thus, *opportunity for education* must be made available to all individuals in society; the right to knowledge is not only a basic human right but is also the key instrument by which society can best solve its problems. By expanding the ranges of cultural appreciation of all citizens, we contribute to our own moral, intellectual, and aesthetic development.

A central value for humanism and democracy is *tolerance*; a just society will allow alternative points of view and a plurality of life styles, beliefs, and moral values, all existing side by side. The chief method of resolving differences should be wherever possible the *peaceful negotiation of differences and compromise*, not force or violence.

A democratic society is one that recognizes the obligation to provide the opportunity and means for all individuals to *satisfy their basic economic and cultural needs*. Thus, an open democratic society will attempt to redress gross inequities in income and provide for the satisfaction of the basic minimal needs for those who are unable, through no fault of their own, to do so. I am referring here to policies of social welfare, unemployment and social security insurance, and aid to the handicapped and disadvantaged. This involves providing both economic and cultural opportunities so that individuals can participate in the democratic society and develop as self-reliant, autonomous, and productive citizens.

The just society will seek *to end discrimination* based on race, gender, creed, sexual orientation, physical handicap, ethnicity, or economic background and accord all of its citizens equal rights. It will provide women with full equality under the law. It will recognize the rights of children.

The preceding is only a thumbnail sketch of some of the principles of humanist social eupraxia. Heretofore, this has been interpreted as applying only to local communities or nation-states, and efforts have been made to democratize these from within. The world has reached such a level of economic and political interdependence today that it is no longer possible to resolve many problems concerning humanity on the local or national level alone. Thus, we need to develop an appreciation for universal (or general) human rights and apply them to all corners of the globe and all members of the human family. We need to build an *ethical commitment to the world community as our highest moral devotion*. There are conservative and reactionary nationalistic, separationist, and ethnic forces throughout the world that oppose this development. Yet it is central, I submit, to the next stage of human civilization.

Notes

1. Paul Kurtz, *Eupraxophy: Living Without Religion* (Buffalo, N.Y., 1989).

2. I have discussed criteria of meaning and proof in detail in the following books: *The Transcendental Temptation* (Buffalo, N.Y., 1986); *Decision and the Condition of Man* (Seattle, 1965); and *The Skeptic's Handbook of Parapsychology* (Buffalo, N.Y., 1985).

3. I have provided more detail in *Forbidden Fruit: The Ethics of Humanism* (Buffalo, N.Y., 1988); *Decision and the Condition of Man;* and *Exuberance: The Philosophy of Happiness* (Los Angeles, 1977).

4. The term *life stance* was first introduced by Harry Stopes-Roe, "Humanism as a Life Stance," *Free Inquiry* 8, no. 1 (Winter 1987/88).

5. For a full discussion, see *Forbidden Fruit*, chapter 4.

6. Karl Marx, *Economic and Philosophic Manuscripts of 1844* (New York, 1964).

7. John Dewey, *Liberalism and Social Action* (New York, 1955); *The Public and Its Problems* (New York, 1927); *Freedom and Culture* (New York, 1939).

Afterword: The Answer of Humanism

Tim Madigan

> I see male and female everywhere,
> I see the serene brotherhood of philosophs,
> I see the constructiveness of my race,
> I see the results of the perseverance and industry of my race,
> I see ranks, colors, barbarisms, civilizations, I go among
>   them, I mix indiscriminately,
> And I salute all the inhabitants of the earth.
>
> Walt Whitman, *Salut au Monde!*

The preceding essays, some favorably disposed toward humanism and others not, present a wide spectrum of views. The attempt to define "humanism" can lead one down many historical, cultural, and linguistic paths. As an avowed secular humanist myself, I was fascinated by the rich tradition and heated controversies that the Brock University series on humanism made evident. In this afterword, I would like to touch upon the three prevalent themes of the series: the varieties of humanism, the challenges to humanism, and the enigmas of humanism. To demonstrate still further the difference of opinion on the subject, I choose to spell the word with a lower-case "h," as the alternative strikes me as being far too reverential.

VARIETIES OF HUMANISM

Just when did humanism first arrive on the scene? This question is a source of endless debate. Some scholars hold that humanism only began during the Renaissance, with its interest in determining the proper place of human beings in the cosmos. Yet the Renaissance humanists themselves looked back with renewed fervor to the philosophies of Ancient Greece and Rome, so a good argument can be made that humanism was inaugurated in such schools as that of the Sophists, the Skeptics, the Stoics and (my own personal favorite) the Cynics. All of these schools, to some extent or another, stopped looking to the stars for answers to the basic questions of human existence and tried to rely upon their own resources for solutions.

And there are scholars who would trace the origins of humanism even further back in time. Martin Bernal, author of the controversial book *Black Athena: The Afroasiatic Roots of Classical Civilization,* speculates that humanism is rooted in the late-Egyptian concept that human beings are capable of becoming gods.

> The belief that humanity has divinity within itself is essentially Egyptian or African, and was transmitted to modern Europe through hermetic texts. These texts drew on Egyptian tradition, are mystical, and place great stress on the divinity of humanity. Some of these texts were known in the West and were referred to by the earliest humanists, but the big wave of neoplatonic thought came about during the 1470s, after a mass of these te..s were discovered. They were extraordinarily influential. They influenced magic, for instance, which in a way is related to humanism in that the magician supposedly has the power to control outside forces, rather than praying to those forces. But they also had a more general influence. So though you could say that the atheist tradition can only be traced back to Greek and Latin thinkers, humanism, in the centrality of the "person," is a very Egyptian idea.[1]

This sentiment of the godlike qualities of human beings is vividly expressed in these lines from Walt Whitman's *Song of Myself:*

> Divine am I inside and out, and I make holy whatever I
>   touch or am touch'd from,
> The scent of these arm-pits aroma finer than prayer,
> This head more than churches, bibles, and all the creeds.

Certainly the centrality of the person is a key humanist attribute. But the notion that human beings have divinity within them does not necessarily follow from it. For, as Bernal rightly points out, humanism also draws upon the atheistic tradition of the Ancients, which stoutly denies that there is a divinity of *any* sort. As Protagoras wrote, "Concerning the gods, I do not know whether they exist or not. For many are the obstacles to knowledge: the obscurity of the subject and the brevity of human life."[2] This position has been a strong undercurrent in the humanist tradition.

To speak of "humanism" at all, one must recognize its evolutionary character, which I will demonstrate by briefly examining five varieties of humanism: Renaissance humanism, Englightenment humanism, Romantic humanism, religious humanism, and secular humanism. Of necessity, I must paint a picture of them in very broad strokes, without doing justice to their infinite sublety.

The Renaissance humanists were chiefly concerned with the idea of *dignitas*—the proper relationship of human beings to God and nature. They turned away from medieval scholasticism's emphasis on theology, and returned to a study of the pre-Christian-era philosophers, under the rallying cry of "the proper study of man is man." There was no longer a burning desire to harmonize pagan teachings with Christian scriptures. Instead, the desire of the Renaissance scholars was to understand these teachings on their own terms, and in their own languages. The irony of this quest, as Edward Synan rightly points out, is that many of these ancient texts had been lovingly preserved by Christian monks. Still, it was the humanists who better understood the significance of them. Petrarch, for instance, referred to the pagan poems he rescued from various monasteries as "gentle prisoners, held in captivity by barbarous jailers."

Renaissance humanists like Petrarch, Erasmus, and Pico della Mirandola did not seek to abolish Christianity, and in fact considered themselves to be good sons of the Church. But they did seek to abolish the Church's impediments to free inquiry and its control over learning. To them, *everything* was worthy of discussion and consideration. In his *Oration on the Dignity of Man,* Pico went so far as to quote favorably from Mohammed, the founder of Christianity's most dreaded competitor. Words of wisdom, they felt, should be cherished, whatever the source.

Another theme pursued by Renaissance humanists was a fascination with the occult. Mysticism of a non-Christian nature had been discouraged since the early days of the Church. But Renaissance humanists hoped to find hidden knowledge through the study of arcane texts, especially those of the mystery cults of the East. Pico's *Oration,* often taken to be the premier expression of Renaissance humanism, is suffused with this gnostic inclination:

> Let us be driven, Fathers, let us be driven by the frenzies of Socrates, that they may so throw us into ecstasy as to put our mind and ourselves in God. Let us be driven by them, if we have first done what is in our power. For if through moral philosophy the forces of our passions have by a fitting agreement become so intent on harmony that they can sing together in undisturbed concord, and if through dialectic our reason has moved progressively in a rhythmical measure, then we shall be stirred by the frenzy of the Muses and drink the heavenly harmony with our inmost hearing. Thereupon Bacchus, the leader of the Muses, by showing in his mysteries, that is, the visible signs of nature, the invisible things of God to us who study philosophy, will intoxicate us with the fulness of God's house, in which, if we prove faithful, like Moses, hallowed theology shall come and inspire us with a doubled frenzy.[3]

Although several popes of the time were more devout followers of Dionysus than of Christ, this mingling of Bacchus and Moses did not sit well with many of the Church fathers. The Renaissance spirit was crushed in the onslaught of religious wars following the Protestant Reformation.

Humanism was revived during the Enlightenment, which began in seventeenth-century France. But Enlightenment thinkers distanced themselves from the Renaissance's mystical tinge and put their trust in sweet reason as the best guide to knowledge. While highly critical of organized religion, the

Enlightenment humanists were, for the most part, deists, believers in a God of reason and order. One could better understand this God through studying the laws of nature than by hoping for miracles or mystical experience. Voltaire, that exemplar par excellence of Enlightenment virtue, held that

> . . . once men have come to embrace a pure and holy religion, superstition becomes, not merely useless, but dangerous. We must not feed on acorns those to whom God offers bread. Superstition is to religion what astrology is to astronomy—the mad daughter of a wise mother. These daughters have too long dominated the earth.[4]

But Enlightenment humanism, with its stoic-like avowal of the primacy of human reason, was itself strongly criticized by the Romantics, who stressed instead the primacy of human emotions. Rousseau, Voltaire's archenemy, went so far as to charge that reason was corrupting. It belonged to civilized humans and marked their estrangement from nature.

Enlightenment and Romantic principles began to intermingle and form a new variety of humanism in the work of John Stuart Mill, a philosopher who originally tried to expound an ethical theory based upon reason alone (and nearly had a nervous breakdown because of it). After reading the Romantic poetry of Wordsworth and Coleridge and after engaging in some romance himself with his beloved Harriet Taylor, he was inspired to broaden his system. Mill's Utilitarianism was a good example of what Paul Kurtz has termed a eupraxophy: not a religion, it nonetheless sought to provide guiding standards for leading a good life.

Mill, himself a nonbeliever (he states in his autobiography that he was brought up without any religious education and "am thus one of the very few examples . . . of one who has, not thrown off religious belief, but never had it"[5]), had hopes that Utilitarianism could replace organized religions as a moral theory. The nineteenth century witnessed a growing dissatisfaction with dogmatic religions. Strauss, Renan, and others offered devastating evaluations of the Bible, demonstrating the historical bases of this "infallible" text, and its connections to the texts of other world religions. Darwin provided a way out for those dissatisfied with the biblical story of human creation. All of this gave rise to religious humanism, which sought to find the common principles that underlie all belief systems. Comte and Feuerbach, among others, wished to keep the trappings of religious ritual while dispensing with the worship of a supernatural deity. Still, for a rising number of humanists, this exercise smacked of throwing out the baby and keeping the bath water.

The final variety I wish to discuss, secular humanism, is ably described by Paul Kurtz in the last essay of this volume. Suffice it to say that secular humanism draws upon its four predecessors. It shares with Renaissance humanism a love for learning and an advocacy of free inquiry, but it is as skeptical of the occult as it is of religion; it agrees with the Enlightenment thinkers that the use of reason is our best guide for understanding, but it tries to avoid the former's near-deification of rationality; it affirms the Romantic stress on the importance of human emotions, but it is wary of the anti-civilization aspects of this movement; and, like religious humanism, it seeks to chart out the common moral decencies found throughout the denominations of humankind, but it does not desire to establish a secular denomination, a Religion of Man, to take their place.

Secular humanism itself has many sources: the pragmatic instrumentalism of Dewey, the Existential focus on human freedom of Sartre, and the logical analysis of Russell have all played a tremendous role. By utilizing the varieties of humanism that preceded it, secular humanism makes clear the evolutionary process of this world view.

One further point needs to be made in discussing the varieties of humanism. While this volume has examined many of these strains, it is by no means all-encompassing. Indeed, by discussing almost exclusively the various movements of the West, a skewed view of humanism is presented. For the East has long had its own varieties of humanism, such as Confucianism, Taoism, and certain branches of Buddhism. Space does not permit me to discuss these, except to say that they have all had a dominant impact upon Oriental thought for thousands of years. In the fifth century B.C.E., Confucius is said to have given the following advice to a student:

> Chi-lu asked how the spirits of the dead and the gods should be served. The Master said, "You are not able even to serve man. How can you serve the spirits?"
> "May I ask about death?"
> "You do not understand even life. How can you understand death?"[6]

How can you serve the gods if you cannot serve human beings? How can you understand death if you don't yet understand life? These two questions have been at the forefront of humanism in *all* its manifestations.

CHALLENGES TO HUMANISM

> God is dead. God remains dead. And we have killed him. How shall we, the murderers of all murderers, comfort ourselves? What was holiest and most powerful of all that the world has yet owned has bled to death under our knives. Who will wipe this blood off us? What water is there for us to clean ourselves? What festivals of atonement, what sacred games shall we have to invent? Is not the greatness of this deed too great for us? Must not we ourselves become gods simply to seem worthy of it?[7]

The above, taken from "the madman's speech" in Nietzsche's *The Gay Science,* contains within it two central challenges to humanism: a religious and a secular reproach. How can one live without God? Let us give an overview of both.

The Religious Challenge

Religious figures have always looked with suspicion upon humanism's de-emphasis of other-worldliness and its questioning of church authority. The debate is often focussed upon the issue of ethics: can there be a moral system which people will adhere to that does not have absolute prescriptions and/ or a divine lawgiver overseeing it?

The notion of a divine lawgiver has had different interpretations in the history of humanism. Renaissance humanists seldom objected to the traditional Christian interpretation of the triune God, although they did try to broaden His domain. Enlightenment humanists were content with a God who set the universe in motion under rational foundations, but who did not intervene in human affairs. Romantic humanists looked to a personal deity, but one who was closer to the joys of life than the austere Judeo-Christian divinity, and whose laws were not merely predicated on the principle of "Thou Shalt Not." Religious humanists wished to discover the life force or world spirit which all human beings could tap into when need be. Secular humanists, taking an atheistic or agnostic stance, agreed with Nietzsche that "God is dead" and put the issue of a divine lawgiver entirely aside, looking instead for ethical principles that arise within human societies.

But Nietzsche asks whether the secularists fully appreciate the significance of the claim that "God is dead." He castigates the deontologists and teleologists, who attempted to come up with an ethic based on reason rather than revelation, for not addressing head-on the opportunities and pitfalls of a godless universe. "Without God, everything is permitted," Dostoyevsky wrote. He bemoaned this, while Nietzsche exulted in it. Where do the humanist stand?

One can first ask: Is life without God even possible? Many religious thinkers would deny this. R.J. McLaughlin's essay presents the Thomistic view that to be fully human requires one to be religious—specifically, Christian, and more specifically, Catholic (and, to be even truer to Aquinas, a medieval Catholic at that). It is through love for one's creator that a person begins to feel love for his/her fellow human beings. Still, even brother Thomas had to admit, in his *Summa Contra Gentiles,* that not everyone takes the existence of God as a given. His famous "five ways" for proving God's existence rely heavily on a belief in an unmoved mover or first cause. If one accepts that basic premise, then grand conclusions can logically follow. But if one doesn't, then the argument is at best valid but unsound. (Thomas's troubles, by the way, were less with unbelievers, who were few and far between in the Middle Ages, than with Muslims, who were happy to accept the first-cause premise, but who arrived at very different conclusions about the nature of that cause and His game plan for His creations.)

But without God, why would anyone bother to act morally? If nothing else, most religions, with their stress on ultimate rewards and punishments, have strong motivating factors for morality. The fear of God's wrath has no doubt kept many potential miscreants in line. What can humanism offer as an alternative? Would not all hell break loose (metaphorically speaking) if God were no more?

Mill addressed this subject in his autobiography. He writes:

On religion in particular the time appears to me to have come, when it is the duty of all who being qualified in point of knowledge, have on mature consideration satisfied themselves that the current opinions are not only false but hurtful, to make their dissent known; at least, if they are among those whose station, or reputation, gives their opinion a chance of being attended to. Such an avowal would put an end, at once and for ever, to the vulgar prejudice, that what is called, very improperly, unbelief, is connected with any bad qualities either of mind or heart. The world would be astonished if it knew how great a proportion of its brightest ornaments—of those most distinguished even in popular estimation for wisdom and virtue—are complete skeptics in religion; many of them refraining from avowal, less from personal considerations, than from a conscientious, though now in my opinion a mistaken apprehension lest by speaking out what would tend to weaken existing beliefs, and by consequence (as they suppose) existing restraints, they should do harm instead of good.[8]

As Mill recognized, "unbeliever" is an unfortunate term. Humanists do have beliefs, perhaps most importantly a belief that human beings do not need the restraining elements of an all-powerful deity in order to act morally. Mill also recognized that the old canard that nonreligious individuals are necessarily evil people could not be eradicated until those individuals were willing to make their views known and to demonstrate by personal example that it is possible to lead a decent, upstanding life without religion. Mill wrote this well over one hundred years ago, yet the number of admitted secular humanists is still quite low, and a good percentage of dictionaries still list "wickedness" as an acceptable definition for "atheism."

Is the motivating factor of humanism strong enough to lead people to an ethical life stance? This is an abstract question. Just what sort of goals are humanists aiming at? If the purpose of life is not to prepare us for an eternal afterlife, then we must return to the time-honored principles addressed by such philosophers as Aristotle, Confucius, and Mill on how to live a good life in the here-and-now.

The Secular Challenge

Svetozar Stojanovic, a member of the Academy of Humanism, in his essay "Some Reflections on Post-Marxism and Post-Christianity," writes: "Atheists should give deep thought to whether the notion of a completely *profane* world gives us any chance at all to avoid the apocalypse. Is it possible to have an atheism for which the continuation of the human species would be a *sacred* cause?"[9] With this, he raises the secular challenge expressed by Nietzsche's madman—is the preservation of the human species a goal worth pursuing?

While humanism has traditionally been criticized from a religious perspective, beginning in the nineteenth century and continuing to the present day, there have been some powerful objections raised from the secular perspective. Three of the main secular critics, whose influence can be seen throughout this volume, are Marx, Nietzsche, and Heidegger. I will touch upon a few of their reproofs, all presented from a temporal point of view.

In his early writings (which were lost for several decades), Marx looked with favor on humanism because he was much influenced by the Enlightenment and Romantic traditions, as well as the religious humanism of Feuerbach. But, as Danny Goldstick and Graeme Nicholson point out, the relationship of the later Marx to humanism is a thorny one. Marx came to see humanism as an ideology which perpetuated the illusion that human beings could gradually better their conditions without concomitantly changing the conditions of power. Humanism, he held, was unable to appreciate the economic, social, and political factors that shape human destiny. By concerning itself with the centrality of the person, humanism overlooked the very circumstances that mold the person. While sharing with humanism a high regard for scientific reasoning, Marx parted company with many humanist theoreticians on the issues of revolution, determinism, and the inevitability of a classless society.

Like Marx, Nietzsche has often been referred to as a "humanist," but this is a misnomer. While his virulent attacks on Christianity gave new ammunition to opponents of organized religion, he had little sympathy for Enlightenment principles. For him, the rational ethics of Kant and the Utilitarianism of Mill were basically nothing more than warmed-over Christianity, new versions of the slave morality that had long oppressed the "higher men." The goal of Kant and Mill was the same as that of Christianity—to bring about a nice, safe, peaceful world where the weak would continue to triumph and the strong would continue to chafe at the bit. Enlightenment humanism, committed to the principles of Apollonian reason, disregarded the Dionysian elements of life. What is more, humanism continued to perpetuate the virtue of compassion, which he saw as a sickly religious attribute, unsuited to the godless environment of self-creating overmen living beyond the contraints of good and evil. The human species is not something to be preserved—it is something to be overcome. As he states in *The AntiChrist:*

> The weak and the failures shall perish: that is the first principle of *our* love of man. And they shall even be given every possible assistance. What is more harmful than any vice? Active pity for all the failures and all the weak: Christianity.[10]

The implications of such a "love of man" are profoundly disturbing.

Martin Heidegger, one of the twentieth century's leading philosophers and a Nietzchean scholar, was another secular figure who spurned humanism, much to the surprise of those who had thought him to be firmly in that camp. Sartre, in his essay *Existentialism is a Humanism,* had attempted to show the connections between the two schools of thought and enlisted Heidegger as a fellow atheistic existentialist and humanist. Heidegger reacted by issuing his "Letter on Humanism." In this letter, and in his later works, Heidegger found fault with humanism's commitment to technological advancement, its deemphasis (and sometimes denial) of the importance of metaphysics, and its latter-day advocacy of democratic political standards.

Thus, we can see the secular challenges to humanism: the Marxist view that humanism is inadequate by dint of its misunderstanding of the vital forces of life; the Nietzschean view that humanism is still not able to appreciate all that the statement "God is dead" entails; and the Heideggerian view that humanism lacks a proper metaphysical grounding, which—along with its hell-bent quest for technological domination of the world—will paradoxically lead to a more and more dehumanizing environment. Many of these challenges have been addressed in the papers within this volume. I have neither the space nor the expertise to deal with them here, except to point out that humanists have grappled with them all. From inside the ranks of Marxism, philosophers such as Adam Schaff have attempted to show that communism *is* a humanism: "[Schaff] distinguishes between God-oriented and man-oriented views. Adopting the latter, he emphasizes, as final goal, a *social eudaemonism,* the pursuit of happiness for the many. And concludes that only Marxist humanism can go that way."[11] From outside the ranks of Marxism, humanist scholars such as Karl Popper have raised serious questions about Marx's own scientific methodology, and the sort of society that Marxist communism would actually bring about.

Nietzsche, perhaps the most discussed philosopher of contemporary times, is a figure all humanists must come to grips with. His sharp objections have to be faced, but one can also raise objections to his own philosophy. Just who are these overmen he advocates? And if God never existed, and human values arose in human contexts, then why should these values be transgressed? Is the "death of God" *really* so disturbing a concept, considering how long the patient had been lingering? And finally, it is debatable whether compassion is a religious attribute. It is surely not only a *Christian* attribute. One can examine the fruits of regimes which have abrogated their respect for human beings *in toto,* in favor of a select few, and see that a policy of compassion is not something which should be easily swept aside. Nietzsche himself, for all the ferociousness of his writings, was a kind-hearted fellow. In *Beyond Good and Evil,* he wrote that: "Indeed, to understand how the abstrusest metaphysical assertions of a philosopher have been arrived at, it is always well (and wise) to first ask oneself: 'What morality do they (or does he) aim at?' "[12] This is a question which it is both well and wise to keep in mind when examining the philosophy of Nietzsche as well.

As for Heidegger, it is certainly true that rampant technological advancement has often had a dehumanizing effect. The photographer Margaret Evans has spent several years chronicling the demise of the American steel mill. Her photos of abandoned steel plants—eerie, empty shells, like the ruins of Ozymandias—are chilling. If such are the fruits of progress, one must wonder about the nature of progress itself. But it is important to note that humanists are well aware of this dehumanizing element and have sought to alleviate it. Richard Francis's essay shows an inadequate appreciation of pragmatic humanism when he asserts that "Pragmatists placed uncritical confidence in the scientific method, expecting that science can do only good and not harm." This strawman view of pragmatism does not account for the actions of individuals like Dewey, James, and Mead, who were in the forefront in the fight for legislation to guarantee workers' rights. They recognized the dangers of unbridled advancement. Today's humanists do not expect science to provide miracles—they leave the hope for miracles to religious-minded folks. But science and technological benefits are the key to providing a better life for human beings. Like it or not, we cannot return to the days of living in forests and caves. Technology has its nice points, too. As Wallace Shawn states in the film *My Dinner With Andre,* "I *like* my electric blanket!"

The criticisms of Marx, Nietzsche, and Heidegger are important for many reasons, not least of all because they are secular in origin. By addressing them, humanism will become better able to meet the challenges of a postmodern world. Humanism *is* committed to the continuation of the human species, for it is from the human species (and not from God on high) that humanism has sprung. This commitment is predicated, as always, on a proper understanding of both the centrality of the person and the environment from which that person springs. The critics of humanism, be they religious or secular, help to keep this understanding in the forefront of humanist thought and action.

ENIGMAS OF HUMANISM

Finally, a look at humanism today. John Luik's essay raises the four questions that Kant attempted to address:
1. What can I know?
2. What ought I to do?
3. What may I hope for?
4. What is man?

These questions are still germane to humanism. I propose that the best approach to answering them is to explore in greater detail the work now being done on evolutionary theories. Michael Ruse, in his book *Taking Darwin Seriously,* shows how the first two questions—pertaining to epistemology and to ethics—can be examined in a naturalistic fashion.

> Now, what we have in the case of Darwinian epistemology is a denial of metaphysical reality—the world of the thing-in-itself, not to mention Platonic forms and eternal mathematical truths just waiting to be discovered—and an affirmation of common-sense reality, in which the enquiring subject plays an active, creative part. What we have in the case of Darwinian ethics is a denial of objectivity, which is surely a denial of metaphysical reality by another name, and an affirmation of subjectivity, which is no less a commitment to common sense, in which the moral subject plays an active creative part.[13]

There is exciting work being done in the fields of evolutionary epistemology and ethics, which humanists would do well to acquaint themselves with.

The third of Kant's questions—"What may I hope for?"—is surely of great importance to humanism. It can perhaps best be summed up by "A Declaration of Interdependence: A New Global Ethics," which was issued at the 10th International Humanist and Ethical Union Congress in 1988. It reads in part:

> The overriding need is to develop a new global ethic—one that seeks to preserve and enhance individual human freedom and emphasizes our com-

mitment to the world community. Although we must recognize our obligations and responsibilities to the local communities, states and nations of which
we are citizens, we also need to develop a new sense of identity with the
planetary society of the future. As we approach the twenty-first century, we
need to ask: How can we work cooperatively to create a peaceful and
prosperous world where combating national allegiances are transcended? How
can we confer dignity upon all human beings? How can we build a genuine
world community?[14]

Is a universal humanism possible? Can we, as it were, get underneath
the various religions, philosophies, and eupraxophies to find the core maxims
to live by? This has always been an enigma of humanism. The Renaissance
scholars looked to the past and to mystical wisdom and hidden knowledge.
The Enlightenment philosophers hoped that reason was the answer, and the
Romantics put their trust in emotions. The Pragmatists looked toward science
and naturalism. Today's secular humanists continue these traditions but are
also willing to deviate from them when they no longer meet the needs of
the day. Examining the origins of human world views, and the connections
among them, is a project that humanists will continue, especially as the world
we all live in becomes more and more interconnected.

Kant's final question—"What is man?"—has been uppermost in humanist concerns. The Renaissance humanists placed man between the animals
and the angels. Today's humanists, having forsworn angels, are now interested in pursuing the evolutionary connections between humans and animals.
Aristotle's definition of humans as "rational animals" may not be such a vital
distinction as was once thought, and contemporary humanists, well-versed
in Freudian theories of the unconscious, are less likely than enlightenment
humanists to promote a religion of reason. But, while we may not hope to
live within the bounds of pure reason alone, we still hold that rationality
is our best beacon light for understanding the universe we find ourselves in,
and the best basis for building a true world community.

Coupled with the question "What is man?" is the question "How can
humans best govern themselves?" Secular humanism is committed to a defense of democracy as the form of government which can best satisfy the
myriad desires of its citizens while protecting their rights. Democracy has had
its critics, dating back at least to the time of Socrates and all the way to
the present. But what are the alternatives, and how can they satisfy these
desires? In discussing Victor Farias's book *Heidegger and Nazism,* which re-
opened the debate about that philosopher's flirtation with fascism, Luc Ferry
and Alain Renaut observe that:

The virtue of Farias' book, whatever its weakness, is to make us rethink
a question that surely would have been once again swept under the rug
by a consensus of intellectuals: under what circumstances can the contemporary world be subjected to criticism that is not inexorably attended by
a sweeping negation of the principles of democratic humanism? We need
to spell this out: the neo-Heideggerians of the 1980s played a game in which
all the moves are familiar. Why can't we see that the main drift of Heidegger's

thinking was that, from the birth of subjectivity to the world of technology, the sequence is inevitable? Why can't we realize that under the circumstances criticism of the contemporary world is basically—*Heidegger himself knew this and said it plainly*—radically incompatible with the minimum of *subjectivity* needed for *democratic* thinking, in whatever form we conceive it?[15]

Ferry and Renault, in their book *French Philosophy of the Sixties: An Essay on Antihumanism,* go on to say that for the past forty years there have been two major critiques of democratic humanism: the Marxist one, conducted in the name of an ideal future, and the Heideggerian one, conducted in the name of an ideal past (namely, that of the pre-Socratic Greeks).[16] Marxism, at least as it has been practiced for the past forty years, appears to be crumbling throughout the world, and Heidegger's philosophy is now undergoing its own severe scrutiny. Perhaps the time has now come to seriously reevaluate democratic humanism as the means for achieving global cooperation.

Whatever may occur, the humanism of the future will differ from that of the past. One of the crucial aspects of humanism is that it is always open to change and to challenge. It is not committed to a set of sacred doctrines or to all-purpose idealistic solutions. Indeed, one of the difficulties of listing the suppositions and principles of humanism lies in the fact that humanism stresses that one should constantly question one's basic suppositions and principles.

The title of this afterword, then, is deliberately vague. "The Answer of Humanism" is dependent not merely upon "What is the question?" but even more so upon "When was that question asked and under what conditions?" This volume has looked at the many varieties of humanism, past and present. How humanism will manifest itself in the future depends upon how it meets the challenges of its time. The Brock University series on humanism, ably orchestrated by David Goicoechea, helped to crystallize many of these challenges. So long as humanists remain aware of their rich tradition and remain open to honest criticism and self-appraisal, they will continue to play a crucial role in world affairs.

The preface to this volume began with a brief poem by John Updike, asserting that "An easy Humanism plagues the land." If this volume demonstrates nothing else, it is that the term "easy" is misapplied to humanism. (And I'm not too thrilled about his coupling it with the term "plagues," either.) While Updike and others of his ilk may choose to take an otherworldly stand, we humanists prefer the James Thurber approach: this is my world, and welcome to it.

In honor of William Blake, whose philosophy graces this volume, I would like to close with my own "fearful symmetry," ending as I began with a poem by Walt Whitman, a man who often declared that nothing human was foreign to him. The following words may help us to chart a better humanist metaphysics, one that does not seek to replace God with humans, but rather gives a renewed interest in the Renaissance question: What is the proper role of human beings in the cosmos? Let us look for understanding not in our stars, but in ourselves.

The Base of All Metaphysics

And now gentlemen
A word I give to remain in your memories and minds,
As base and finalè too for all metaphysics.

(So to the students the old professor,
At the close of his crowded course.)

Having studied the new and antique, the Greek and
    Germanic systems,
Kant having studied and stated, Fichte and Schelling and
    Hegel,
Stated the lore of Plato, and Socrates greater than Plato,
And greater than Socrates sought and stated, Christ divine
    having studied long,
I see reminiscent to-day those Greek and Germanic
    systems,
See the philosophies all, Christian churches and tenets see,
Yet underneath Socrates clearly see, and underneath Christ
    the divine I see,
The dear love of man for his comrade, the attraction of
    friend to friend,
Of the well-married husband and wife, of children and
    parents,
Of city for city and land for land.

Notes

1. "Black Athena: An Interview with Martin Bernal," *Free Inquiry* 10/2 (Spring 1990): 19.

2. John Mansley Robinson, *An Introduction to Early Greek Philosophy* (Boston, 1968), 269.

3. Karl F. Thompson, ed., *Middle Ages, Renaissance, and Reformation,* vol. 2 of *Classics of Western Thought* (New York, 1988), 261.

4. Paul Edwards, ed., *Voltaire Selections* (New York, 1989), 117.

5. John Stuart Mill, *Autobiography* (Boston, 1969), 28–29.

6. Confucius, *The Analects,* trans. D.C. Lau (London, 1988), 107.

7. Friedrich Nietzsche, *The Portable Nietzsche,* ed. and trans. Walter Kaufmann (London, 1979), 95–96.

8. Mill, *Autobiography,* 28–29.

9. Svetozar Stojanovic, "Some Reflections on Post-Marxism and Post-Christianity: A Response to Professor Arthur McGovern," *Dialectics and Humanism* 16/3–4 (Summer/Autumn 1989): 106.

10. *The Portable Nietzsche,* 570.

11. Helio Jaguaribe, "The Social Humanism of Adam Schaff," *Dialectics and Humanism,* 16/2 (Spring 1989): 31.

12. Friedrich Nietzsche, *Beyond Good and Evil,* trans. Helen Zimmern (Edinburgh, 1907), 11.

13. Michael Ruse, *Taking Darwin Seriously* (New York, 1987), 269.

14. "A Declaration of Interdependence: A New Global Ethics," *Free Inquiry* 8/4 (Fall 1988): 7.

15. Luc Ferry and Alain Renaut, *Heidegger and Modernity,* trans. Franklin Philip (Chicago, 1990), 16–17.

16. Luc Ferry and Alain Renaut, *French Philosophy of the Sixties: An Essay on Antihumanism,* trans. Mary Schnackenberg Cattani (Boston, 1990).

List of Contributors

Dean Cecil Abrahams
Dean, Division of Humanities
Brock University
St. Catharines, Ontario

Professor Zygmunt Adamczewski
Department of Philosophy
Brock University
St. Catharines, Ontario

Professor Samuel Ajzenstat
Department of Philosophy
McMaster University
Hamilton, Ontario

Professor Martin Andic
Department of Philosophy
University of Massachusetts
Boston, Massachusetts

Professor Allan Booth
Department of Classics
Brock University
St. Catharines, Ontario

Professor Richard S. G. Brown
Department of Philosophy
Brock University
St. Catharines, Ontario

Professor Michael Cardy
Department of French, Italian, and
    Spanish
Brock University
St. Catharines, Ontario

Professor Kenneth Dorter
Department of Philosophy
University of Guelph
Guelph, Ontario

Professor Richard Francis
Department of Philosophy
University of Colorado
Colorado Springs, Colorado

Professor David Goicoechea
Department of Philosophy
Brock University
St. Catharines, Ontario

Professor Danny Goldstick
Department of Philosophy
University of Toronto
Toronto, Ontario

Mr. Calvin Hayes
Department of Philosophy
Brock University
St. Catharines, Ontario

Professor Marsha Hewitt
Department of Religious Studies
Trinity College
University of Toronto
Toronto, Ontario

Dr. Monica Hornyansky
Department of Philosophy
Brock University
St. Catharines, Ontario

Professor Paul Kurtz
Department of Philosophy
State University of New York at
    Buffalo
Buffalo, New York

Professor James Lawler
Department of Philosophy
State University of New York at
    Buffalo
Buffalo, New York

Professor John Luik
Department of Philosophy
Brock University
St. Catharines, Ontario

Mr. Tim Madigan
Executive Editor
Free Inquiry
Buffalo, New York

Professor Robert McLaughlin
Department of Philosophy
Saint John Fisher College
Rochester, New York

Professor Graeme Nicholson
Department of Philosophy
University of Toronto
Toronto, Ontario

Professor Zaid Orudjev
Department of Philosophy
Moscow State University
Moscow, U.S.S.R.

Professor Robert Perkins
Department of Philosophy
Stetson University
Deland, Florida

Professor Charles Scott
Department of Philosophy
Vanderbilt University
Nashville, Tennessee

Professor Edward A. Synan
Pontifical Institute of Medieval
    Studies
Toronto, Ontario